VOLUME 2

by
Nami Akimoto

HAMBURG // LONDON // LOS ANGELES // TOKYO

Ultra Cute Vol. 2
Created by Nami Akimoto

Translation - Emi Onishi
English Adaptation - Hope Donovan
Copy Editor - Hope Donovan
Retouch and Lettering - Mike Grainel & Erika "Skooter" Terriquez
Production Artist - Alyson Stetz
Cover Design - James Lee

Editor - Troy Lewter
Digital Imaging Manager - Chris Buford
Production Manager - Jennifer Miller
Managing Editor - Lindsey Johnston
VP of Production - Ron Klamert
Publisher and E.I.C. - Mike Kiley
President and C.O.O. - John Parker
C.E.O. and Chief Creative Officer - Stuart Levy

A  Manga

TOKYOPOP Inc.
5900 Wilshire Blvd. Suite 2000
Los Angeles, CA 90036

E-mail: info@TOKYOPOP.com
Come visit us online at www.TOKYOPOP.com

ISBN: 1-59532-957-9

First TOKYOPOP printing: April 2006
10 9 8 7 6 5 4 3 2 1
Printed in the USA

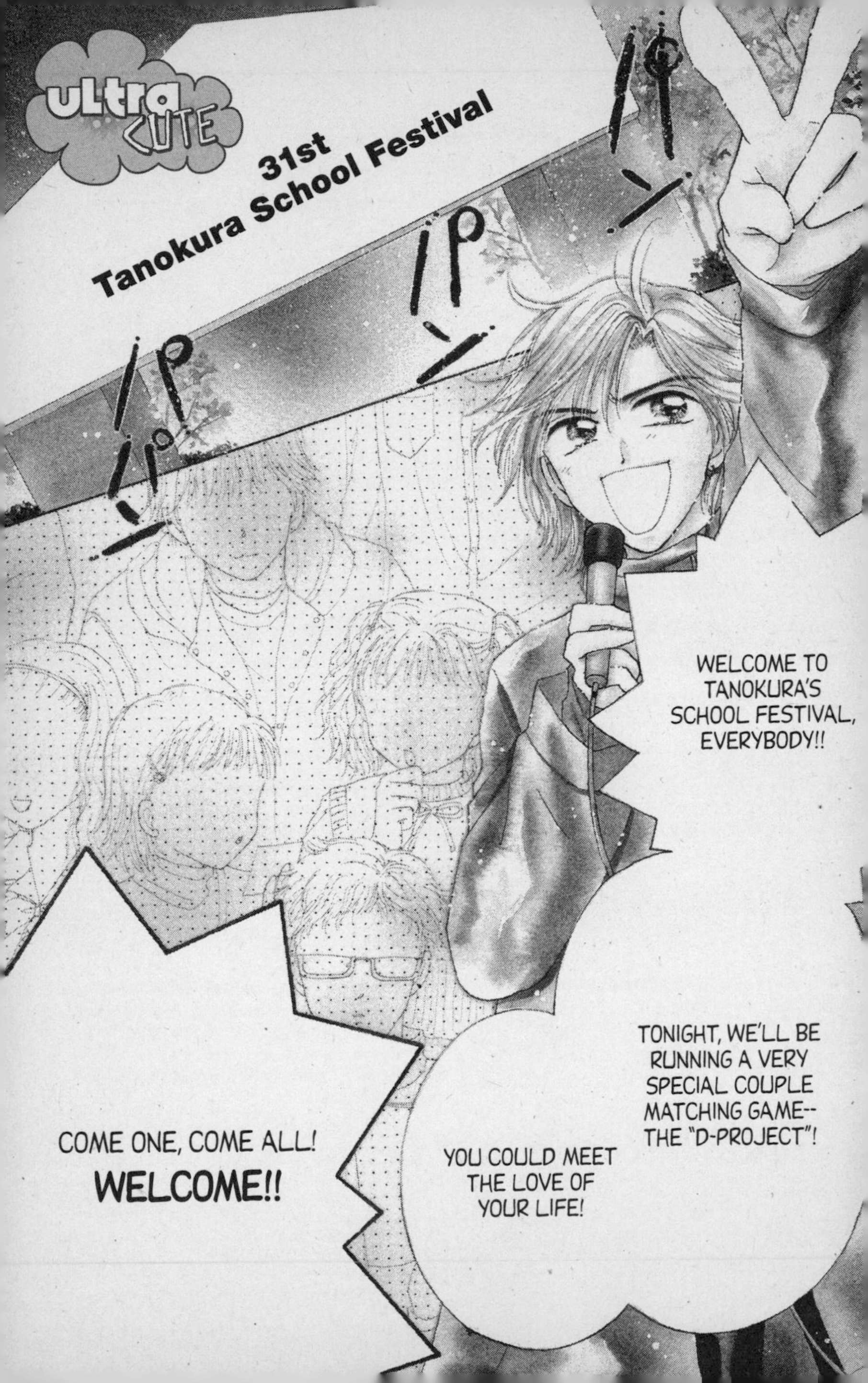
ultra CUTE
31st
Tanokura School Festival
WELCOME TO TANOKURA'S SCHOOL FESTIVAL, EVERYBODY!!
TONIGHT, WE'LL BE RUNNING A VERY SPECIAL COUPLE MATCHING GAME-- THE "D-PROJECT"!
YOU COULD MEET THE LOVE OF YOUR LIFE!
COME ONE, COME ALL!
WELCOME!!

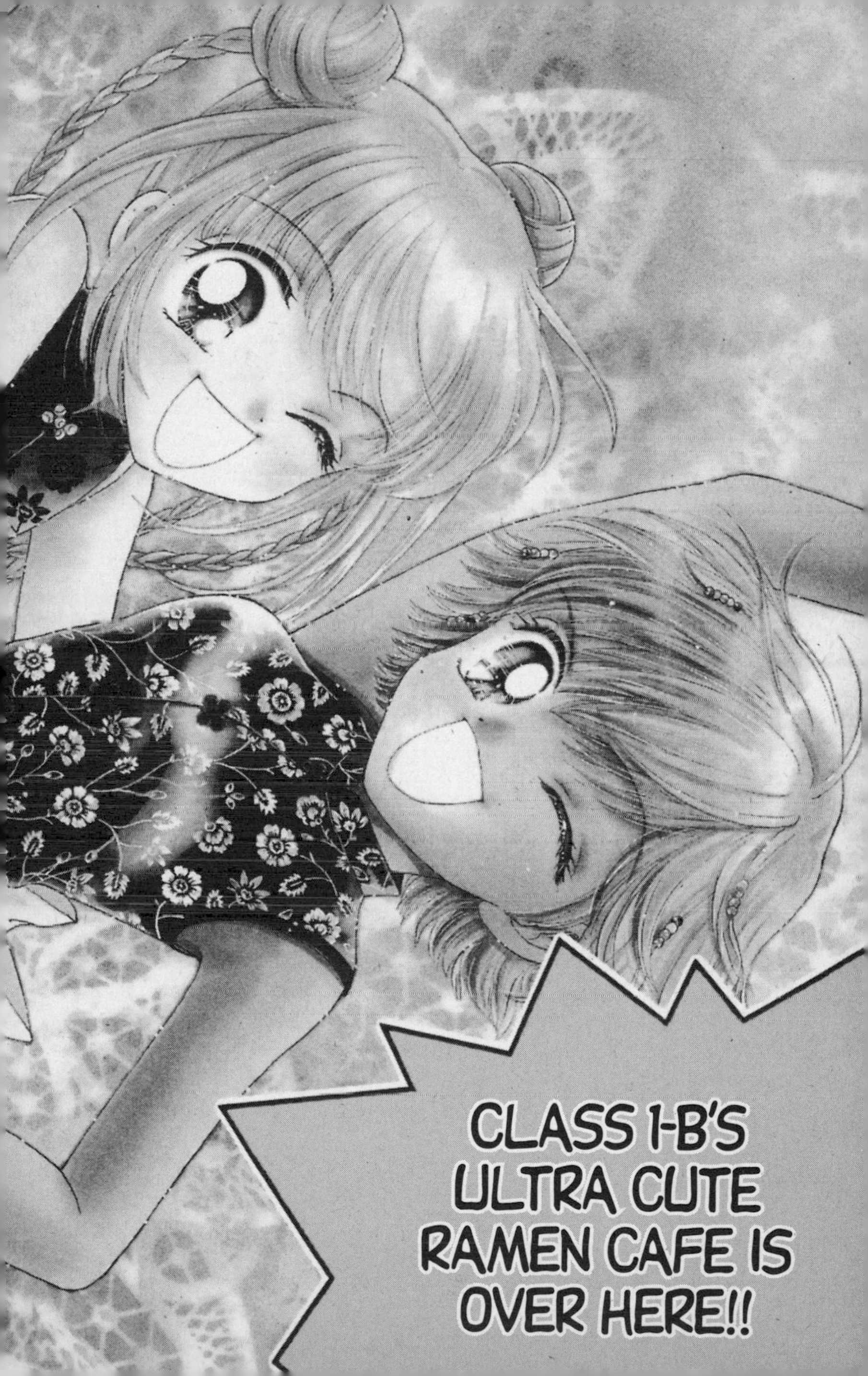
CLASS 1-B'S ULTRA CUTE RAMEN CAFE IS OVER HERE!!

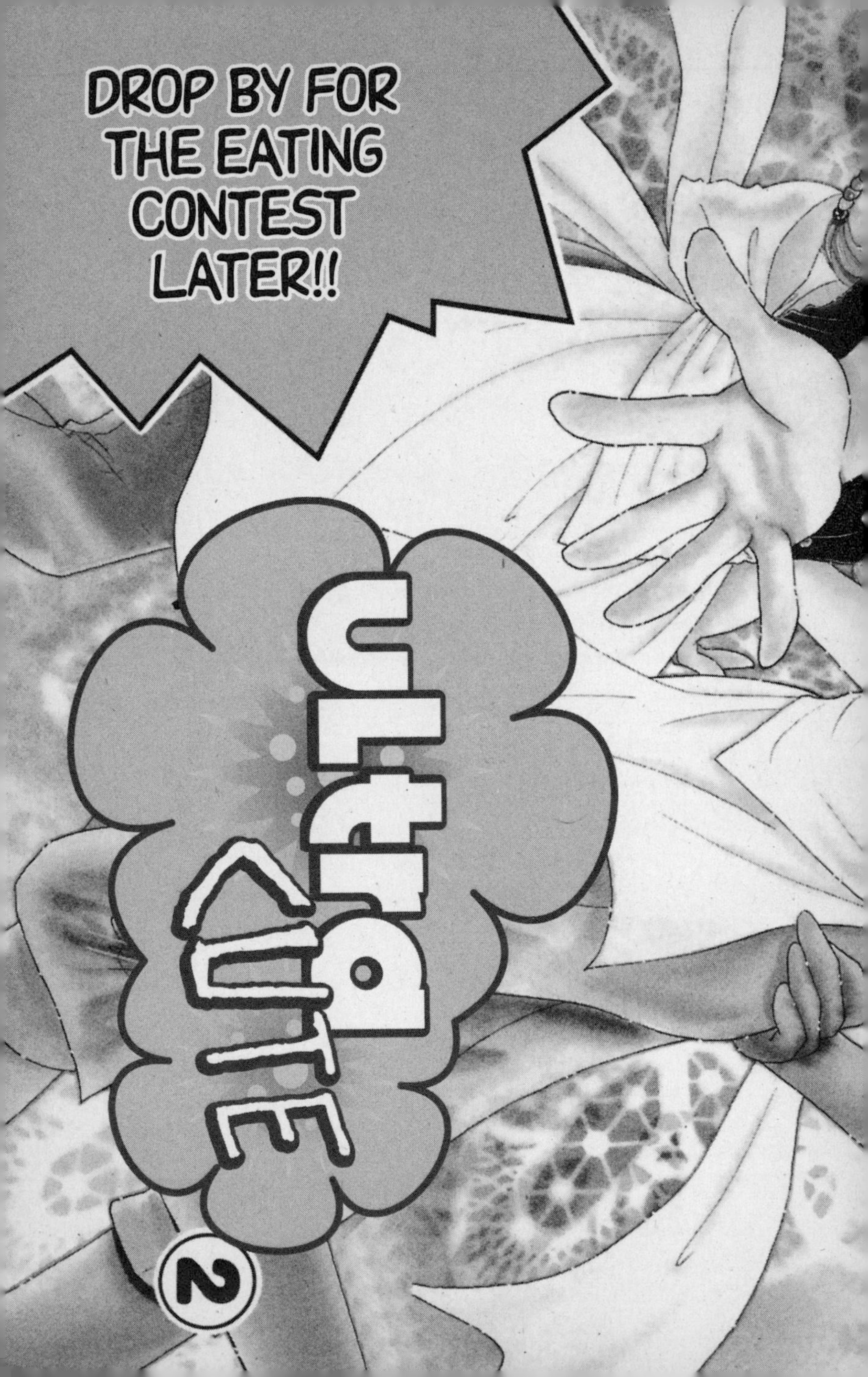
DROP BY FOR THE EATING CONTEST LATER!!
ultra CUTE
2

Hiroyuki Miyamura
A TEACHER AT TANOKURA HIGH SCHOOL. HIS NICKNAME IS CHUCKY.

Ami Uzuki
A HIGH SCHOOL FRESHMAN. SHE MAY LOOK DELICATE, BUT SHE'S A VERY ACTIVE GIRL WHO ALSO HAS A VERY HEALTHY APPETITE. LOOKING FOR A BOYFRIEND.

Tamon Okazaki
THE GUY AMI HAS A CRUSH ON.

Tomohiro Nakatsu
THE GUY NOA HAS A CRUSH ON.

Noa Kurosawa
A HIGH SCHOOL FRESHMAN. SHE'S ALWAYS TAN AND SUPER SMART. ALSO LOOKING FOR A BOYFRIEND.

Mika Tsukishima
TAMON'S EX-GIRLFRIEND. SHE GOES TO A PREPPY SCHOOL.

ULTRA CUTE

The Dish on Ami and Noa's Love Hunt

AMI AND NOA HAVE ALWAYS BEEN RIVALS WHEN IT COMES TO LOVE. HOWEVER, ONE DAY THEY WERE LUCKY ENOUGH TO MEET TWO SUPER HOT GUYS, TAMON AND TOMOHIRO, AT A KARAOKE CLUB AND NOT (FOR ONCE) BE ATTRACTED TO THE SAME ONE.

UNFORTUNATELY, TAMON AND TOMOHIRO ARE PLAYERS WHO TREAT RELATIONSHIPS LIKE A GAME. AMI'S DETERMINED TO MAKE TAMON FALL IN LOVE WITH HER FOR REAL, BUT TOMOHIRO HASN'T COME CLEAN WITH NOA YET.

BOTH GIRLS INVITED THE BOYS TO THE SCHOOL FESTIVAL THEY HAD BEEN PLANNING. HOWEVER, TAMON'S EX-GIRLFRIEND, MIKA, INVITED TAMON TO HER SCHOOL FESTIVAL, AND IT'S BEING HELD THE SAME DAY. WILL TAMON SHOW UP FOR EITHER OF THEM?

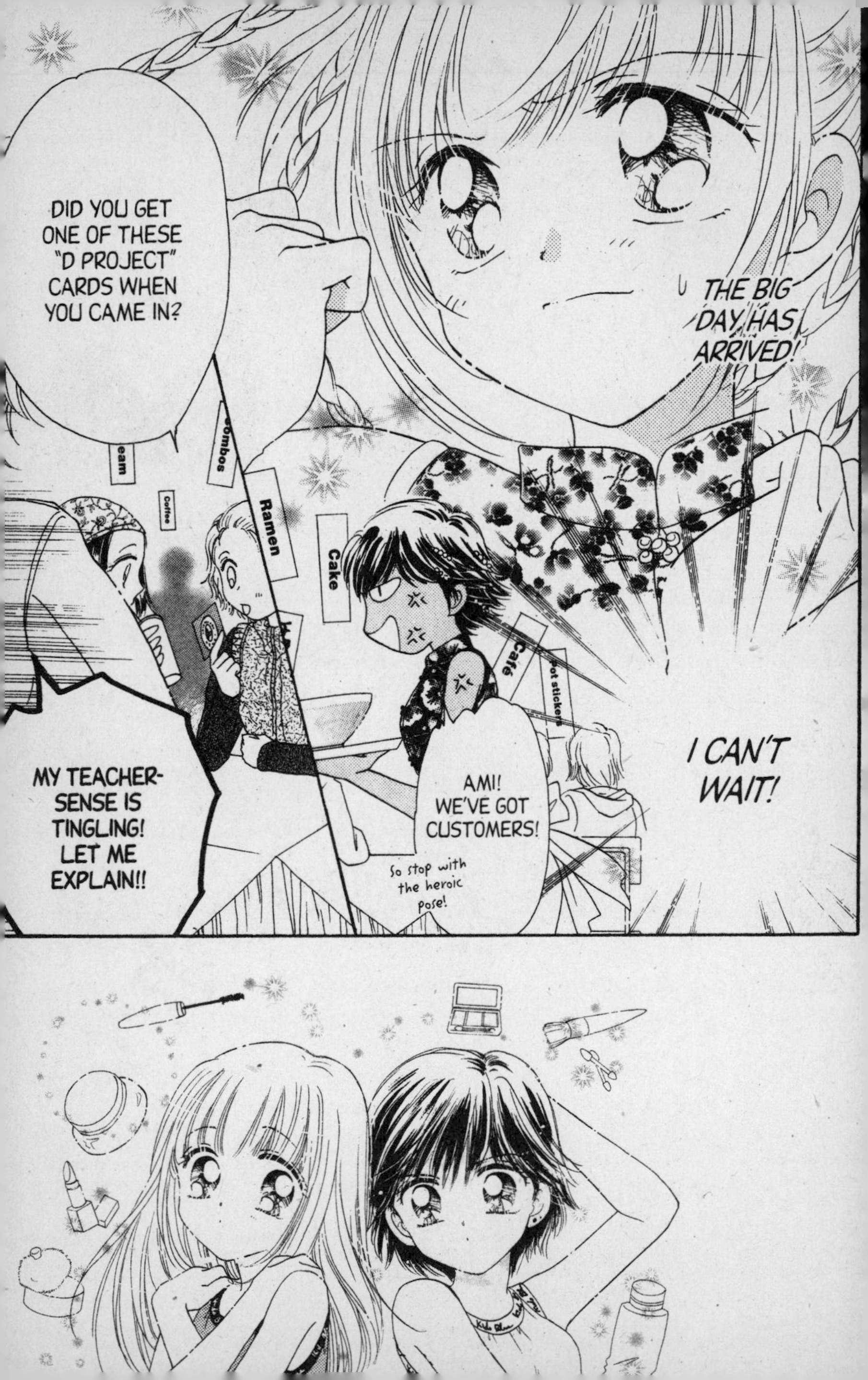
THE BIG DAY HAS ARRIVED!
I CAN'T WAIT!
Café
Cake
Ramen
AMI! WE'VE GOT CUSTOMERS!
So stop with the heroic pose!
Coffee
DID YOU GET ONE OF THESE "D PROJECT" CARDS WHEN YOU CAME IN?
MY TEACHER-SENSE IS TINGLING! LET ME EXPLAIN!!

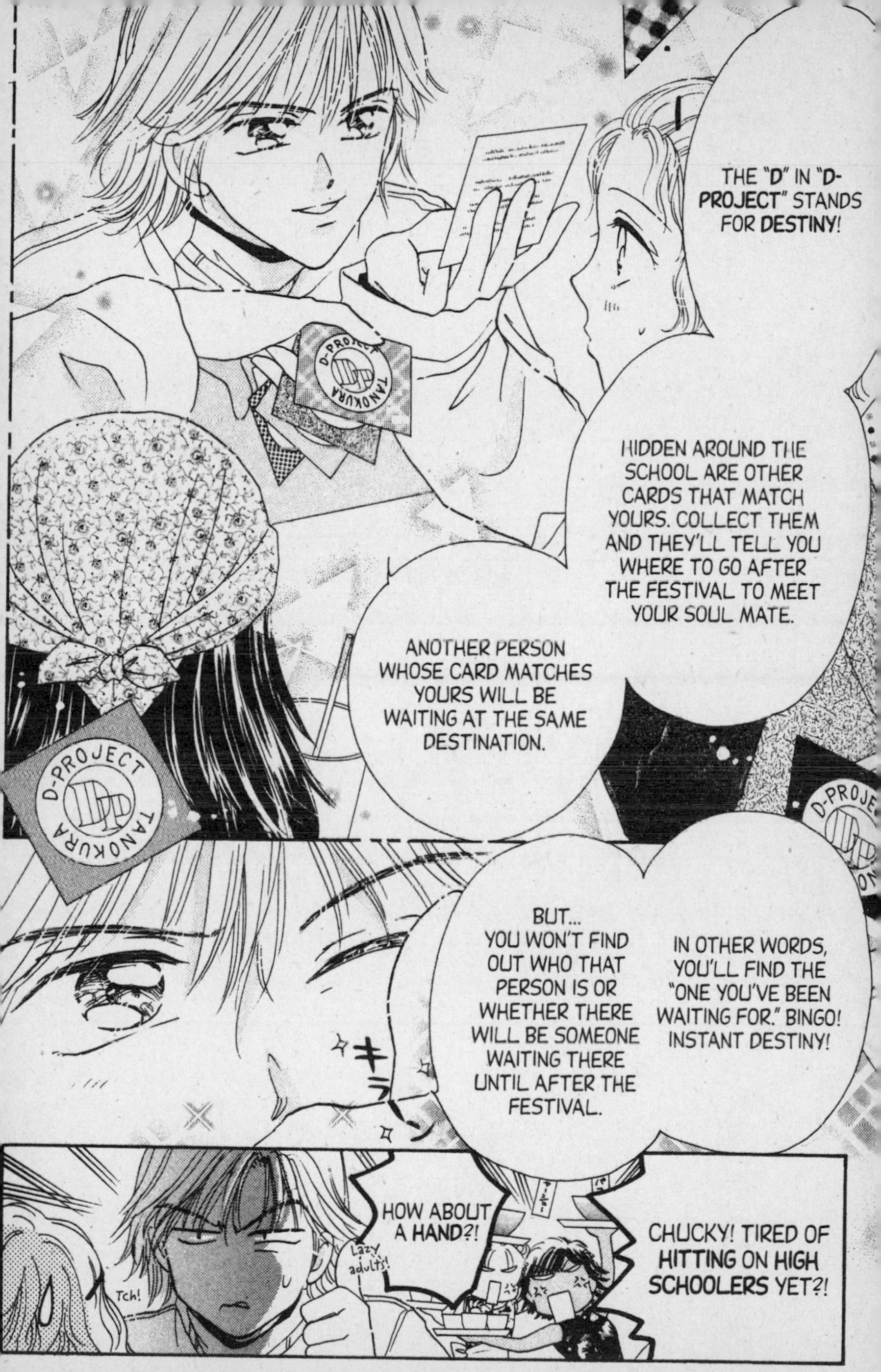
THE "D" IN "D-PROJECT" STANDS FOR DESTINY!
HIDDEN AROUND THE SCHOOL ARE OTHER CARDS THAT MATCH YOURS. COLLECT THEM AND THEY'LL TELL YOU WHERE TO GO AFTER THE FESTIVAL TO MEET YOUR SOUL MATE.
ANOTHER PERSON WHOSE CARD MATCHES YOURS WILL BE WAITING AT THE SAME DESTINATION.
D-PROJECT TANOKURA
IN OTHER WORDS, YOU'LL FIND THE "ONE YOU'VE BEEN WAITING FOR." BINGO! INSTANT DESTINY!
BUT... YOU WON'T FIND OUT WHO THAT PERSON IS OR WHETHER THERE WILL BE SOMEONE WAITING THERE UNTIL AFTER THE FESTIVAL.
CHUCKY! TIRED OF HITTING ON HIGH SCHOOLERS YET?!
Lazy adults!
HOW ABOUT A HAND?!
Tch!

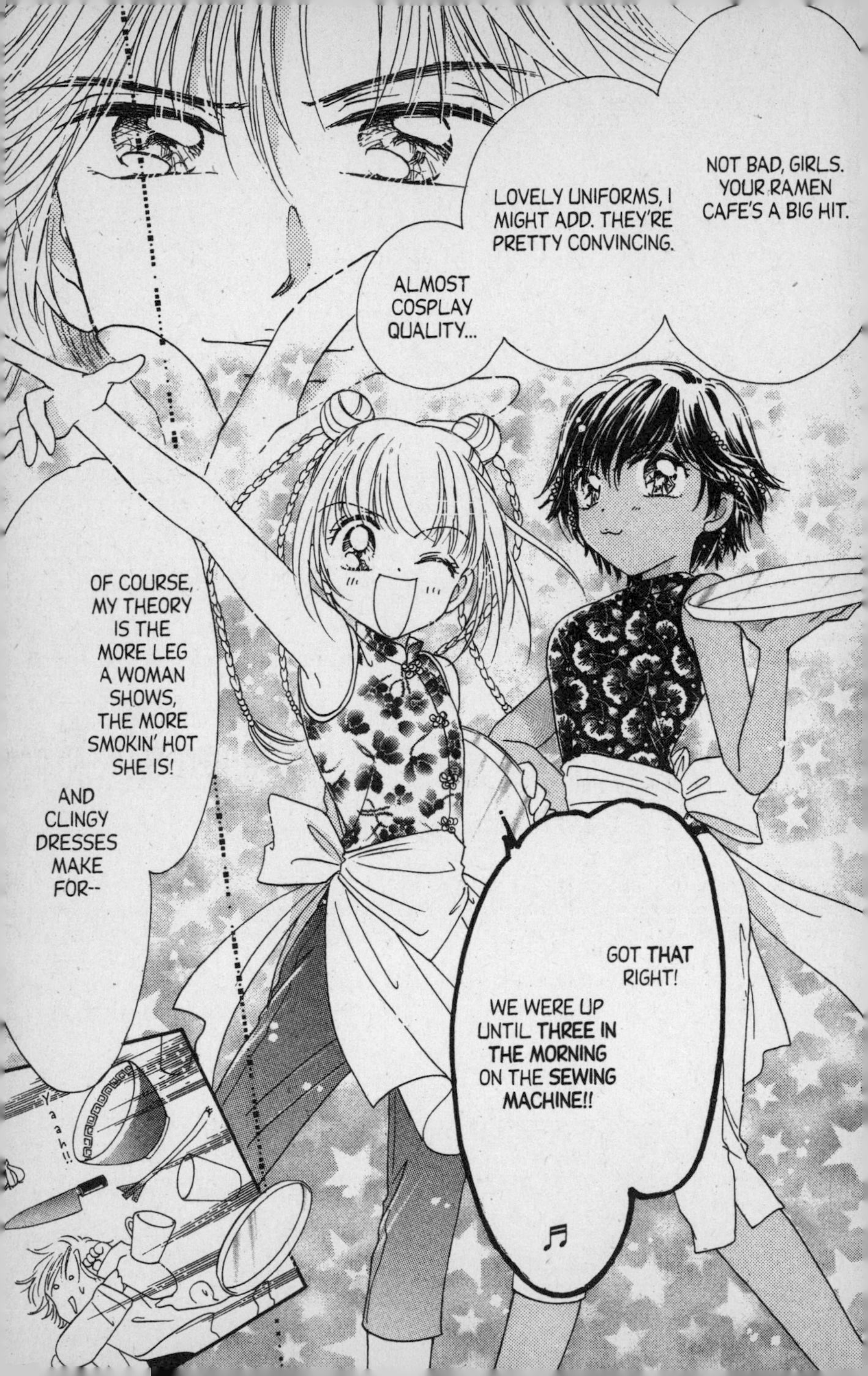
NOT BAD, GIRLS. YOUR RAMEN CAFE'S A BIG HIT.
LOVELY UNIFORMS, I MIGHT ADD. THEY'RE PRETTY CONVINCING.
ALMOST COSPLAY QUALITY...
GOT THAT RIGHT!
WE WERE UP UNTIL THREE IN THE MORNING ON THE SEWING MACHINE!!
OF COURSE, MY THEORY IS THE MORE LEG A WOMAN SHOWS, THE MORE SMOKIN' HOT SHE IS!
AND CLINGY DRESSES MAKE FOR--
Yaah!!

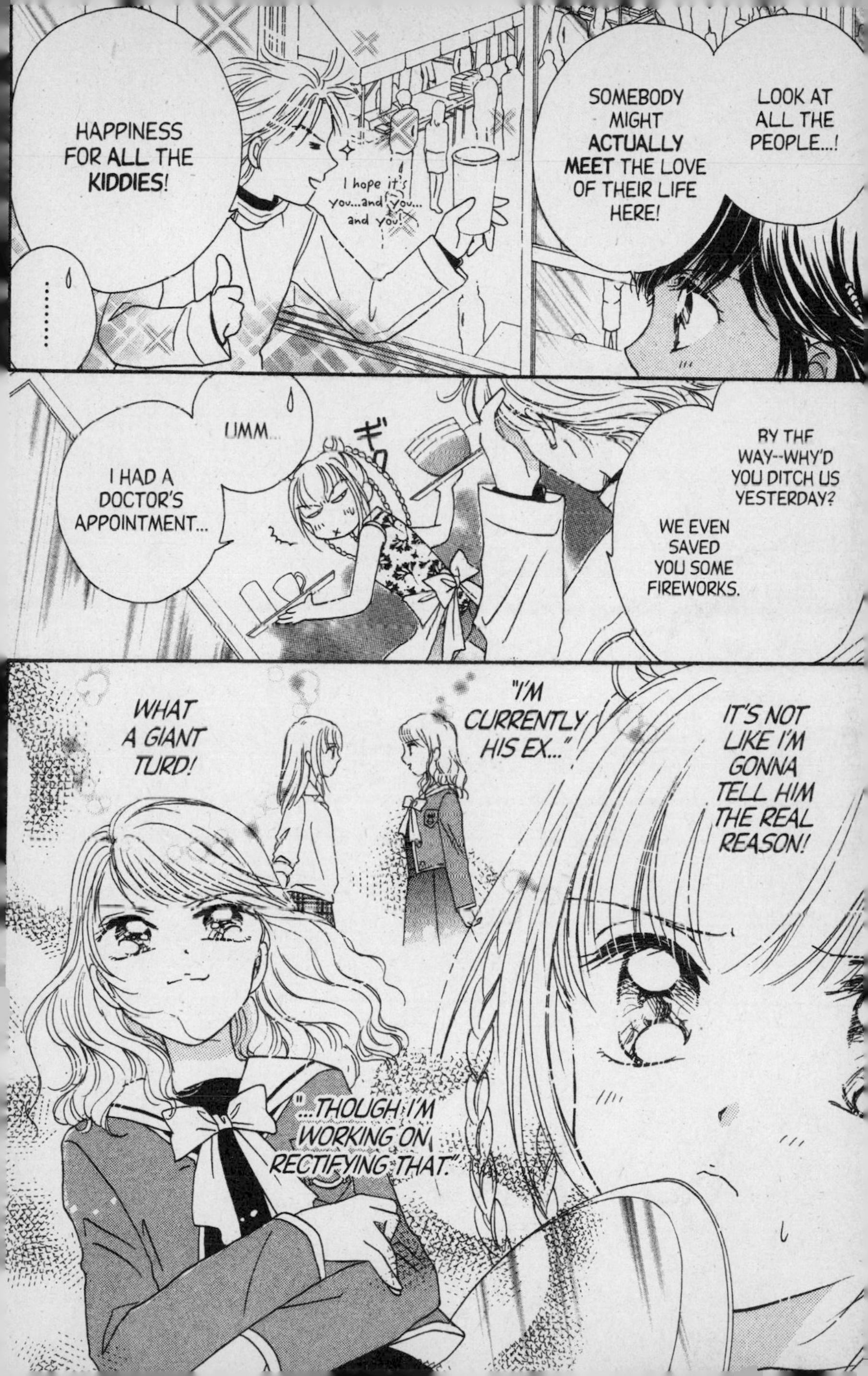
LOOK AT ALL THE PEOPLE...!
SOMEBODY MIGHT ACTUALLY MEET THE LOVE OF THEIR LIFE HERE!
HAPPINESS FOR ALL THE KIDDIES!
I hope it's you...and you... and you!
......
BY THE WAY--WHY'D YOU DITCH US YESTERDAY?
WE EVEN SAVED YOU SOME FIREWORKS.
ギク
UMM...
I HAD A DOCTOR'S APPOINTMENT...
IT'S NOT LIKE I'M GONNA TELL HIM THE REAL REASON!
"I'M CURRENTLY HIS EX..."
"...THOUGH I'M WORKING ON RECTIFYING THAT."
WHAT A GIANT TURD!

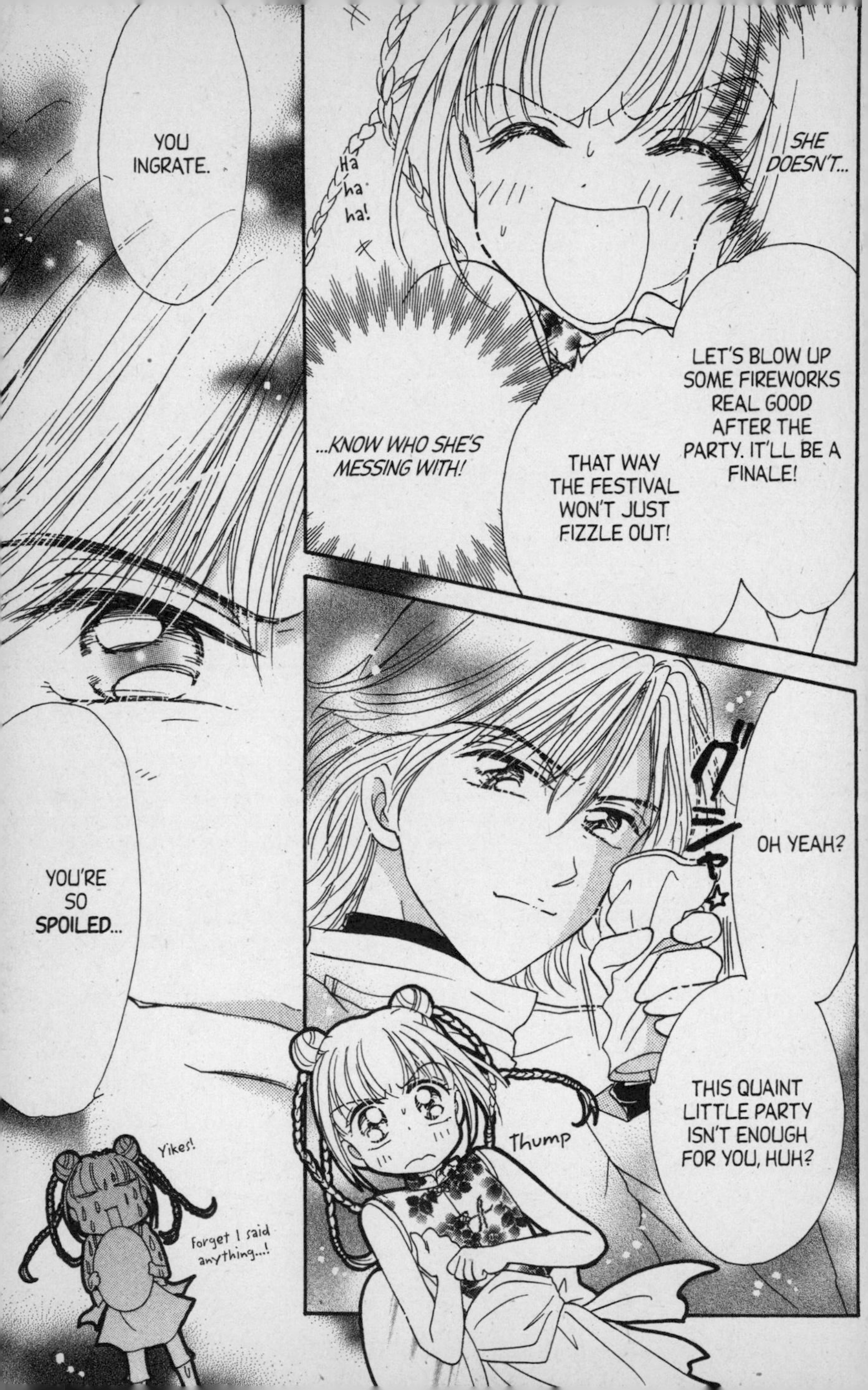
SHE DOESN'T...
Ha ha ha!
LET'S BLOW UP SOME FIREWORKS REAL GOOD AFTER THE PARTY. IT'LL BE A FINALE!
THAT WAY THE FESTIVAL WON'T JUST FIZZLE OUT!
...KNOW WHO SHE'S MESSING WITH!
OH YEAH?
THIS QUAINT LITTLE PARTY ISN'T ENOUGH FOR YOU, HUH?
Thump
YOU INGRATE.
YOU'RE SO SPOILED...
Yikes!
Forget I said anything...!

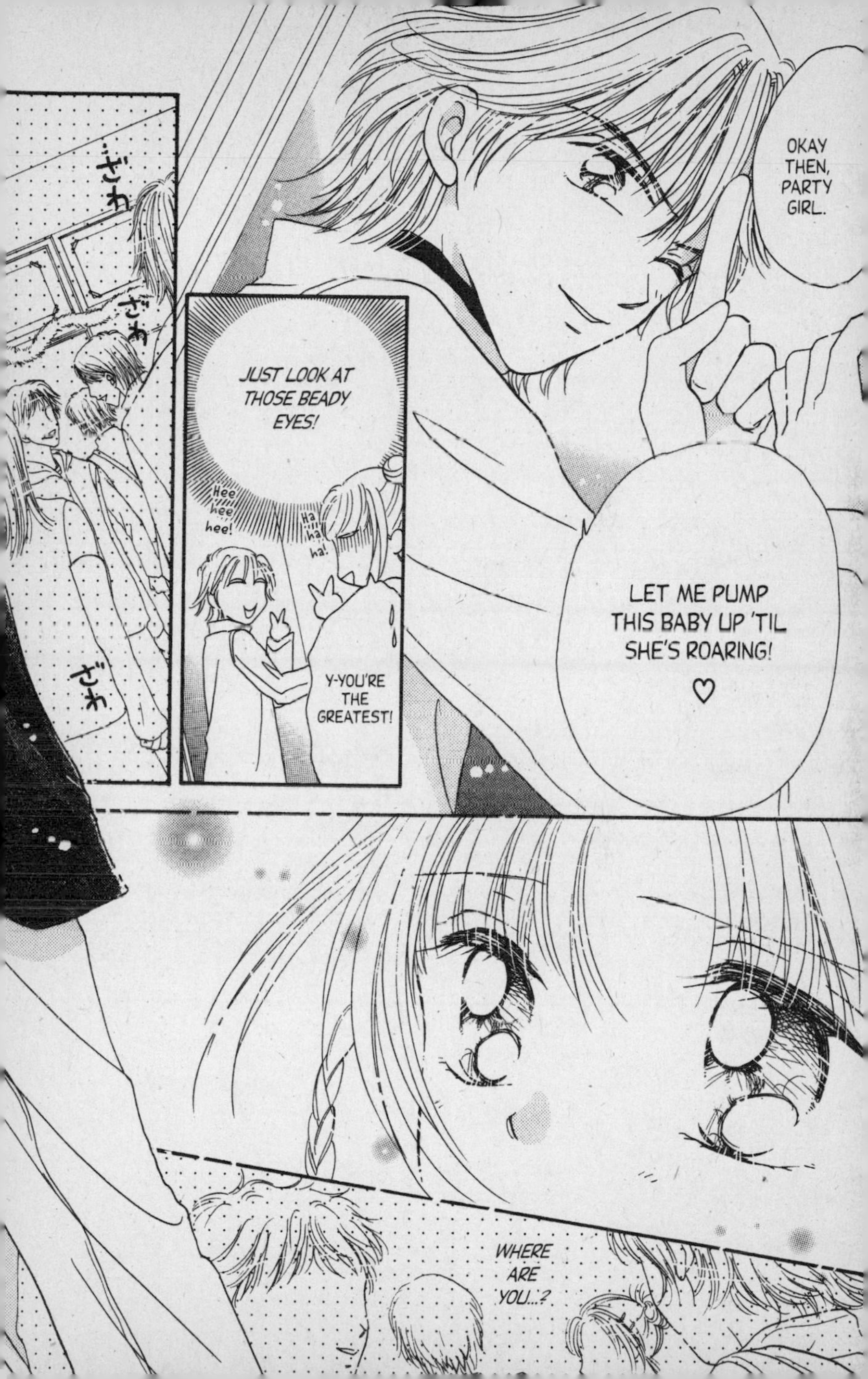
OKAY THEN, PARTY GIRL.
LET ME PUMP THIS BABY UP 'TIL SHE'S ROARING! ♡
JUST LOOK AT THOSE BEADY EYES!
Ha ha ha!
Hee hee hee!
Y-YOU'RE THE GREATEST!
ざわ
ざわ
ざわ
WHERE ARE YOU...?

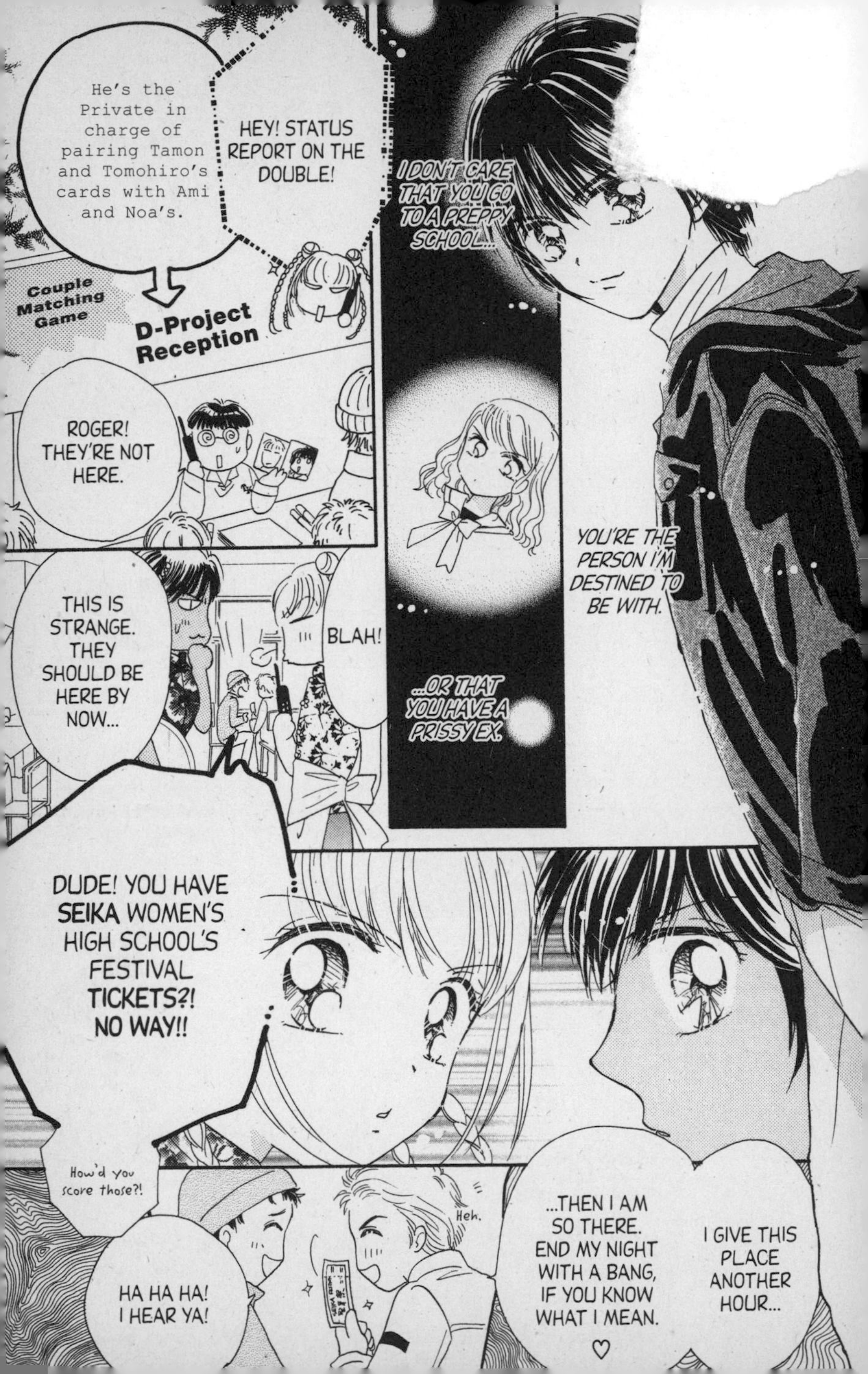
I DON'T CARE THAT YOU GO TO A PREPPY SCHOOL...
...OR THAT YOU HAVE A PRISSY EX.
YOU'RE THE PERSON I'M DESTINED TO BE WITH.
HEY! STATUS REPORT ON THE DOUBLE!
He's the Private in charge of pairing Tamon and Tomohiro's cards with Ami and Noa's.
Couple Matching Game
D-Project Reception
ROGER! THEY'RE NOT HERE.
BLAH!
THIS IS STRANGE. THEY SHOULD BE HERE BY NOW...
DUDE! YOU HAVE SEIKA WOMEN'S HIGH SCHOOL'S FESTIVAL TICKETS?! NO WAY!!
I GIVE THIS PLACE ANOTHER HOUR...
...THEN I AM SO THERE. END MY NIGHT WITH A BANG, IF YOU KNOW WHAT I MEAN. ♡
Heh.
How'd you score those?!
HA HA HA! I HEAR YA!

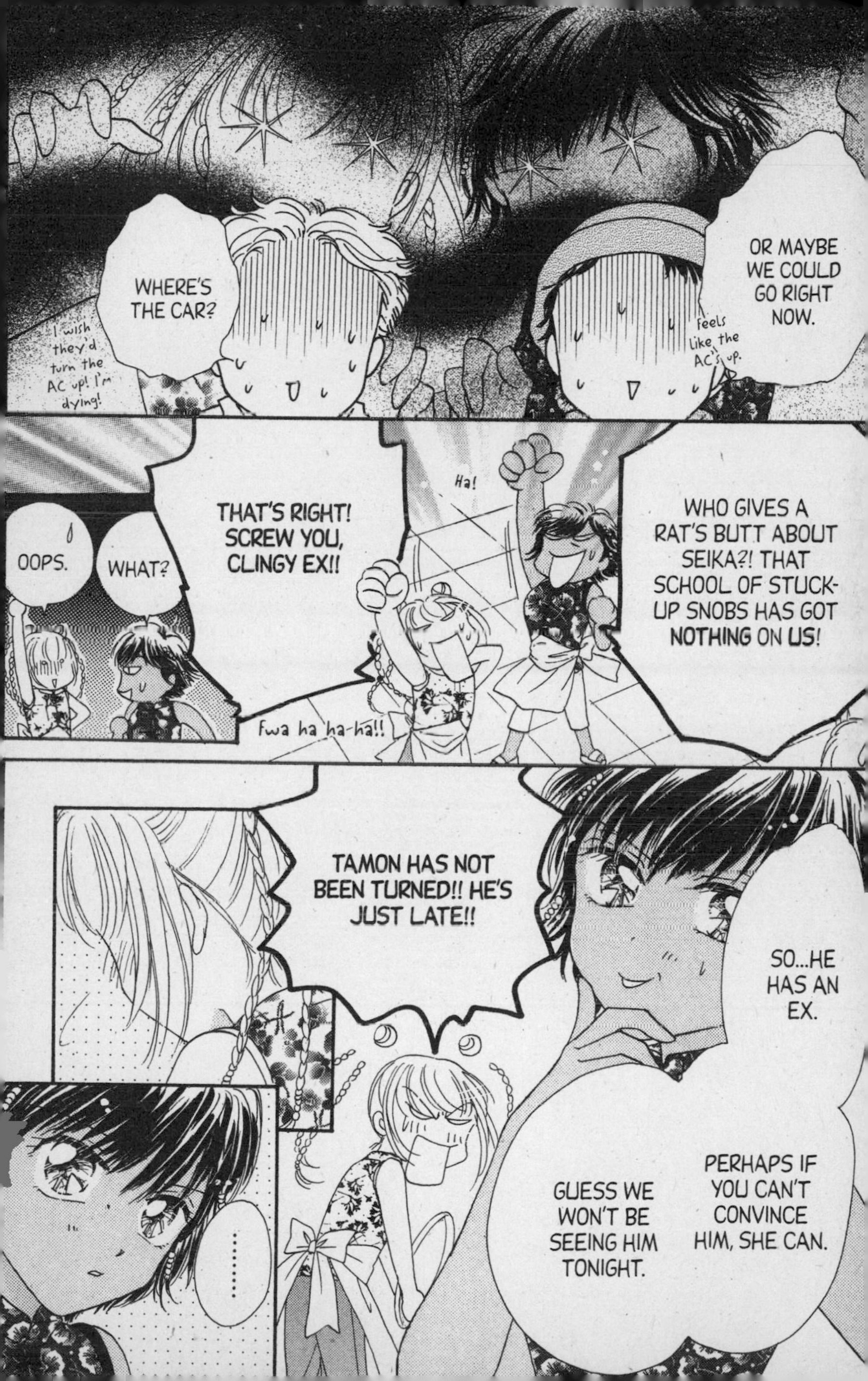
OR MAYBE WE COULD GO RIGHT NOW.
Feels like the AC's up.
WHERE'S THE CAR?
I wish they'd turn the AC up! I'm dying!
WHO GIVES A RAT'S BUTT ABOUT SEIKA?! THAT SCHOOL OF STUCK-UP SNOBS HAS GOT NOTHING ON US!
Ha!
THAT'S RIGHT! SCREW YOU, CLINGY EX!!
Fwa ha ha-ha!!
WHAT?
OOPS.
SO...HE HAS AN EX.
TAMON HAS NOT BEEN TURNED!! HE'S JUST LATE!!
PERHAPS IF YOU CAN'T CONVINCE HIM, SHE CAN.
GUESS WE WON'T BE SEEING HIM TONIGHT.
......

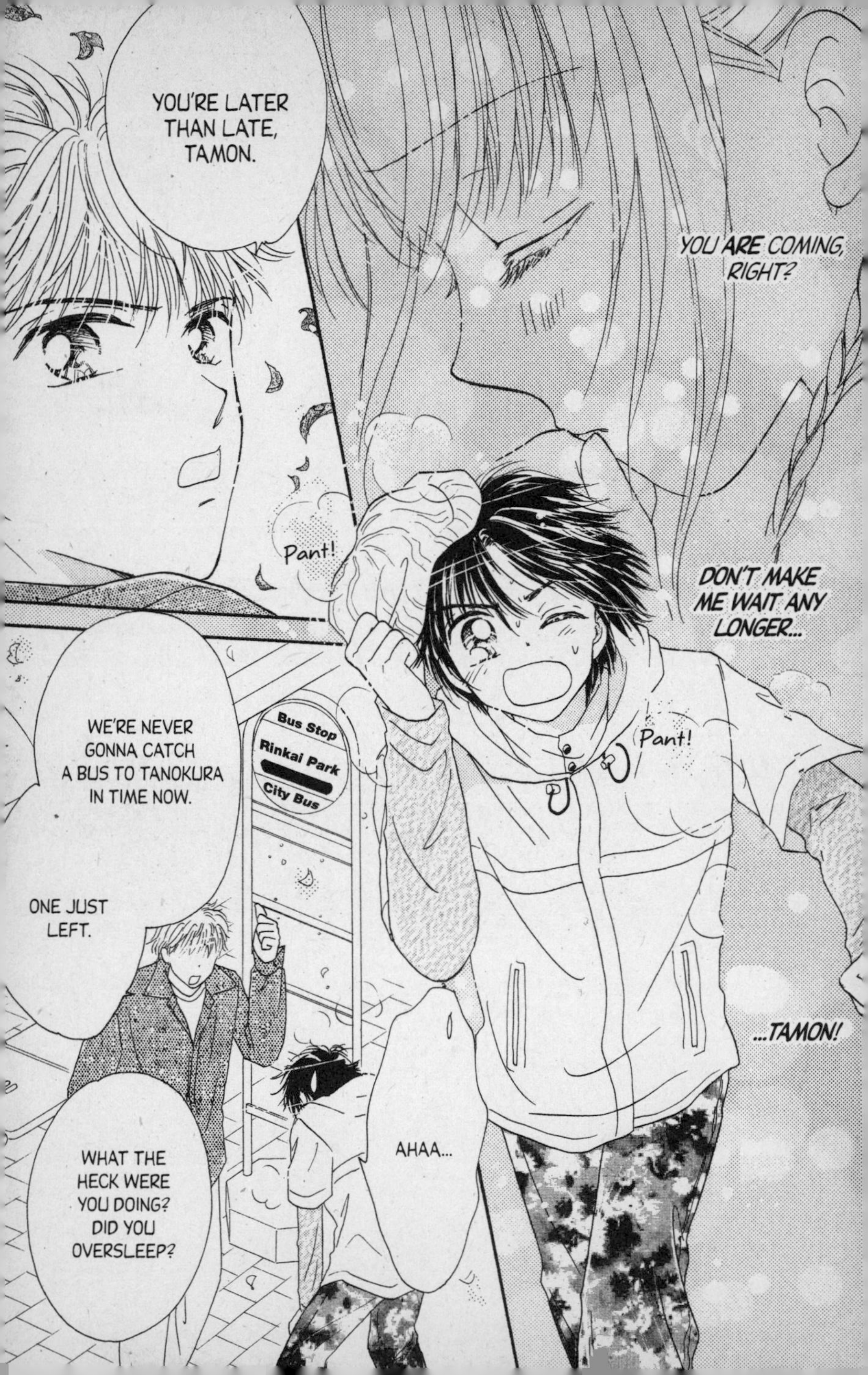
YOU ARE COMING, RIGHT?
DON'T MAKE ME WAIT ANY LONGER...
...TAMON!
Pant!
Pant!
YOU'RE LATER THAN LATE, TAMON.
WE'RE NEVER GONNA CATCH A BUS TO TANOKURA IN TIME NOW.
ONE JUST LEFT.
Bus Stop
Rinkai Park
City Bus
WHAT THE HECK WERE YOU DOING? DID YOU OVERSLEEP?
AHAA...

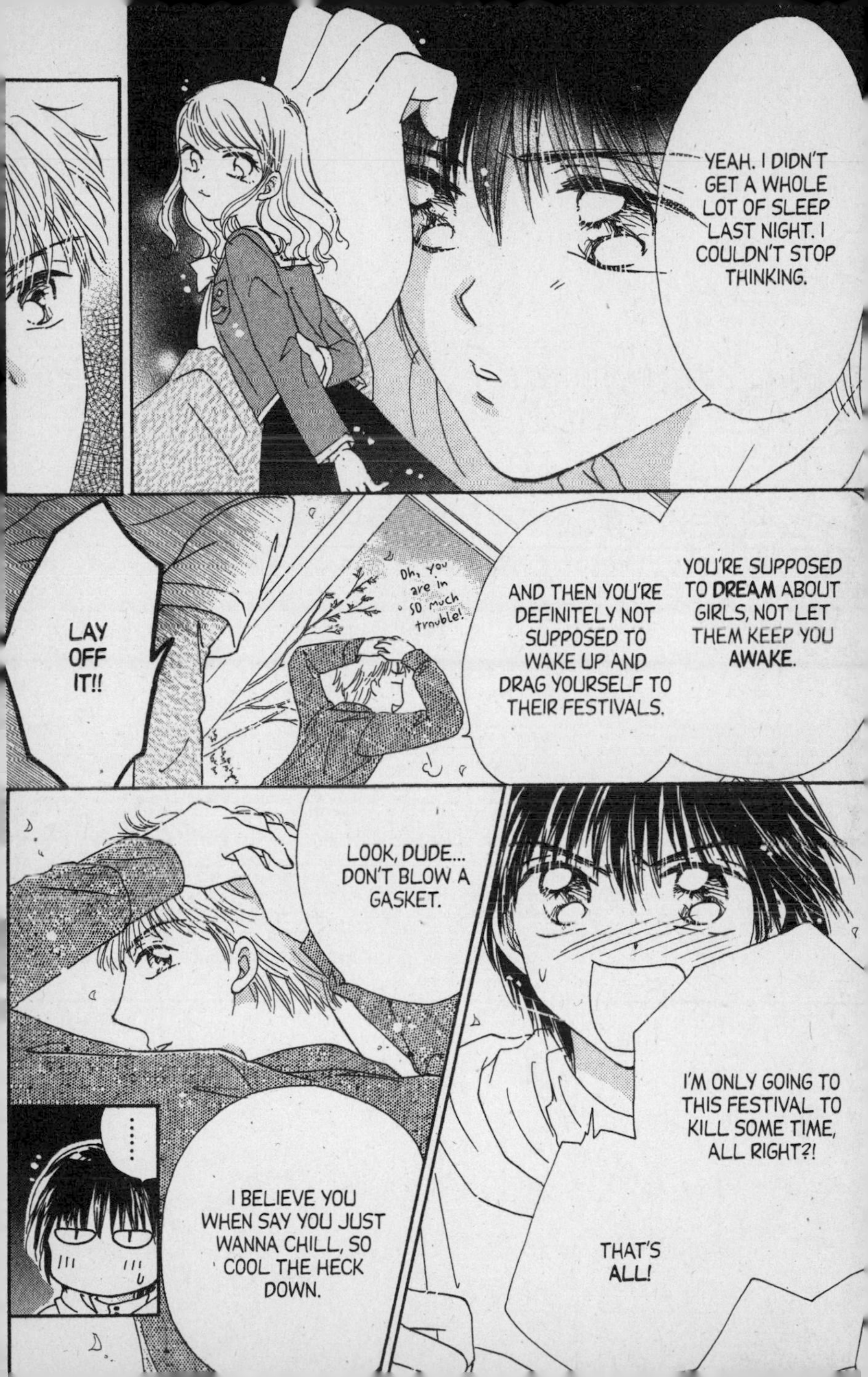
YEAH. I DIDN'T GET A WHOLE LOT OF SLEEP LAST NIGHT. I COULDN'T STOP THINKING.
YOU'RE SUPPOSED TO DREAM ABOUT GIRLS, NOT LET THEM KEEP YOU AWAKE.
AND THEN YOU'RE DEFINITELY NOT SUPPOSED TO WAKE UP AND DRAG YOURSELF TO THEIR FESTIVALS.
Oh, you are in SO much trouble!
LAY OFF IT!!
I'M ONLY GOING TO THIS FESTIVAL TO KILL SOME TIME, ALL RIGHT?!
THAT'S ALL!
LOOK, DUDE... DON'T BLOW A GASKET.
......
I BELIEVE YOU WHEN SAY YOU JUST WANNA CHILL, SO COOL THE HECK DOWN.

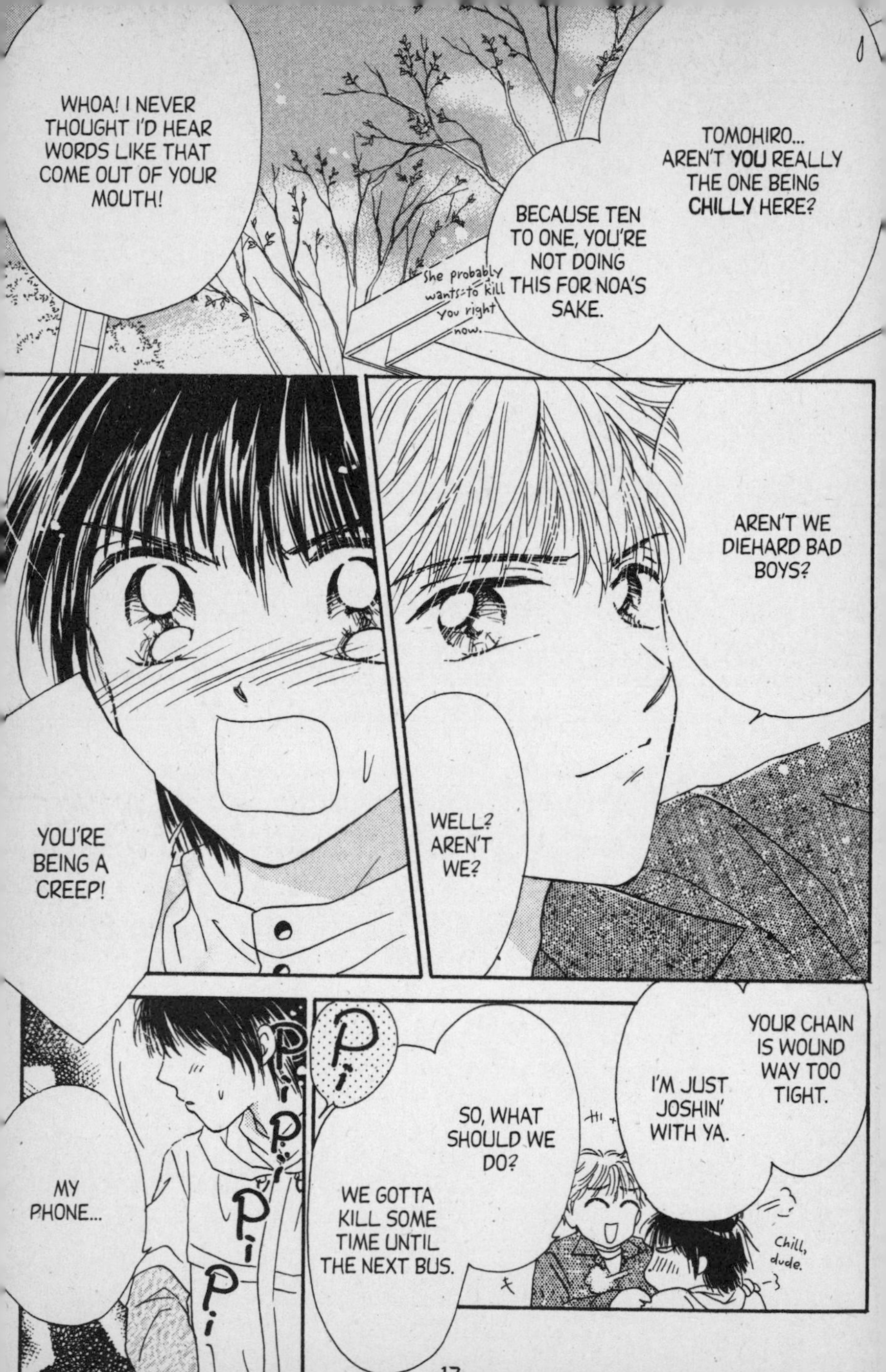
TOMOHIRO... AREN'T YOU REALLY THE ONE BEING CHILLY HERE?
BECAUSE TEN TO ONE, YOU'RE NOT DOING THIS FOR NOA'S SAKE.
She probably wants to kill you right now.
WHOA! I NEVER THOUGHT I'D HEAR WORDS LIKE THAT COME OUT OF YOUR MOUTH!
AREN'T WE DIEHARD BAD BOYS?
WELL? AREN'T WE?
YOU'RE BEING A CREEP!
YOUR CHAIN IS WOUND WAY TOO TIGHT.
I'M JUST JOSHIN' WITH YA.
Chill, dude.
SO, WHAT SHOULD WE DO?
WE GOTTA KILL SOME TIME UNTIL THE NEXT BUS.
Pi
Pi Pi Pi Pi
MY PHONE...

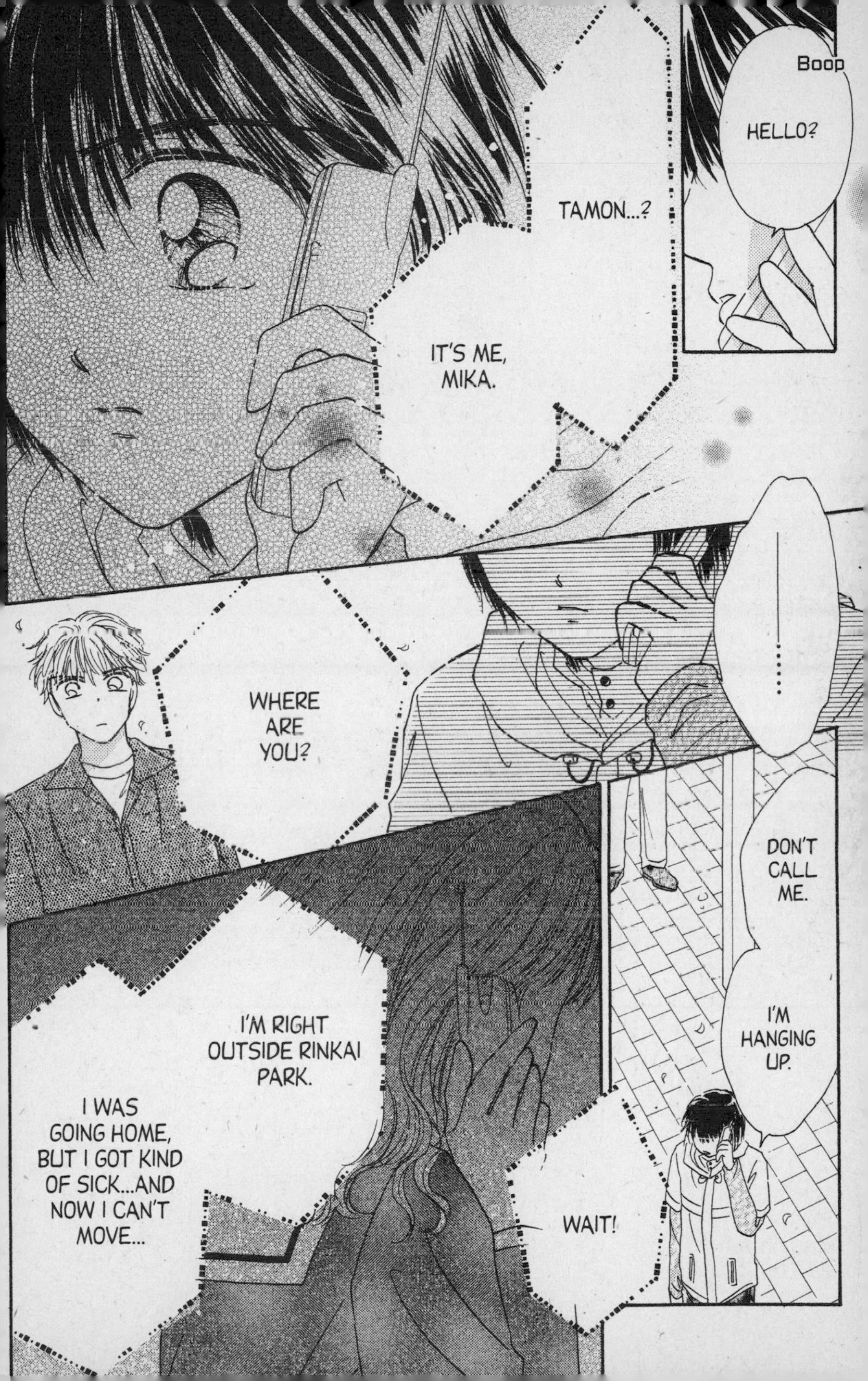

Boop
HELLO?
TAMON...?
IT'S ME, MIKA.
......
WHERE ARE YOU?
DON'T CALL ME.
I'M HANGING UP.
WAIT!
I'M RIGHT OUTSIDE RINKAI PARK.
I WAS GOING HOME, BUT I GOT KIND OF SICK...AND NOW I CAN'T MOVE...

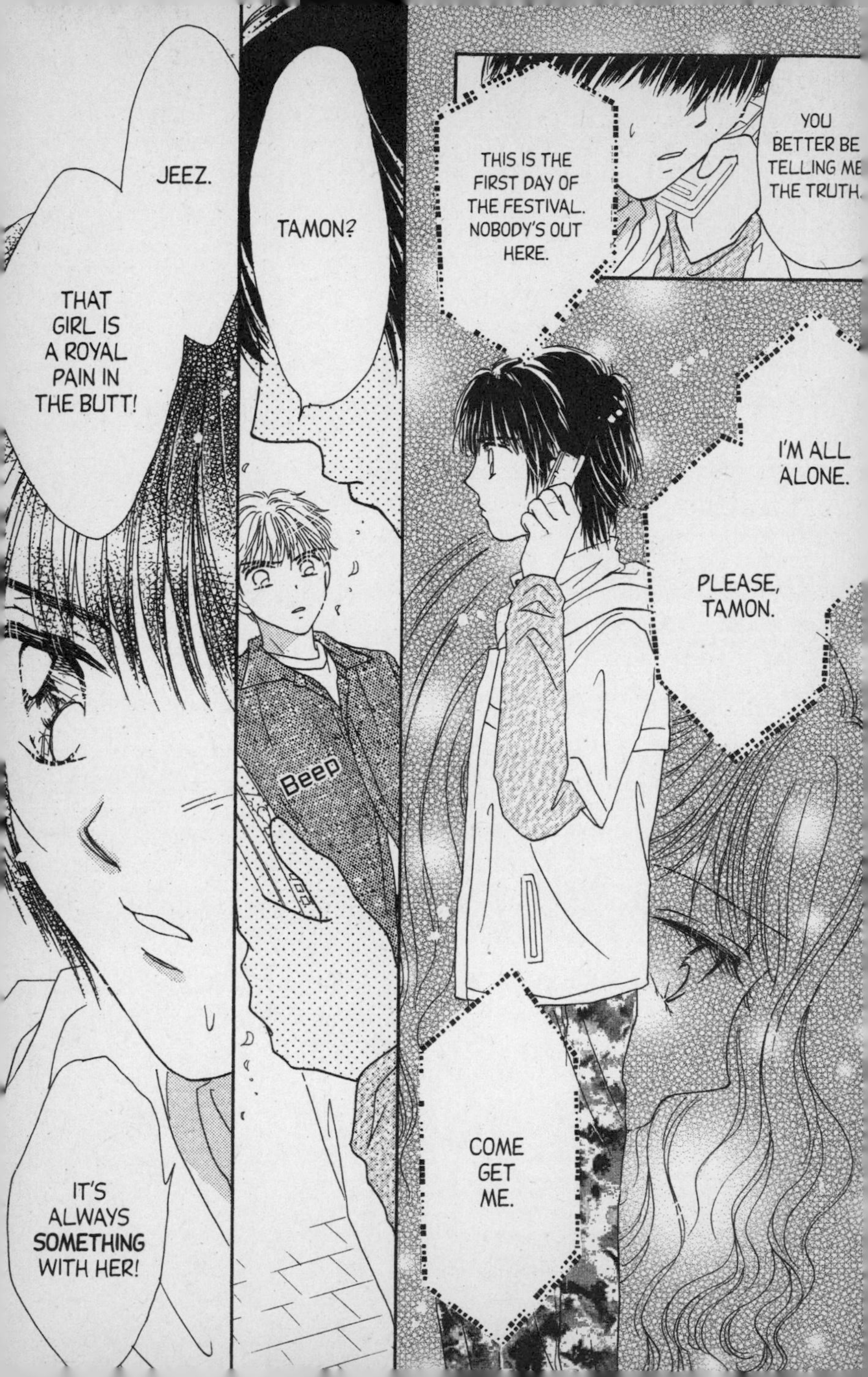
YOU BETTER BE TELLING ME THE TRUTH.
THIS IS THE FIRST DAY OF THE FESTIVAL. NOBODY'S OUT HERE.
I'M ALL ALONE.
PLEASE, TAMON.
COME GET ME.
TAMON?
Beep
JEEZ.
THAT GIRL IS A ROYAL PAIN IN THE BUTT!
IT'S ALWAYS SOMETHING WITH HER!

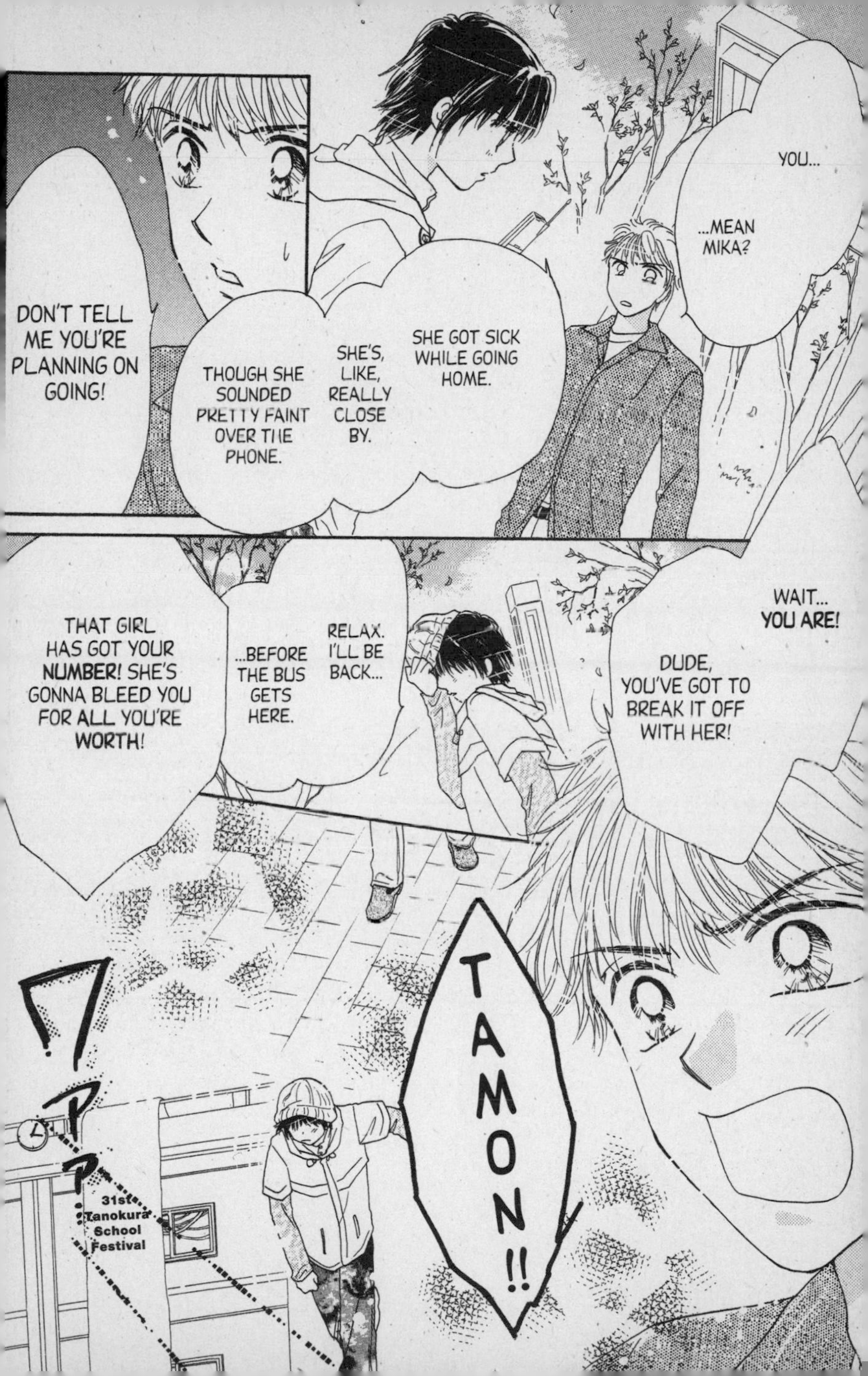
YOU...
...MEAN MIKA?
SHE GOT SICK WHILE GOING HOME.
SHE'S, LIKE, REALLY CLOSE BY.
THOUGH SHE SOUNDED PRETTY FAINT OVER THE PHONE.
DON'T TELL ME YOU'RE PLANNING ON GOING!
WAIT... **YOU ARE!**
DUDE, YOU'VE GOT TO BREAK IT OFF WITH HER!
RELAX. I'LL BE BACK...
...BEFORE THE BUS GETS HERE.
THAT GIRL HAS GOT YOUR **NUMBER!** SHE'S GONNA BLEED YOU FOR ALL YOU'RE **WORTH!**
TAMON!!
31st Tanokura School Festival

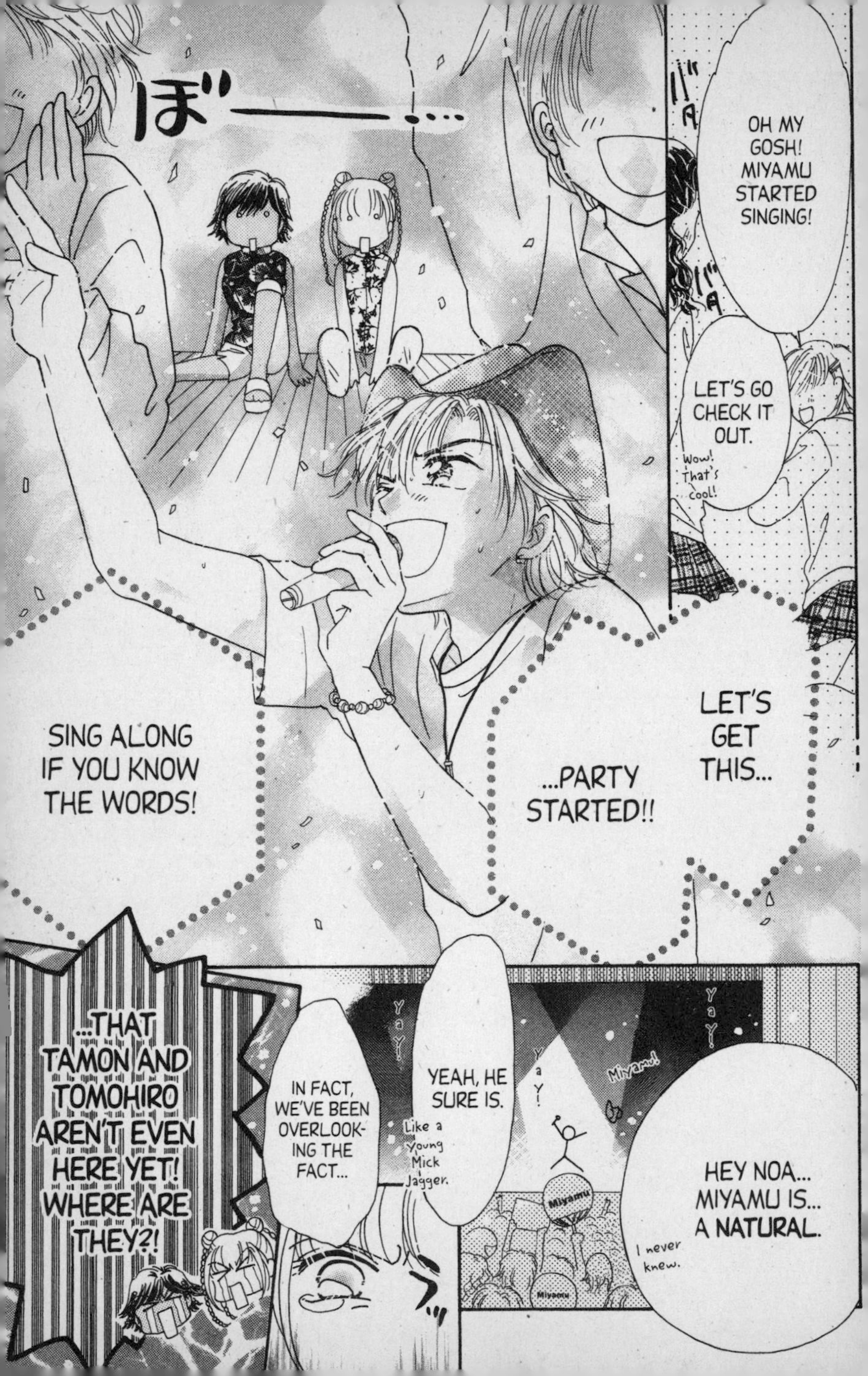
OH MY GOSH! MIYAMU STARTED SINGING!
LET'S GO CHECK IT OUT.
Wow! That's cool!
ぼー…
LET'S GET THIS...
...PARTY STARTED!!
SING ALONG IF YOU KNOW THE WORDS!
HEY NOA... MIYAMU IS... A NATURAL.
I never knew.
Yay!
Miyamu!
Yay!
Yay!
Miyamu
Miyamu
YEAH, HE SURE IS.
Like a Young Mick Jagger.
IN FACT, WE'VE BEEN OVERLOOKING THE FACT...
...THAT TAMON AND TOMOHIRO AREN'T EVEN HERE YET! WHERE ARE THEY?!

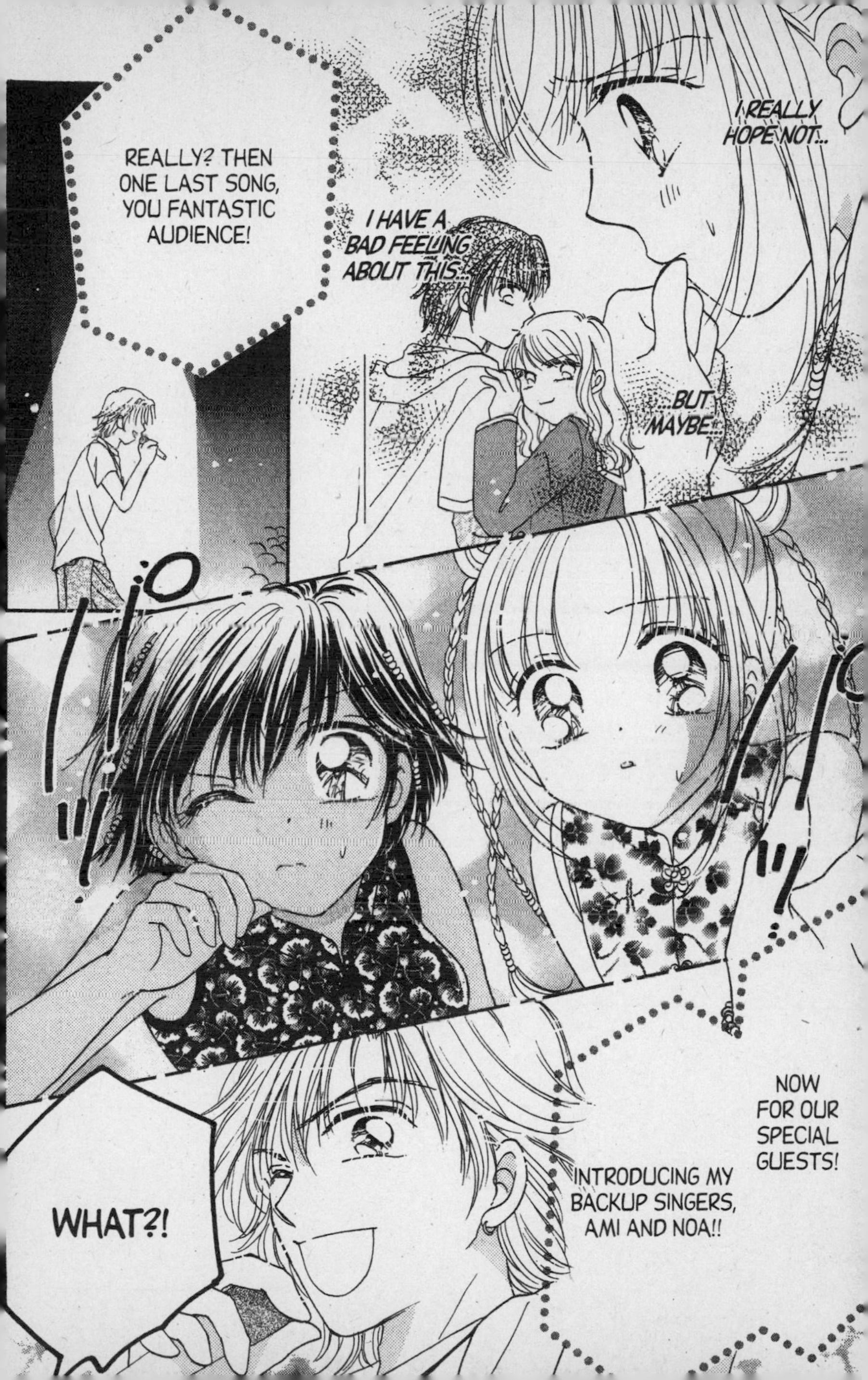
I HAVE A BAD FEELING ABOUT THIS...
I REALLY HOPE NOT...
...BUT MAYBE...
REALLY? THEN ONE LAST SONG, YOU FANTASTIC AUDIENCE!
NOW FOR OUR SPECIAL GUESTS!
INTRODUCING MY BACKUP SINGERS, AMI AND NOA!!
WHAT?!

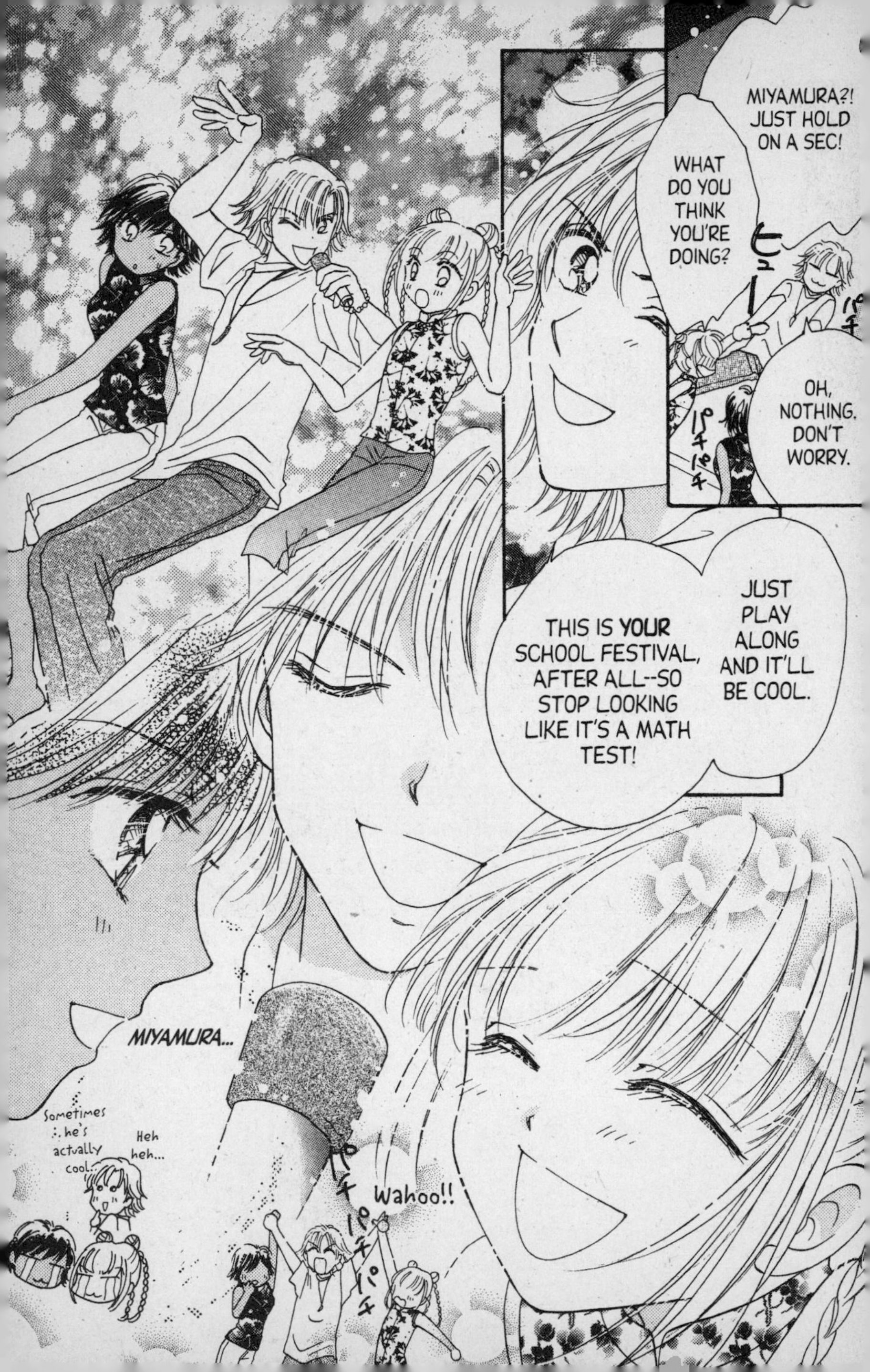
MIYAMURA?! JUST HOLD ON A SEC!
WHAT DO YOU THINK YOU'RE DOING?
OH, NOTHING. DON'T WORRY.
JUST PLAY ALONG AND IT'LL BE COOL.
THIS IS **YOUR** SCHOOL FESTIVAL, AFTER ALL--SO STOP LOOKING LIKE IT'S A MATH TEST!
MIYAMURA...
Wahoo!!
Heh heh...
Sometimes he's actually cool...

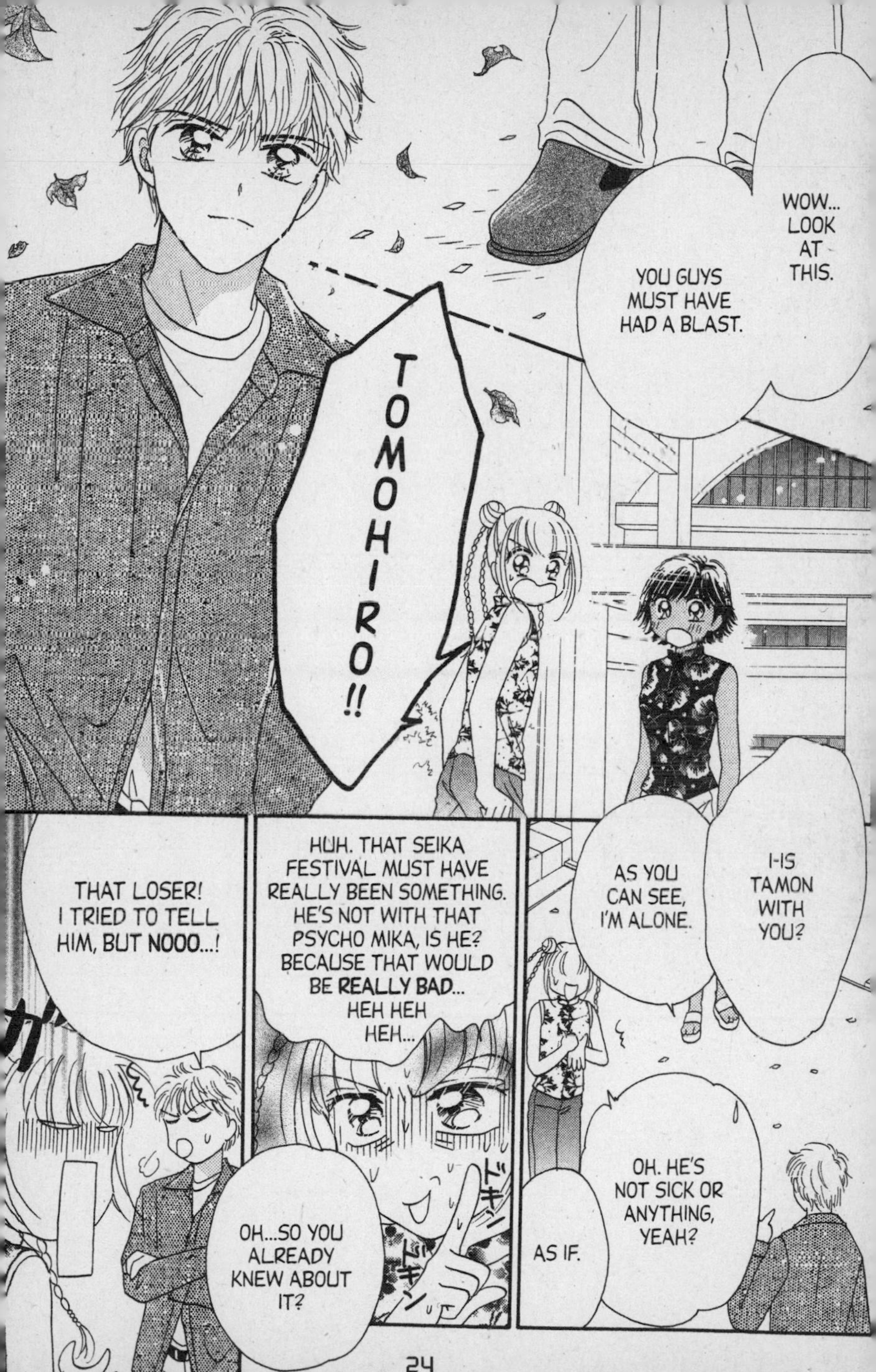
WOW... LOOK AT THIS.
YOU GUYS MUST HAVE HAD A BLAST.
TOMOHIRO!!
I-IS TAMON WITH YOU?
AS YOU CAN SEE, I'M ALONE.
OH. HE'S NOT SICK OR ANYTHING, YEAH?
AS IF.
HUH. THAT SEIKA FESTIVAL MUST HAVE REALLY BEEN SOMETHING. HE'S NOT WITH THAT PSYCHO MIKA, IS HE? BECAUSE THAT WOULD BE **REALLY BAD**... HEH HEH HEH...
ドキン
ドキン
OH...SO YOU ALREADY KNEW ABOUT IT?
THAT LOSER! I TRIED TO TELL HIM, BUT **NOOO**...!

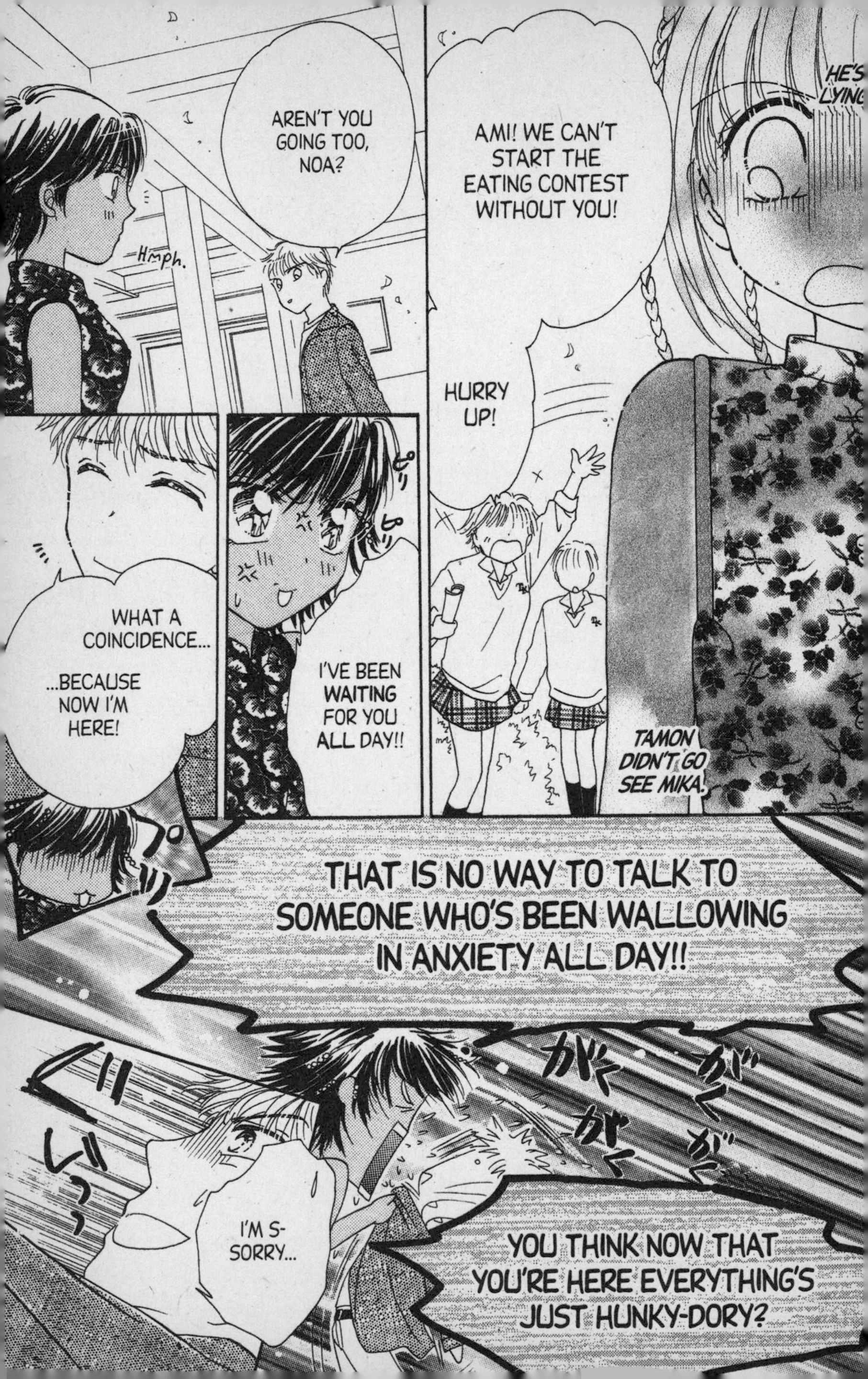
HE'S LYING
AMI! WE CAN'T START THE EATING CONTEST WITHOUT YOU!
HURRY UP!
TAMON DIDN'T GO SEE MIKA.
AREN'T YOU GOING TOO, NOA?
Hmph.
I'VE BEEN WAITING FOR YOU ALL DAY!!
WHAT A COINCIDENCE...
...BECAUSE NOW I'M HERE!
THAT IS NO WAY TO TALK TO SOMEONE WHO'S BEEN WALLOWING IN ANXIETY ALL DAY!!
YOU THINK NOW THAT YOU'RE HERE EVERYTHING'S JUST HUNKY-DORY?
I'M S-SORRY...

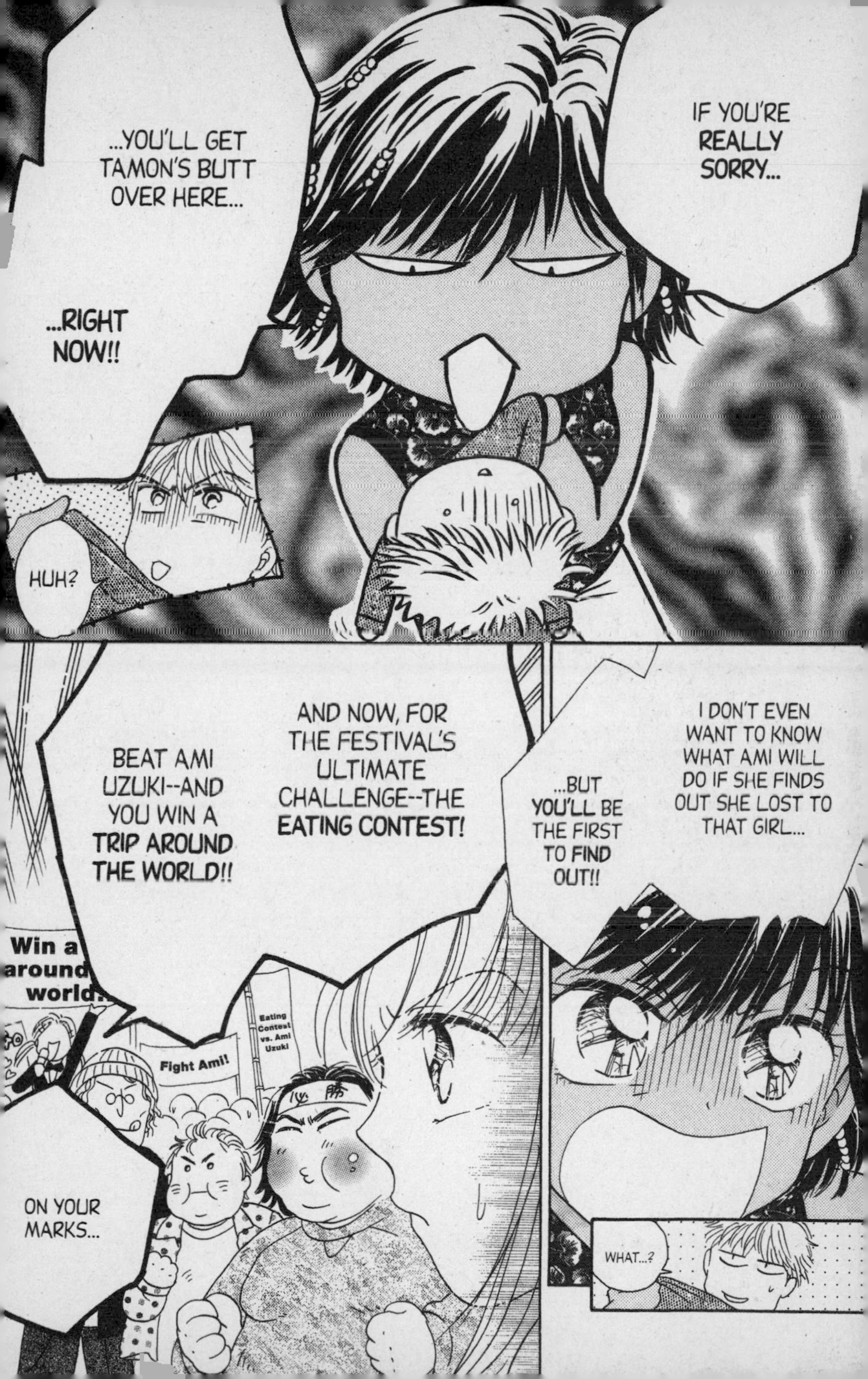
IF YOU'RE REALLY SORRY...
...YOU'LL GET TAMON'S BUTT OVER HERE...
...RIGHT NOW!!
HUH?
I DON'T EVEN WANT TO KNOW WHAT AMI WILL DO IF SHE FINDS OUT SHE LOST TO THAT GIRL...
...BUT YOU'LL BE THE FIRST TO FIND OUT!!
WHAT...?
AND NOW, FOR THE FESTIVAL'S ULTIMATE CHALLENGE--THE EATING CONTEST!
BEAT AMI UZUKI--AND YOU WIN A TRIP AROUND THE WORLD!!
Win a
around
world!!
Eating Contest vs. Ami Uzuki
Fight Ami!
ON YOUR MARKS...

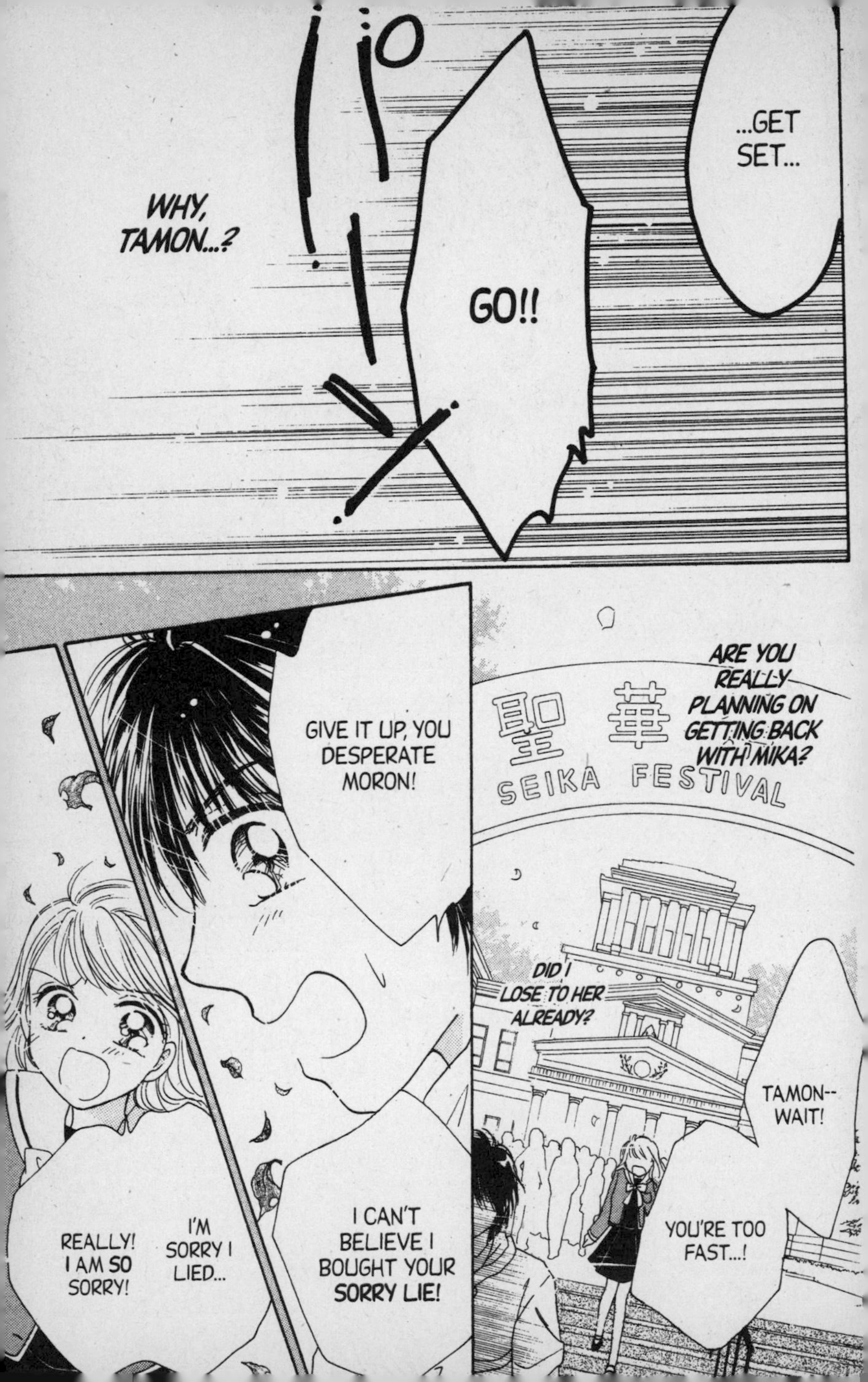
...GET SET...
GO!!
WHY, TAMON...?
ARE YOU REALLY PLANNING ON GETTING BACK WITH MIKA?
聖 華
SEIKA FESTIVAL
TAMON-- WAIT!
DID I LOSE TO HER ALREADY?
YOU'RE TOO FAST...!
GIVE IT UP, YOU DESPERATE MORON!
I CAN'T BELIEVE I BOUGHT YOUR SORRY LIE!
I'M SORRY I LIED...
REALLY! I AM SO SORRY!

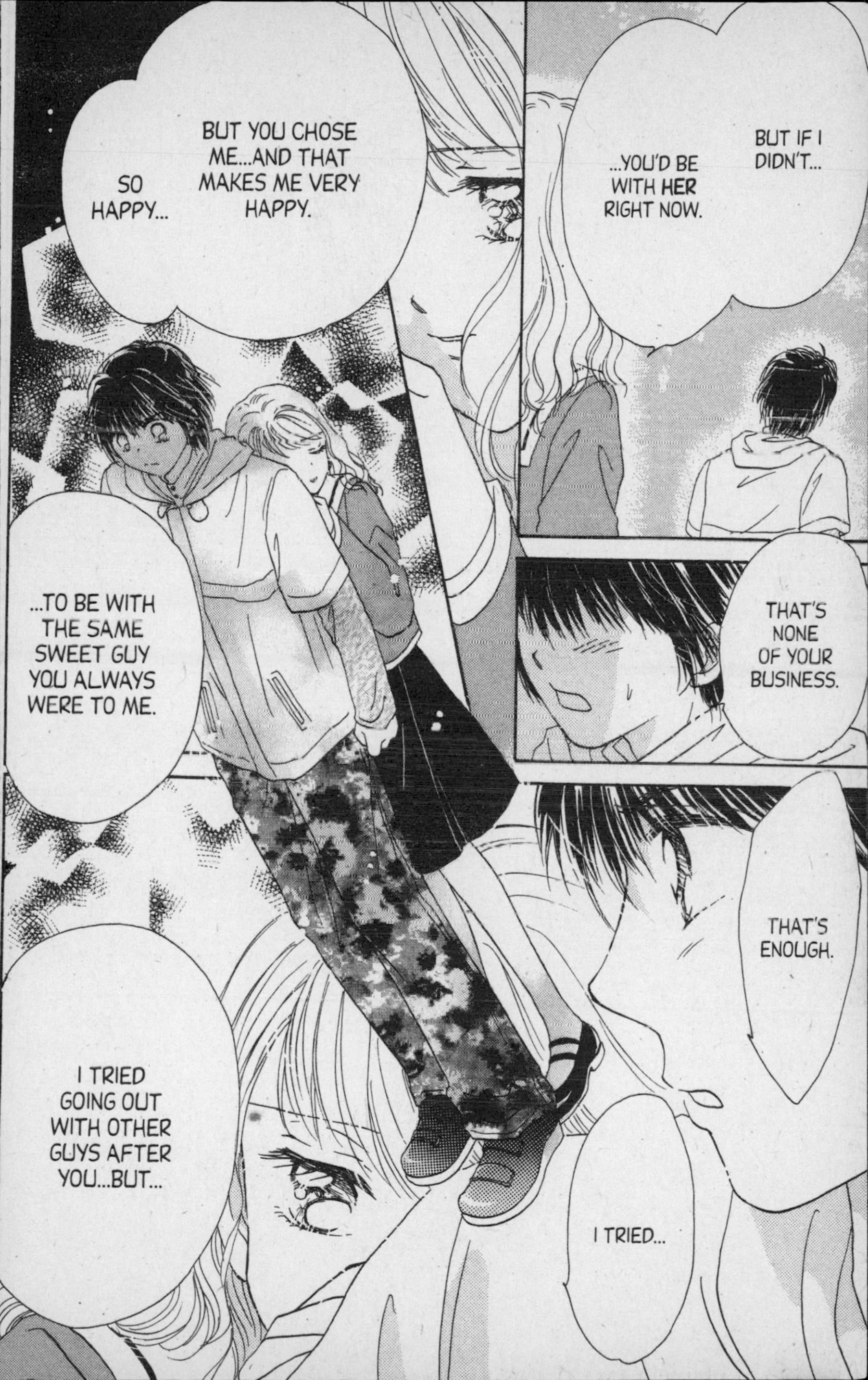
BUT IF I DIDN'T...
...YOU'D BE WITH **HER** RIGHT NOW.
THAT'S NONE OF YOUR BUSINESS.
BUT YOU CHOSE ME...AND THAT MAKES ME VERY HAPPY.
SO HAPPY...
...TO BE WITH THE SAME SWEET GUY YOU ALWAYS WERE TO ME.
THAT'S ENOUGH.
I TRIED...
I TRIED GOING OUT WITH OTHER GUYS AFTER YOU...BUT...

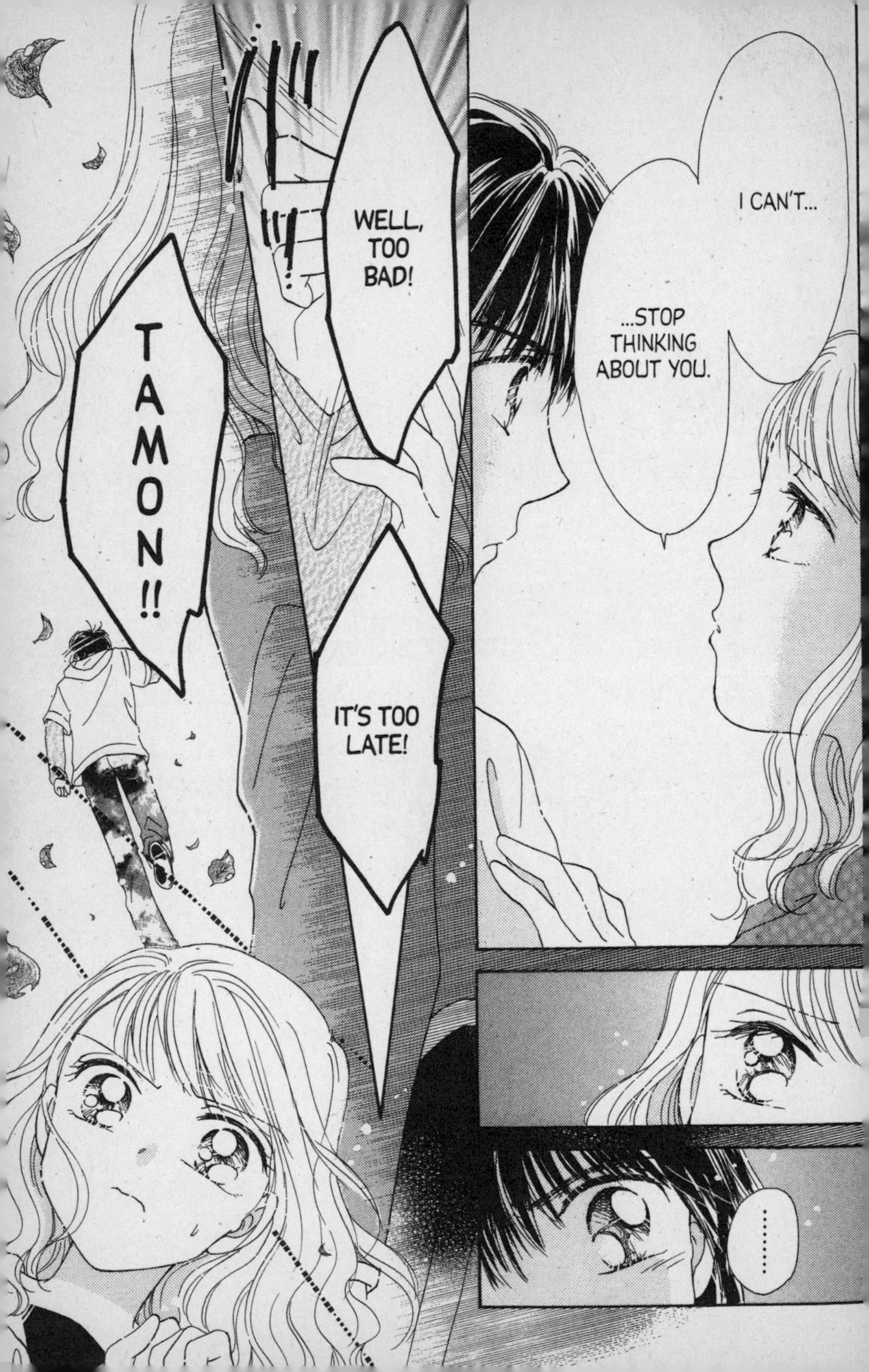
I CAN'T...
...STOP THINKING ABOUT YOU.
......
WELL, TOO BAD!
IT'S TOO LATE!
TAMON!!

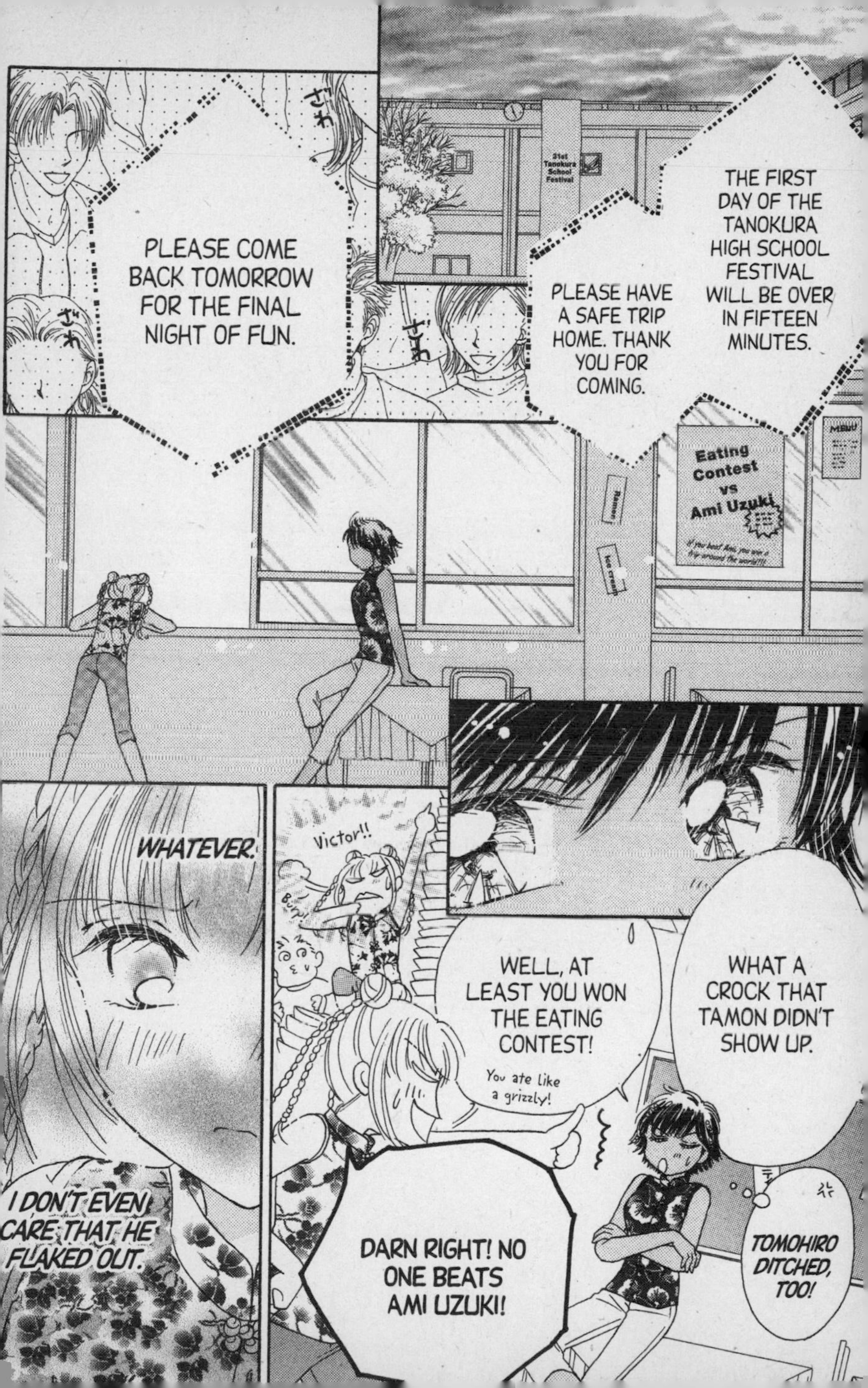
31st Tanokura School Festival
THE FIRST DAY OF THE TANOKURA HIGH SCHOOL FESTIVAL WILL BE OVER IN FIFTEEN MINUTES.
PLEASE HAVE A SAFE TRIP HOME. THANK YOU FOR COMING.
ざわ
ざわ
ざわ
PLEASE COME BACK TOMORROW FOR THE FINAL NIGHT OF FUN.
MENU
Eating Contest vs Ami Uzuki
If you beat Ami, you win a trip around the world!!!
Ramen
Ice cream
WHAT A CROCK THAT TAMON DIDN'T SHOW UP.
TOMOHIRO DITCHED, TOO!
Victor!!
Burp!
WELL, AT LEAST YOU WON THE EATING CONTEST!
You ate like a grizzly!
DARN RIGHT! NO ONE BEATS AMI UZUKI!
WHATEVER.
I DON'T EVEN CARE THAT HE FLAKED OUT.

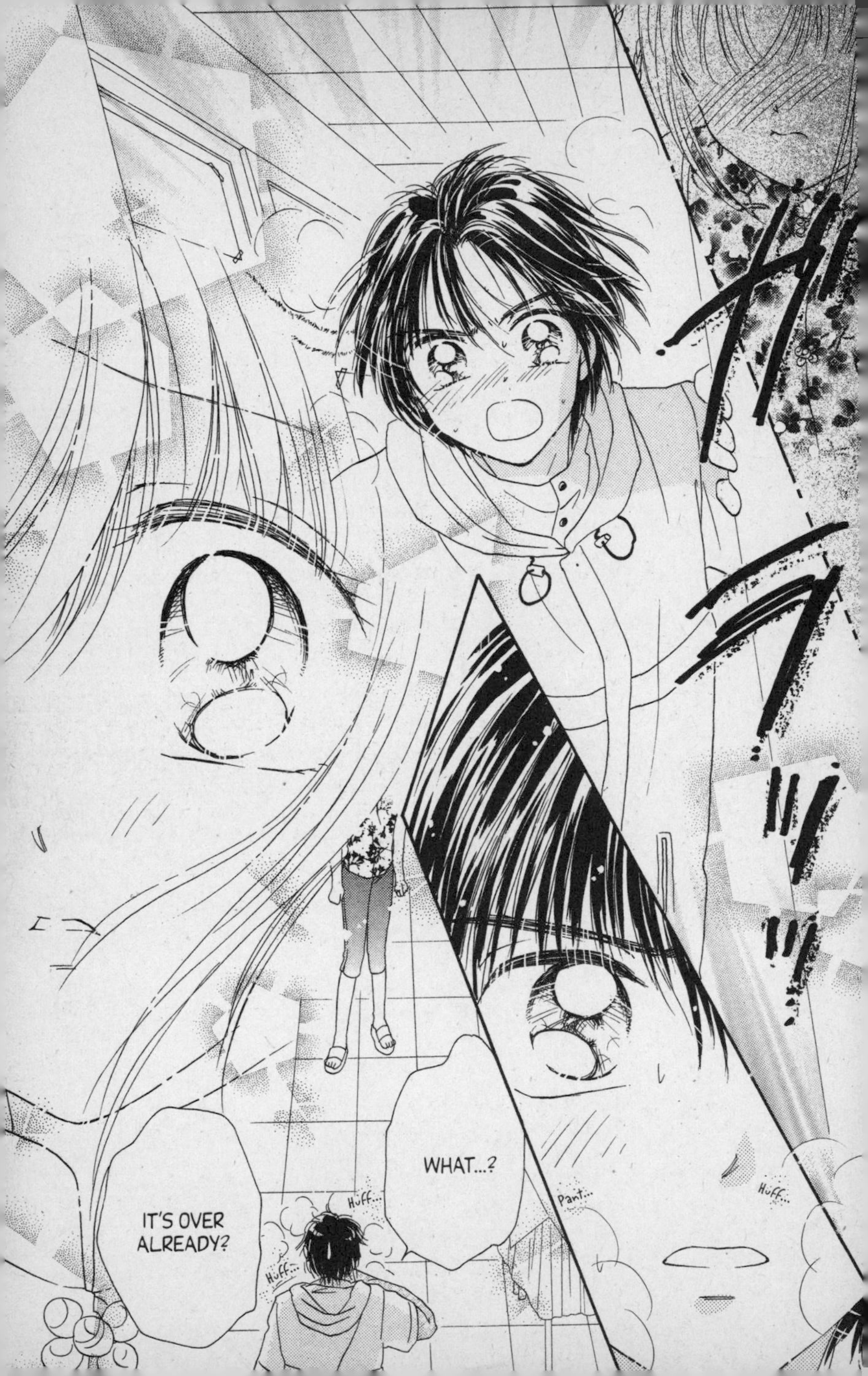
Huff...
Pant...
WHAT...?
Huff...
Huff...
IT'S OVER ALREADY?

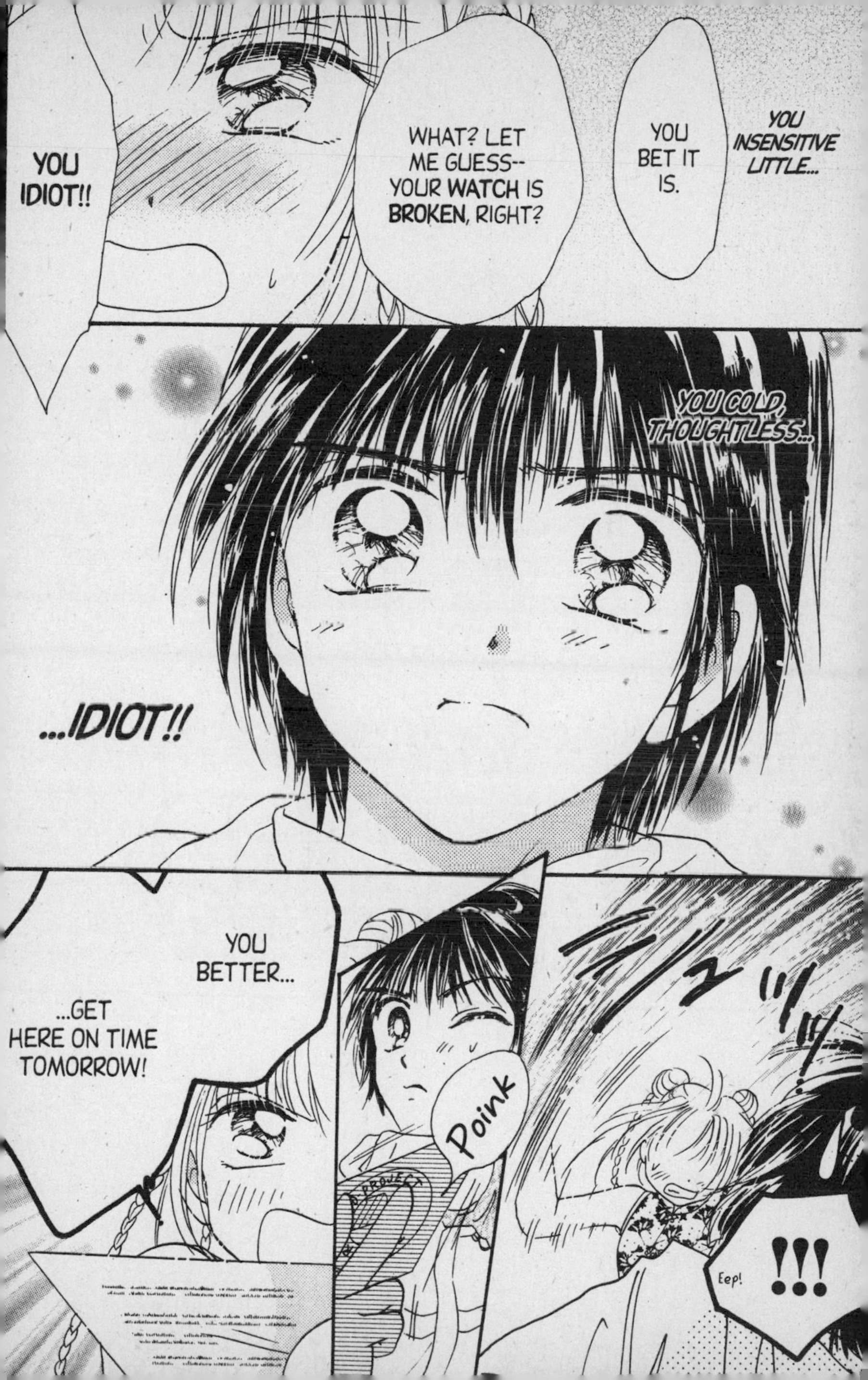
YOU INSENSITIVE LITTLE...
YOU BET IT IS.
WHAT? LET ME GUESS-- YOUR WATCH IS BROKEN, RIGHT?
YOU IDIOT!!
YOU COLD, THOUGHTLESS...
...IDIOT!!
!!!
Eep!
Poink
YOU BETTER...
...GET HERE ON TIME TOMORROW!

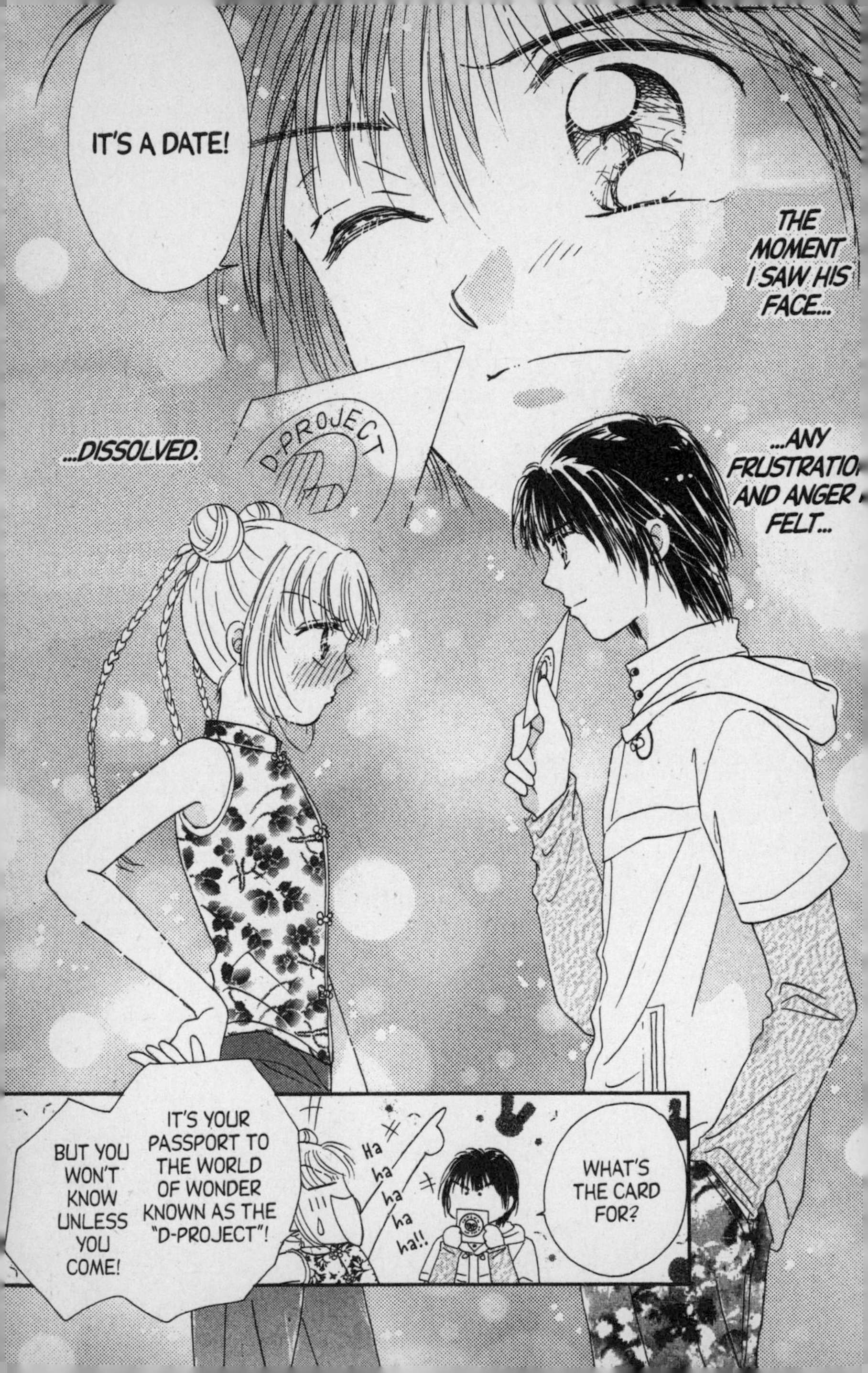
IT'S A DATE!
THE MOMENT I SAW HIS FACE...
...ANY FRUSTRATIO AND ANGER FELT...
...DISSOLVED.
D-PROJECT
WHAT'S THE CARD FOR?
Ha ha ha ha ha!!
IT'S YOUR PASSPORT TO THE WORLD OF WONDER KNOWN AS THE "D-PROJECT"!
BUT YOU WON'T KNOW UNLESS YOU COME!

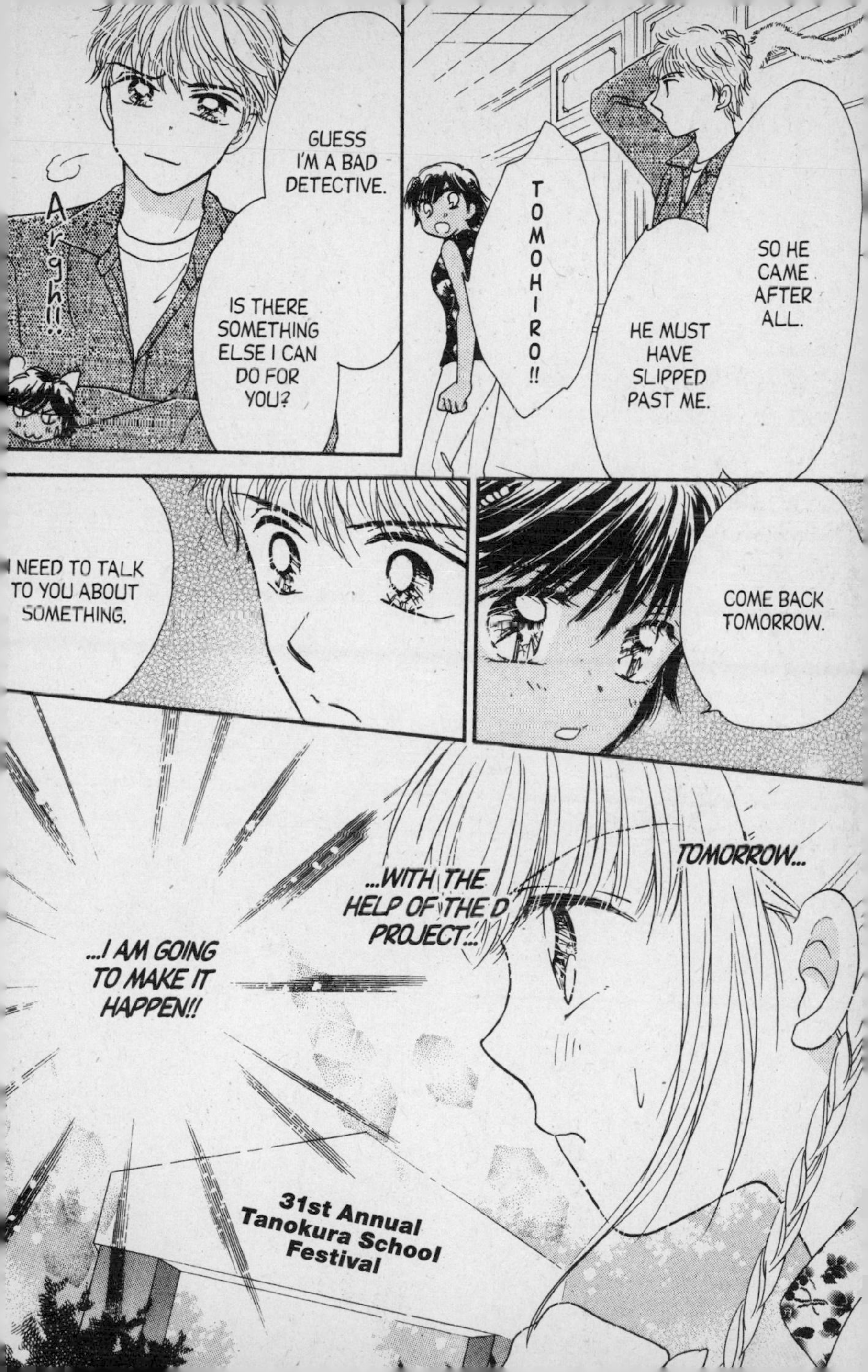
SO HE CAME AFTER ALL.
HE MUST HAVE SLIPPED PAST ME.
TOMOHIRO!!
GUESS I'M A BAD DETECTIVE.
Argh!!
IS THERE SOMETHING ELSE I CAN DO FOR YOU?
COME BACK TOMORROW.
I NEED TO TALK TO YOU ABOUT SOMETHING.
TOMORROW...
...WITH THE HELP OF THE D PROJECT...
...I AM GOING TO MAKE IT HAPPEN!!
31st Annual Tanokura School Festival

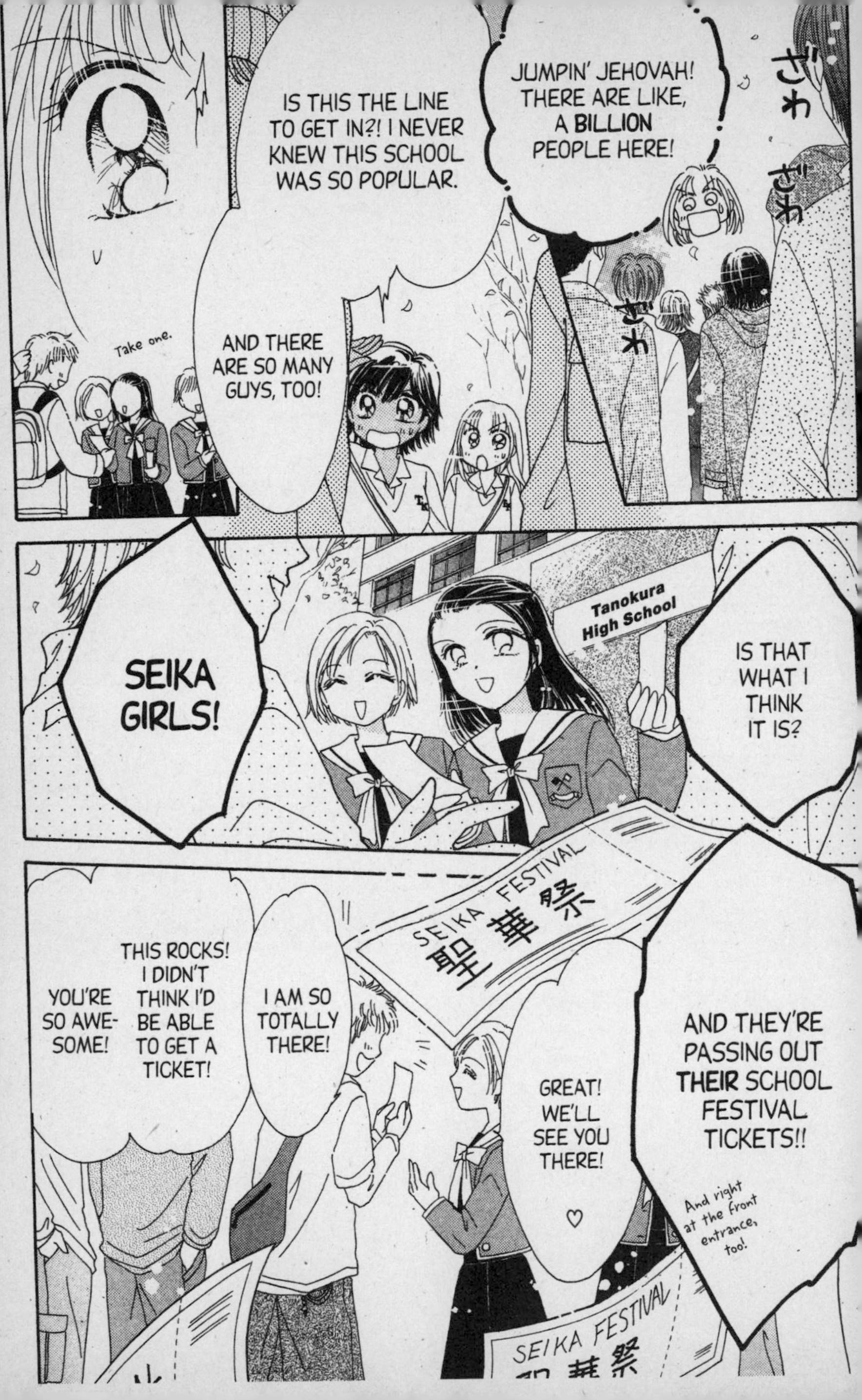
ざわ ざわ
JUMPIN' JEHOVAH! THERE ARE LIKE, A **BILLION** PEOPLE HERE!
IS THIS THE LINE TO GET IN?! I NEVER KNEW THIS SCHOOL WAS SO POPULAR.
ざわ
AND THERE ARE SO MANY GUYS, TOO!
Take one.
IS THAT WHAT I THINK IT IS?
Tanokura High School
SEIKA GIRLS!
AND THEY'RE PASSING OUT **THEIR** SCHOOL FESTIVAL TICKETS!!
And right at the front entrance, too!
SEIKA FESTIVAL
聖華祭
GREAT! WE'LL SEE YOU THERE!
I AM SO TOTALLY THERE!
THIS ROCKS! I DIDN'T THINK I'D BE ABLE TO GET A TICKET!
YOU'RE SO AWE-SOME!
SEIKA FESTIVAL

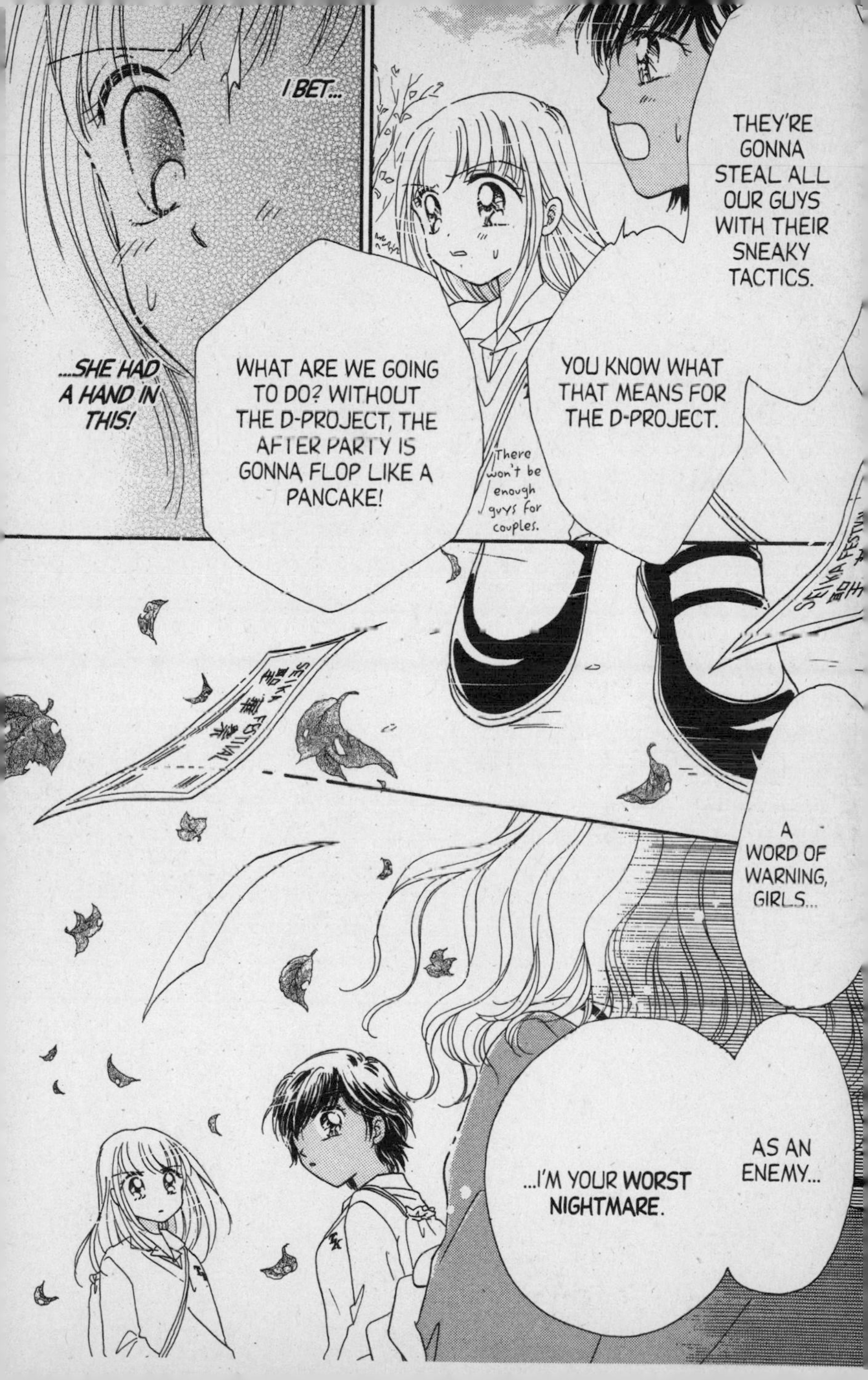
THEY'RE GONNA STEAL ALL OUR GUYS WITH THEIR SNEAKY TACTICS.
YOU KNOW WHAT THAT MEANS FOR THE D-PROJECT.
There won't be enough guys for couples.
WHAT ARE WE GOING TO DO? WITHOUT THE D-PROJECT, THE AFTER PARTY IS GONNA FLOP LIKE A PANCAKE!
I BET...
...SHE HAD A HAND IN THIS!
SEIKA 聖華祭 FESTIVAL
A WORD OF WARNING, GIRLS...
AS AN ENEMY...
...I'M YOUR WORST NIGHTMARE.

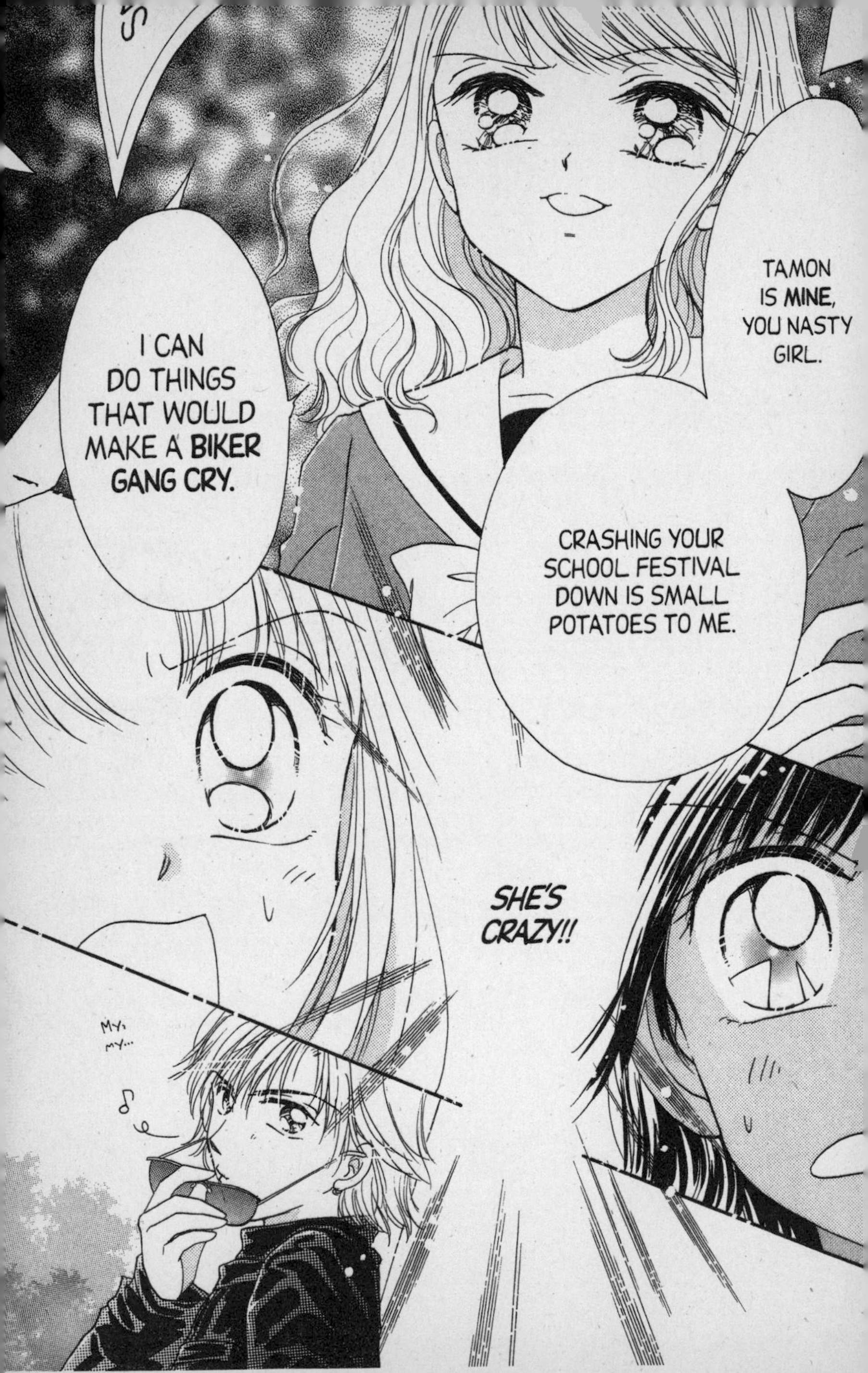
TAMON IS MINE, YOU NASTY GIRL.
CRASHING YOUR SCHOOL FESTIVAL DOWN IS SMALL POTATOES TO ME.
I CAN DO THINGS THAT WOULD MAKE A BIKER GANG CRY.
SHE'S CRAZY!!
MY, MY...

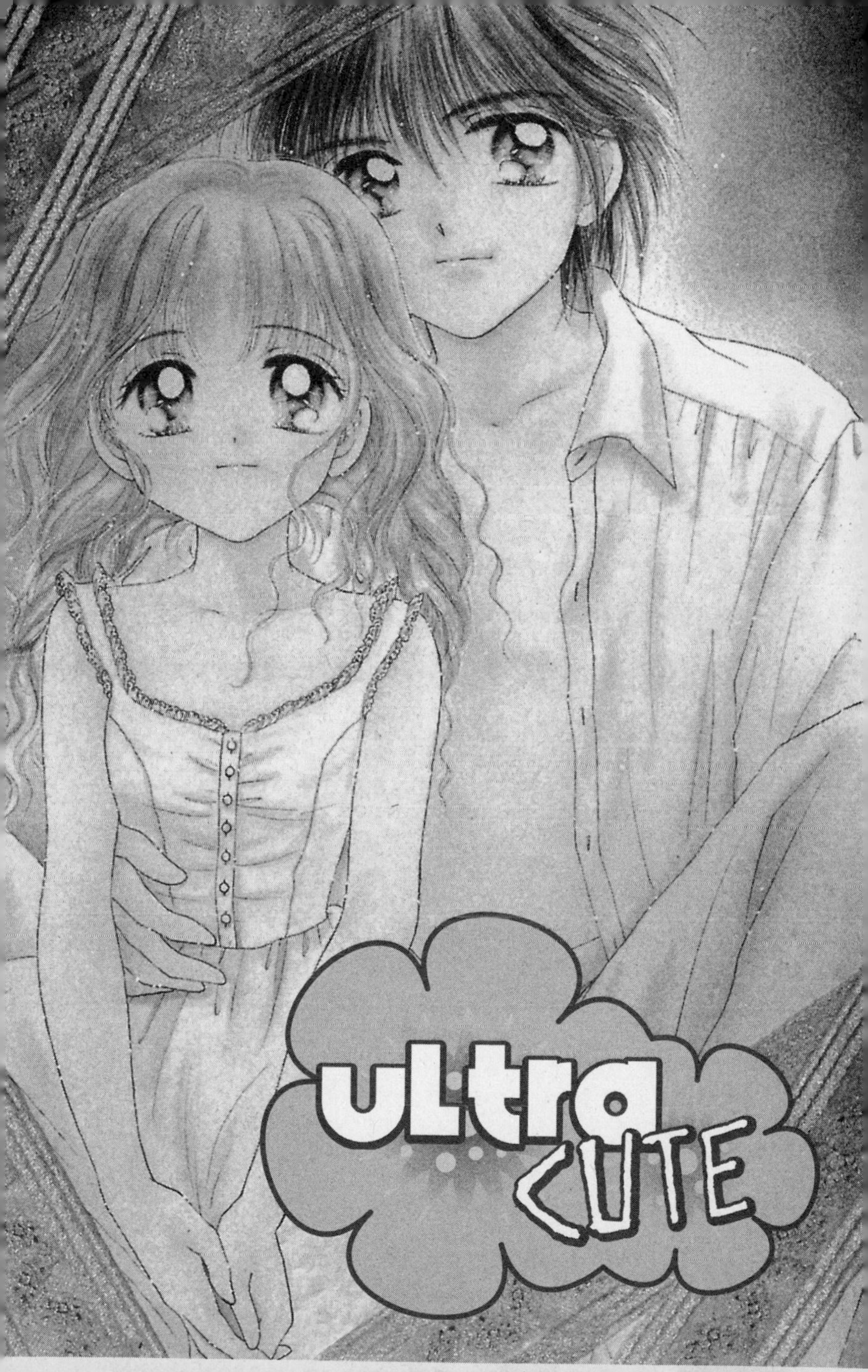
ultra
CUTE

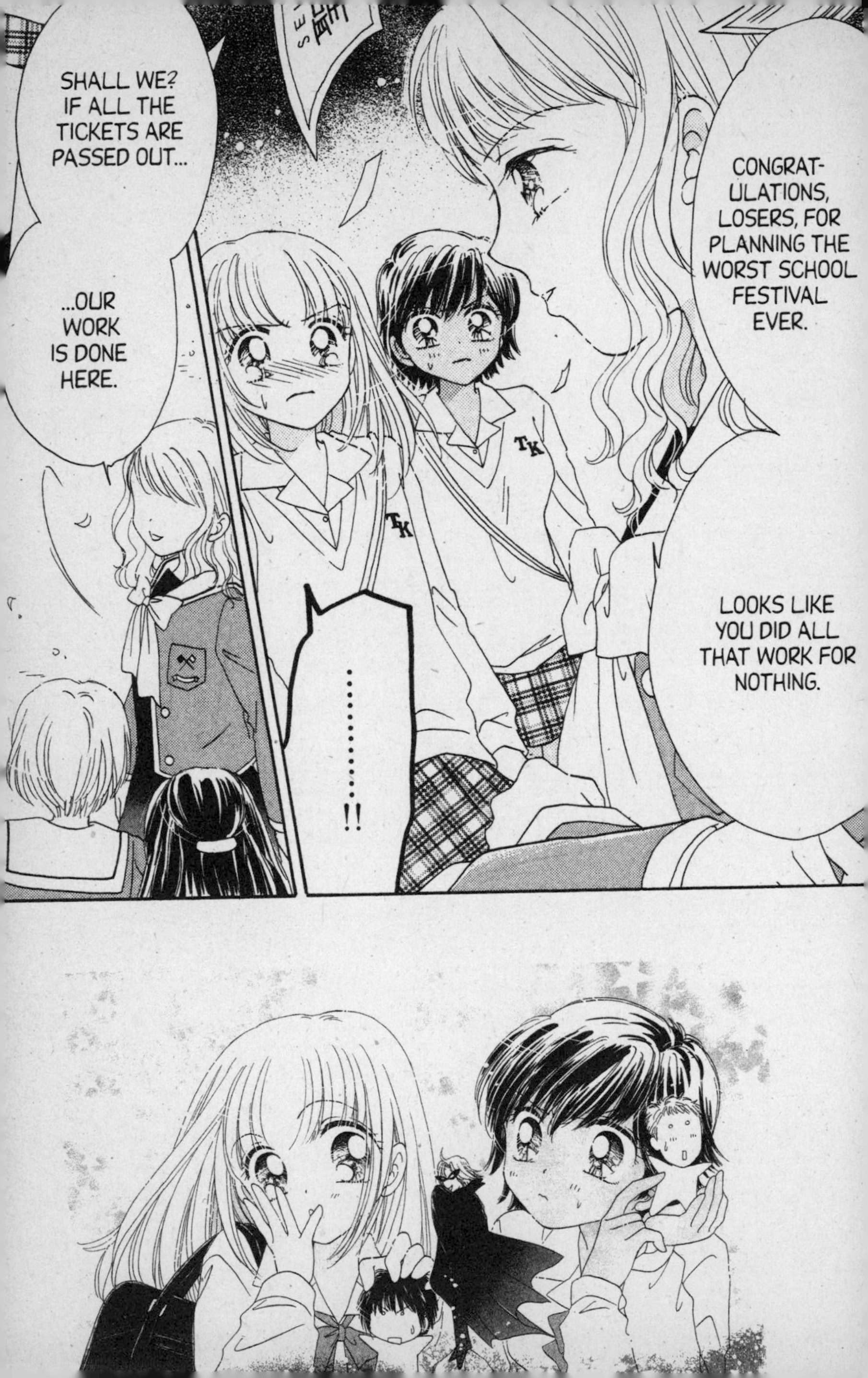
CONGRAT-ULATIONS, LOSERS, FOR PLANNING THE WORST SCHOOL FESTIVAL EVER.
LOOKS LIKE YOU DID ALL THAT WORK FOR NOTHING.
......!!
SHALL WE? IF ALL THE TICKETS ARE PASSED OUT...
...OUR WORK IS DONE HERE.

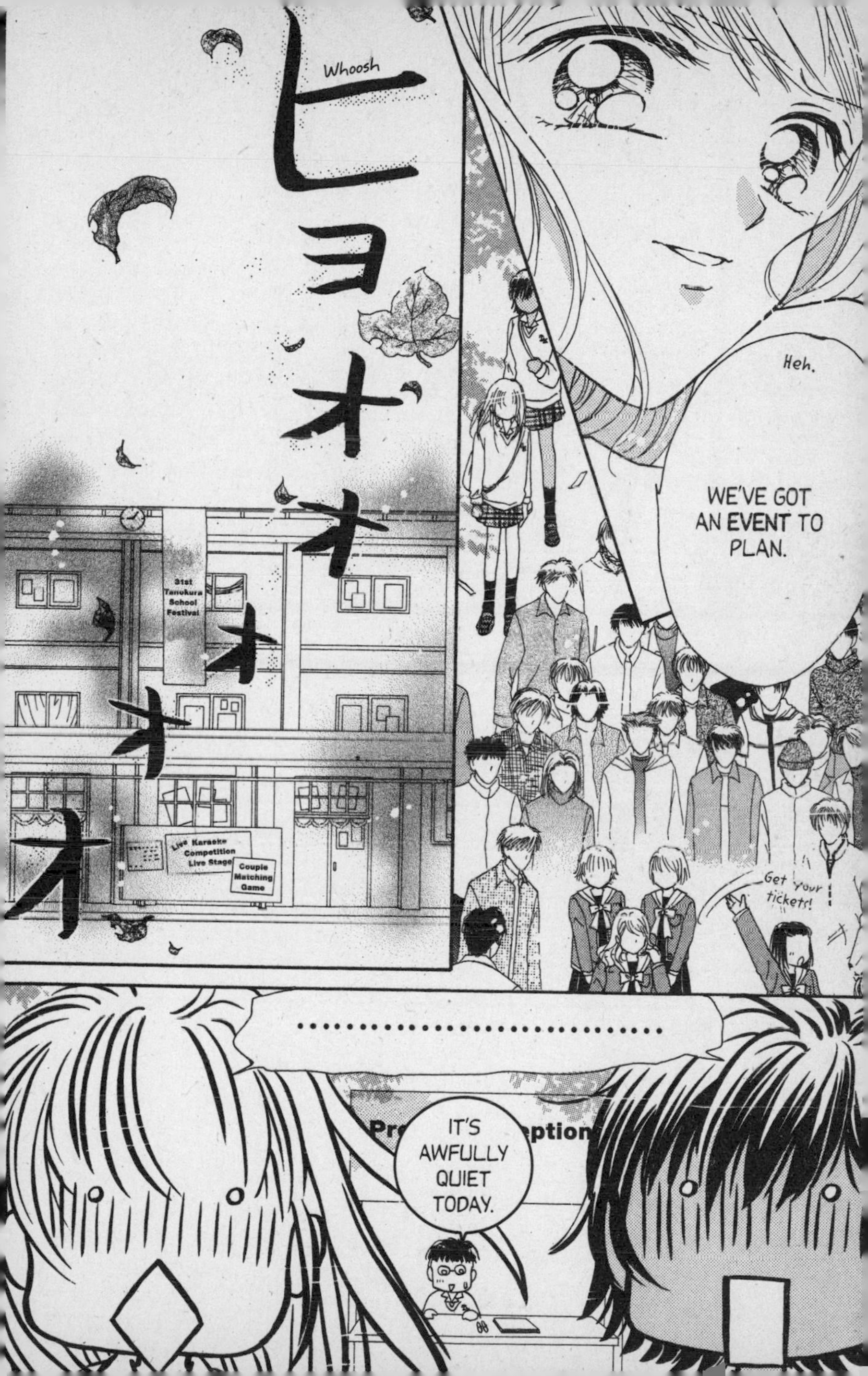
Heh.
WE'VE GOT AN EVENT TO PLAN.
Get your tickets!
Whoosh
ヒョオオオオ
31st Tanokura School Festival
Live Karaoke Competition Live Stage
Couple Matching Game
....
IT'S AWFULLY QUIET TODAY.

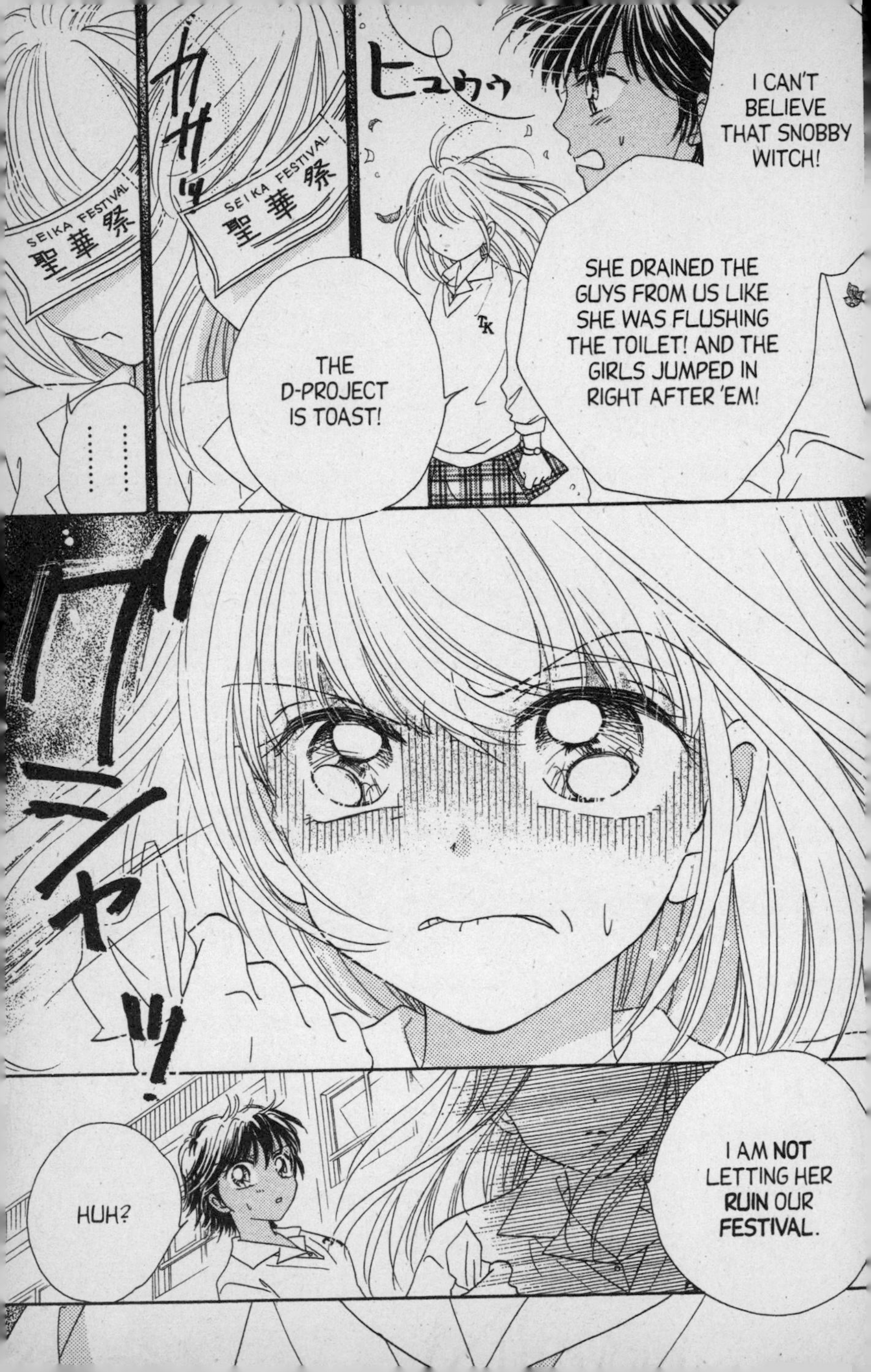
I CAN'T BELIEVE THAT SNOBBY WITCH!
SHE DRAINED THE GUYS FROM US LIKE SHE WAS FLUSHING THE TOILET! AND THE GIRLS JUMPED IN RIGHT AFTER 'EM!
ヒュウウ
THE D-PROJECT IS TOAST!
SEIKA FESTIVAL 聖華祭
カサッ
SEIKA FESTIVAL 聖華祭
……
グシャッ
I AM **NOT** LETTING HER **RUIN** OUR **FESTIVAL**.
HUH?

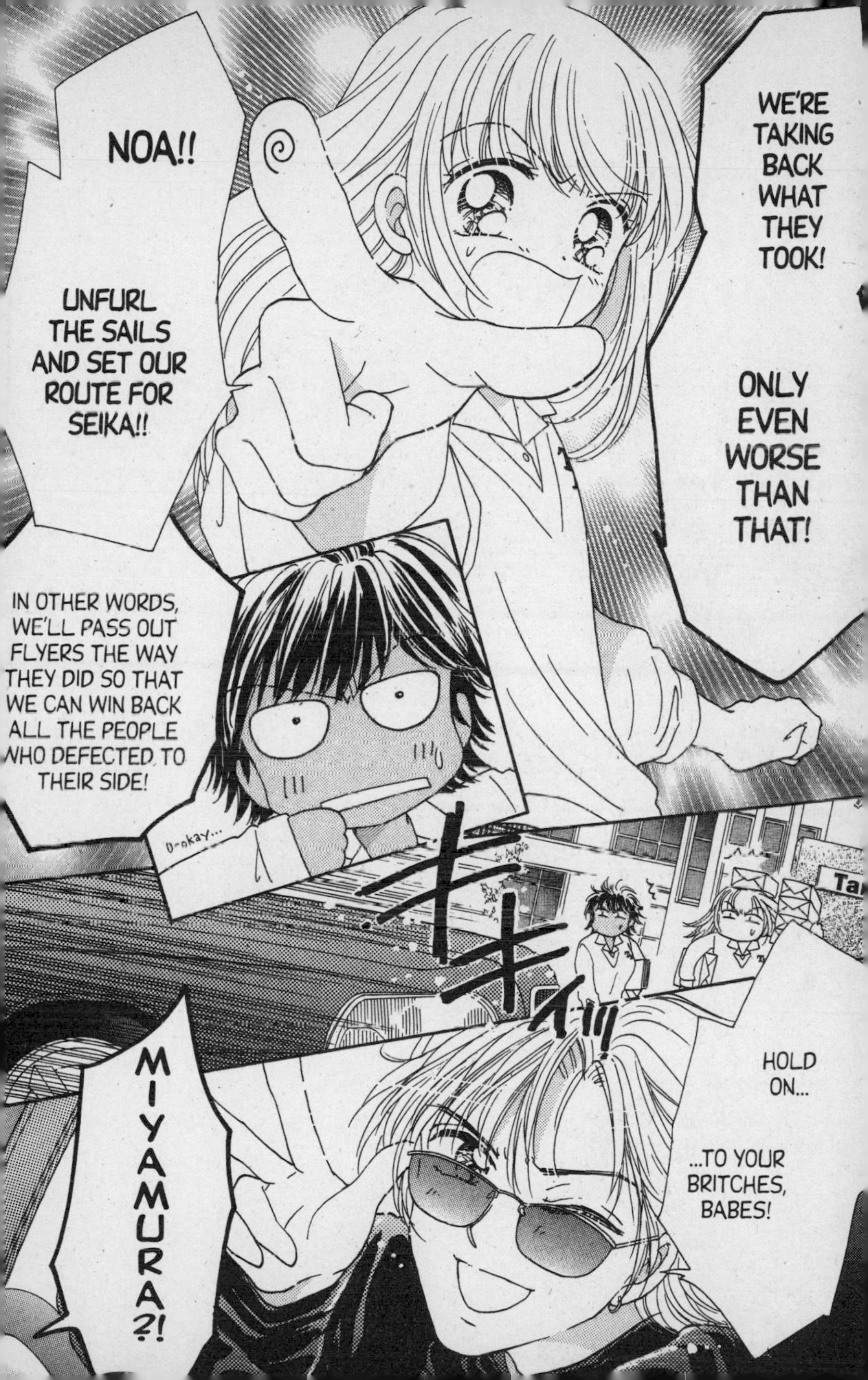

WE'RE TAKING BACK WHAT THEY TOOK!
ONLY EVEN WORSE THAN THAT!
NOA!!
UNFURL THE SAILS AND SET OUR ROUTE FOR SEIKA!!
IN OTHER WORDS, WE'LL PASS OUT FLYERS THE WAY THEY DID SO THAT WE CAN WIN BACK ALL THE PEOPLE WHO DEFECTED TO THEIR SIDE!
D-okay...
キキイ!!
HOLD ON...
...TO YOUR BRITCHES, BABES!
MIYAMURA?!

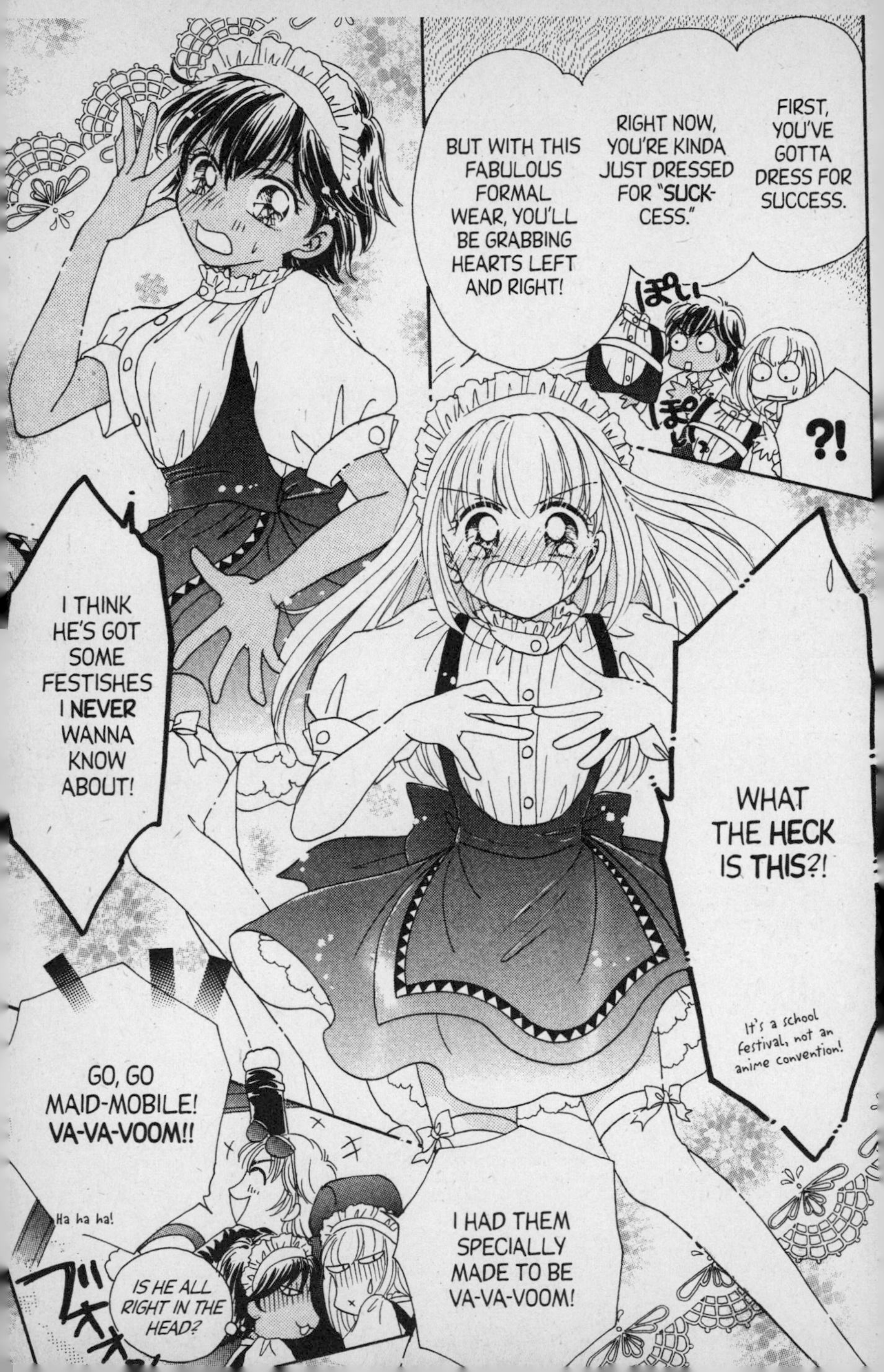
FIRST, YOU'VE GOTTA DRESS FOR SUCCESS.
RIGHT NOW, YOU'RE KINDA JUST DRESSED FOR "SUCK-CESS."
BUT WITH THIS FABULOUS FORMAL WEAR, YOU'LL BE GRABBING HEARTS LEFT AND RIGHT!
ぽい
ぽい
?!
WHAT THE HECK IS THIS?!
I THINK HE'S GOT SOME FESTISHES I NEVER WANNA KNOW ABOUT!
It's a school festival, not an anime convention!
I HAD THEM SPECIALLY MADE TO BE VA-VA-VOOM!
GO, GO MAID-MOBILE! VA-VA-VOOM!!
Ha ha ha!
IS HE ALL RIGHT IN THE HEAD?

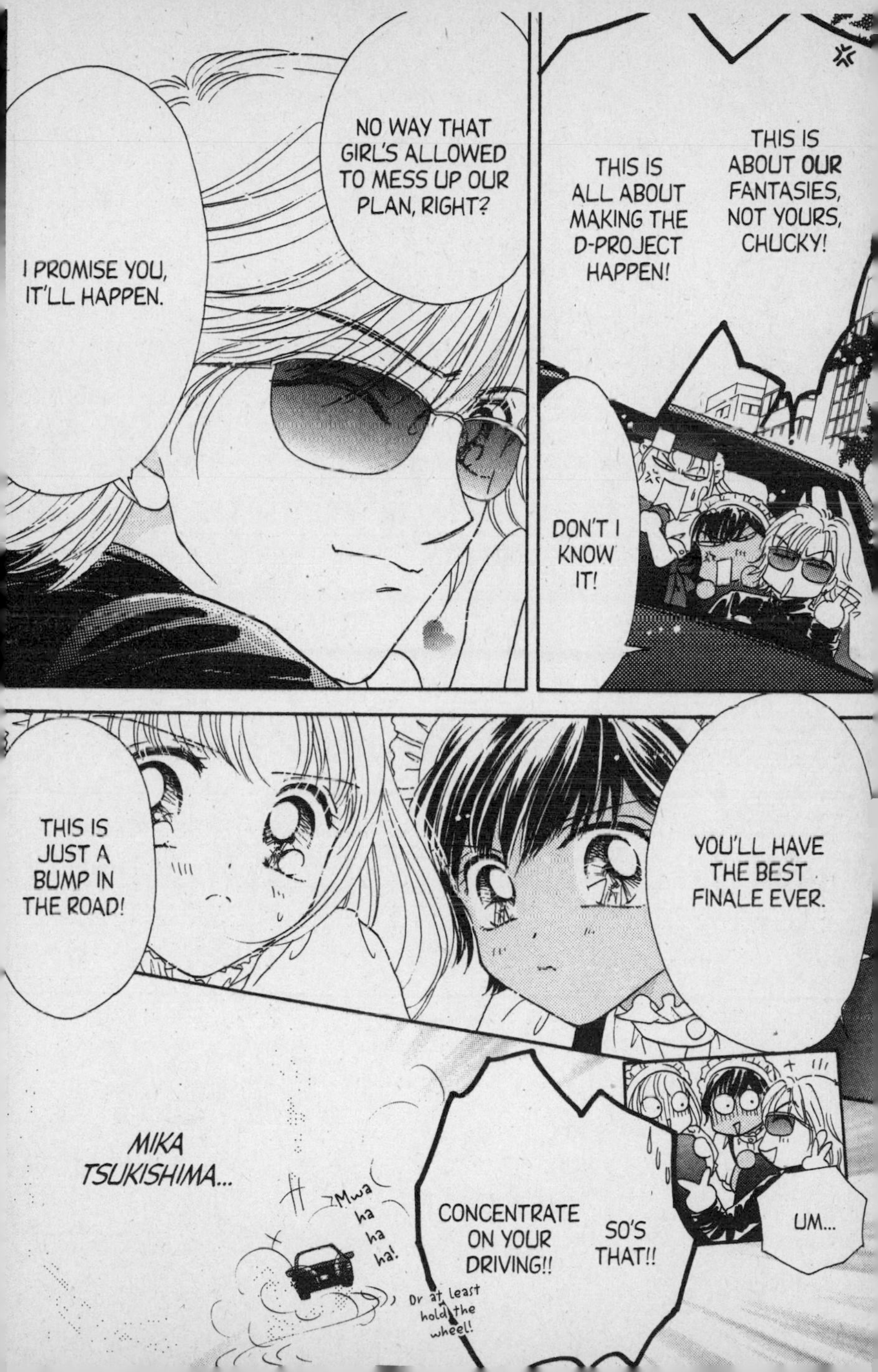
THIS IS ABOUT OUR FANTASIES, NOT YOURS, CHUCKY!
THIS IS ALL ABOUT MAKING THE D-PROJECT HAPPEN!
DON'T I KNOW IT!
NO WAY THAT GIRL'S ALLOWED TO MESS UP OUR PLAN, RIGHT?
I PROMISE YOU, IT'LL HAPPEN.
YOU'LL HAVE THE BEST FINALE EVER.
THIS IS JUST A BUMP IN THE ROAD!
UM...
SO'S THAT!!
CONCENTRATE ON YOUR DRIVING!!
Or at least hold the wheel!
Mwa ha ha ha!
MIKA TSUKISHIMA...

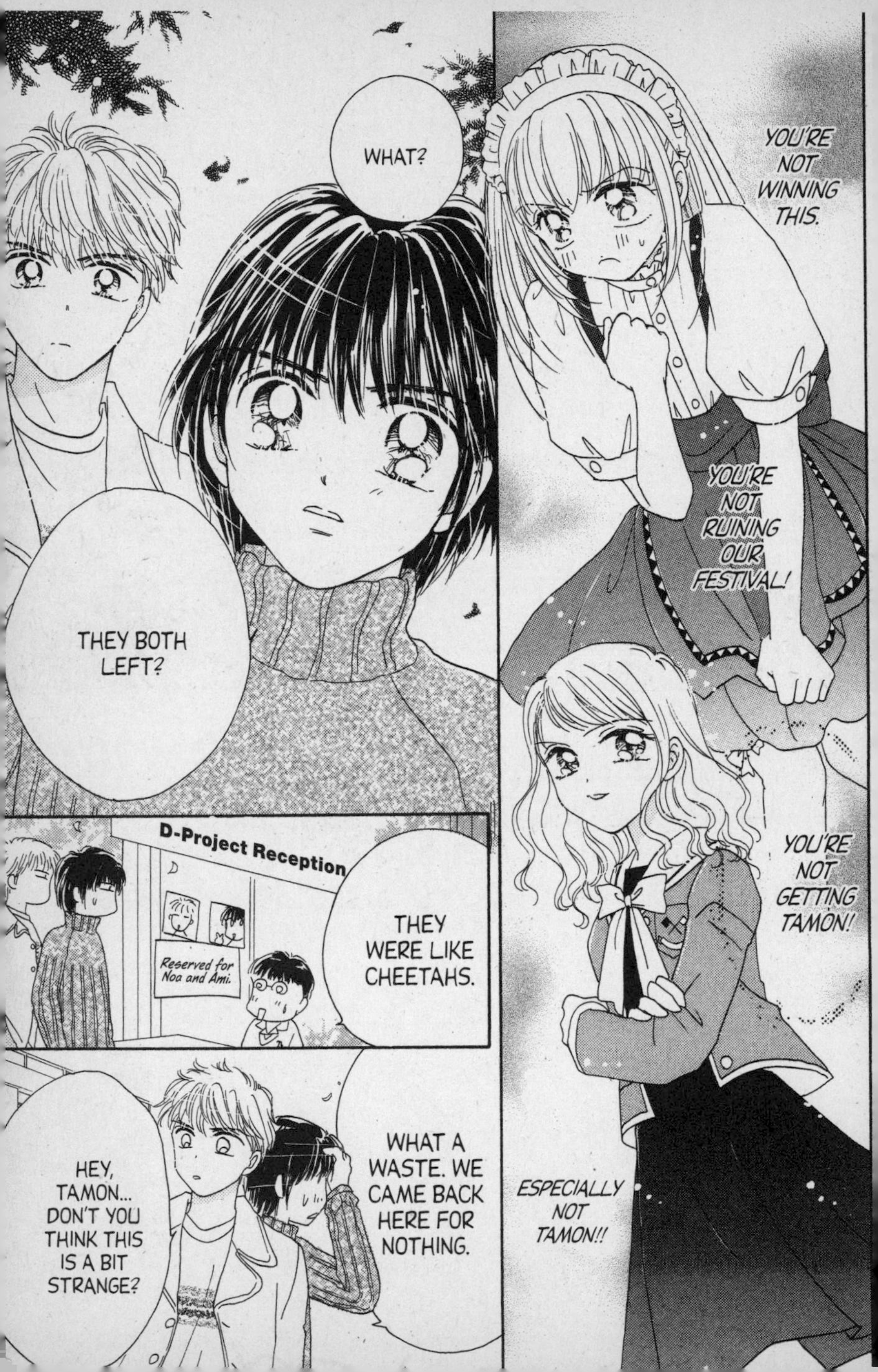
YOU'RE NOT WINNING THIS.
YOU'RE NOT RUINING OUR FESTIVAL!
YOU'RE NOT GETTING TAMON!
ESPECIALLY NOT TAMON!!
WHAT?
THEY BOTH LEFT?
D-Project Reception
Reserved for Noa and Ami.
THEY WERE LIKE CHEETAHS.
WHAT A WASTE. WE CAME BACK HERE FOR NOTHING.
HEY, TAMON... DON'T YOU THINK THIS IS A BIT STRANGE?

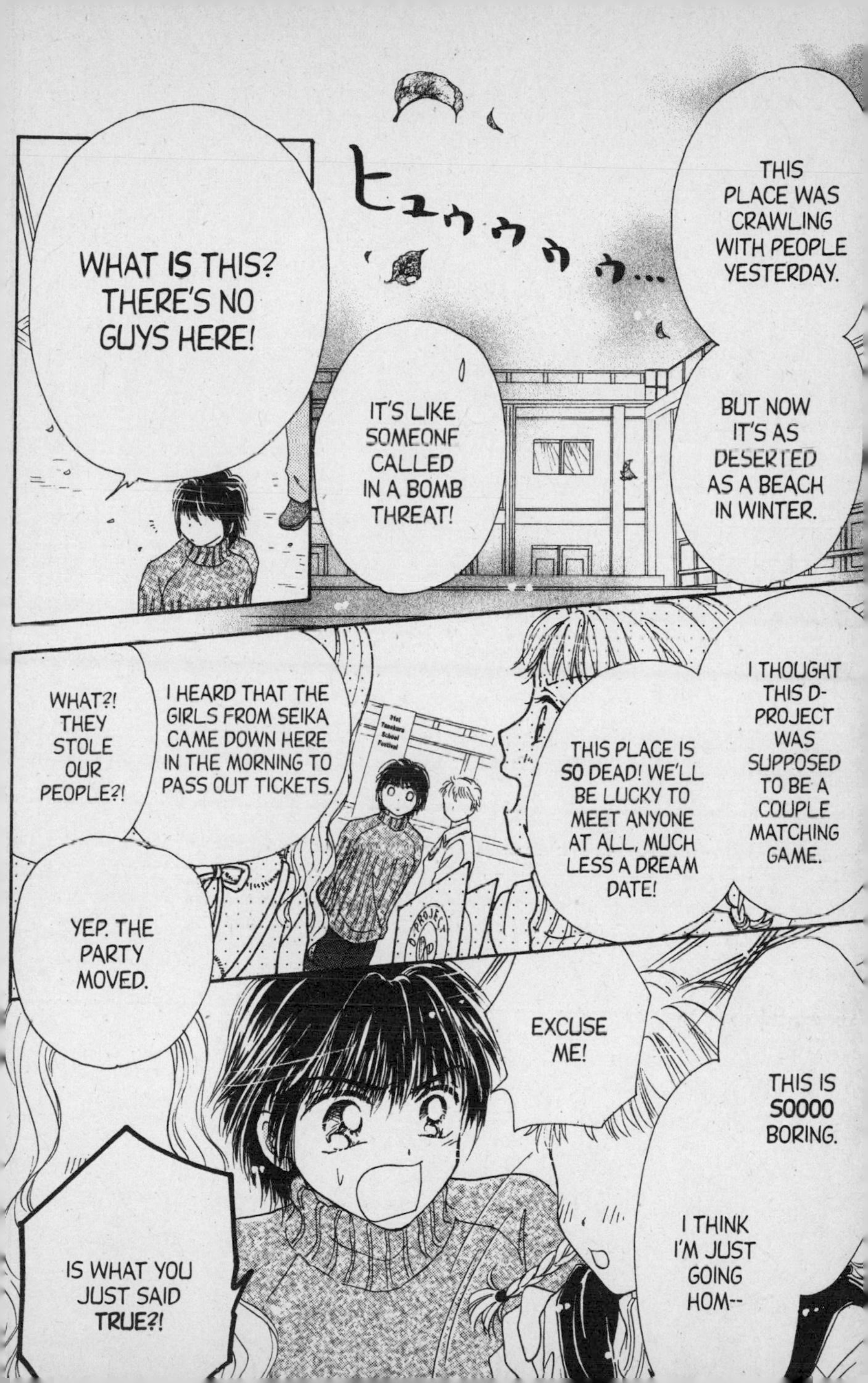
ヒュウウウウ…
THIS PLACE WAS CRAWLING WITH PEOPLE YESTERDAY.
BUT NOW IT'S AS DESERTED AS A BEACH IN WINTER.
IT'S LIKE SOMEONF CALLED IN A BOMB THREAT!
WHAT IS THIS? THERE'S NO GUYS HERE!
I THOUGHT THIS D-PROJECT WAS SUPPOSED TO BE A COUPLE MATCHING GAME.
THIS PLACE IS SO DEAD! WE'LL BE LUCKY TO MEET ANYONE AT ALL, MUCH LESS A DREAM DATE!
I HEARD THAT THE GIRLS FROM SEIKA CAME DOWN HERE IN THE MORNING TO PASS OUT TICKETS.
WHAT?! THEY STOLE OUR PEOPLE?!
YEP. THE PARTY MOVED.
THIS IS SOOOO BORING.
I THINK I'M JUST GOING HOM--
EXCUSE ME!
IS WHAT YOU JUST SAID TRUE?!

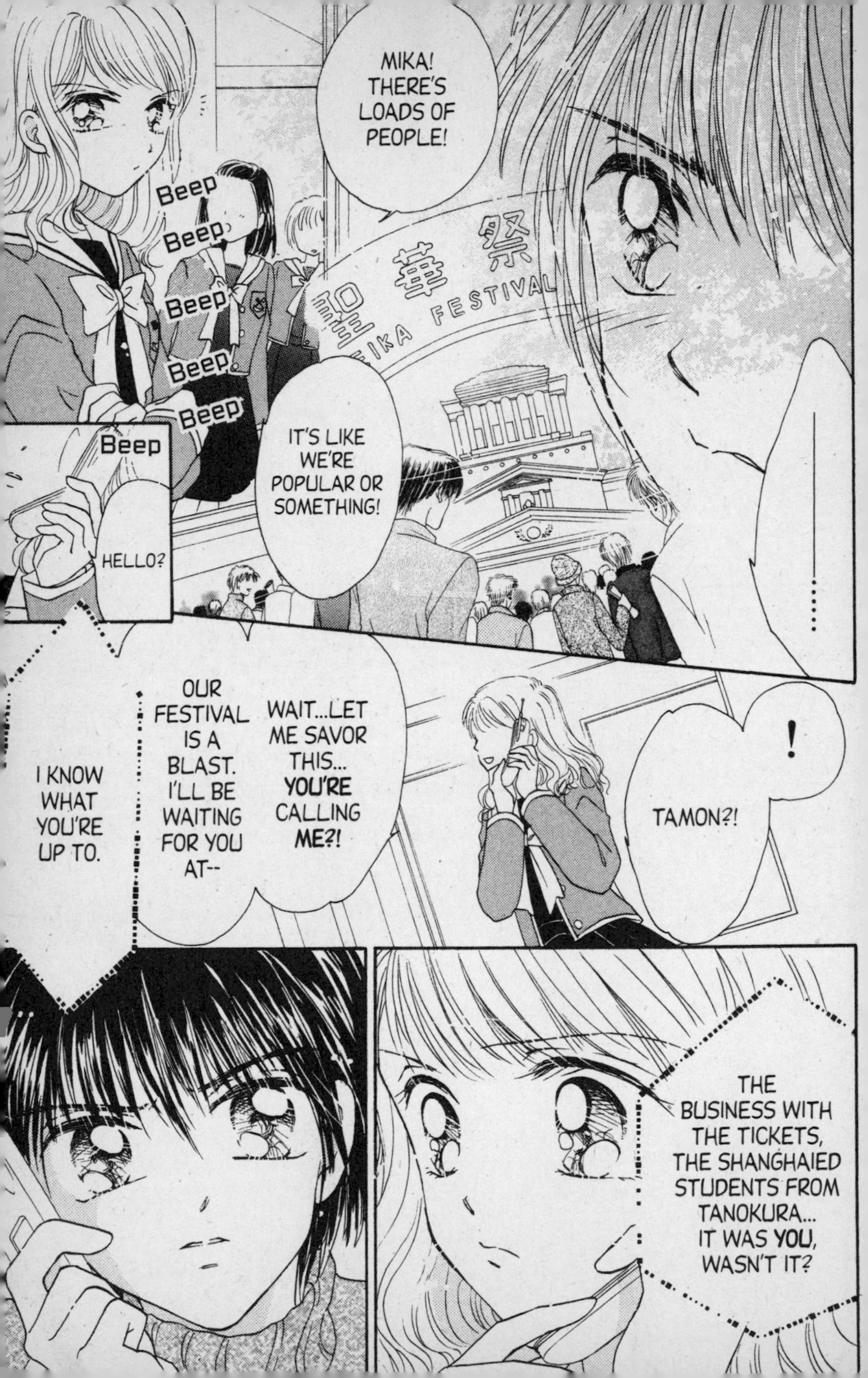
MIKA! THERE'S LOADS OF PEOPLE!
聖華祭
IKA FESTIVAL
IT'S LIKE WE'RE POPULAR OR SOMETHING!
......
Beep
Beep
Beep
Beep
Beep
Beep
HELLO?
!
TAMON?!
WAIT...LET ME SAVOR THIS... YOU'RE CALLING ME?!
OUR FESTIVAL IS A BLAST. I'LL BE WAITING FOR YOU AT--
I KNOW WHAT YOU'RE UP TO.
THE BUSINESS WITH THE TICKETS, THE SHANGHAIED STUDENTS FROM TANOKURA... IT WAS YOU, WASN'T IT?

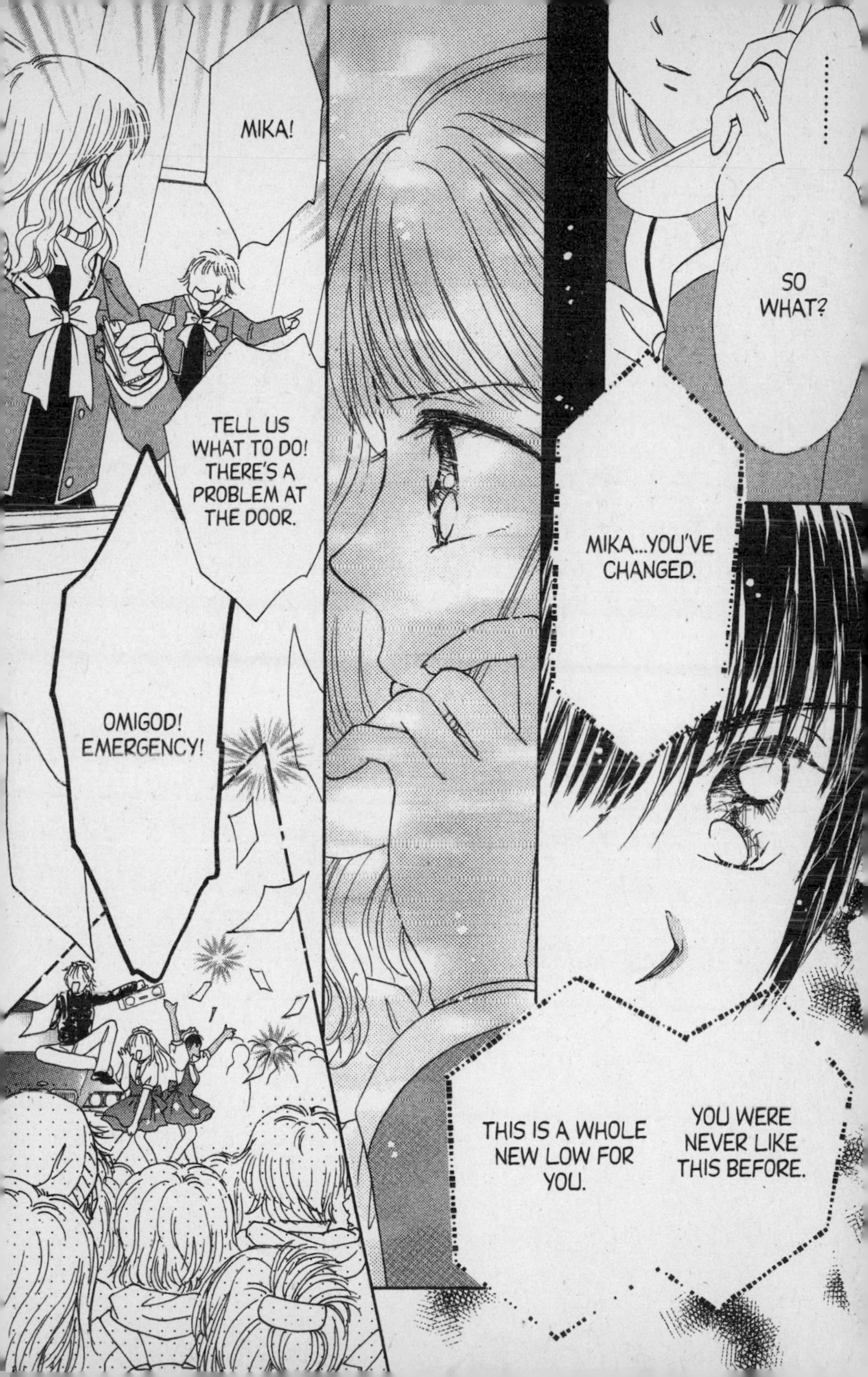
......
SO WHAT?
MIKA...YOU'VE CHANGED.
YOU WERE NEVER LIKE THIS BEFORE.
THIS IS A WHOLE NEW LOW FOR YOU.
MIKA!
TELL US WHAT TO DO! THERE'S A PROBLEM AT THE DOOR.
OMIGOD! EMERGENCY!

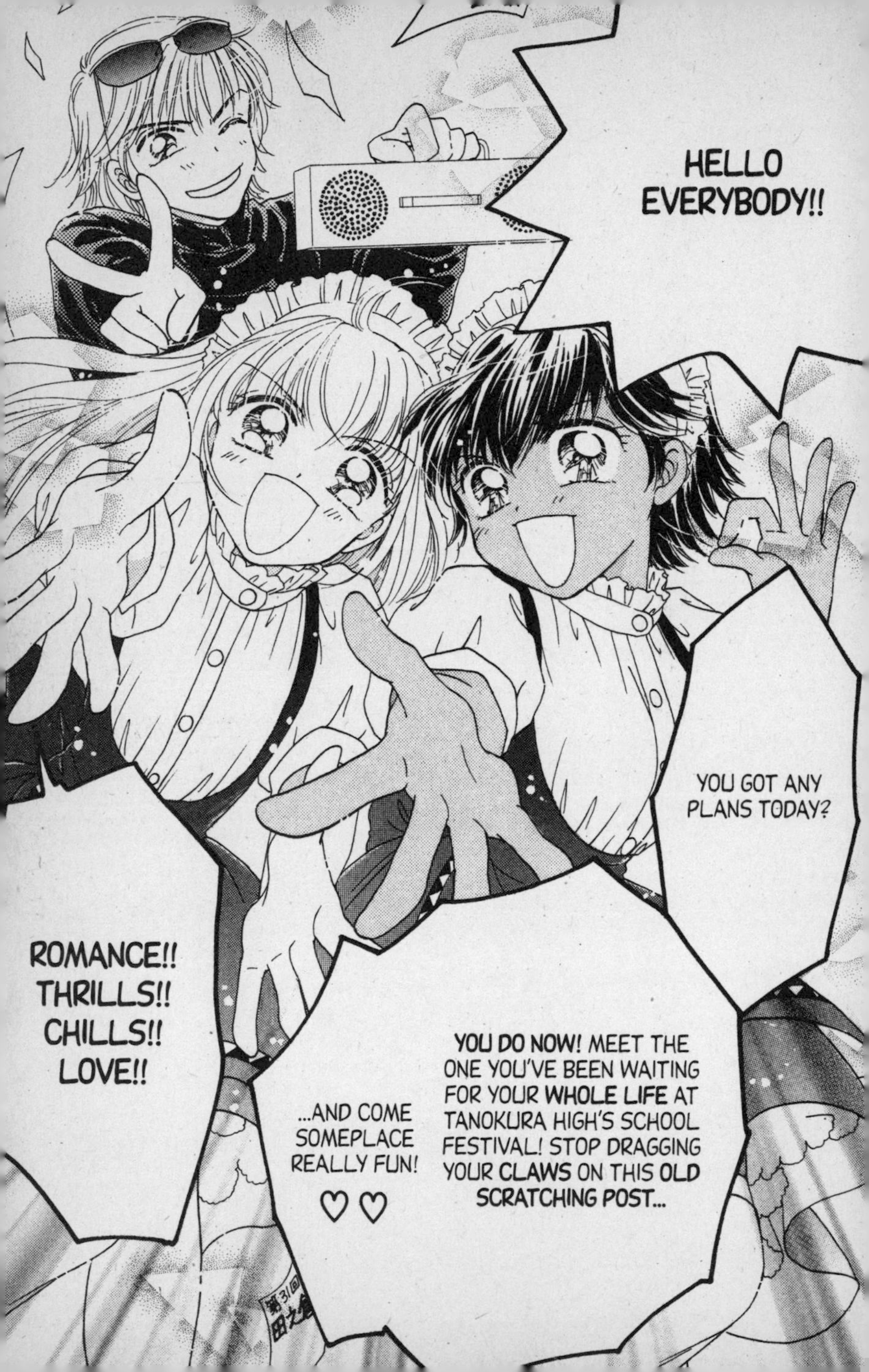
HELLO EVERYBODY!!
YOU GOT ANY PLANS TODAY?
YOU DO NOW! MEET THE ONE YOU'VE BEEN WAITING FOR YOUR WHOLE LIFE AT TANOKURA HIGH'S SCHOOL FESTIVAL! STOP DRAGGING YOUR CLAWS ON THIS OLD SCRATCHING POST...
...AND COME SOMEPLACE REALLY FUN! ♡ ♡
ROMANCE!! THRILLS!! CHILLS!! LOVE!!
第31回 田之倉

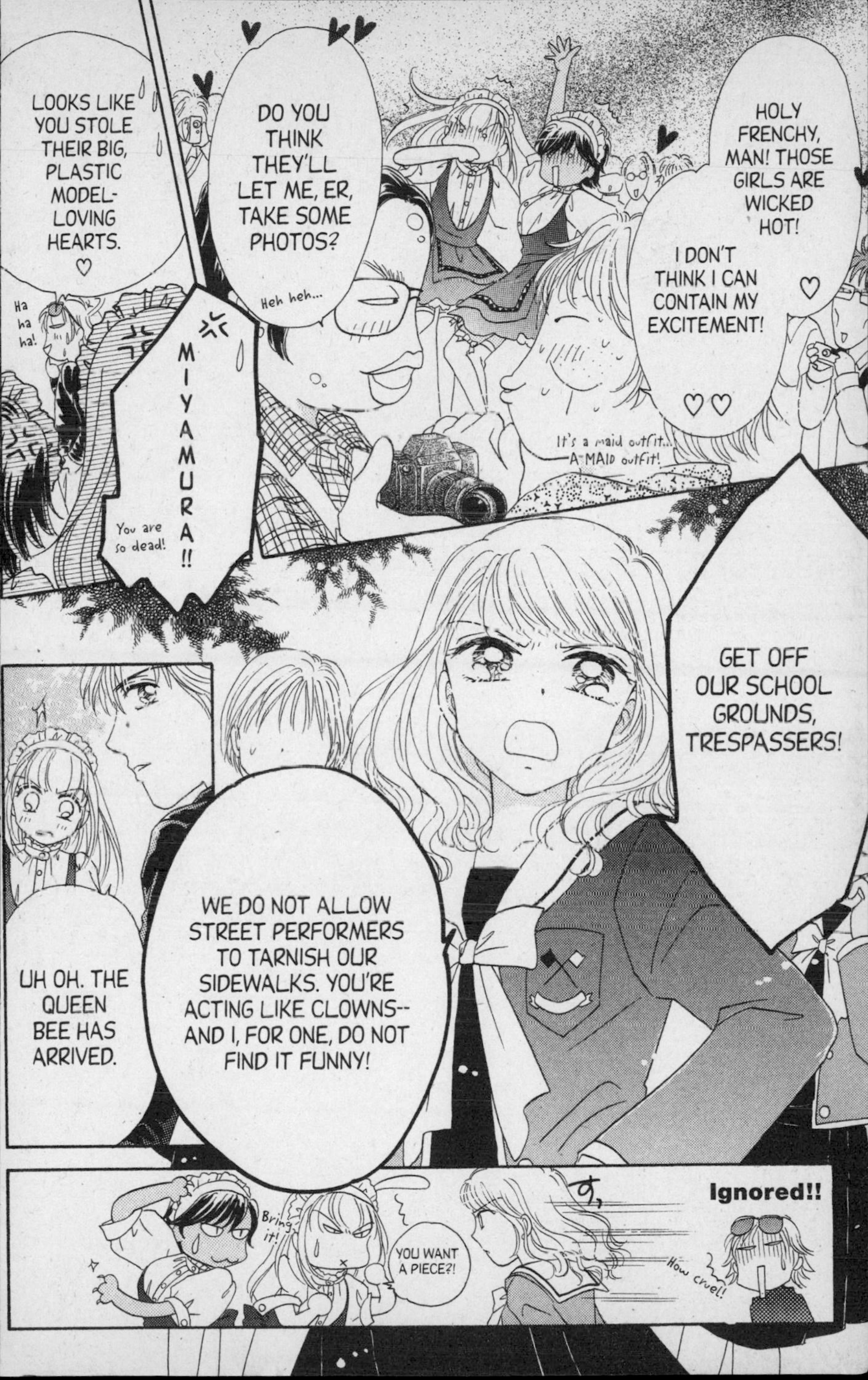
HOLY FRENCHY, MAN! THOSE GIRLS ARE WICKED HOT!
I DON'T THINK I CAN CONTAIN MY EXCITEMENT!
It's a maid outfit... A-MAID outfit!
DO YOU THINK THEY'LL LET ME, ER, TAKE SOME PHOTOS?
Heh heh...
LOOKS LIKE YOU STOLE THEIR BIG, PLASTIC MODEL-LOVING HEARTS.
Ha ha ha!
MIYAMURA!!
You are so dead!
GET OFF OUR SCHOOL GROUNDS, TRESPASSERS!
WE DO NOT ALLOW STREET PERFORMERS TO TARNISH OUR SIDEWALKS. YOU'RE ACTING LIKE CLOWNS--AND I, FOR ONE, DO NOT FIND IT FUNNY!
UH OH. THE QUEEN BEE HAS ARRIVED.
Ignored!!
How cruel!
す
YOU WANT A PIECE?!
Bring it!

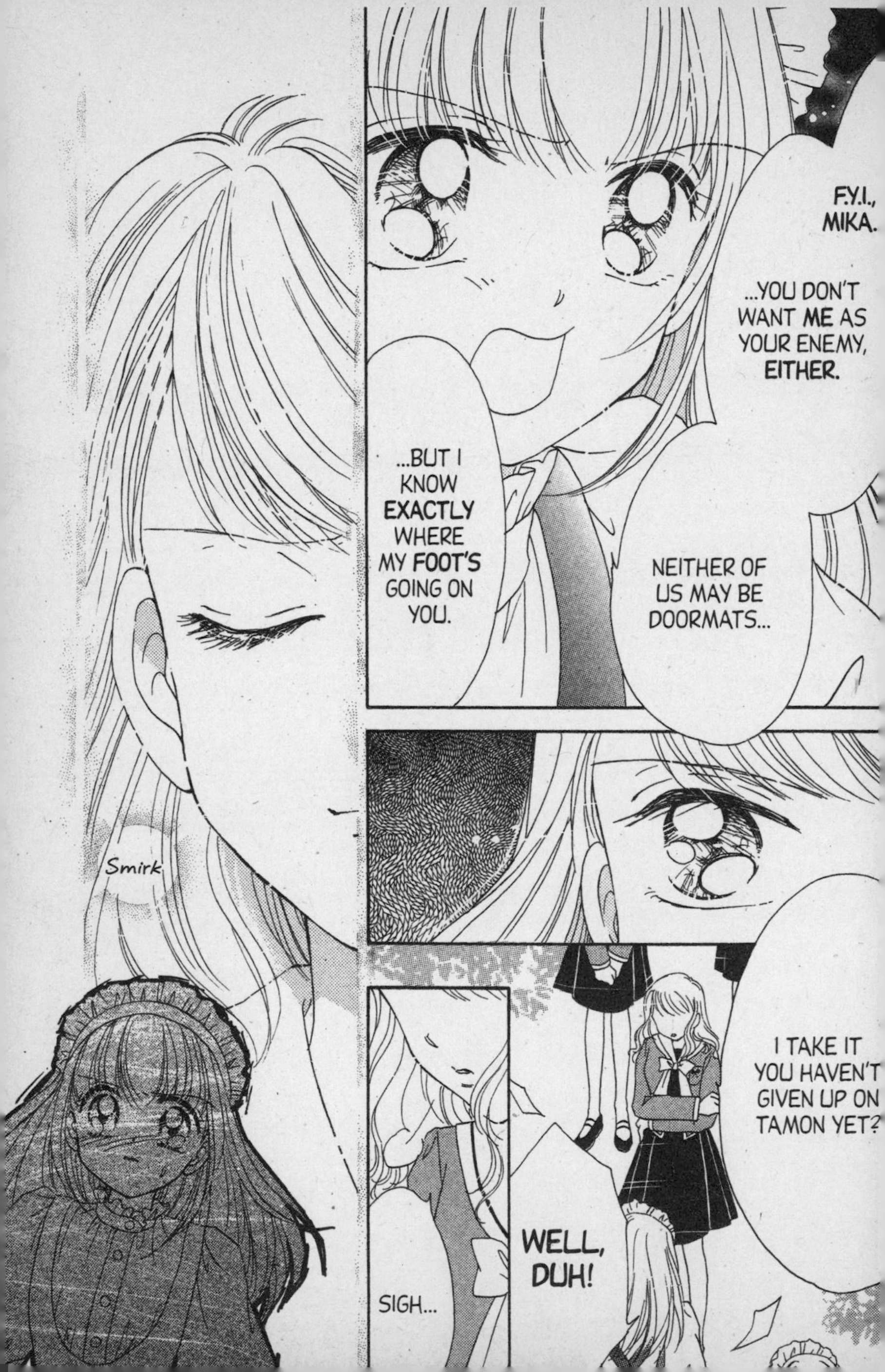
F.Y.I., MIKA.
...YOU DON'T WANT ME AS YOUR ENEMY, EITHER.
NEITHER OF US MAY BE DOORMATS...
...BUT I KNOW EXACTLY WHERE MY FOOT'S GOING ON YOU.
I TAKE IT YOU HAVEN'T GIVEN UP ON TAMON YET?
WELL, DUH!
SIGH...
Smirk

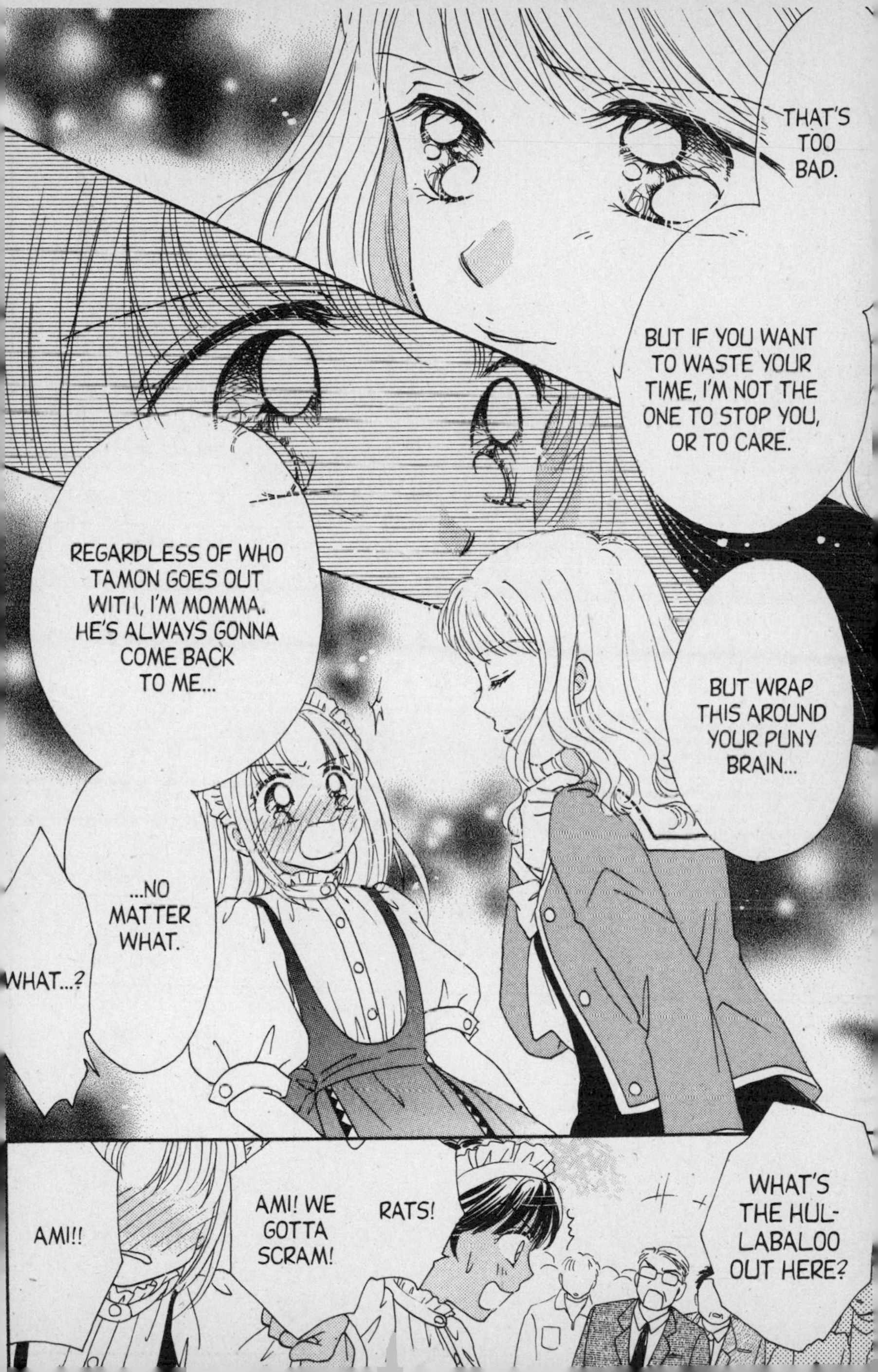
THAT'S TOO BAD.
BUT IF YOU WANT TO WASTE YOUR TIME, I'M NOT THE ONE TO STOP YOU, OR TO CARE.
BUT WRAP THIS AROUND YOUR PUNY BRAIN...
REGARDLESS OF WHO TAMON GOES OUT WITH, I'M MOMMA. HE'S ALWAYS GONNA COME BACK TO ME...
...NO MATTER WHAT.
WHAT...?
WHAT'S THE HUL-LABALOO OUT HERE?
RATS!
AMI! WE GOTTA SCRAM!
AMI!!

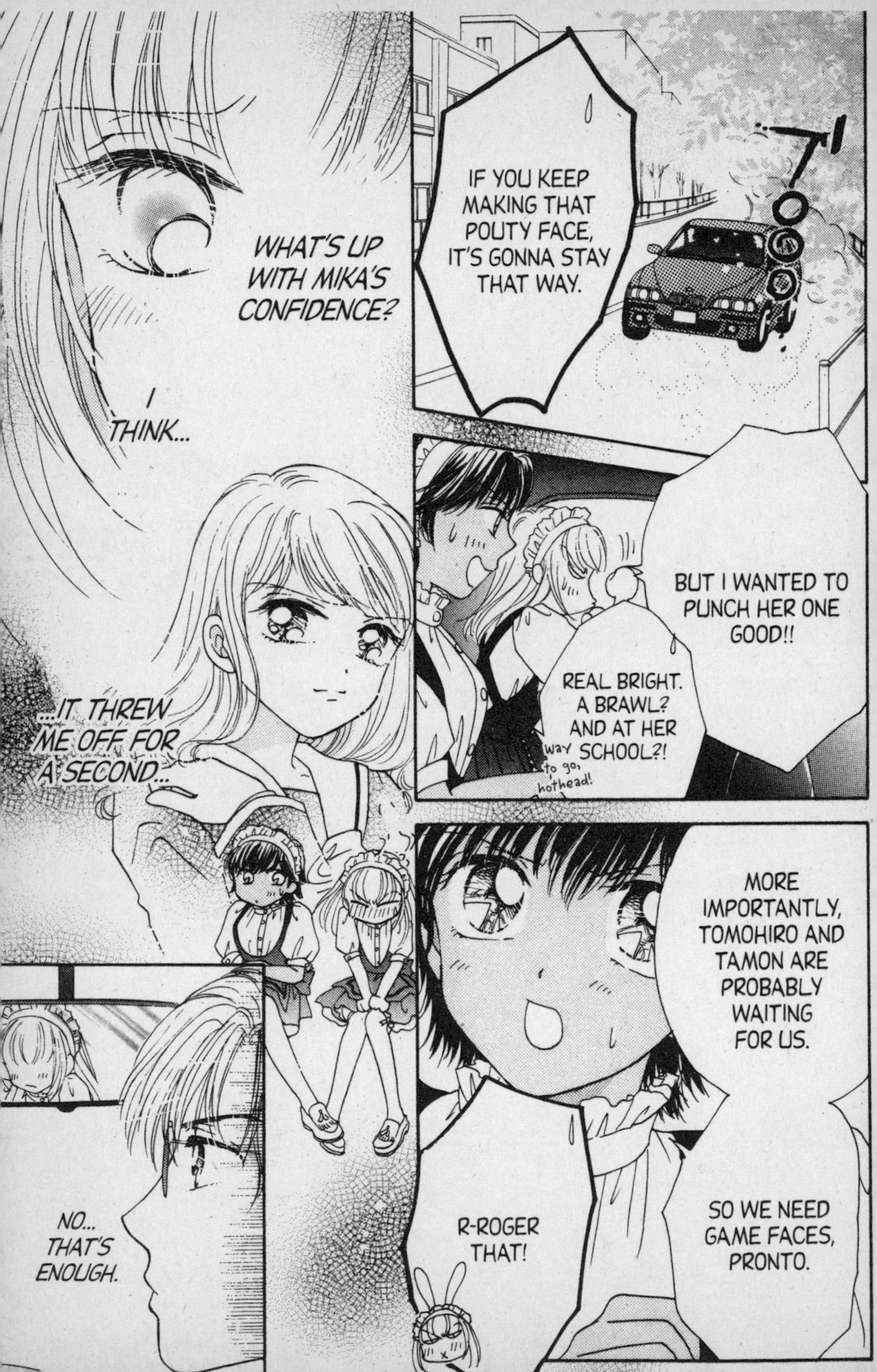
IF YOU KEEP MAKING THAT POUTY FACE, IT'S GONNA STAY THAT WAY.
BUT I WANTED TO PUNCH HER ONE GOOD!!
REAL BRIGHT. A BRAWL? AND AT HER SCHOOL?!
way to go, hothead!
MORE IMPORTANTLY, TOMOHIRO AND TAMON ARE PROBABLY WAITING FOR US.
SO WE NEED GAME FACES, PRONTO.
R-ROGER THAT!
WHAT'S UP WITH MIKA'S CONFIDENCE?
I THINK...
...IT THREW ME OFF FOR A SECOND...
NO... THAT'S ENOUGH.

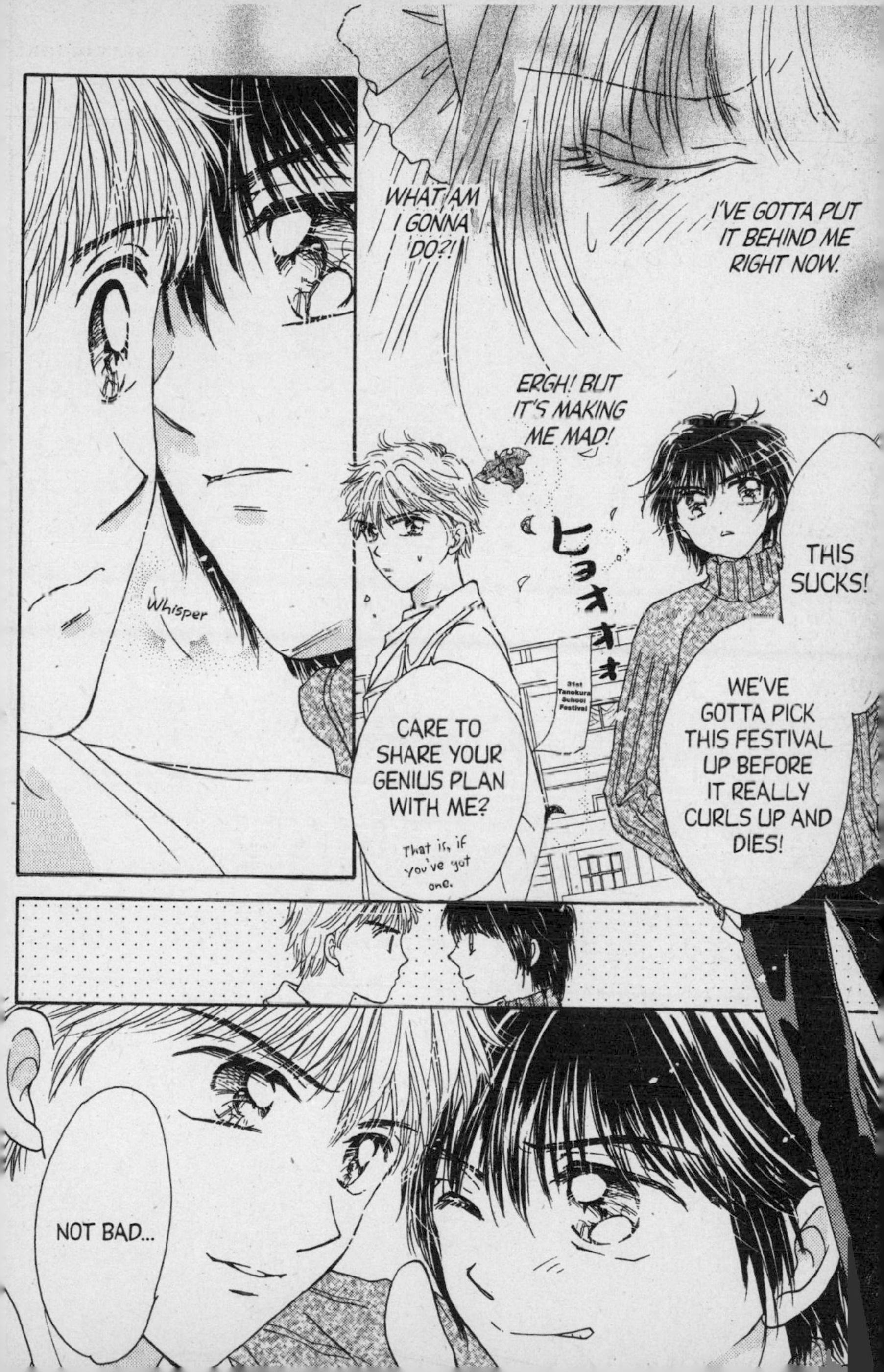
I'VE GOTTA PUT IT BEHIND ME RIGHT NOW.
WHAT AM I GONNA DO?!
ERGH! BUT IT'S MAKING ME MAD!
THIS SUCKS!
WE'VE GOTTA PICK THIS FESTIVAL UP BEFORE IT REALLY CURLS UP AND DIES!
ヒョオオオ
31st Tanokura School Festival
CARE TO SHARE YOUR GENIUS PLAN WITH ME?
That is, if you've got one.
Whisper
NOT BAD...

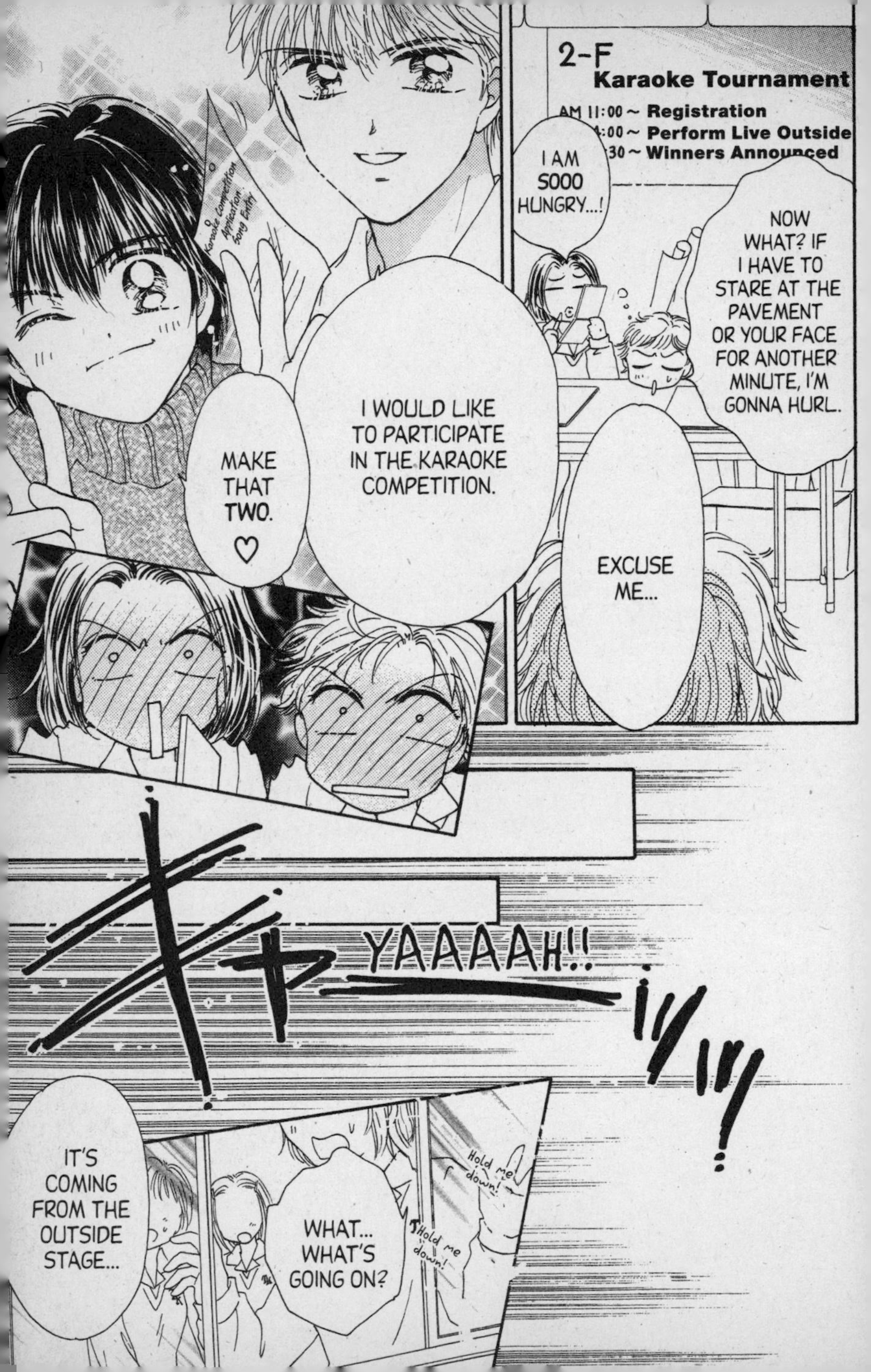
2-F
Karaoke Tournament
AM 11:00 ~ Registration
4:00 ~ Perform Live Outside
30 ~ Winners Announced
NOW WHAT? IF I HAVE TO STARE AT THE PAVEMENT OR YOUR FACE FOR ANOTHER MINUTE, I'M GONNA HURL.
I AM SOOO HUNGRY...!
EXCUSE ME...
I WOULD LIKE TO PARTICIPATE IN THE KARAOKE COMPETITION.
Karaoke Competition Application: Song Entry
MAKE THAT TWO. ♡
YAAAAH!!
Hold me down!
Hold me down!
WHAT... WHAT'S GOING ON?
IT'S COMING FROM THE OUTSIDE STAGE...

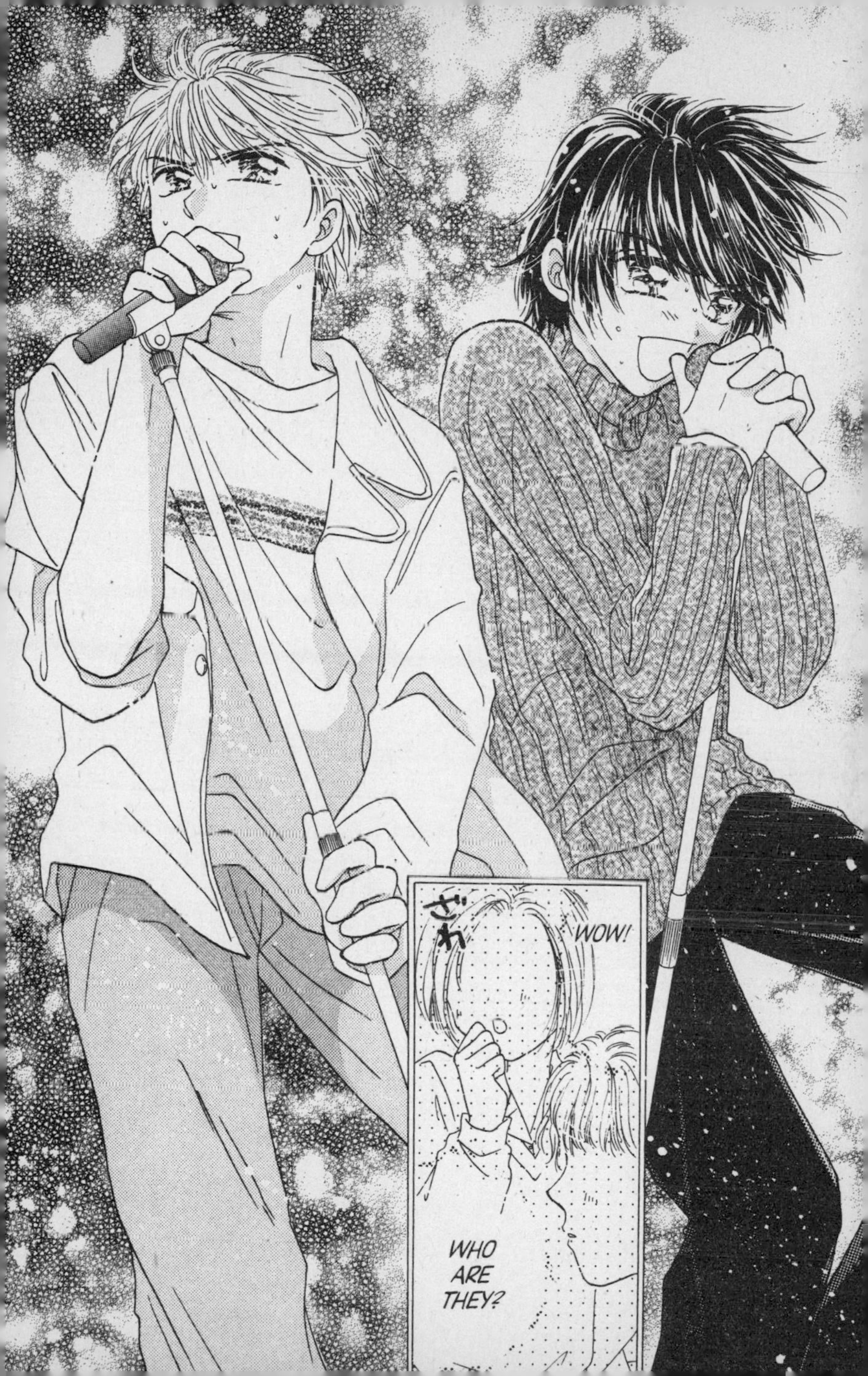
ざわ
WOW!
WHO ARE THEY?

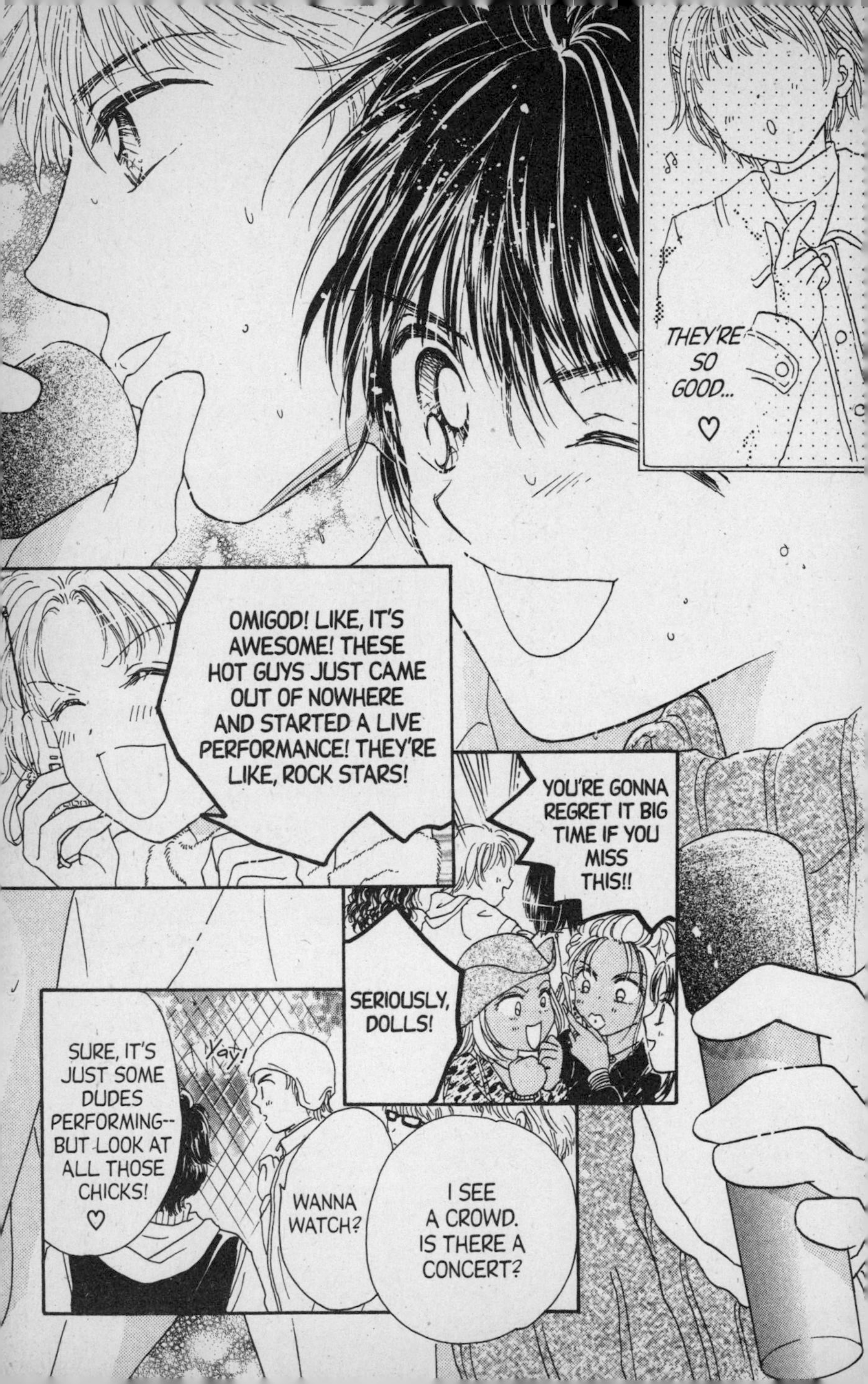
THEY'RE SO GOOD... ♡
YOU'RE GONNA REGRET IT BIG TIME IF YOU MISS THIS!!
SERIOUSLY, DOLLS!
OMIGOD! LIKE, IT'S AWESOME! THESE HOT GUYS JUST CAME OUT OF NOWHERE AND STARTED A LIVE PERFORMANCE! THEY'RE LIKE, ROCK STARS!
I SEE A CROWD. IS THERE A CONCERT?
WANNA WATCH?
Yay!
SURE, IT'S JUST SOME DUDES PERFORMING-- BUT LOOK AT ALL THOSE CHICKS! ♡

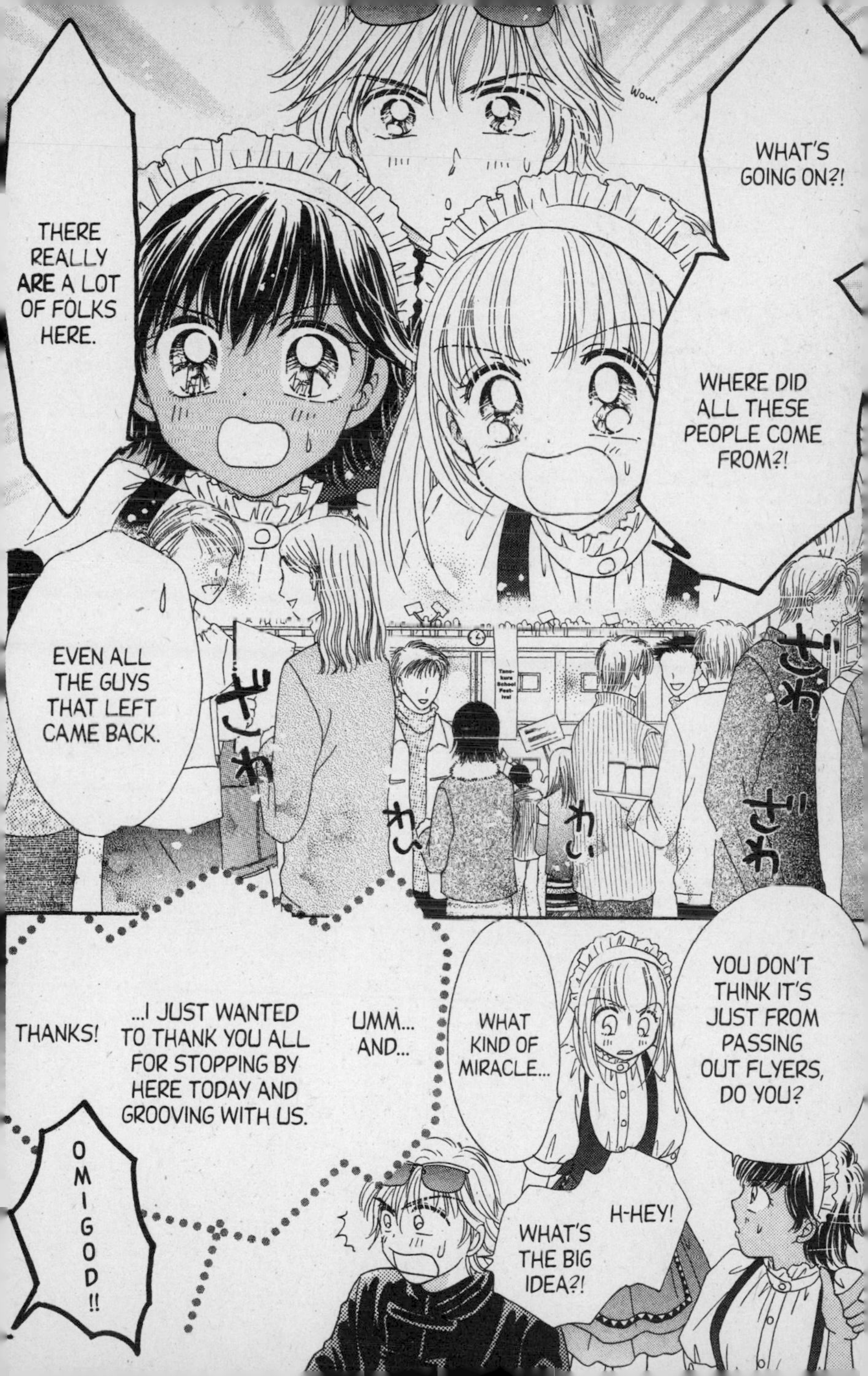
WHAT'S GOING ON?!
Wow.
WHERE DID ALL THESE PEOPLE COME FROM?!
THERE REALLY ARE A LOT OF FOLKS HERE.
EVEN ALL THE GUYS THAT LEFT CAME BACK.
YOU DON'T THINK IT'S JUST FROM PASSING OUT FLYERS, DO YOU?
WHAT KIND OF MIRACLE...
UMM... AND...
...I JUST WANTED TO THANK YOU ALL FOR STOPPING BY HERE TODAY AND GROOVING WITH US.
THANKS!
H-HEY!
WHAT'S THE BIG IDEA?!
OMIGOD!!

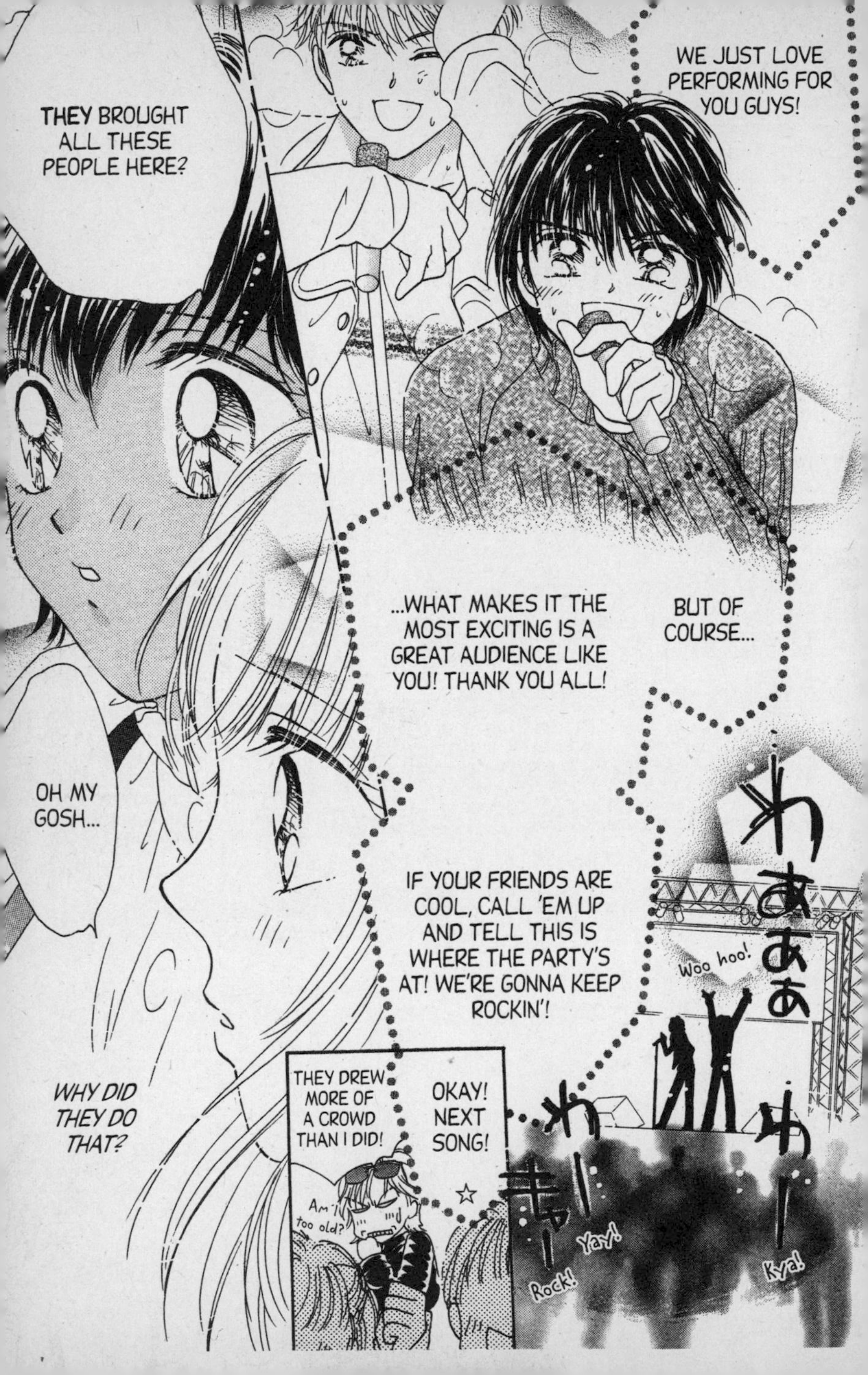
WE JUST LOVE PERFORMING FOR YOU GUYS!
THEY BROUGHT ALL THESE PEOPLE HERE?
BUT OF COURSE...
...WHAT MAKES IT THE MOST EXCITING IS A GREAT AUDIENCE LIKE YOU! THANK YOU ALL!
IF YOUR FRIENDS ARE COOL, CALL 'EM UP AND TELL THIS IS WHERE THE PARTY'S AT! WE'RE GONNA KEEP ROCKIN'!
OH MY GOSH...
わあぁぁ
Woo hoo!
わー
わー
きゃー
Kya!
Yay!
Rock!
OKAY! NEXT SONG!
THEY DREW MORE OF A CROWD THAN I DID!
Am I too old?
WHY DID THEY DO THAT?

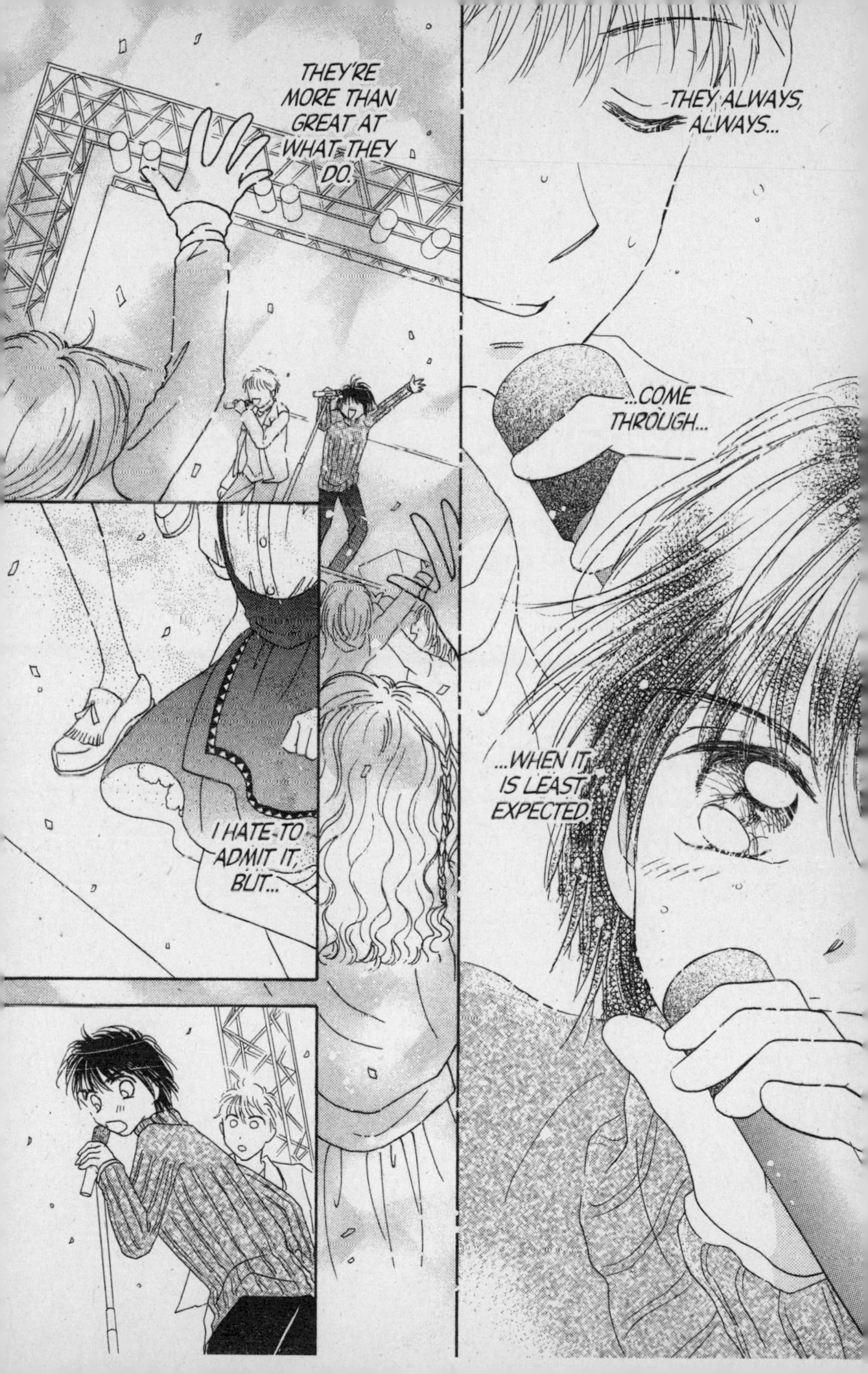
THEY ALWAYS, ALWAYS...
...COME THROUGH...
...WHEN IT IS LEAST EXPECTED.
THEY'RE MORE THAN GREAT AT WHAT THEY DO.
I HATE TO ADMIT IT, BUT...

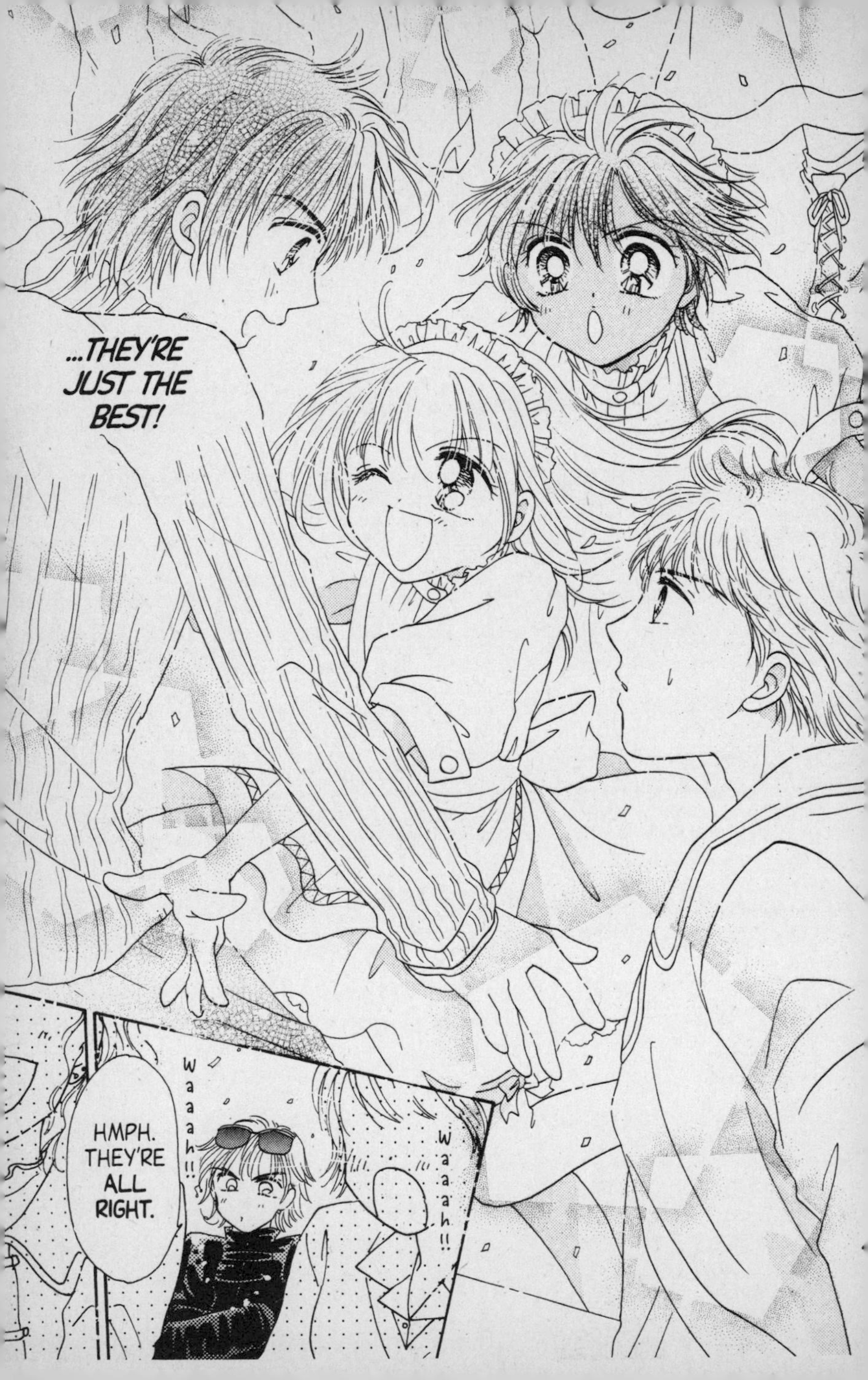
...THEY'RE JUST THE BEST!
Waaah!!
Waaah!!
HMPH. THEY'RE ALL RIGHT.

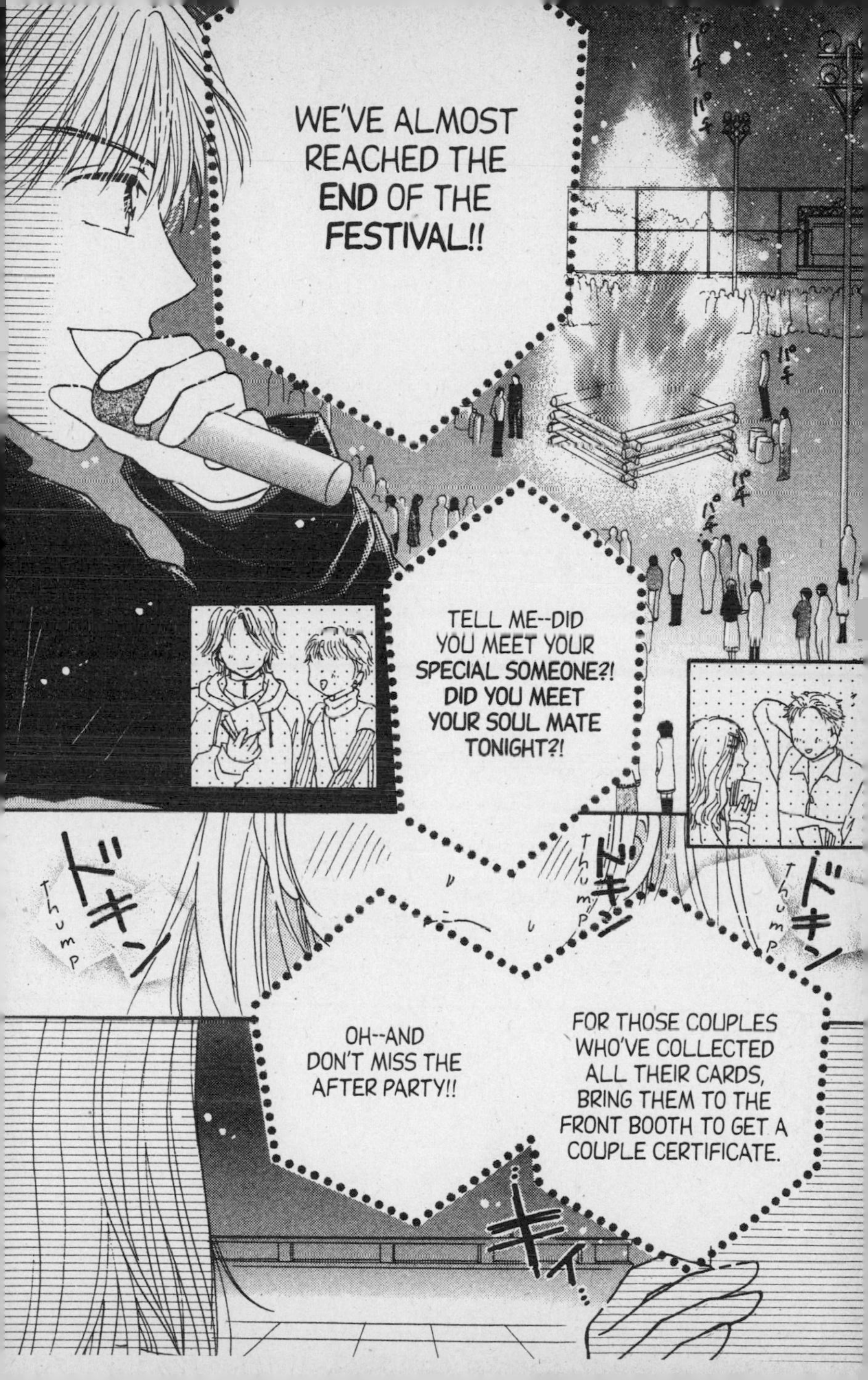
WE'VE ALMOST REACHED THE END OF THE FESTIVAL!!
TELL ME--DID YOU MEET YOUR SPECIAL SOMEONE?! DID YOU MEET YOUR SOUL MATE TONIGHT?!
thump
thump
thump
FOR THOSE COUPLES WHO'VE COLLECTED ALL THEIR CARDS, BRING THEM TO THE FRONT BOOTH TO GET A COUPLE CERTIFICATE.
OH--AND DON'T MISS THE AFTER PARTY!!

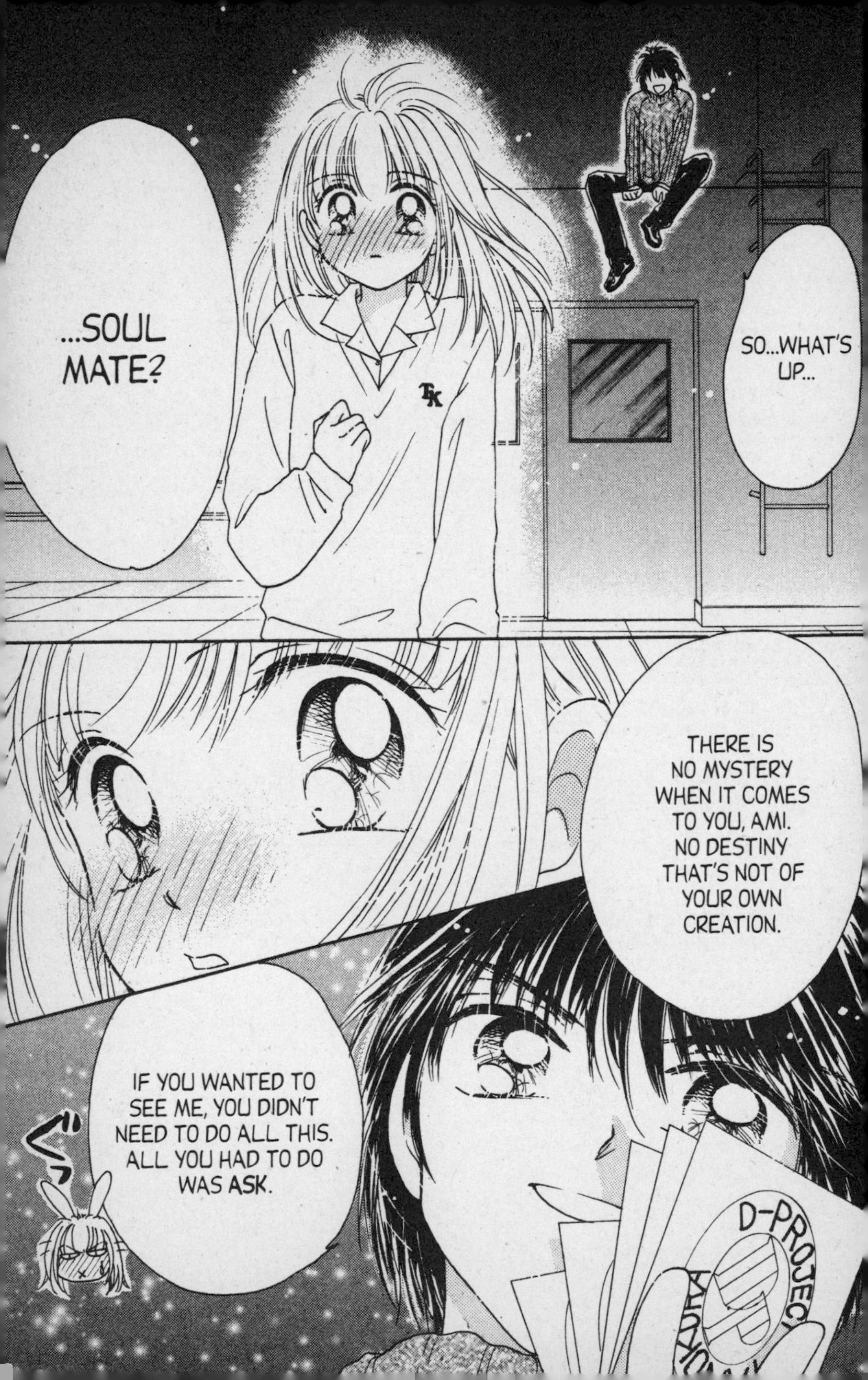
SO...WHAT'S UP...
...SOUL MATE?
THERE IS NO MYSTERY WHEN IT COMES TO YOU, AMI. NO DESTINY THAT'S NOT OF YOUR OWN CREATION.
IF YOU WANTED TO SEE ME, YOU DIDN'T NEED TO DO ALL THIS. ALL YOU HAD TO DO WAS ASK.

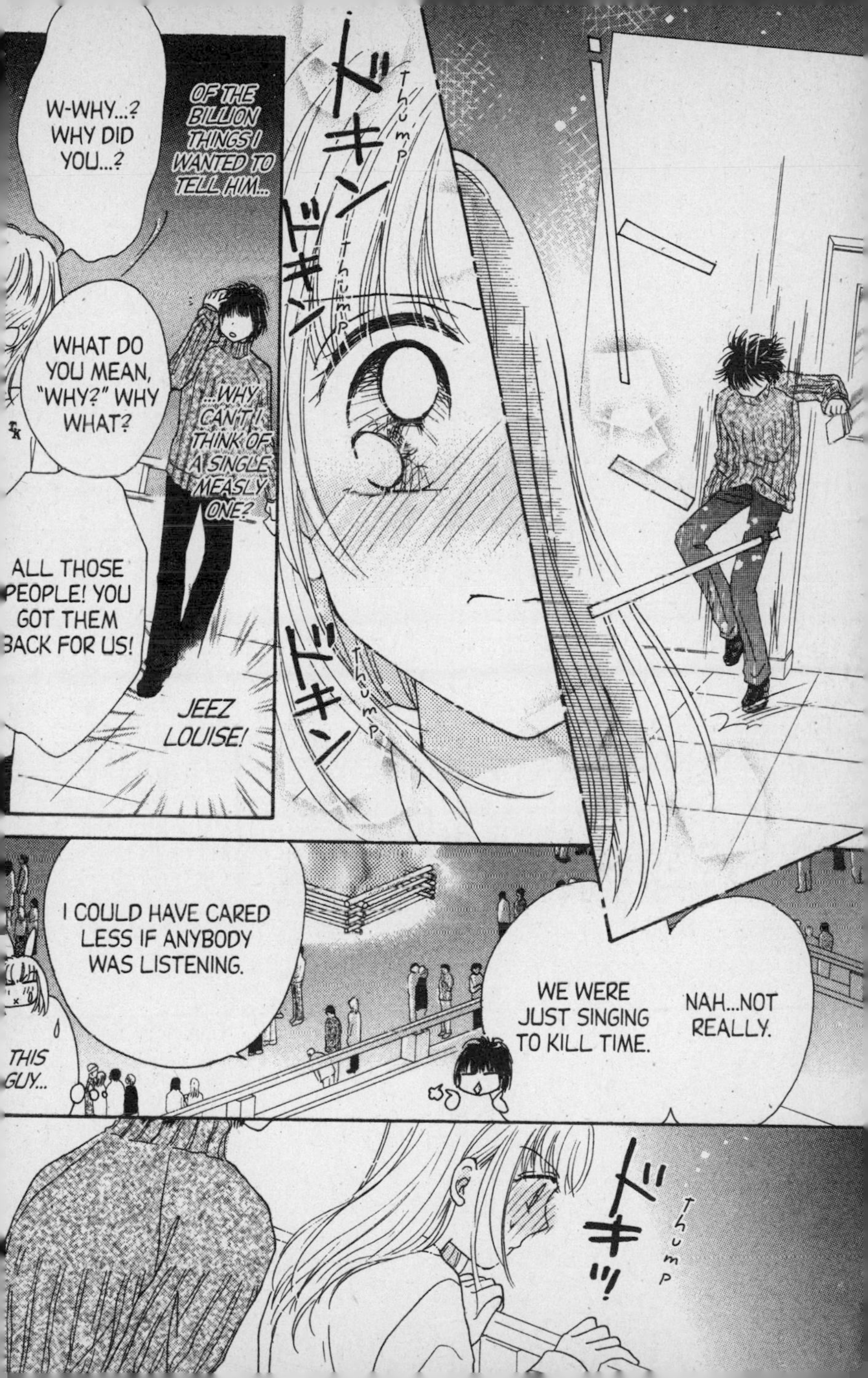
ドキン
THUMP
ドキン
THUMP
ドキン
THUMP
W-WHY...? WHY DID YOU...?
OF THE BILLION THINGS I WANTED TO TELL HIM...
WHAT DO YOU MEAN, "WHY?" WHY WHAT?
...WHY CAN'T I THINK OF A SINGLE MEASLY ONE?
ALL THOSE PEOPLE! YOU GOT THEM BACK FOR US!
JEEZ LOUISE!
NAH...NOT REALLY.
WE WERE JUST SINGING TO KILL TIME.
I COULD HAVE CARED LESS IF ANYBODY WAS LISTENING.
THIS GUY...
ドキッ!
THUMP

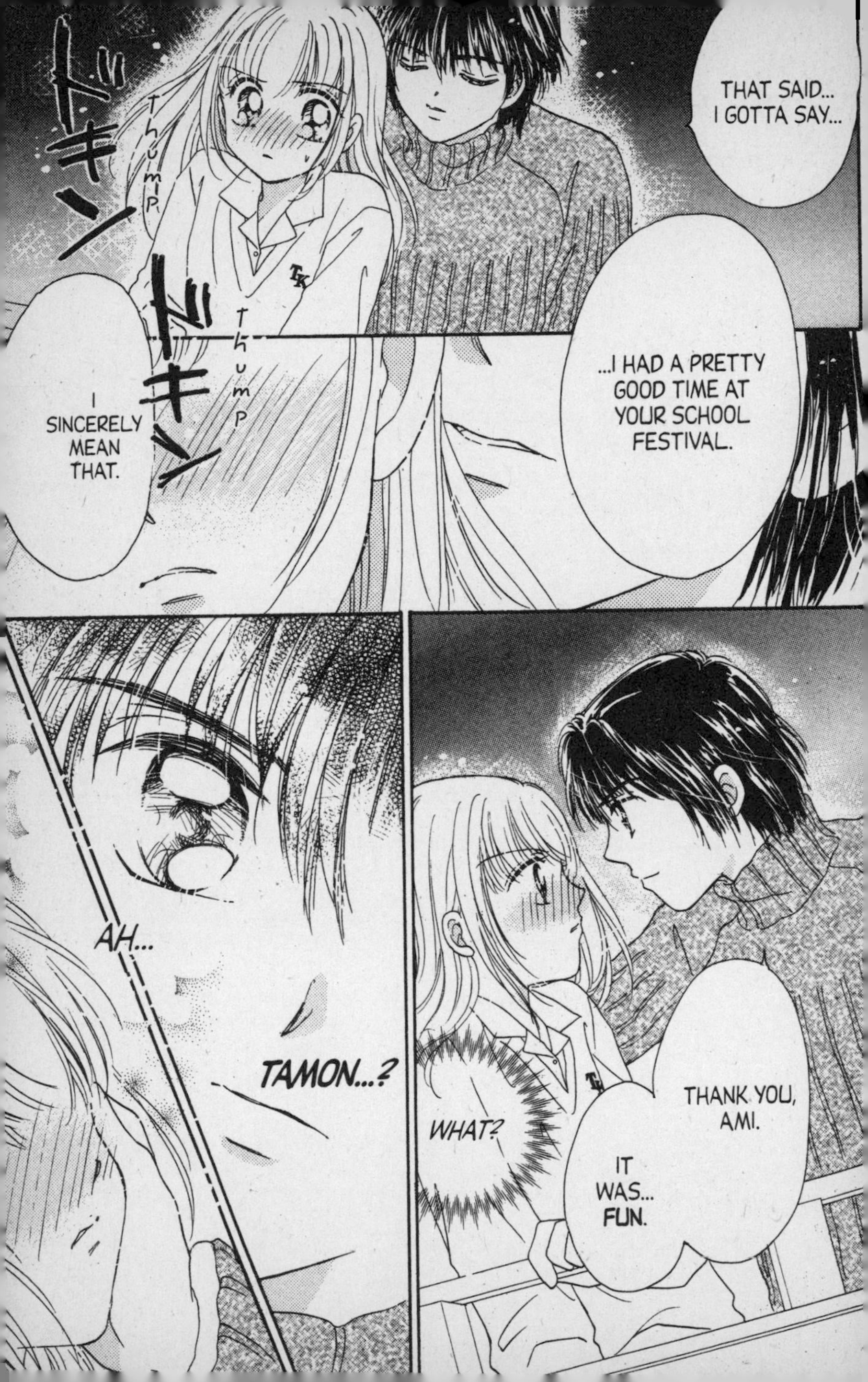
THAT SAID... I GOTTA SAY...
ドキン
THUMP
...I HAD A PRETTY GOOD TIME AT YOUR SCHOOL FESTIVAL.
I SINCERELY MEAN THAT.
ドキン
THUMP
THANK YOU, AMI.
IT WAS... FUN.
WHAT?
AH...
TAMON...?

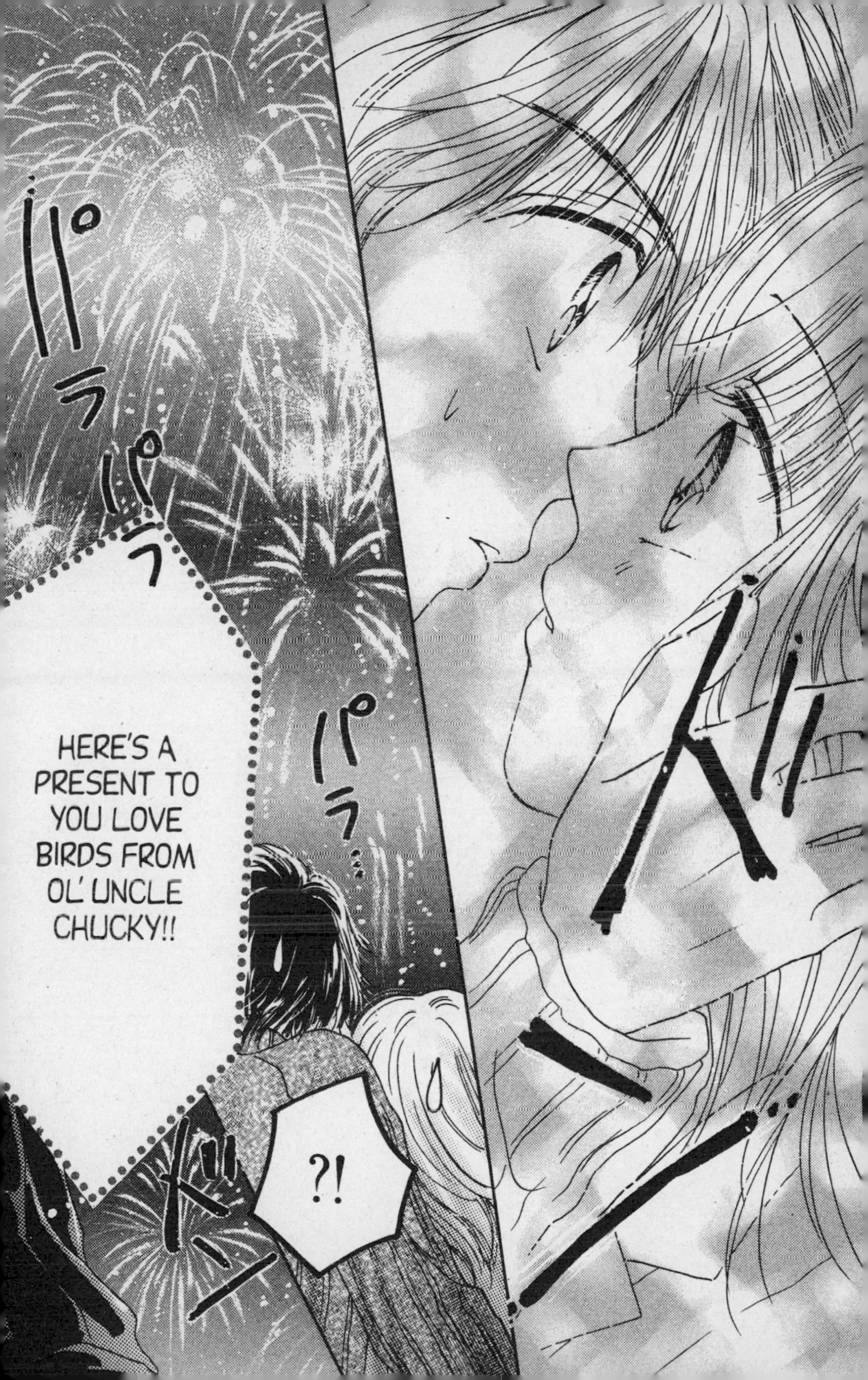
パラパラ
HERE'S A PRESENT TO YOU LOVE BIRDS FROM OL' UNCLE CHUCKY!!
パラ...
?!

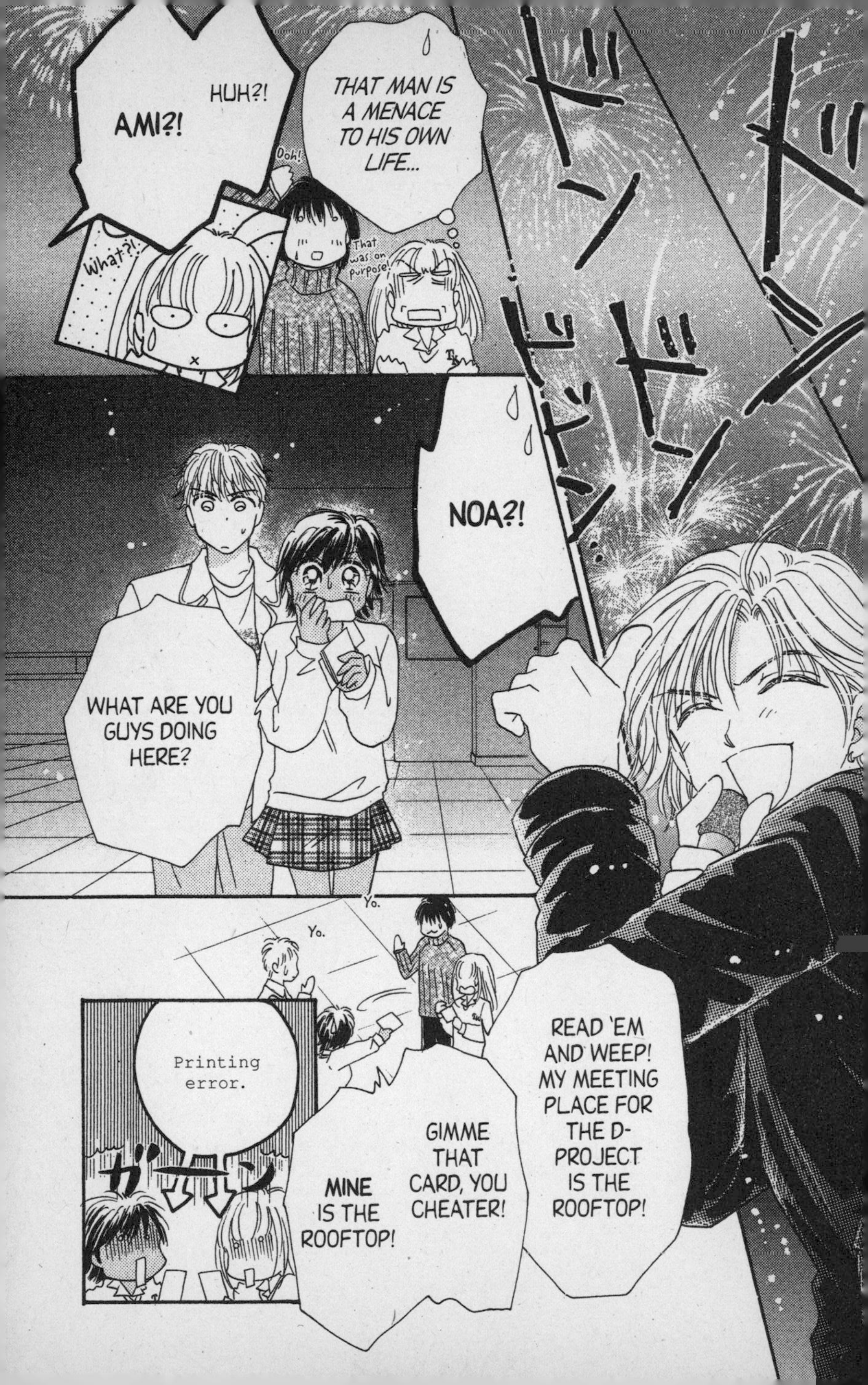
THAT MAN IS A MENACE TO HIS OWN LIFE...
That was on purpose!
Ooh!
HUH?!
AMI?!
What?!
NOA?!
READ 'EM AND WEEP! MY MEETING PLACE FOR THE D-PROJECT IS THE ROOFTOP!
WHAT ARE YOU GUYS DOING HERE?
Yo.
Yo.
GIMME THAT CARD, YOU CHEATER!
MINE IS THE ROOFTOP!
Printing error.

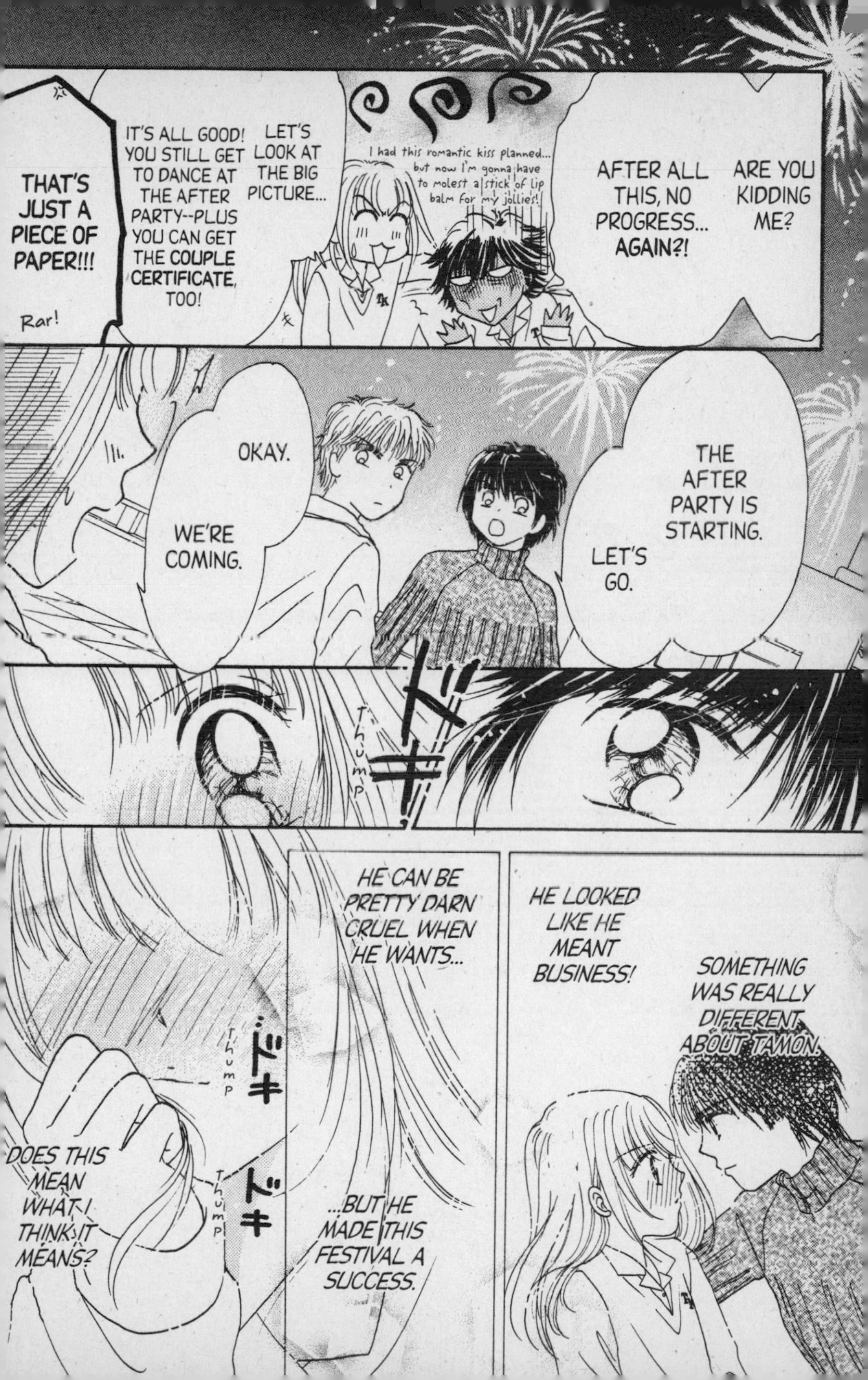

ARE YOU KIDDING ME?
AFTER ALL THIS, NO PROGRESS... AGAIN?!
I had this romantic kiss planned... but now I'm gonna have to molest a stick of lip balm for my jollies!
LET'S LOOK AT THE BIG PICTURE...
IT'S ALL GOOD! YOU STILL GET TO DANCE AT THE AFTER PARTY--PLUS YOU CAN GET THE COUPLE CERTIFICATE, TOO!
THAT'S JUST A PIECE OF PAPER!!!
Rar!
THE AFTER PARTY IS STARTING.
LET'S GO.
OKAY.
WE'RE COMING.
ドキ
THUMP
SOMETHING WAS REALLY DIFFERENT ABOUT TAMON.
HE LOOKED LIKE HE MEANT BUSINESS!
HE CAN BE PRETTY DARN CRUEL WHEN HE WANTS...
...BUT HE MADE THIS FESTIVAL A SUCCESS.
ドキ
THUMP
ドキ
THUMP
DOES THIS MEAN WHAT I THINK IT MEANS?

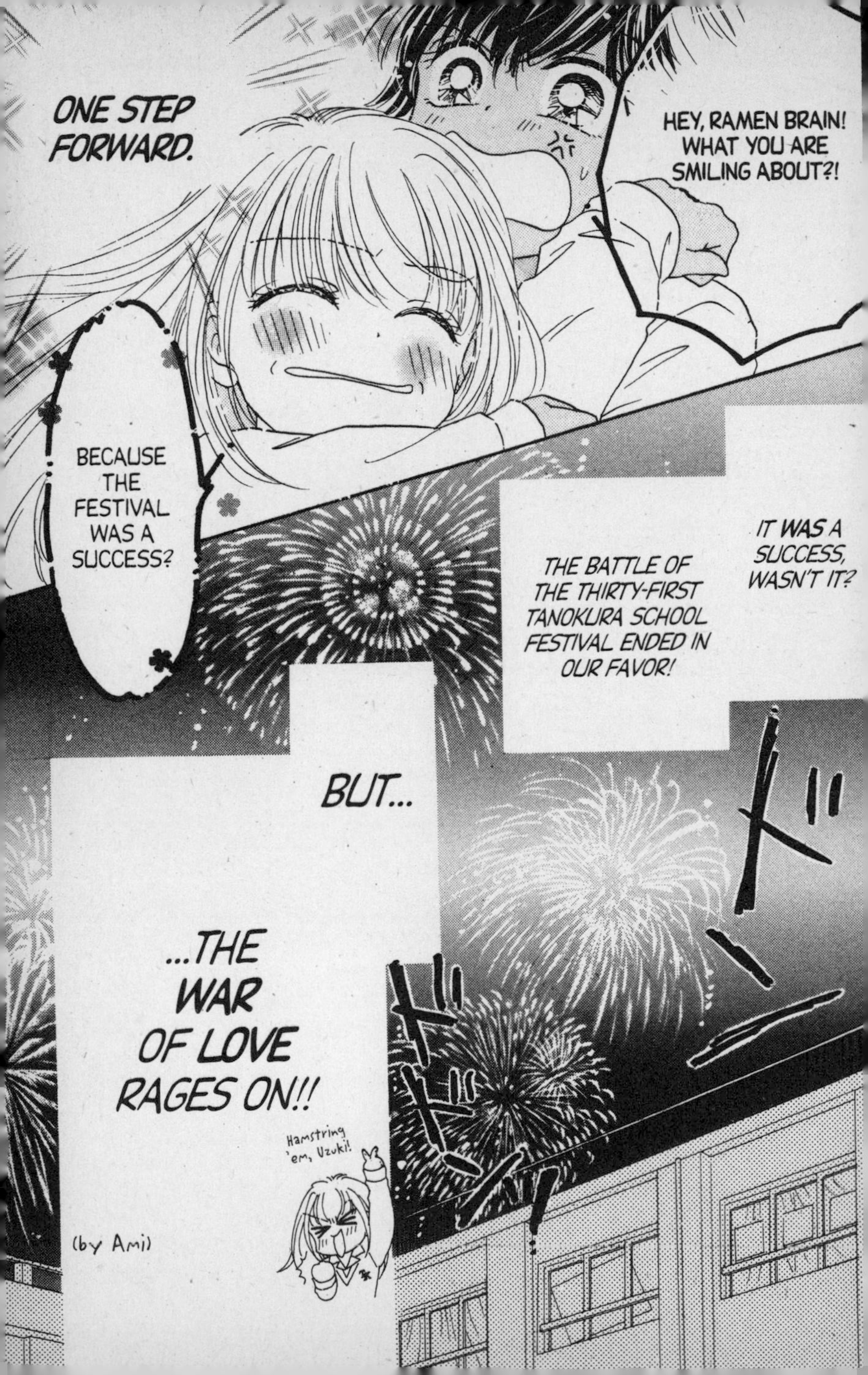
HEY, RAMEN BRAIN! WHAT YOU ARE SMILING ABOUT?!
ONE STEP FORWARD.
BECAUSE THE FESTIVAL WAS A SUCCESS?
IT WAS A SUCCESS, WASN'T IT?
THE BATTLE OF THE THIRTY-FIRST TANOKURA SCHOOL FESTIVAL ENDED IN OUR FAVOR!
BUT...
...THE WAR OF LOVE RAGES ON!!
Hamstring 'em, Uzuki!
(by Ami)

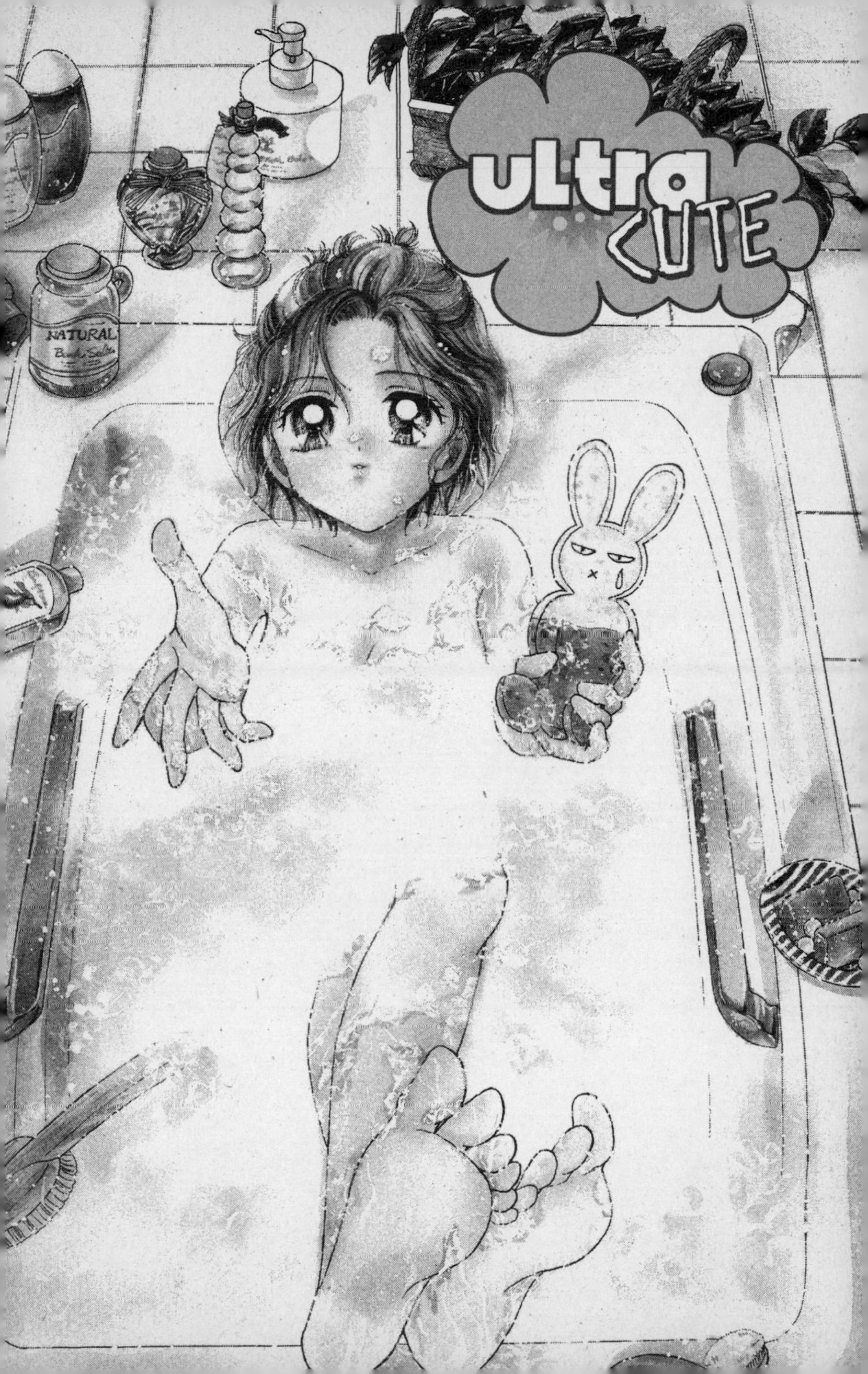
ultra CUTE
NATURAL
Bath Salts

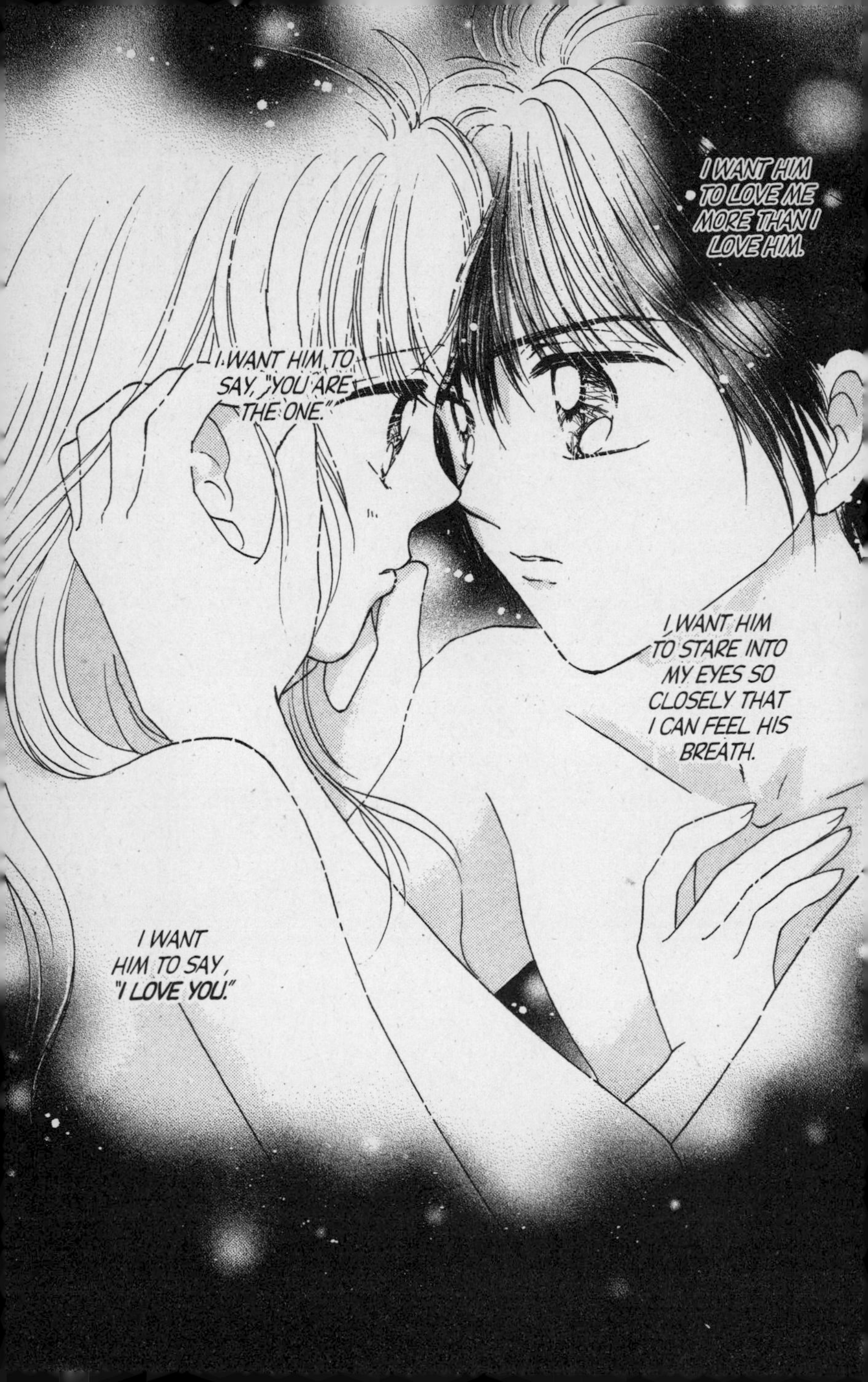
I WANT HIM TO LOVE ME MORE THAN I LOVE HIM.
I WANT HIM TO SAY, "YOU ARE THE ONE."
I WANT HIM TO STARE INTO MY EYES SO CLOSELY THAT I CAN FEEL HIS BREATH.
I WANT HIM TO SAY, "I LOVE YOU."

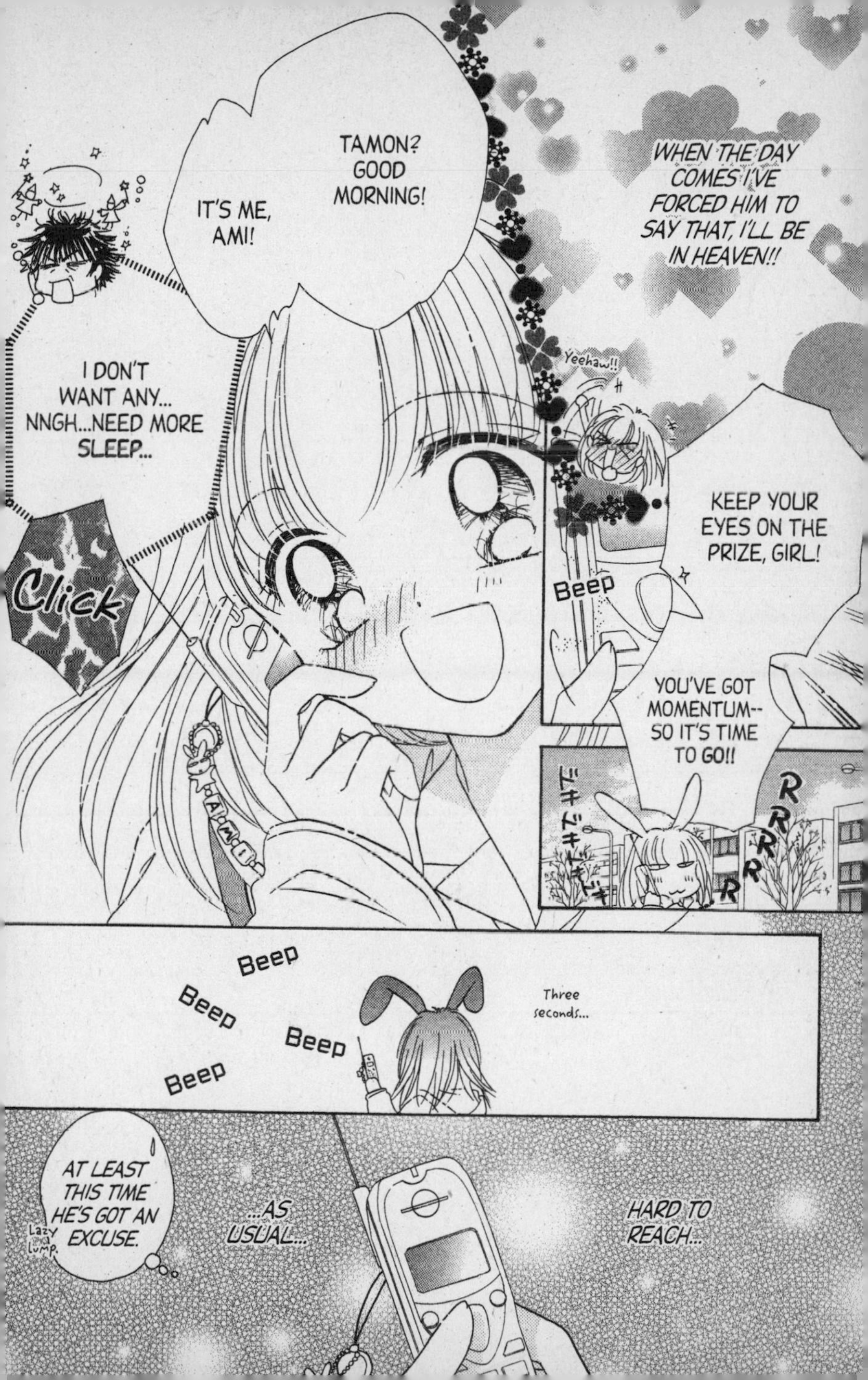

WHEN THE DAY COMES I'VE FORCED HIM TO SAY THAT, I'LL BE IN HEAVEN!!
Yeehaw!!
Beep
KEEP YOUR EYES ON THE PRIZE, GIRL!
YOU'VE GOT MOMENTUM-- SO IT'S TIME TO GO!!
RRRRR
TAMON? GOOD MORNING!
IT'S ME, AMI!
I DON'T WANT ANY... NNGH...NEED MORE SLEEP...
Click
Beep
Beep
Beep
Beep
Three seconds...
HARD TO REACH...
...AS USUAL...
AT LEAST THIS TIME HE'S GOT AN EXCUSE.
Lazy lump.

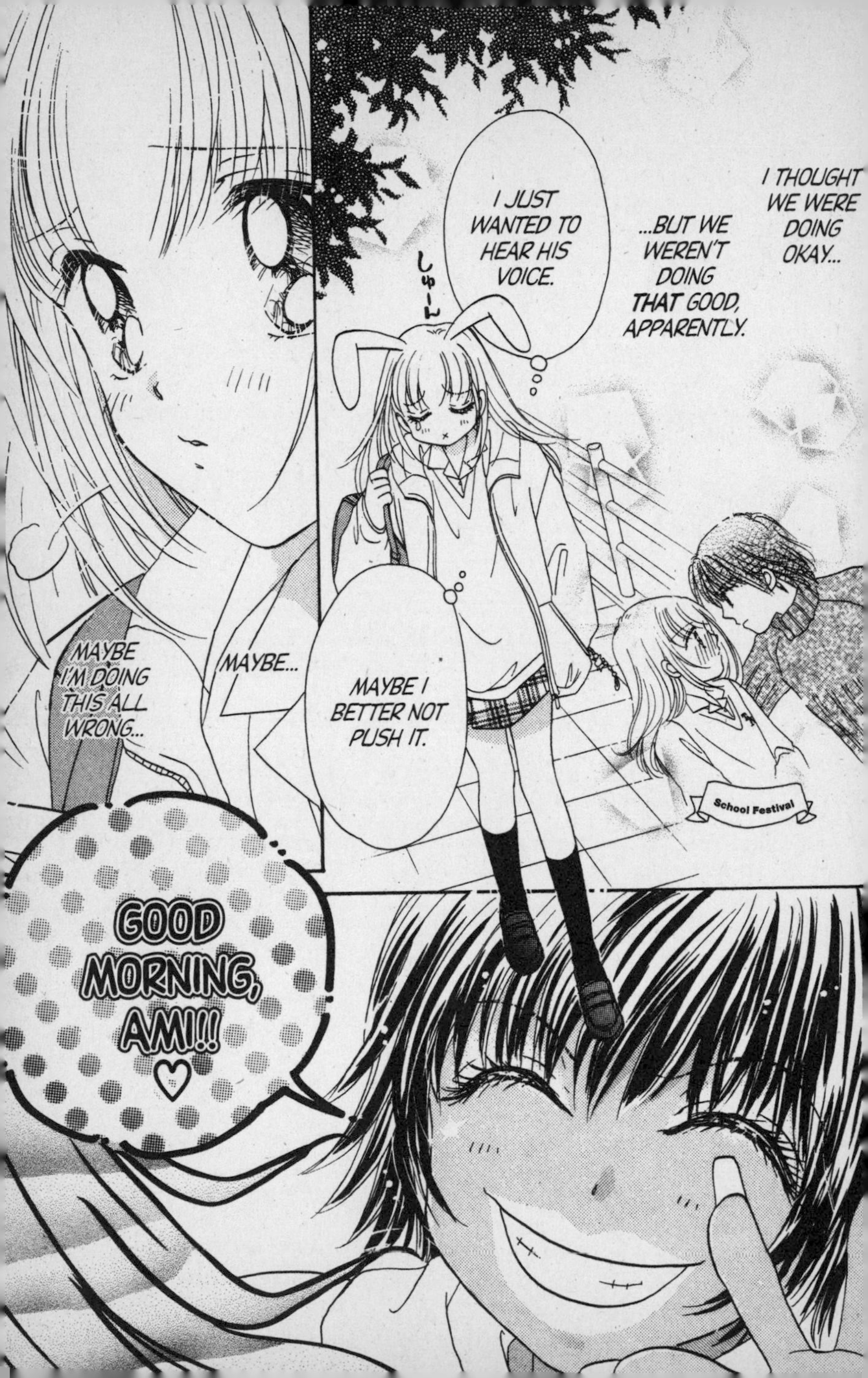
I THOUGHT WE WERE DOING OKAY...
...BUT WE WEREN'T DOING THAT GOOD, APPARENTLY.
I JUST WANTED TO HEAR HIS VOICE.
しゅーん
MAYBE I BETTER NOT PUSH IT.
School Festival
MAYBE...
MAYBE I'M DOING THIS ALL WRONG...
GOOD MORNING, AMI!! ♡

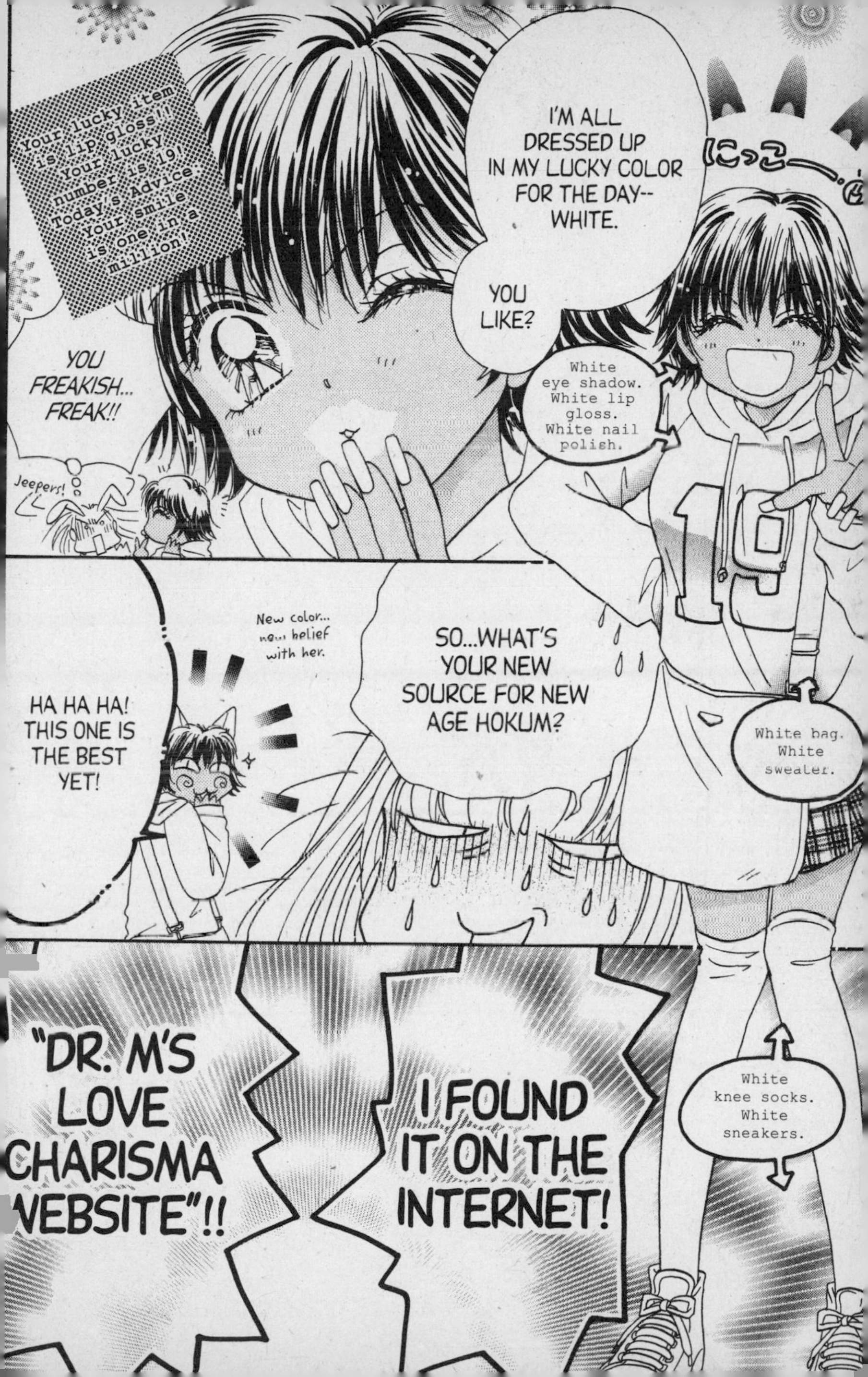
にっこー
I'M ALL DRESSED UP IN MY LUCKY COLOR FOR THE DAY-- WHITE.
YOU LIKE?
White eye shadow. White lip gloss. White nail polish.
Your lucky item is lip gloss!! Your lucky number is 19! Today's Advice: Your smile is one in a million!
YOU FREAKISH... FREAK!!
Jeepers!
White bag. White sweater.
SO...WHAT'S YOUR NEW SOURCE FOR NEW AGE HOKUM?
New color... new belief with her.
HA HA HA! THIS ONE IS THE BEST YET!
White knee socks. White sneakers.
I FOUND IT ON THE INTERNET!
"DR. M'S LOVE CHARISMA WEBSITE"!!

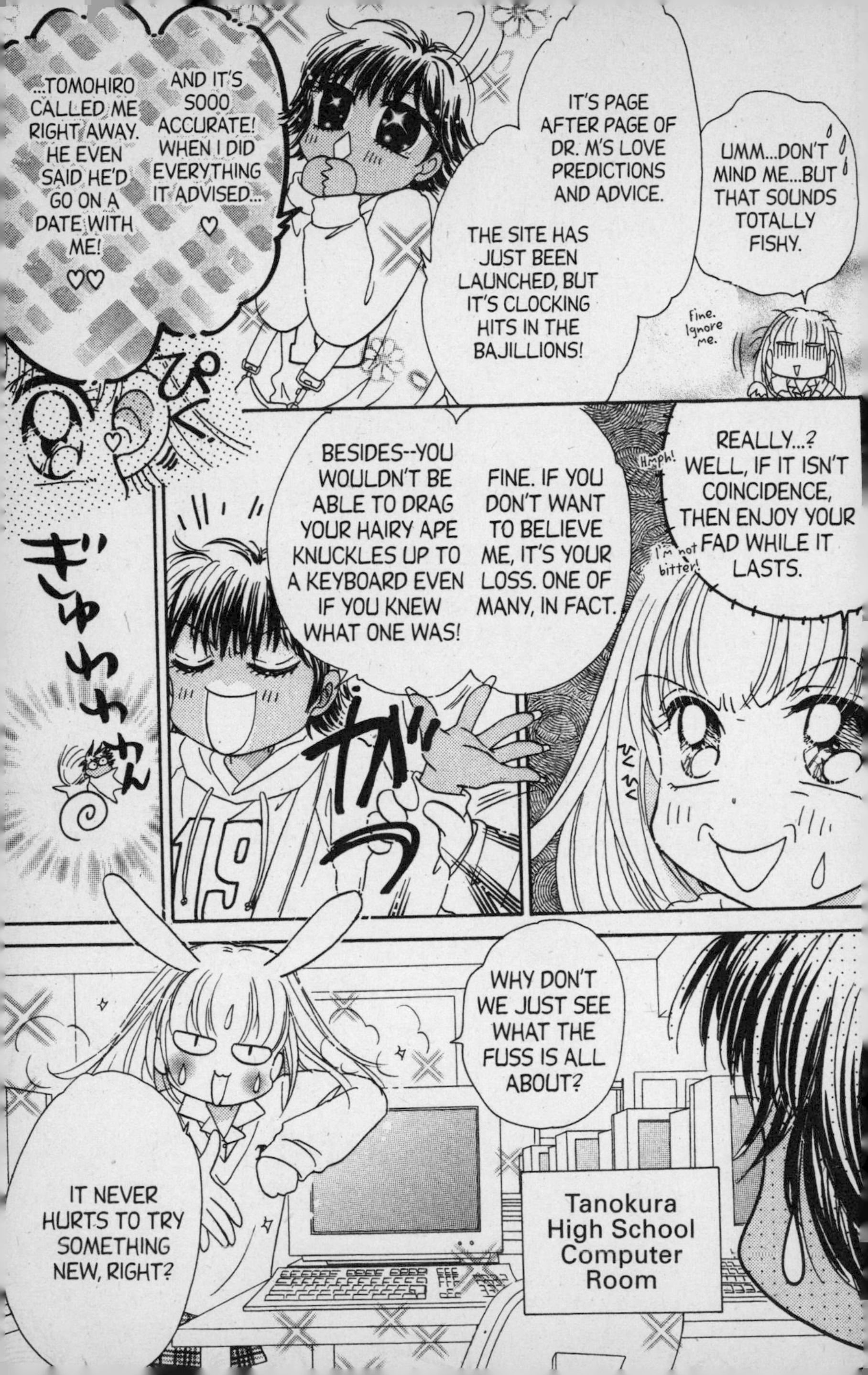
IT'S PAGE AFTER PAGE OF DR. M'S LOVE PREDICTIONS AND ADVICE.
THE SITE HAS JUST BEEN LAUNCHED, BUT IT'S CLOCKING HITS IN THE BAJILLIONS!
UMM...DON'T MIND ME...BUT THAT SOUNDS TOTALLY FISHY.
Fine. Ignore me.
AND IT'S SOOO ACCURATE! WHEN I DID EVERYTHING IT ADVISED...
...TOMOHIRO CALLED ME RIGHT AWAY. HE EVEN SAID HE'D GO ON A DATE WITH ME!
ぴく
REALLY...? WELL, IF IT ISN'T COINCIDENCE, THEN ENJOY YOUR FAD WHILE IT LASTS.
Hmph!
I'm not bitter!
FINE. IF YOU DON'T WANT TO BELIEVE ME, IT'S YOUR LOSS. ONE OF MANY, IN FACT.
BESIDES--YOU WOULDN'T BE ABLE TO DRAG YOUR HAIRY APE KNUCKLES UP TO A KEYBOARD EVEN IF YOU KNEW WHAT ONE WAS!
がっ
WHY DON'T WE JUST SEE WHAT THE FUSS IS ALL ABOUT?
Tanokura High School Computer Room
IT NEVER HURTS TO TRY SOMETHING NEW, RIGHT?

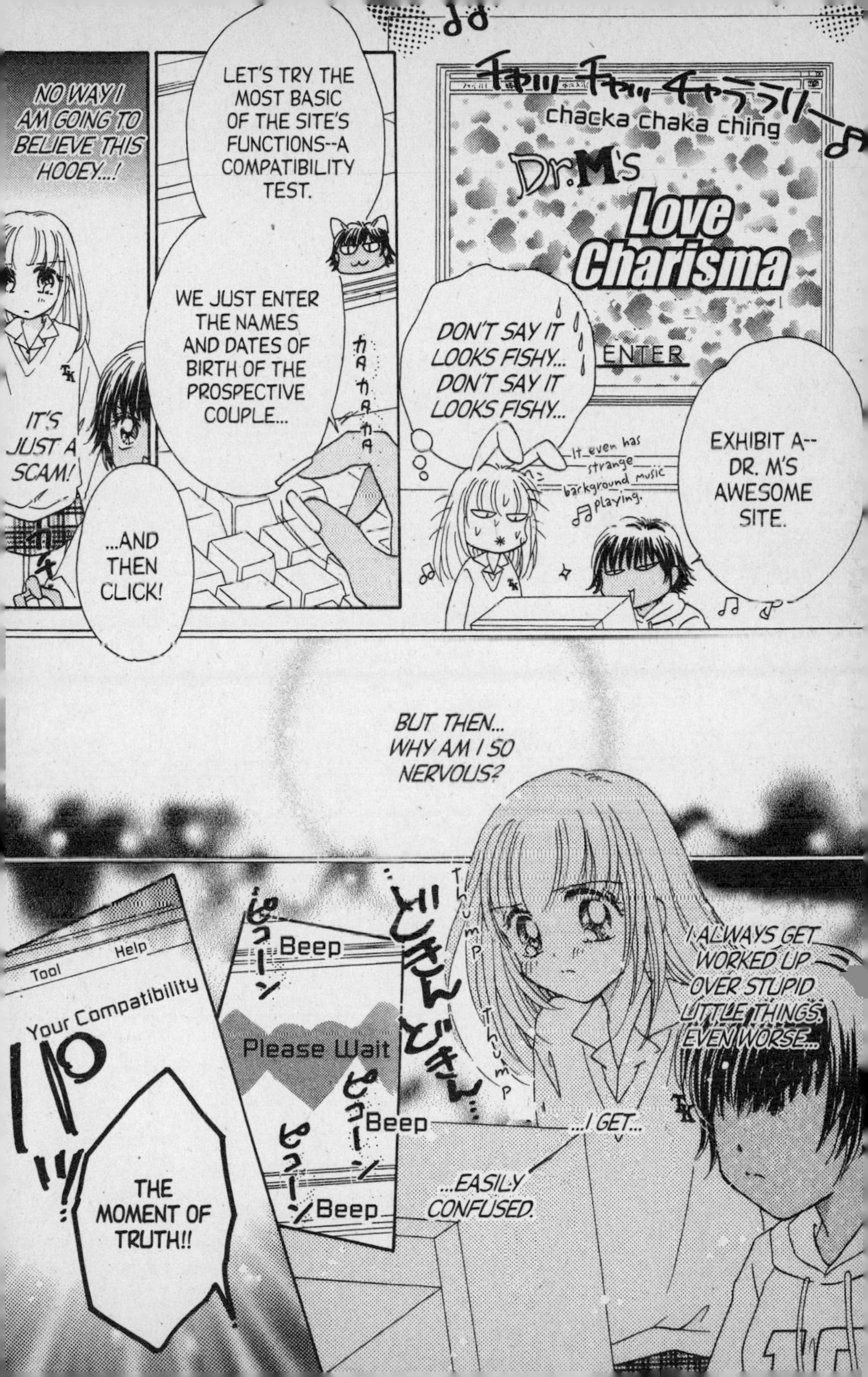
chacka chaka ching
Dr. M's Love Charisma
ENTER
EXHIBIT A-- DR. M'S AWESOME SITE.
DON'T SAY IT LOOKS FISHY... DON'T SAY IT LOOKS FISHY...
It even has strange background music playing.
LET'S TRY THE MOST BASIC OF THE SITE'S FUNCTIONS--A COMPATIBILITY TEST.
WE JUST ENTER THE NAMES AND DATES OF BIRTH OF THE PROSPECTIVE COUPLE...
...AND THEN CLICK!
NO WAY I AM GOING TO BELIEVE THIS HOOEY...!
IT'S JUST A SCAM!
BUT THEN... WHY AM I SO NERVOUS?
I ALWAYS GET WORKED UP OVER STUPID LITTLE THINGS. EVEN WORSE...
...I GET...
...EASILY CONFUSED.
THUMP THUMP
Beep
Please Wait
Beep
Beep
Tool
Help
Your Compatibility
THE MOMENT OF TRUTH!!

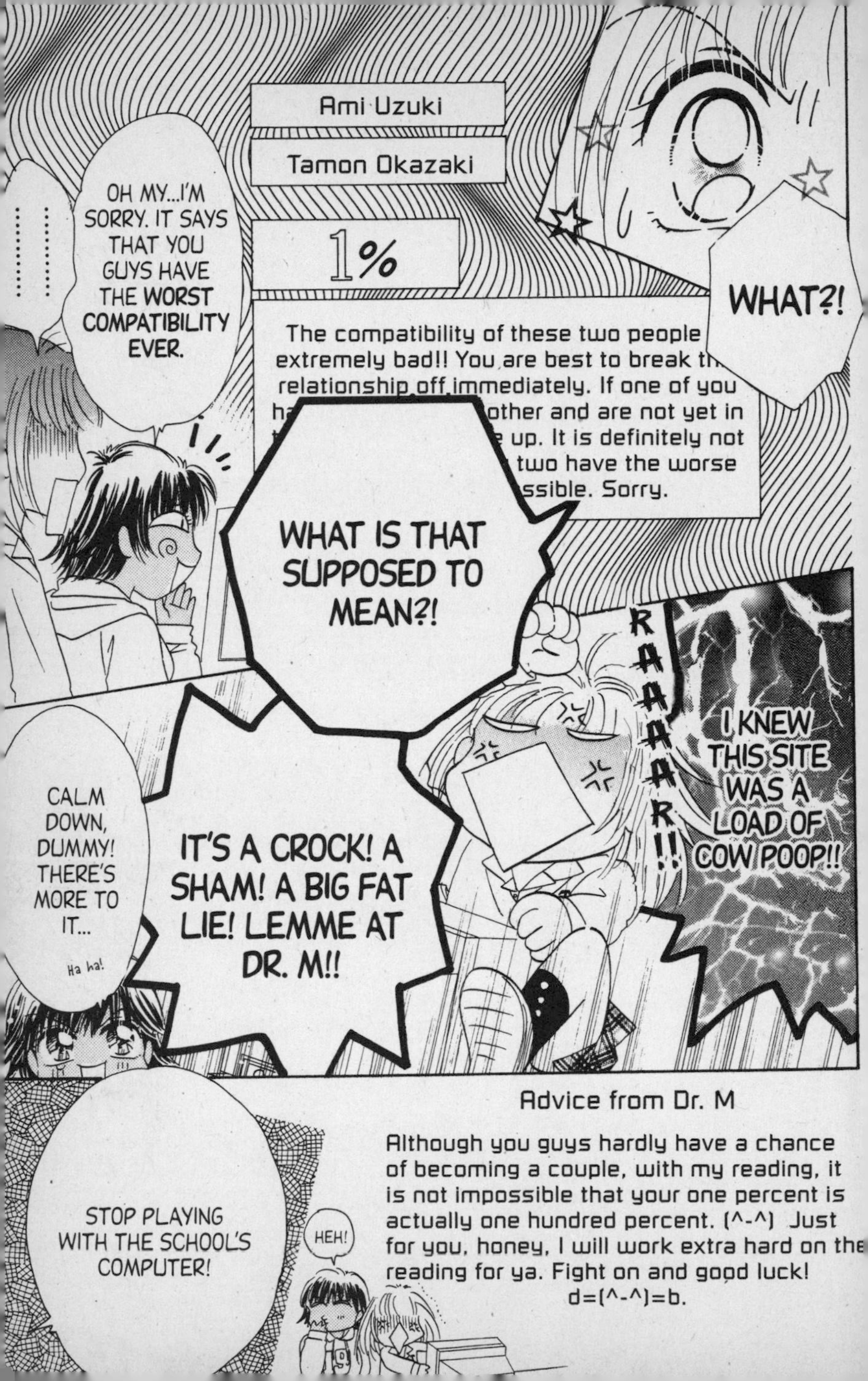

WHAT?!
Ami Uzuki
Tamon Okazaki
1%
The compatibility of these two people
extremely bad!! You are best to break
relationship off immediately. If one of you
other and are not yet in
up. It is definitely not
two have the worse
Sorry.
OH MY...I'M SORRY. IT SAYS THAT YOU GUYS HAVE THE WORST COMPATIBILITY EVER.
......
WHAT IS THAT SUPPOSED TO MEAN?!
RAAAAR!!
I KNEW THIS SITE WAS A LOAD OF COW POOP!!
IT'S A CROCK! A SHAM! A BIG FAT LIE! LEMME AT DR. M!!
CALM DOWN, DUMMY! THERE'S MORE TO IT...
Ha ha!
Advice from Dr. M
Although you guys hardly have a chance of becoming a couple, with my reading, it is not impossible that your one percent is actually one hundred percent. (^-^) Just for you, honey, I will work extra hard on the reading for ya. Fight on and good luck!
d=(^-^)=b.
HEH!
STOP PLAYING WITH THE SCHOOL'S COMPUTER!

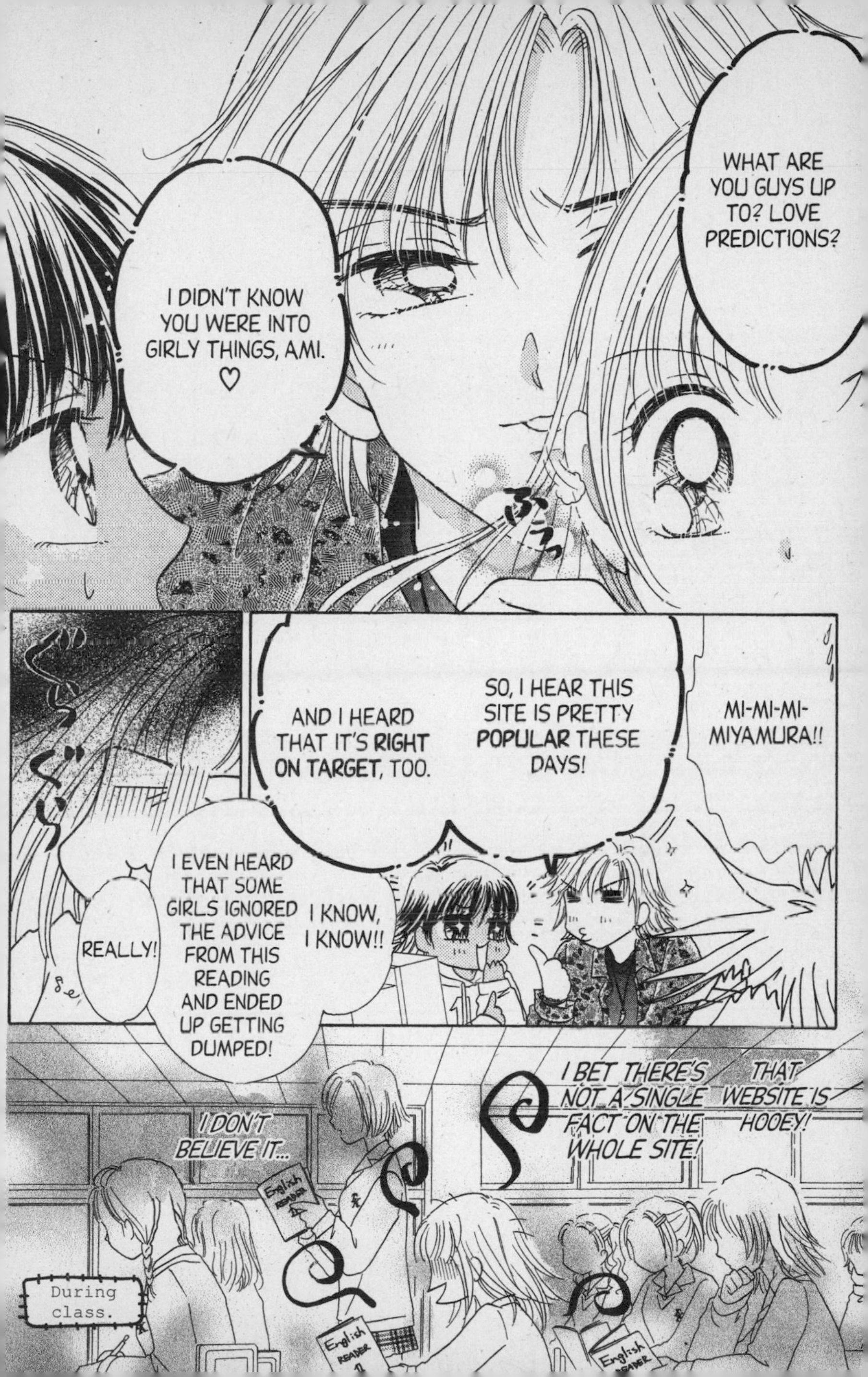
WHAT ARE YOU GUYS UP TO? LOVE PREDICTIONS?
I DIDN'T KNOW YOU WERE INTO GIRLY THINGS, AMI. ♡
MI-MI-MI-MIYAMURA!!
SO, I HEAR THIS SITE IS PRETTY POPULAR THESE DAYS!
AND I HEARD THAT IT'S RIGHT ON TARGET, TOO.
I KNOW, I KNOW!!
I EVEN HEARD THAT SOME GIRLS IGNORED THE ADVICE FROM THIS READING AND ENDED UP GETTING DUMPED!
REALLY!
THAT WEBSITE IS HOOEY!
I BET THERE'S NOT A SINGLE FACT ON THE WHOLE SITE!
I DON'T BELIEVE IT...
During class.

FROM AKIMOTO

Hello! Akimoto here. I hope you are enjoying *Ultra Cute* Volume Two. I know it's sudden, but it seems like the first signs of spring are here. What signs, you ask? Well, hay fever, for one--and I've got it! I'm not positive, but I'd say chances are pretty high that hay fever's what I've got. So a big shout out to all my fellow hay fever sufferers out there!

Noooo!!

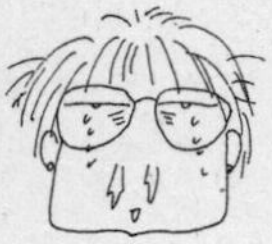

Blah! It's so hard to concentrate on my work (and it's so not funny)! I have a hard time dressing up, too. Anyhow, this spring of the year 2000 has been bad for me. I want to go out and find something fun to do, but unfortunately I've been pretty tied up with work, so I haven't had any chance to do so. Pollen is everywhere, too--so I'm doubly stuck at home. So anyhow, I'm hooked on internet shopping and animal prints, lately. I love tiger print the most!! (And especially anything in mint condition.) I had started collecting all these little things and handbags, and was being all happy about it when my friend goes, "Because you are a **monster**, you love **monster stuff**." Tigers aren't monsters!! (Did I just totally change the subject?)

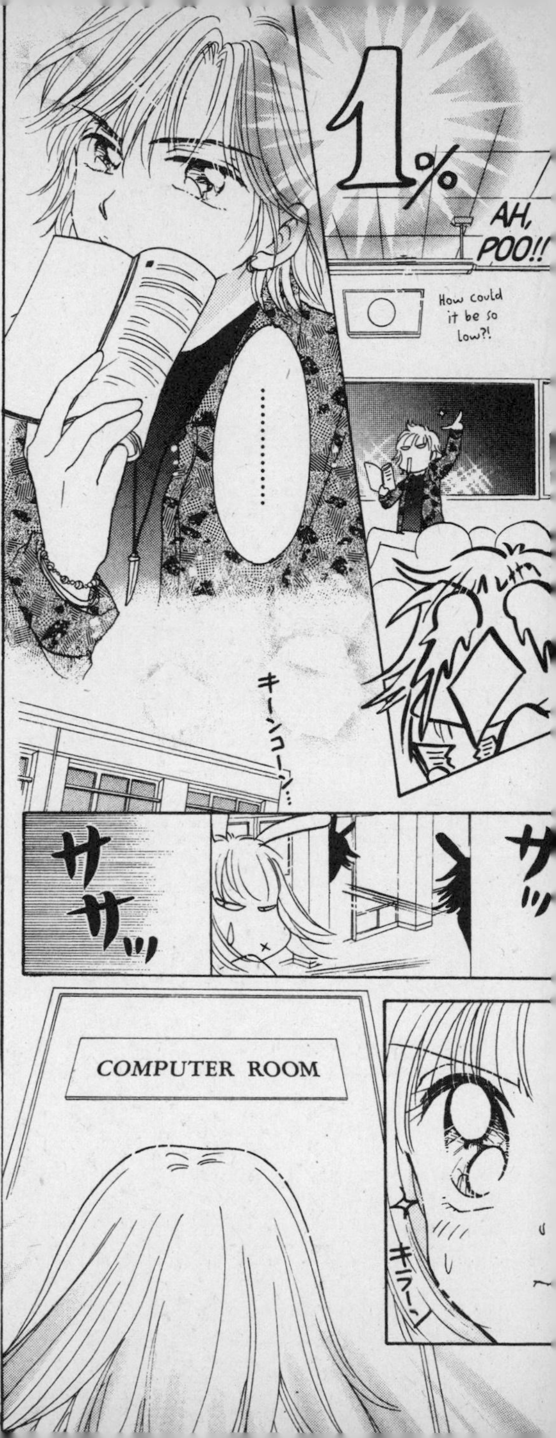
1%
AH, POO!!
How could it be so low?!
......
キーンコーン…
サッ
ササッ
COMPUTER ROOM
キラ〜ン

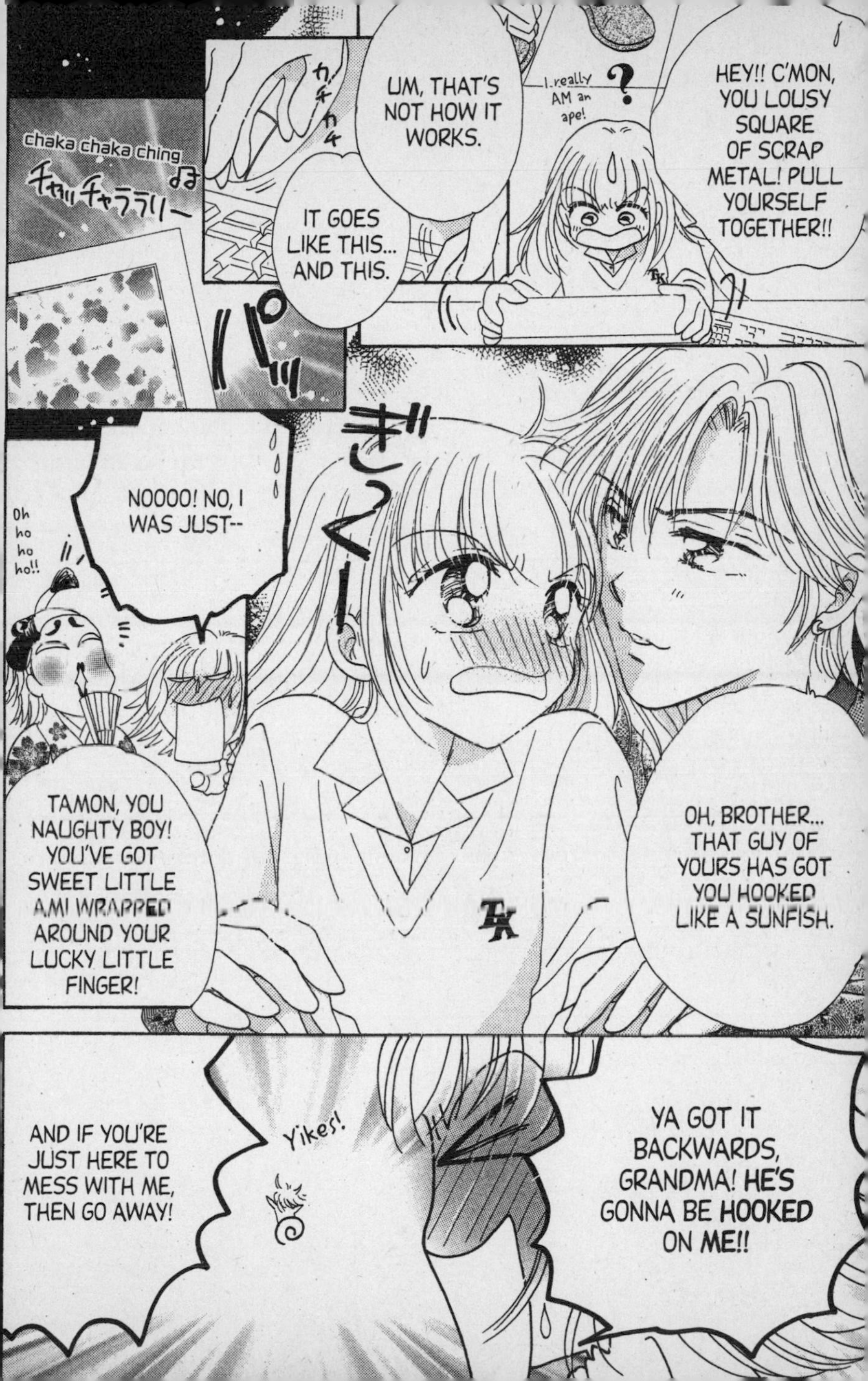
HEY!! C'MON, YOU LOUSY SQUARE OF SCRAP METAL! PULL YOURSELF TOGETHER!!
I really AM an ape!
UM, THAT'S NOT HOW IT WORKS.
IT GOES LIKE THIS... AND THIS.
カチカチ
chaka chaka ching
チャッチャラララリー
パッ
ぎっくー
OH, BROTHER... THAT GUY OF YOURS HAS GOT YOU HOOKED LIKE A SUNFISH.
NOOOO! NO, I WAS JUST--
Oh ho ho ho!!
TAMON, YOU NAUGHTY BOY! YOU'VE GOT SWEET LITTLE AMI WRAPPED AROUND YOUR LUCKY LITTLE FINGER!
YA GOT IT BACKWARDS, GRANDMA! HE'S GONNA BE HOOKED ON ME!!
Yikes!
AND IF YOU'RE JUST HERE TO MESS WITH ME, THEN GO AWAY!

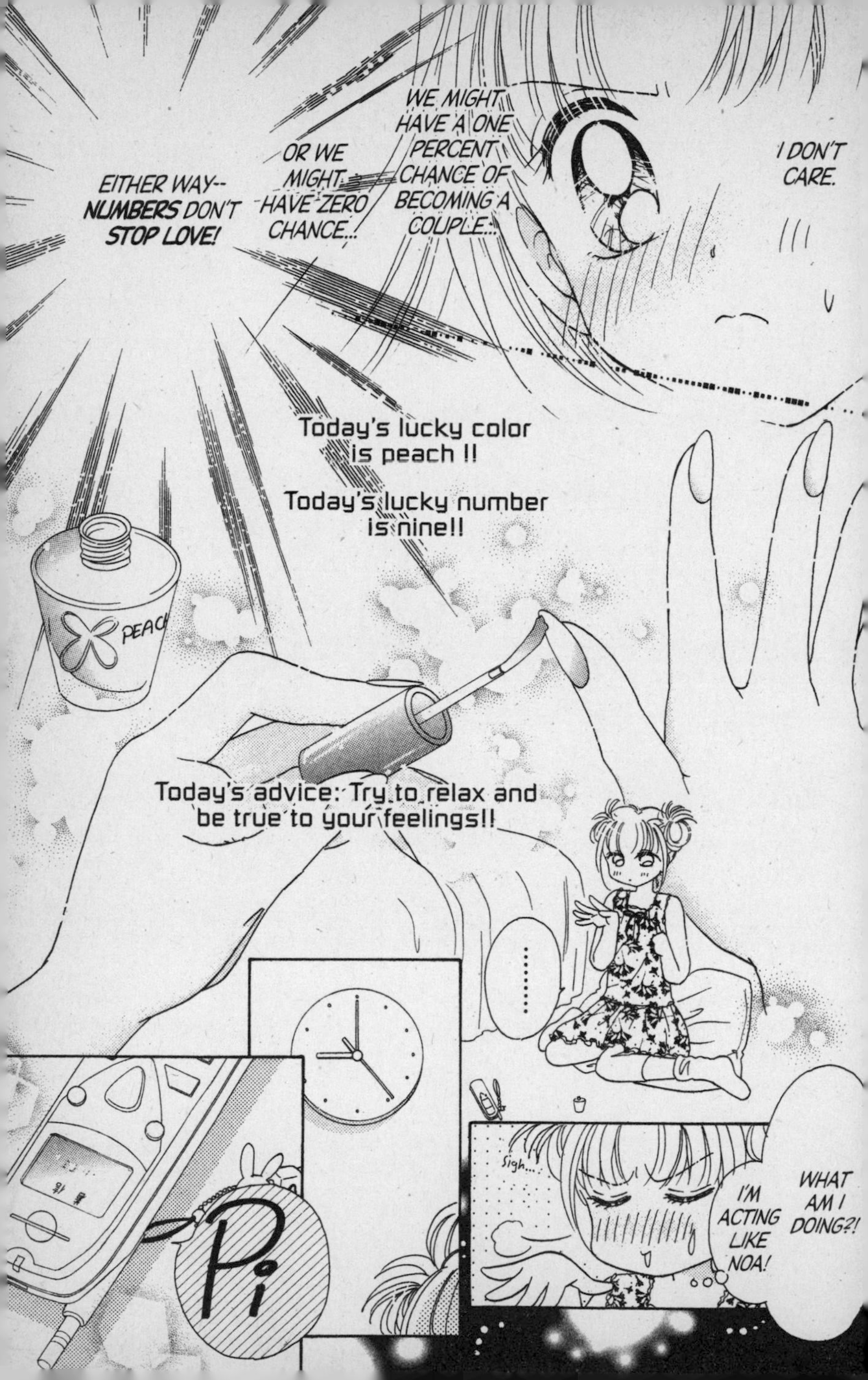
I DON'T CARE.
WE MIGHT HAVE A ONE PERCENT CHANCE OF BECOMING A COUPLE...
OR WE MIGHT HAVE ZERO CHANCE...
EITHER WAY-- NUMBERS DON'T STOP LOVE!
Today's lucky color is peach !!
Today's lucky number is nine!!
PEACH
Today's advice: Try to relax and be true to your feelings!!
......
WHAT AM I DOING?!
I'M ACTING LIKE NOA!
Sigh...
Pi

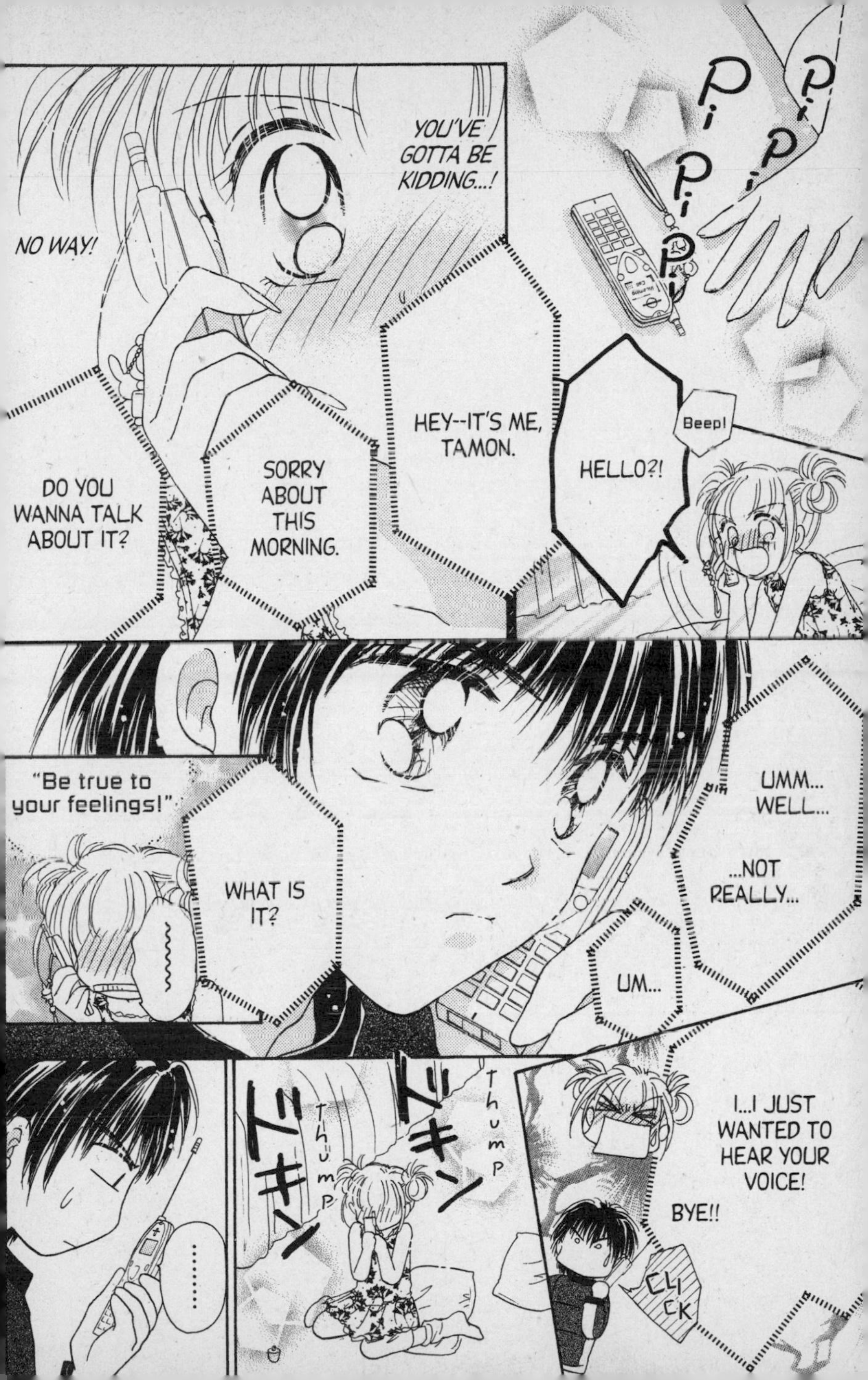

Pi Pi Pi Pi Pi
Beep!
HELLO?!
HEY--IT'S ME, TAMON.
YOU'VE GOTTA BE KIDDING...!
NO WAY!
SORRY ABOUT THIS MORNING.
DO YOU WANNA TALK ABOUT IT?
UMM... WELL...
...NOT REALLY...
UM...
WHAT IS IT?
"Be true to your feelings!"
I...I JUST WANTED TO HEAR YOUR VOICE!
BYE!!
CLICK
Thump
ドキン
Thump
ドキン
......

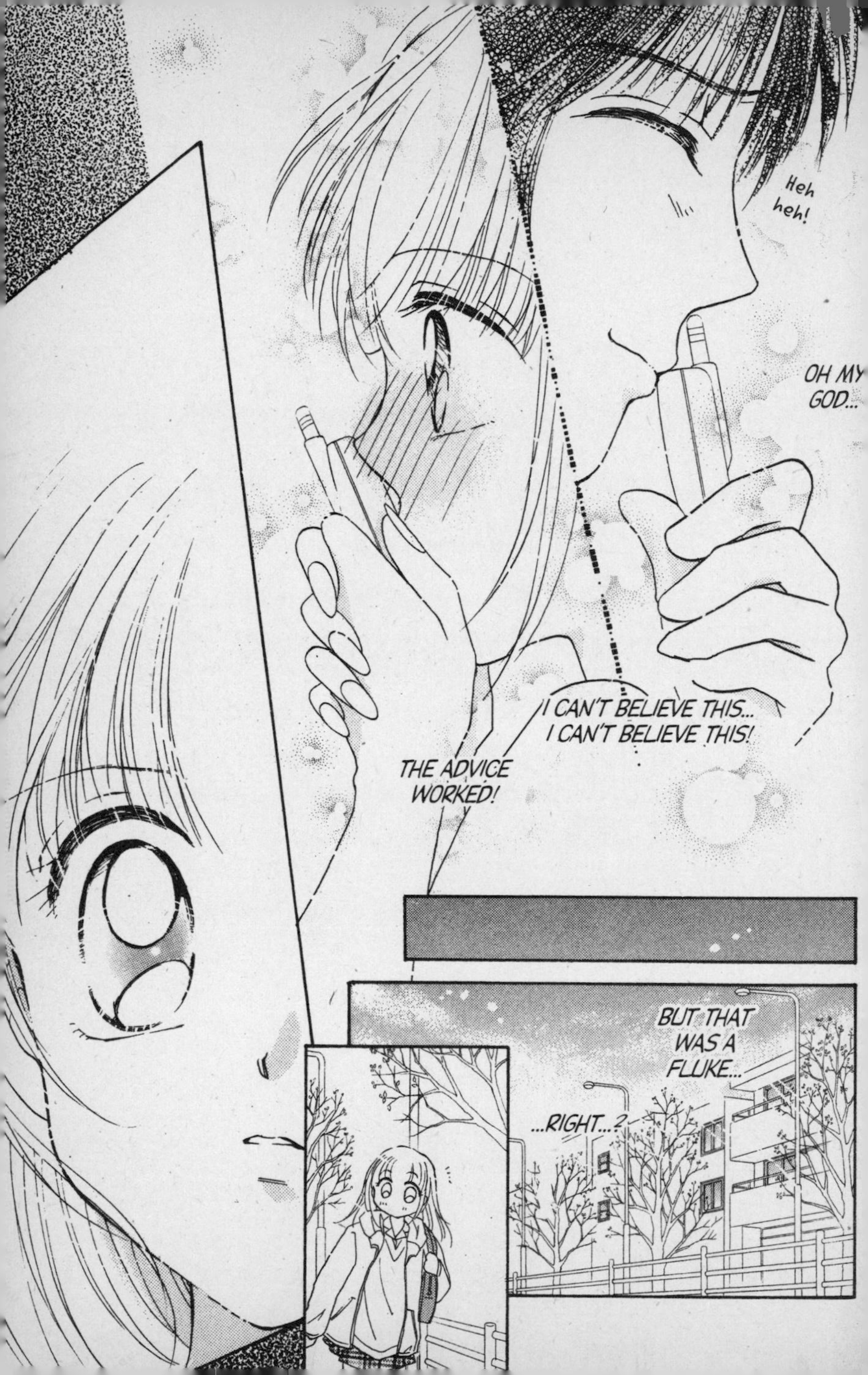
Heh heh!
OH MY GOD...
I CAN'T BELIEVE THIS... I CAN'T BELIEVE THIS!
THE ADVICE WORKED!
BUT THAT WAS A FLUKE...
...RIGHT...?

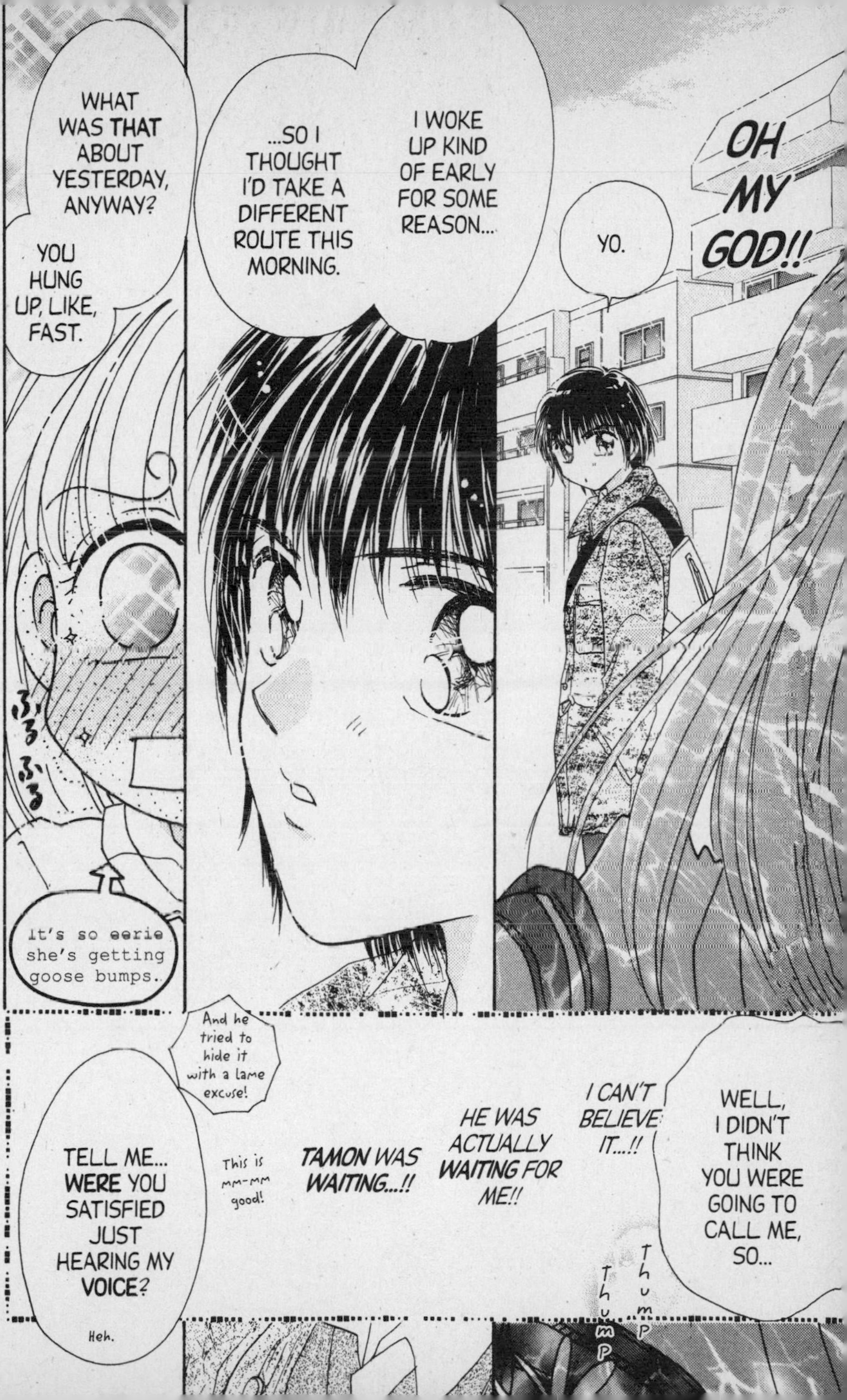
OH MY GOD!!
YO.
I WOKE UP KIND OF EARLY FOR SOME REASON...
...SO I THOUGHT I'D TAKE A DIFFERENT ROUTE THIS MORNING.
WHAT WAS THAT ABOUT YESTERDAY, ANYWAY?
YOU HUNG UP, LIKE, FAST.
ふるふる
It's so eerie she's getting goose bumps.
WELL, I DIDN'T THINK YOU WERE GOING TO CALL ME, SO...
Thump Thump
I CAN'T BELIEVE IT...!!
HE WAS ACTUALLY WAITING FOR ME!!
TAMON WAS WAITING...!!
And he tried to hide it with a lame excuse!
This is mm-mm good!
TELL ME... WERE YOU SATISFIED JUST HEARING MY VOICE?
Heh.

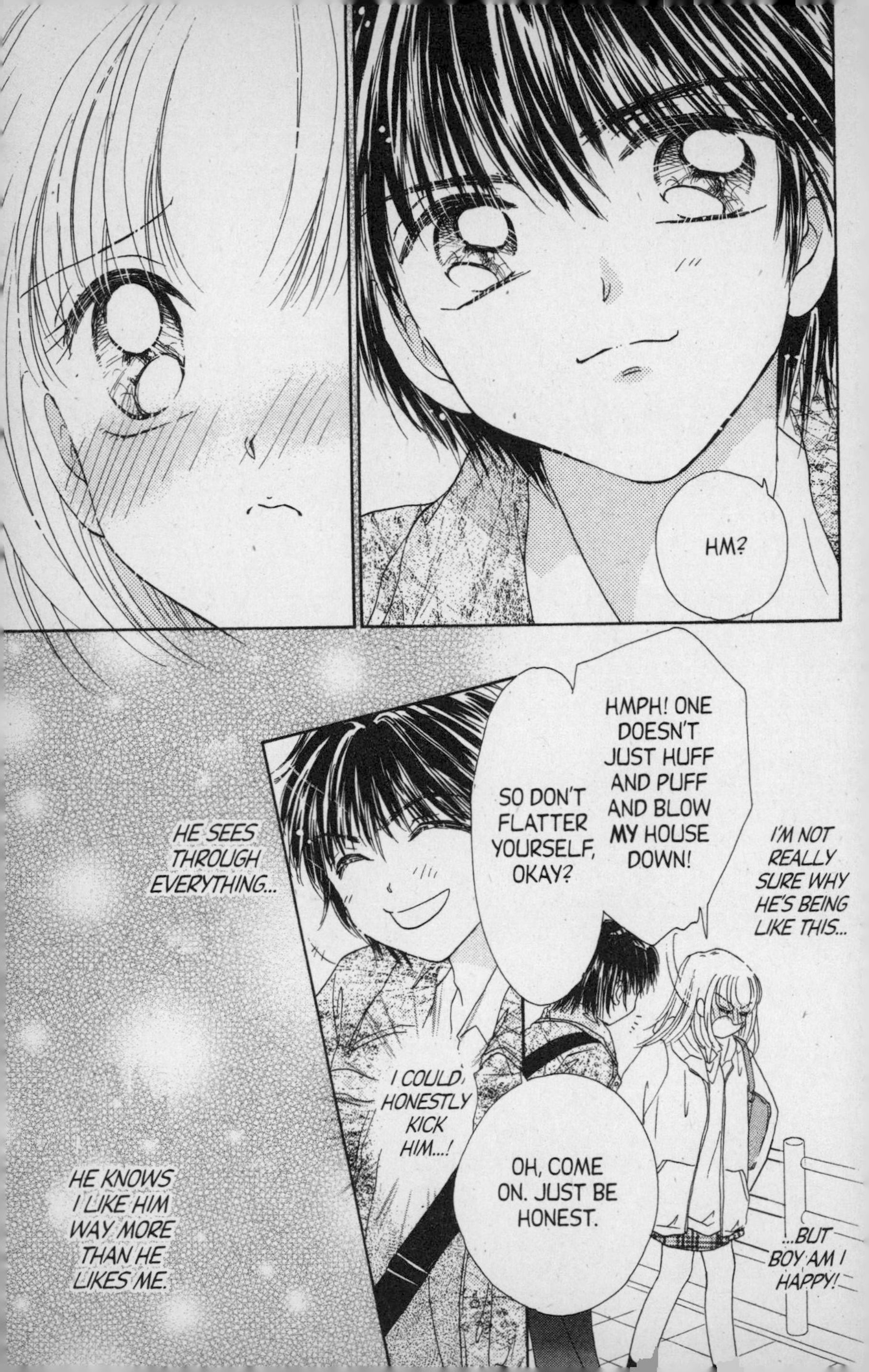
HM?
I'M NOT REALLY SURE WHY HE'S BEING LIKE THIS...
HMPH! ONE DOESN'T JUST HUFF AND PUFF AND BLOW MY HOUSE DOWN!
SO DON'T FLATTER YOURSELF, OKAY?
HE SEES THROUGH EVERYTHING...
...BUT BOY AM I HAPPY!
OH, COME ON. JUST BE HONEST.
I COULD HONESTLY KICK HIM...!
HE KNOWS I LIKE HIM WAY MORE THAN HE LIKES ME.

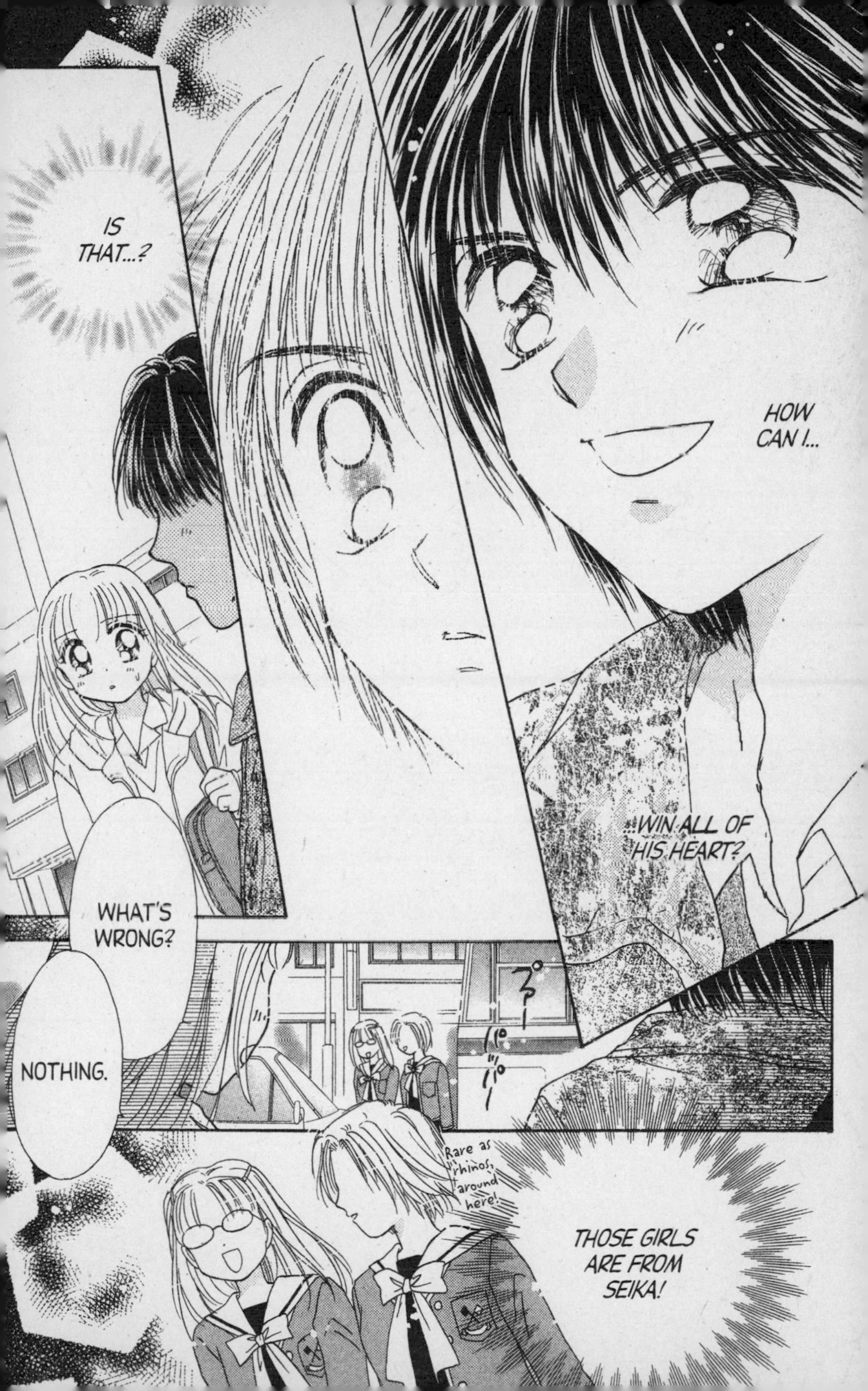
HOW CAN I...
...WIN ALL OF HIS HEART?
IS THAT...?
WHAT'S WRONG?
NOTHING.
THOSE GIRLS ARE FROM SEIKA!
Rare as rhinos, around here!

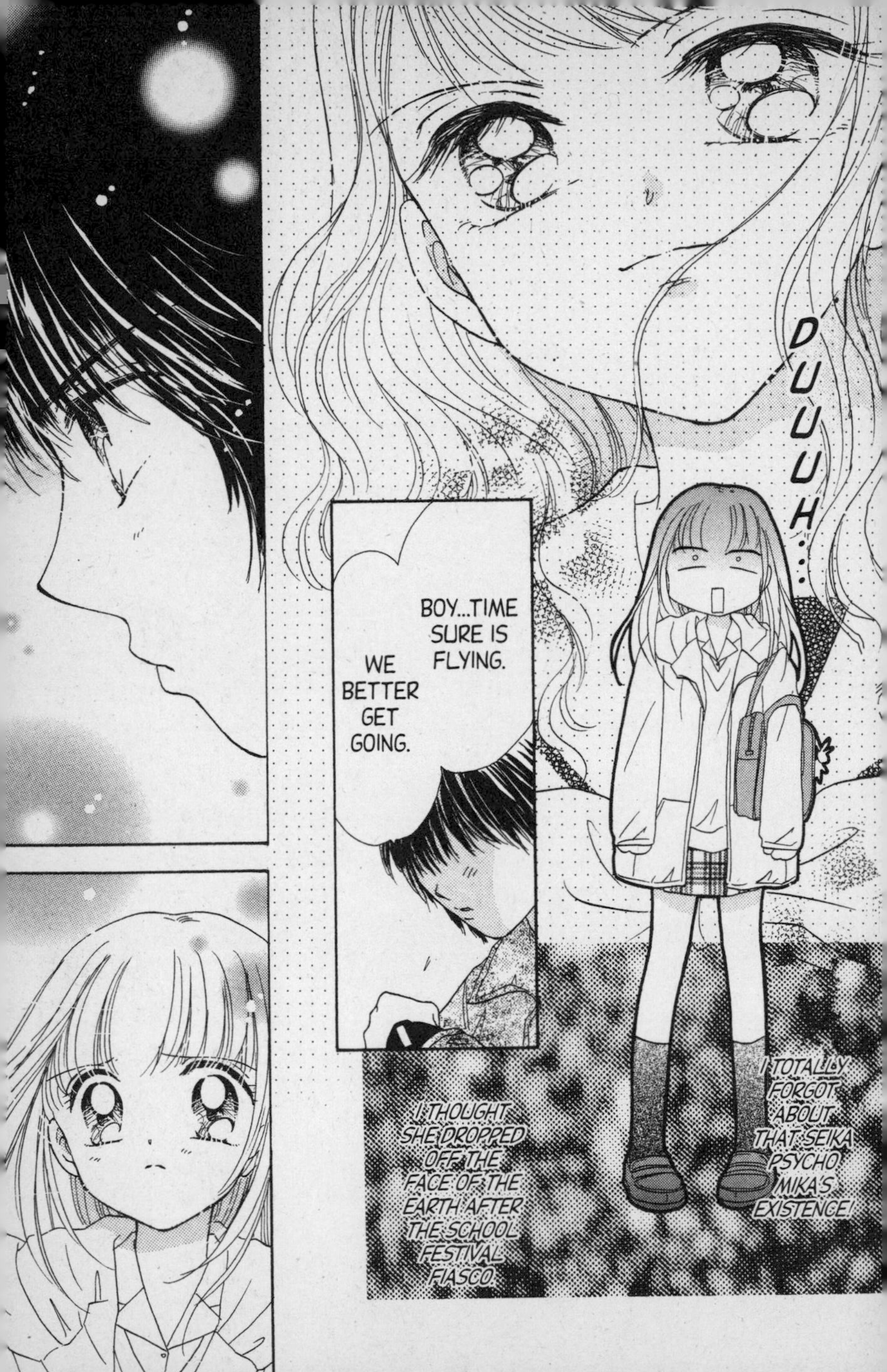
DUUUUH...
I TOTALLY FORGOT ABOUT THAT SEIKA PSYCHO MIKA'S EXISTENCE!
I THOUGHT SHE DROPPED OFF THE FACE OF THE EARTH AFTER THE SCHOOL FESTIVAL FIASCO.
BOY...TIME SURE IS FLYING.
WE BETTER GET GOING.

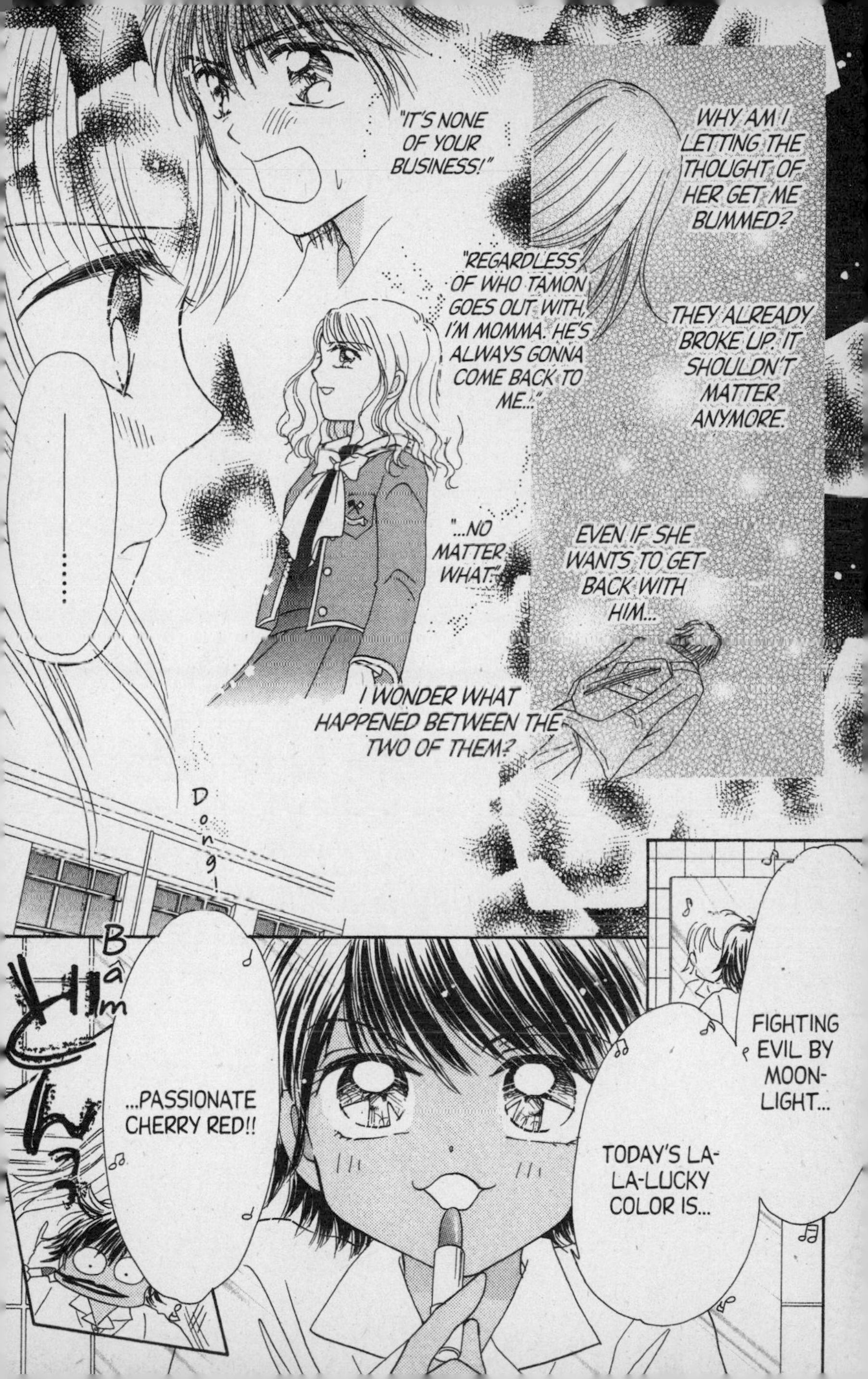
WHY AM I LETTING THE THOUGHT OF HER GET ME BUMMED?
"IT'S NONE OF YOUR BUSINESS!"
"REGARDLESS OF WHO TAMON GOES OUT WITH, I'M MOMMA. HE'S ALWAYS GONNA COME BACK TO ME..."
THEY ALREADY BROKE UP. IT SHOULDN'T MATTER ANYMORE.
"...NO MATTER WHAT."
EVEN IF SHE WANTS TO GET BACK WITH HIM...
I WONDER WHAT HAPPENED BETWEEN THE TWO OF THEM?
......
Dong!
FIGHTING EVIL BY MOON-LIGHT...
TODAY'S LA-LA-LUCKY COLOR IS...
...PASSIONATE CHERRY RED!!
Bam

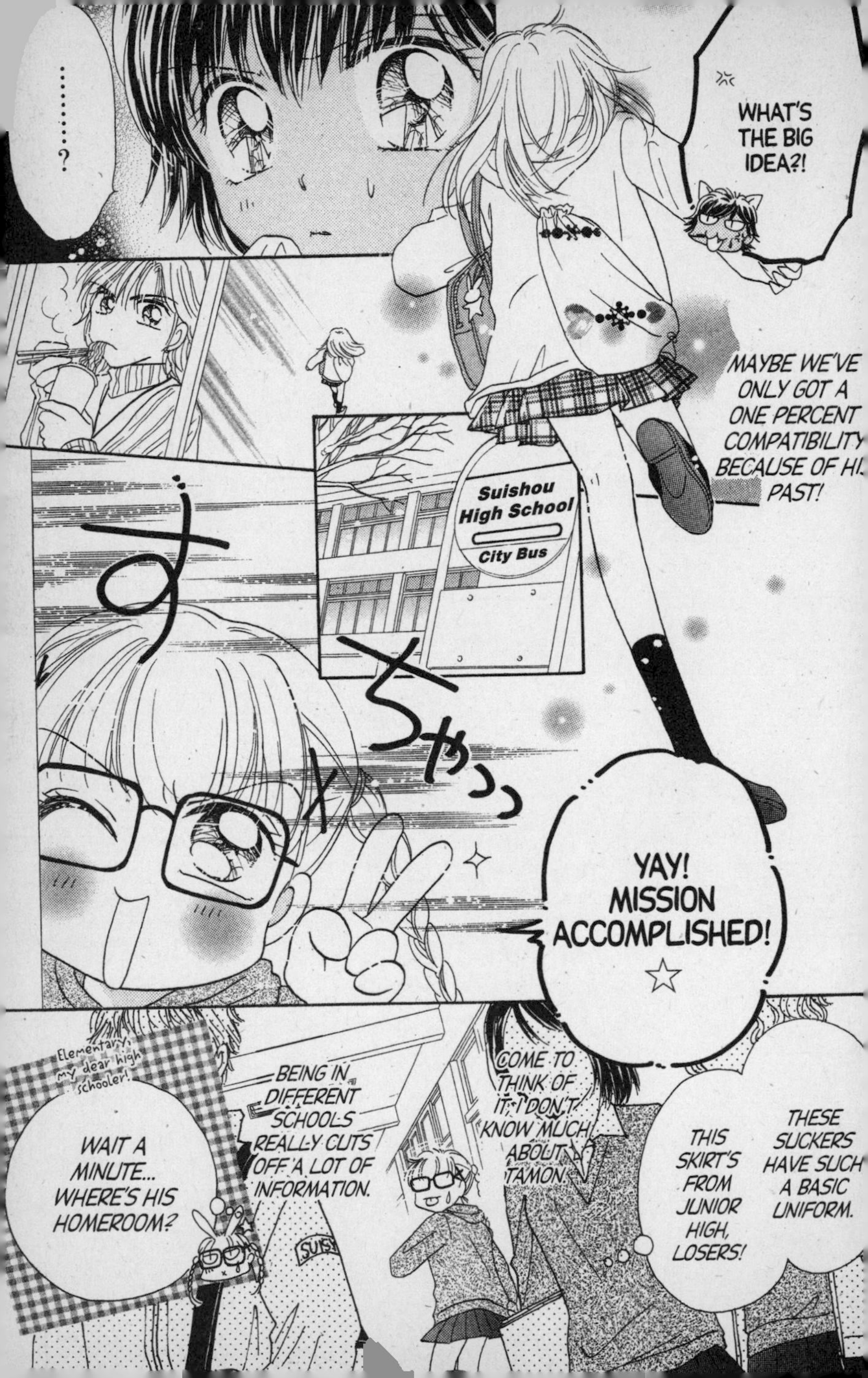
WHAT'S THE BIG IDEA?!
......?
MAYBE WE'VE ONLY GOT A ONE PERCENT COMPATIBILITY BECAUSE OF HI PAST!
Suishou High School
City Bus
すちゃっ
YAY! MISSION ACCOMPLISHED! ☆
THESE SUCKERS HAVE SUCH A BASIC UNIFORM.
THIS SKIRT'S FROM JUNIOR HIGH, LOSERS!
COME TO THINK OF IT, I DON'T KNOW MUCH ABOUT TAMON.
BEING IN DIFFERENT SCHOOLS REALLY CUTS OFF A LOT OF INFORMATION.
WAIT A MINUTE... WHERE'S HIS HOMEROOM?
Elementary, my dear high schooler!

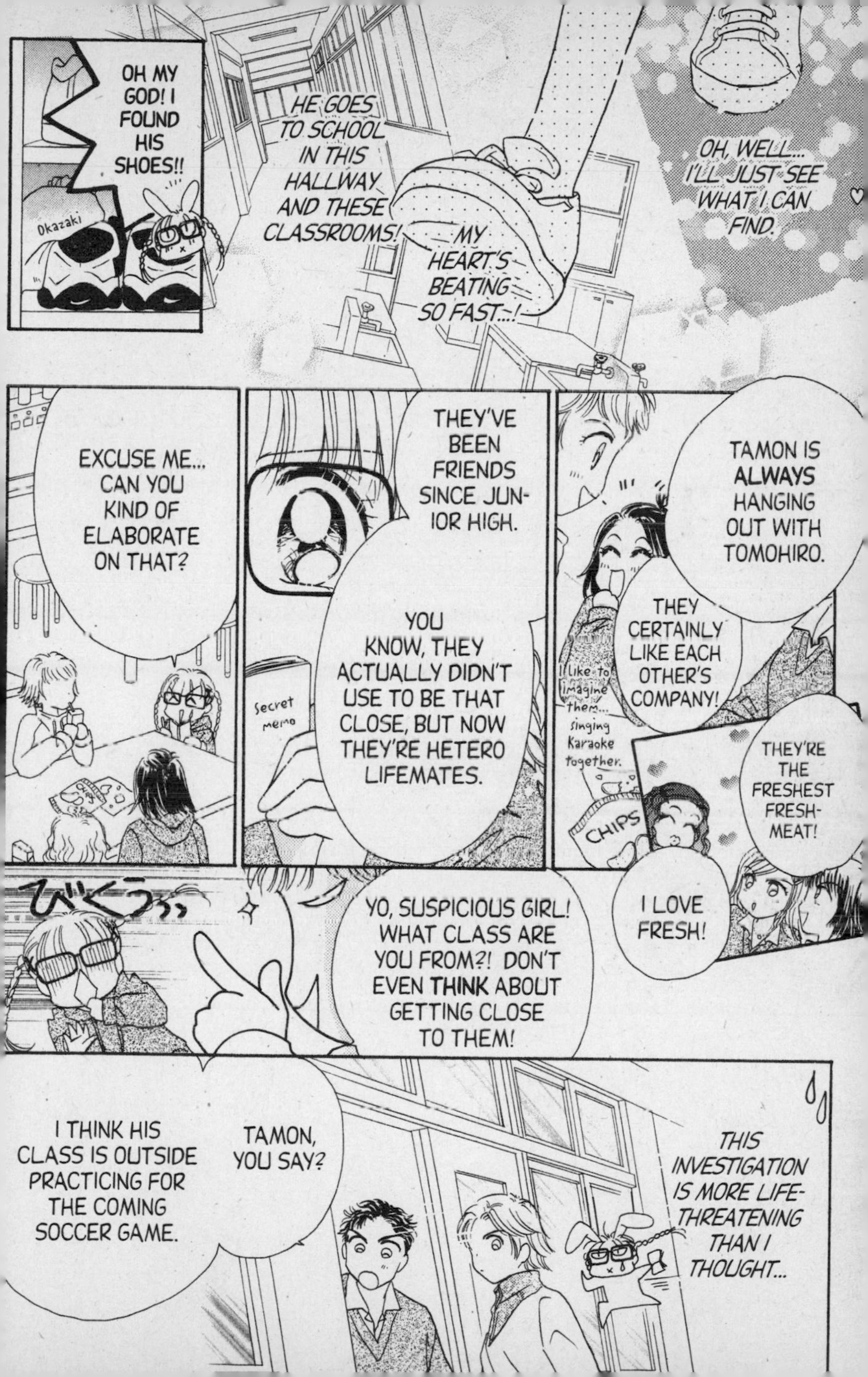

OH, WELL... I'LL JUST SEE WHAT I CAN FIND.
HE GOES TO SCHOOL IN THIS HALLWAY AND THESE CLASSROOMS!
MY HEART'S BEATING SO FAST...!
OH MY GOD! I FOUND HIS SHOES!!
Okazaki
TAMON IS ALWAYS HANGING OUT WITH TOMOHIRO.
THEY CERTAINLY LIKE EACH OTHER'S COMPANY!
I like to imagine them... singing Karaoke together.
THEY'RE THE FRESHEST FRESH-MEAT!
CHIPS
I LOVE FRESH!
THEY'VE BEEN FRIENDS SINCE JUNIOR HIGH.
YOU KNOW, THEY ACTUALLY DIDN'T USE TO BE THAT CLOSE, BUT NOW THEY'RE HETERO LIFEMATES.
Secret memo
EXCUSE ME... CAN YOU KIND OF ELABORATE ON THAT?
YO, SUSPICIOUS GIRL! WHAT CLASS ARE YOU FROM?! DON'T EVEN THINK ABOUT GETTING CLOSE TO THEM!
びくぅ
THIS INVESTIGATION IS MORE LIFE-THREATENING THAN I THOUGHT...
TAMON, YOU SAY?
I THINK HIS CLASS IS OUTSIDE PRACTICING FOR THE COMING SOCCER GAME.

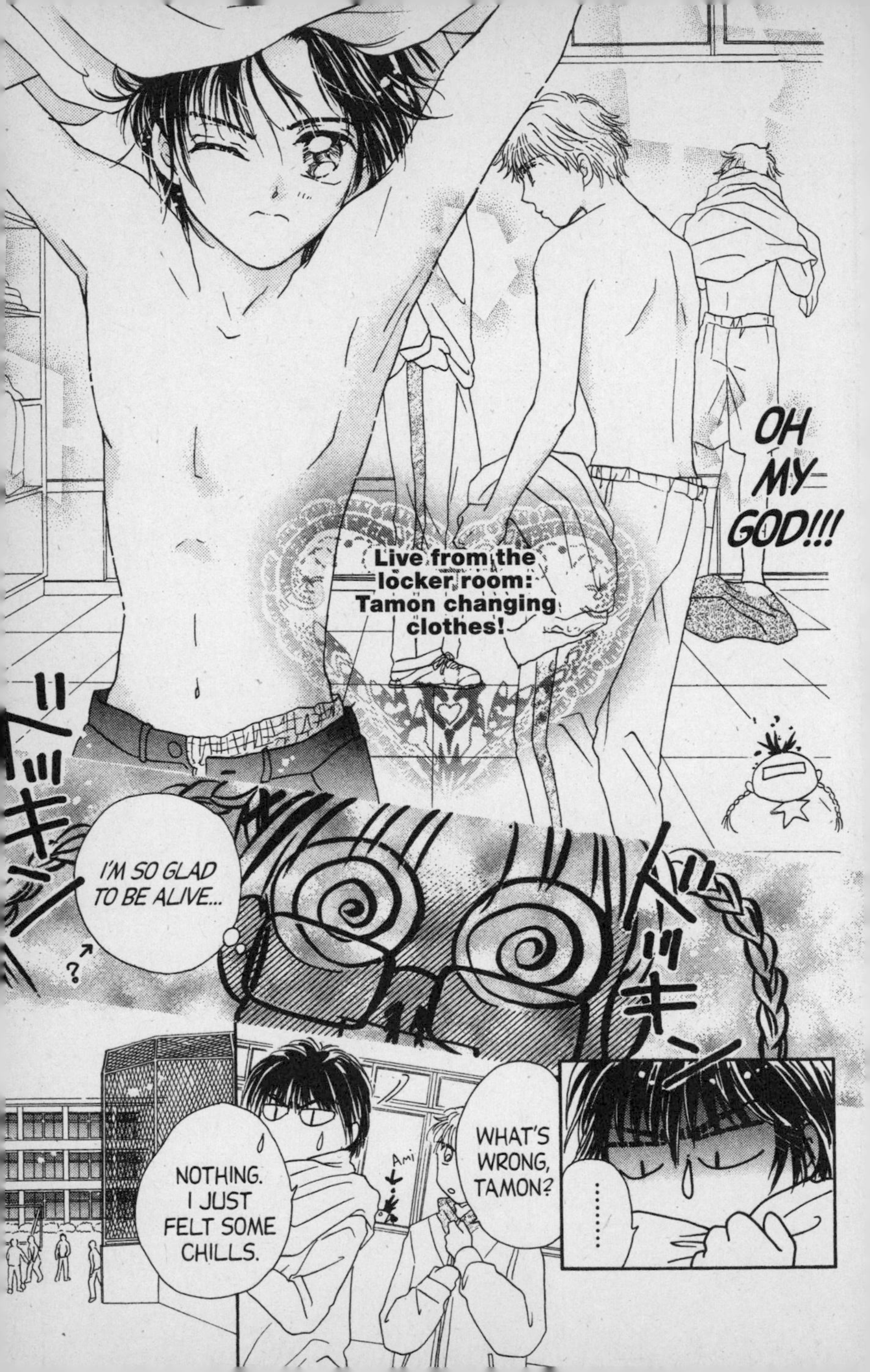
OH MY GOD!!!
Live from the locker room: Tamon changing clothes!
I'M SO GLAD TO BE ALIVE...
?
......
WHAT'S WRONG, TAMON?
Ami
NOTHING. I JUST FELT SOME CHILLS.

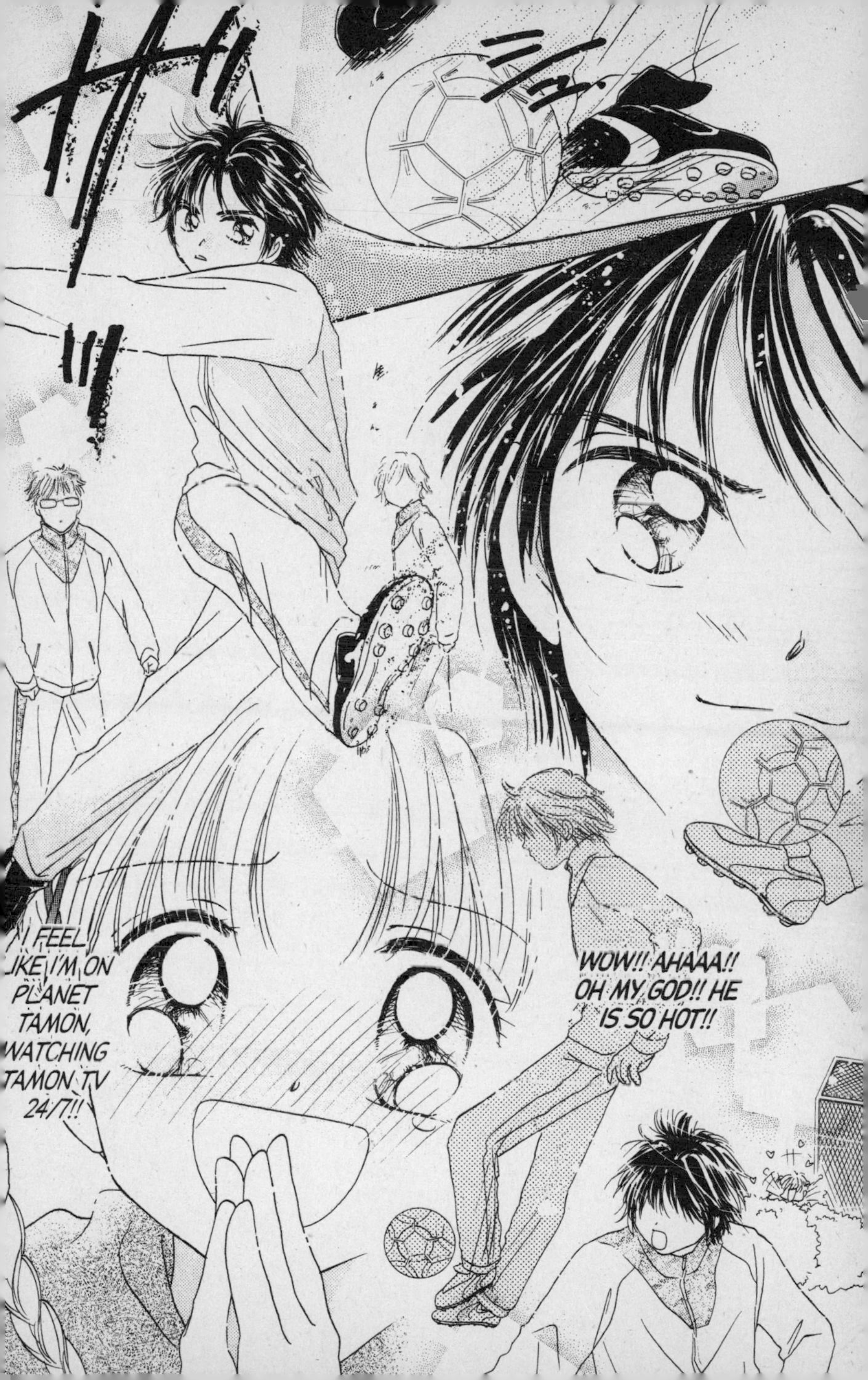
WOW!! AHAAA!! OH MY GOD!! HE IS SO HOT!!
I FEEL LIKE I'M ON PLANET TAMON, WATCHING TAMON TV 24/7!!

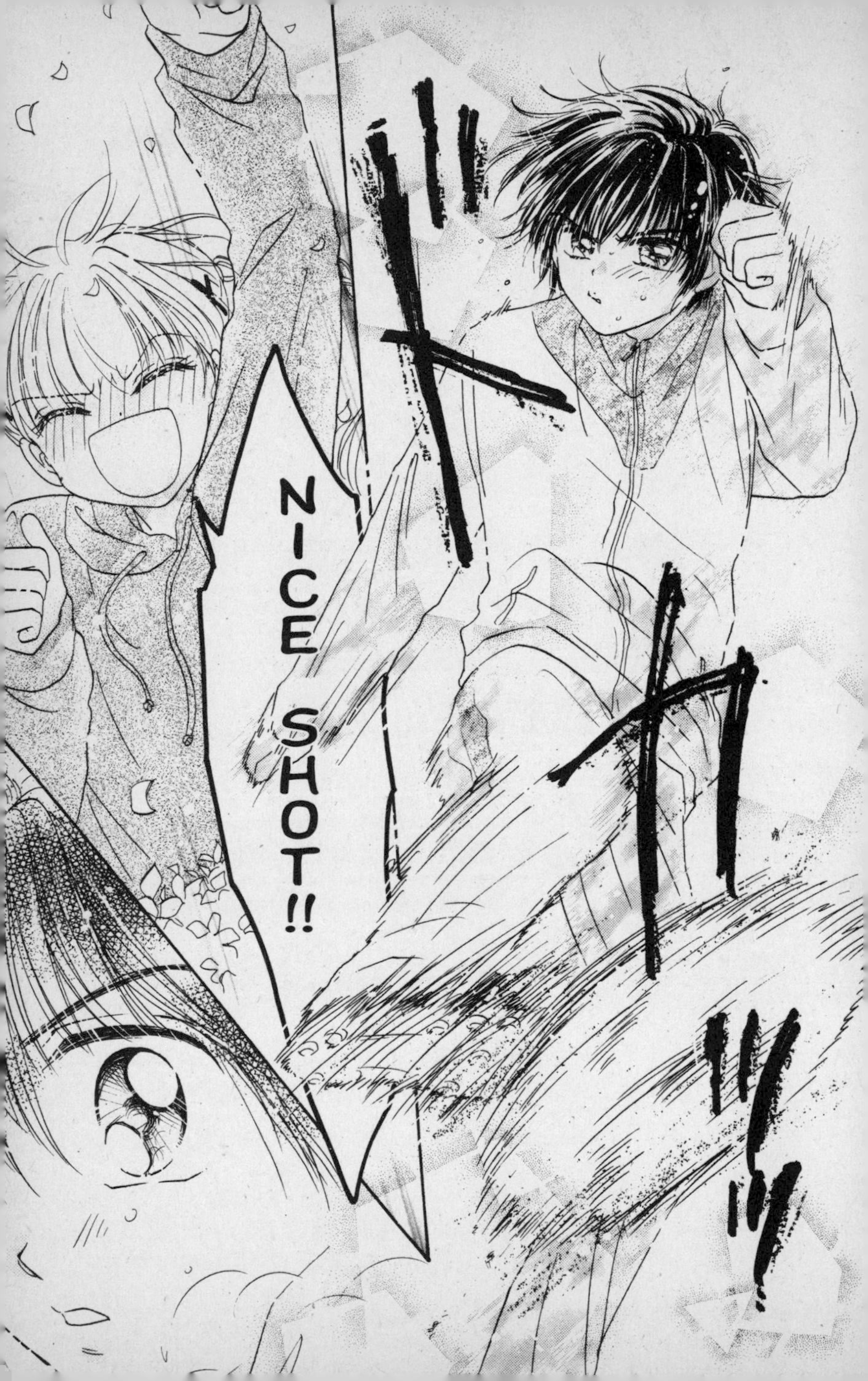
NICE SHOT!!

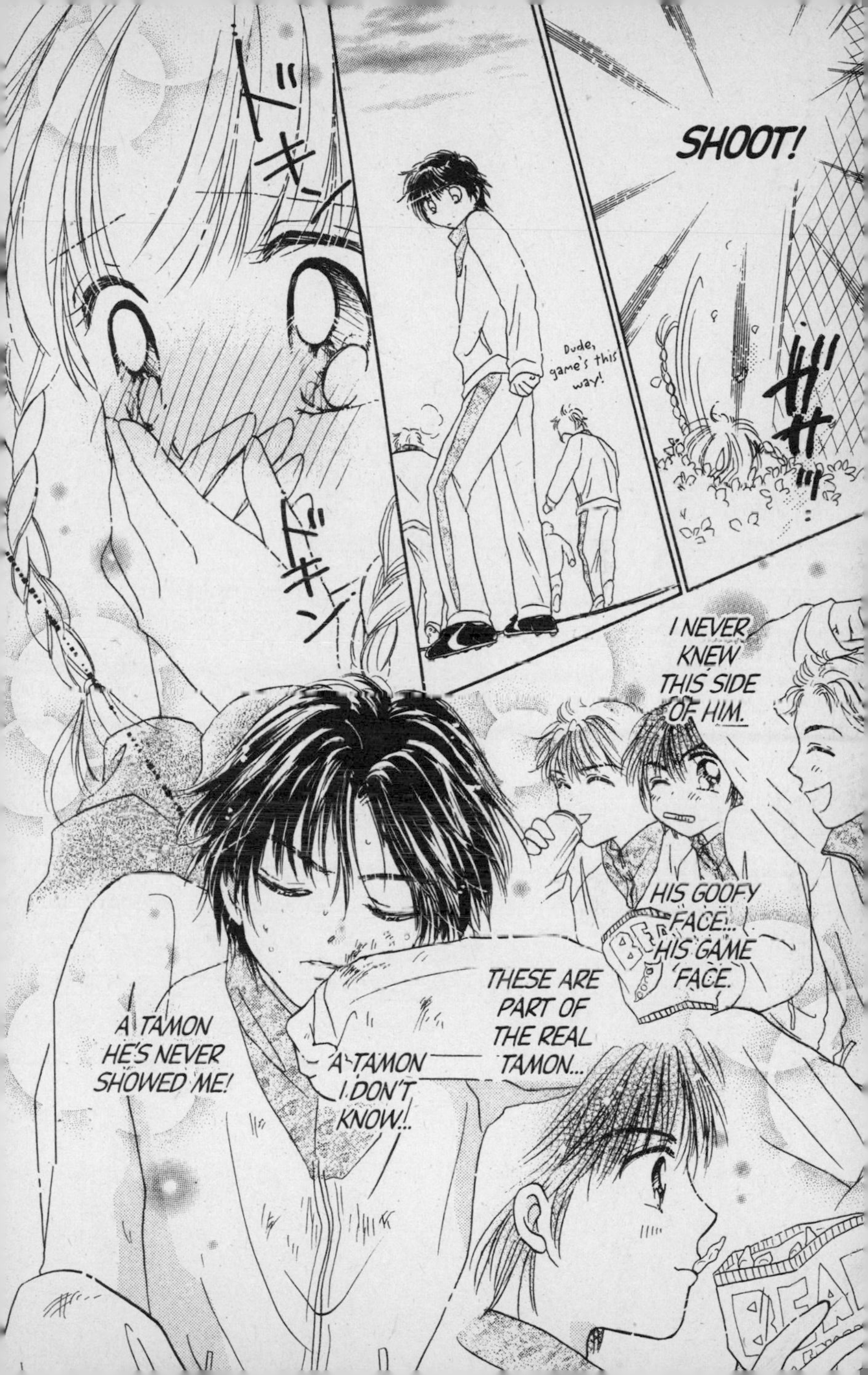
SHOOT!
ザザッ
Dude, game's this way!
ドキン
ドキン
I NEVER KNEW THIS SIDE OF HIM.
HIS GOOFY FACE... HIS GAME FACE.
THESE ARE PART OF THE REAL TAMON...
A TAMON I DON'T KNOW!..
A TAMON HE'S NEVER SHOWED ME!

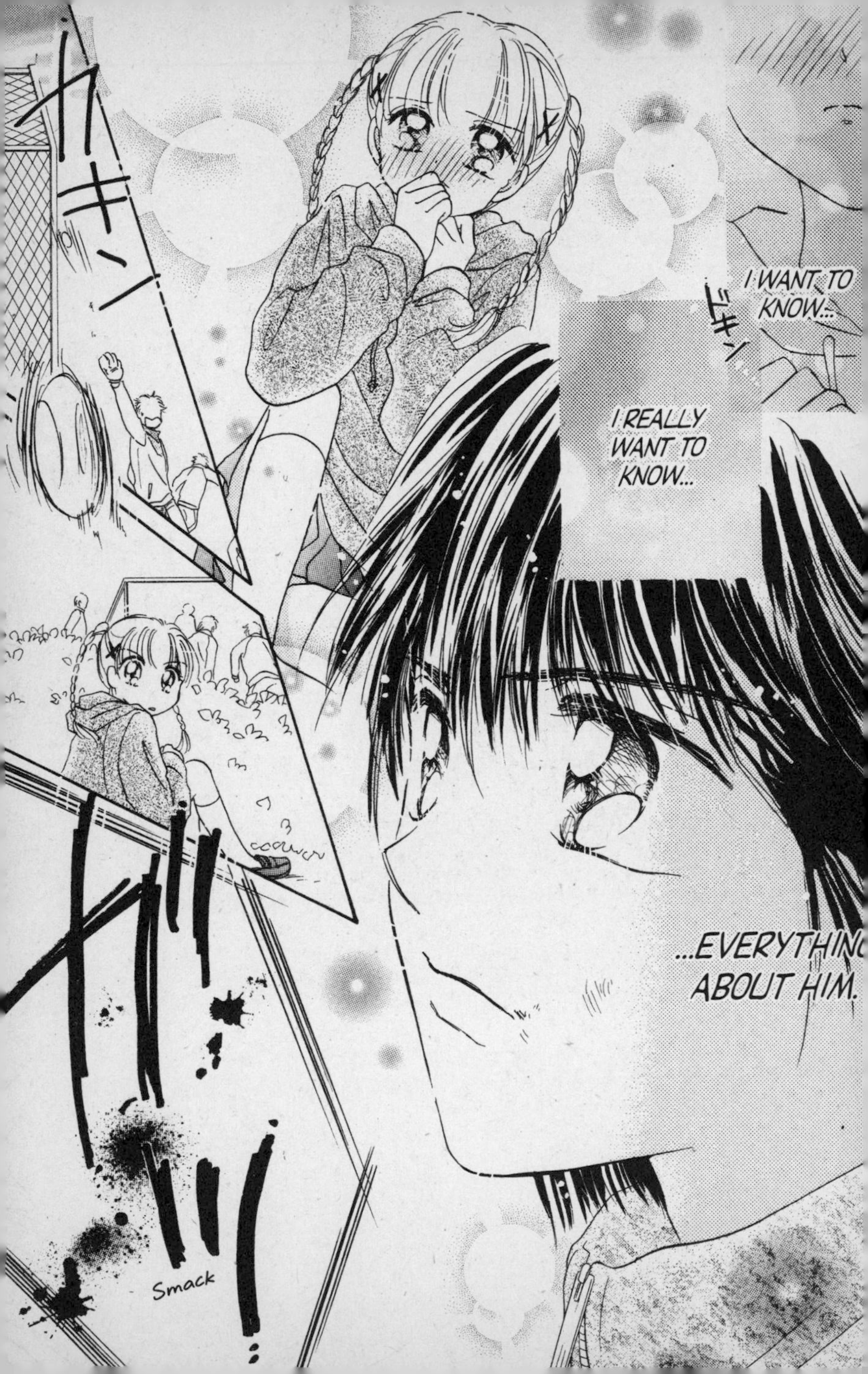
I WANT TO KNOW...
I REALLY WANT TO KNOW...
...EVERYTHING ABOUT HIM.
Smack

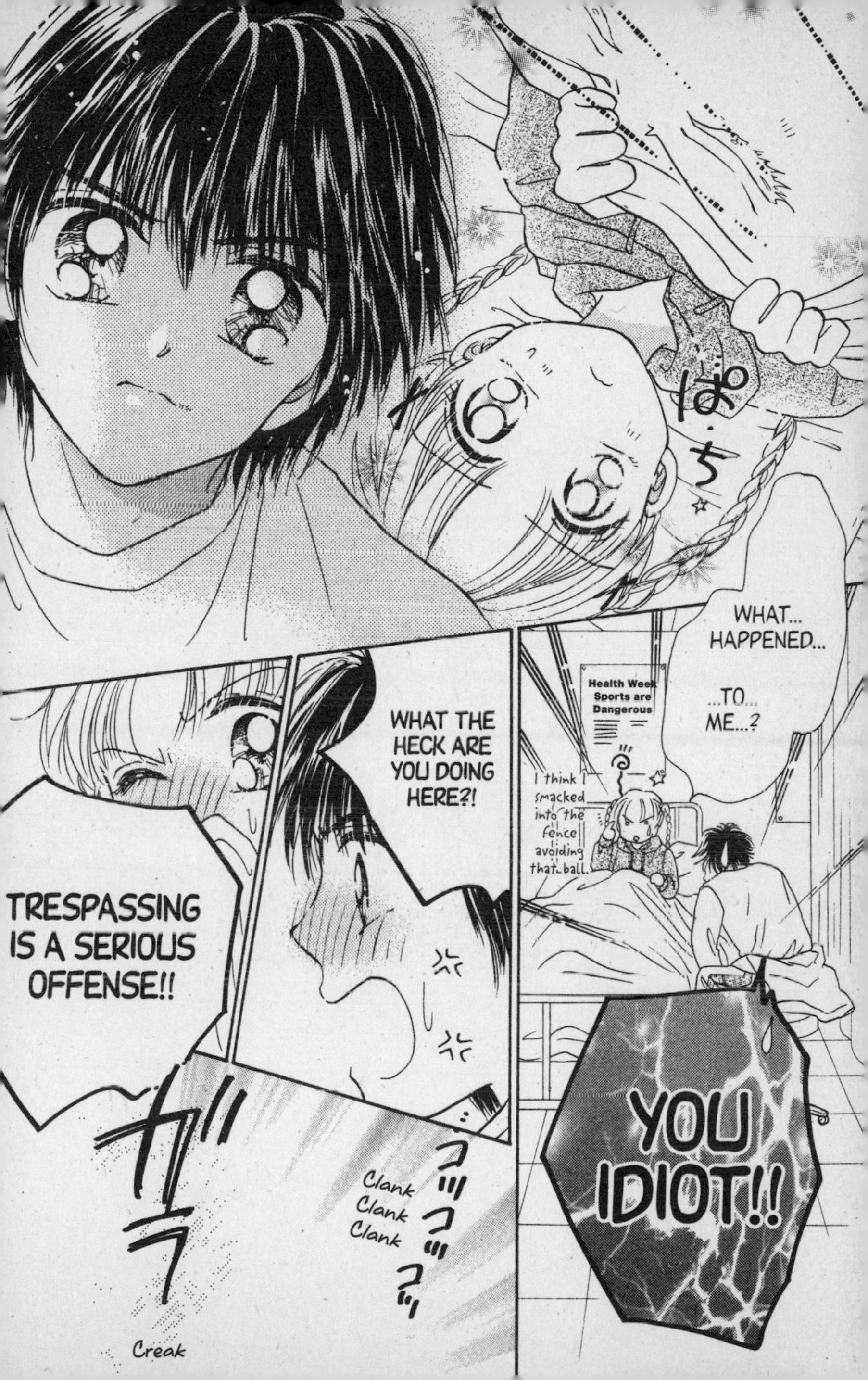
ぱ・ち☆
WHAT... HAPPENED...
...TO... ME...?
Health Week Sports are Dangerous
I think I smacked into the fence avoiding that ball.
YOU IDIOT!!
WHAT THE HECK ARE YOU DOING HERE?!
コッコッコッ
Clank Clank Clank
TRESPASSING IS A SERIOUS OFFENSE!!
ガラ
Creak

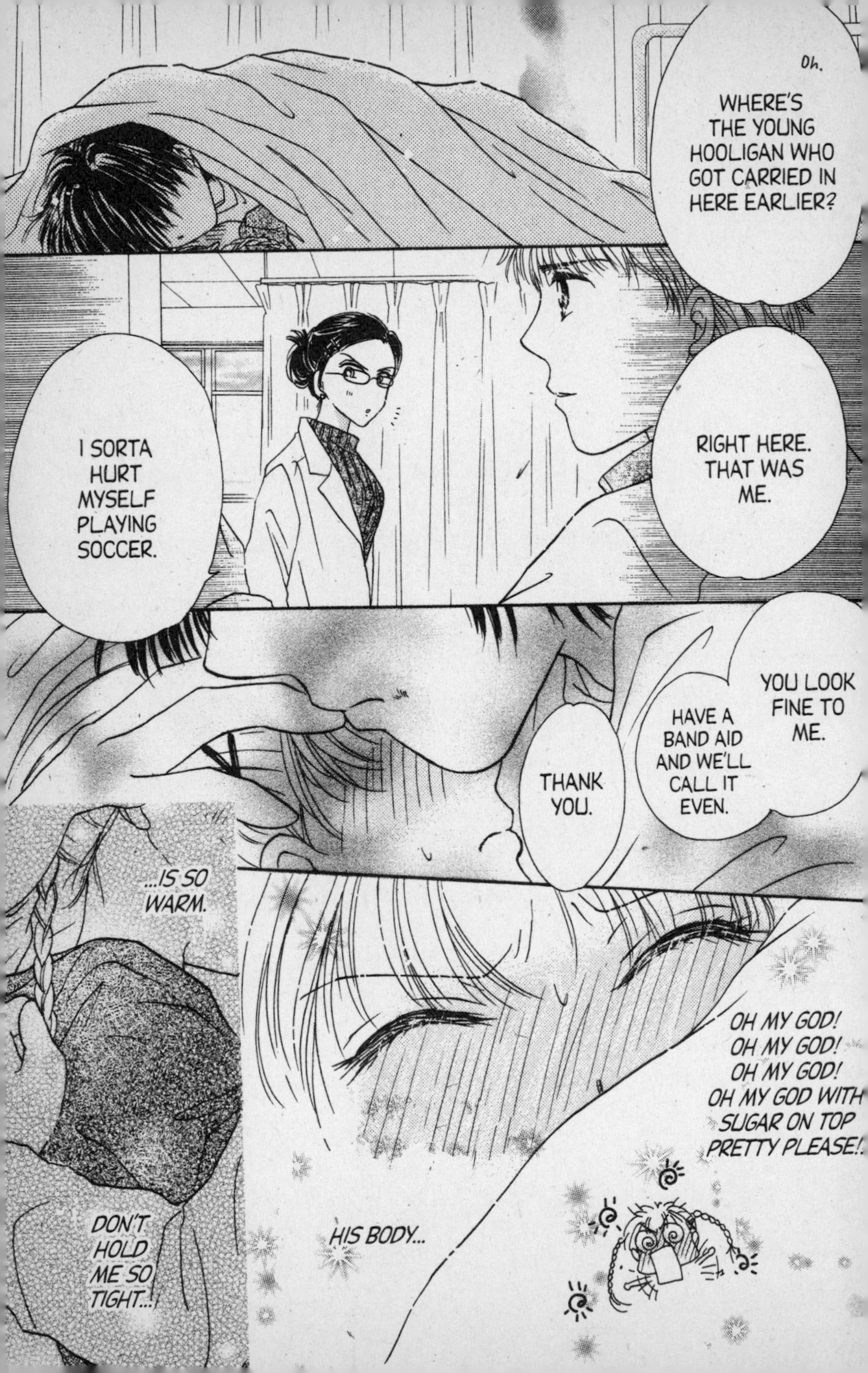
Oh.
WHERE'S THE YOUNG HOOLIGAN WHO GOT CARRIED IN HERE EARLIER?
RIGHT HERE. THAT WAS ME.
I SORTA HURT MYSELF PLAYING SOCCER.
YOU LOOK FINE TO ME.
HAVE A BAND AID AND WE'LL CALL IT EVEN.
THANK YOU.
OH MY GOD! OH MY GOD! OH MY GOD! OH MY GOD WITH SUGAR ON TOP PRETTY PLEASE!.
HIS BODY...
...IS SO WARM.
DON'T HOLD ME SO TIGHT...

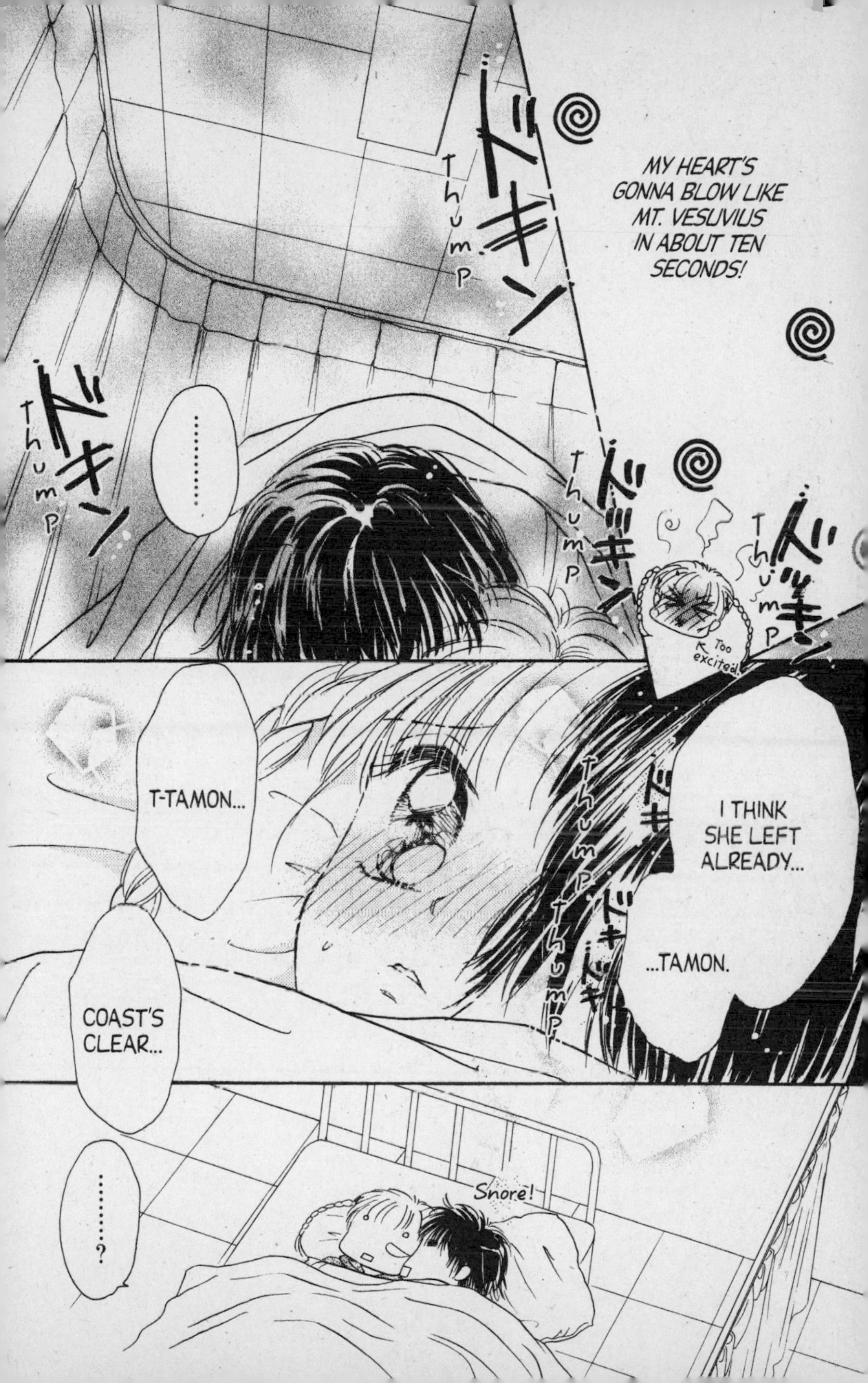

MY HEART'S GONNA BLOW LIKE MT. VESUVIUS IN ABOUT TEN SECONDS!
Thump
Thump
Thump
Too excited.
Thump
......
Thump
I THINK SHE LEFT ALREADY...
...TAMON.
Thump Thump
T-TAMON...
COAST'S CLEAR...
Snore!
......?

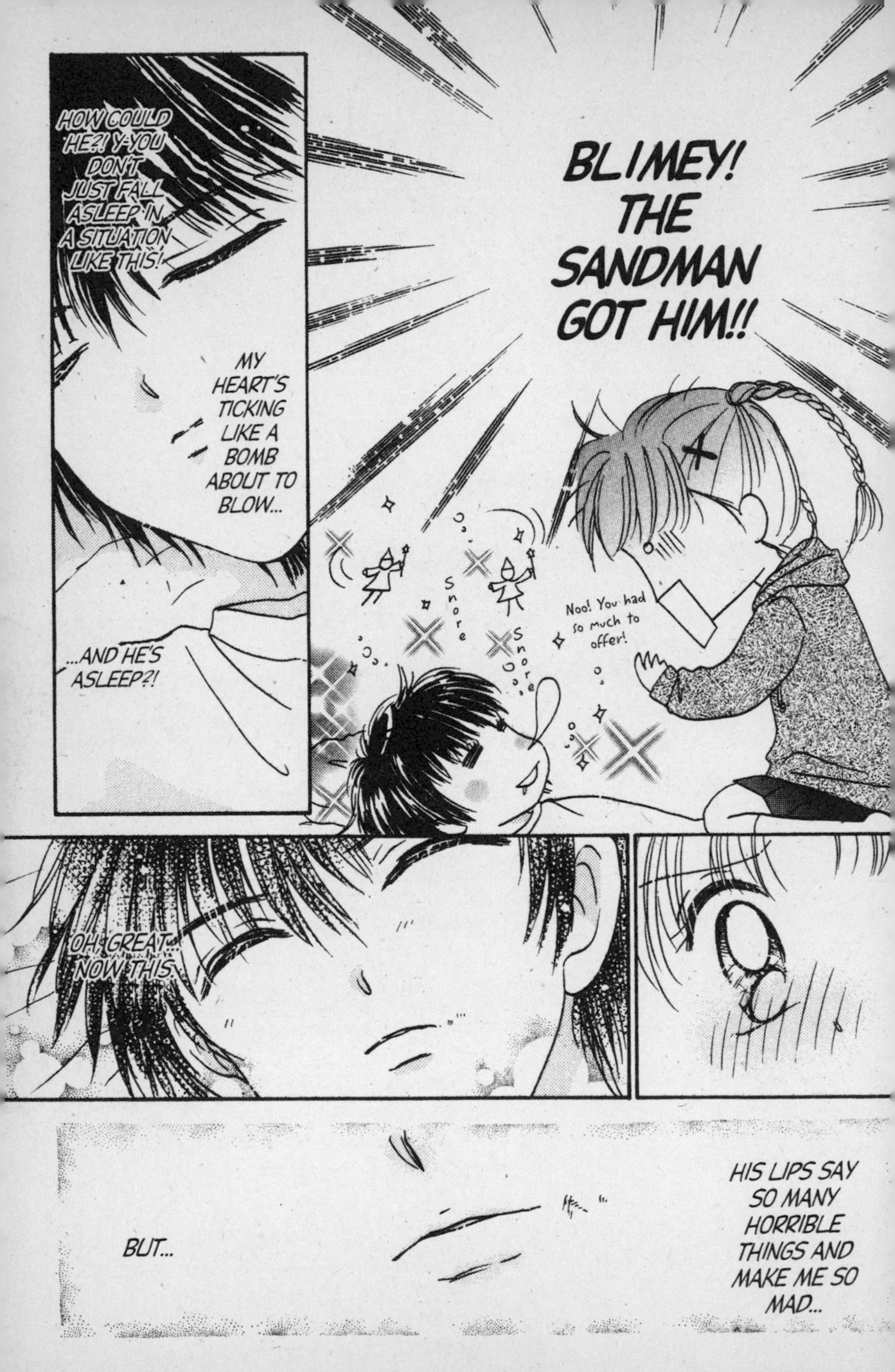
BLIMEY! THE SANDMAN GOT HIM!!
Noo! You had so much to offer!
Snore
Snore
HOW COULD HE?! Y-YOU DON'T JUST FALL ASLEEP IN A SITUATION LIKE THIS!
MY HEART'S TICKING LIKE A BOMB ABOUT TO BLOW...
...AND HE'S ASLEEP?!
OH GREAT. NOW THIS.
HIS LIPS SAY SO MANY HORRIBLE THINGS AND MAKE ME SO MAD...
BUT...

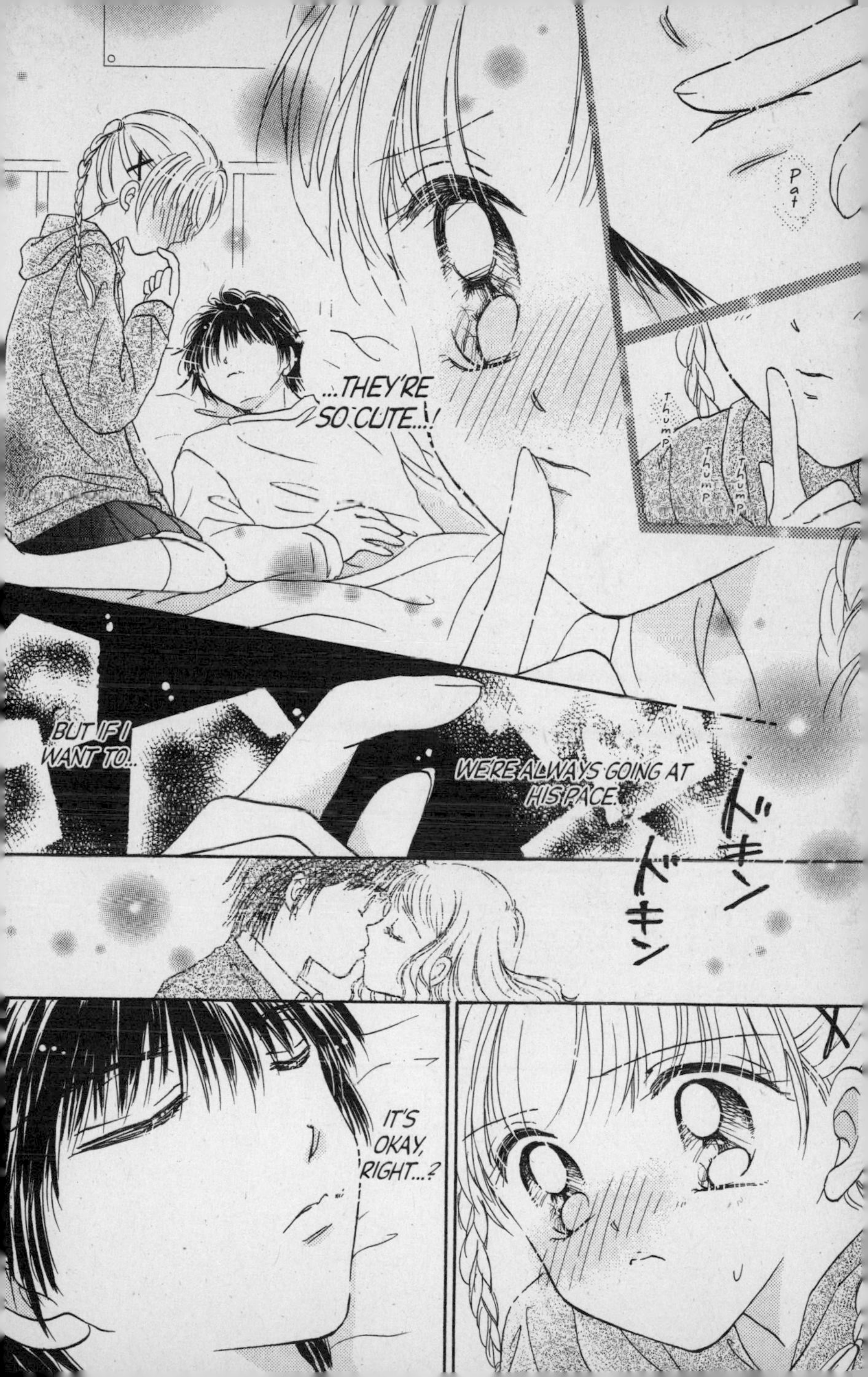
Pat
Thump
Thump
Thump
...THEY'RE SO CUTE...!
WE'RE ALWAYS GOING AT HIS PACE.
BUT IF I WANT TO...
ドキン
ドキン
IT'S OKAY, RIGHT...?

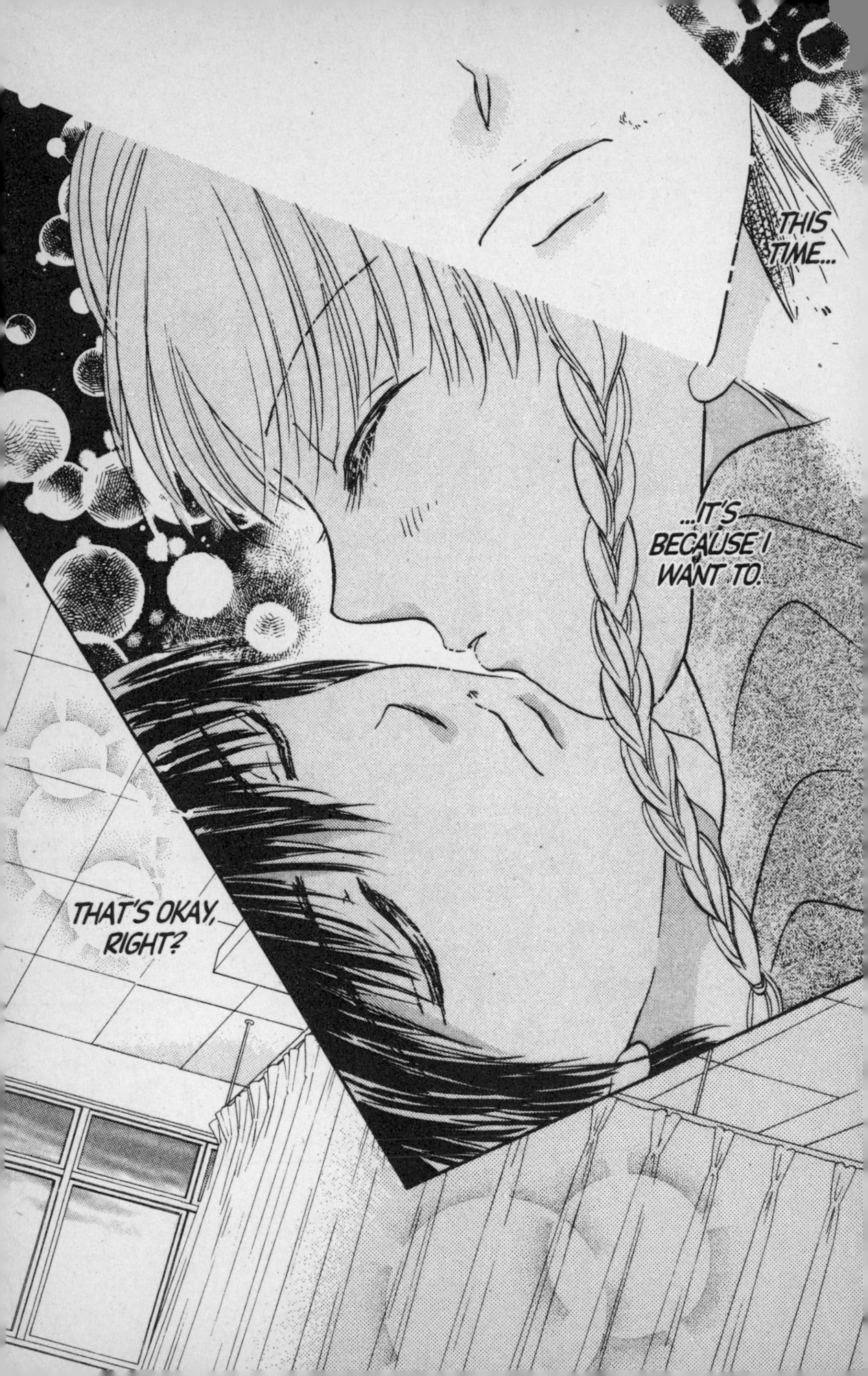
THIS TIME...
...IT'S BECAUSE I WANT TO.
THAT'S OKAY, RIGHT?

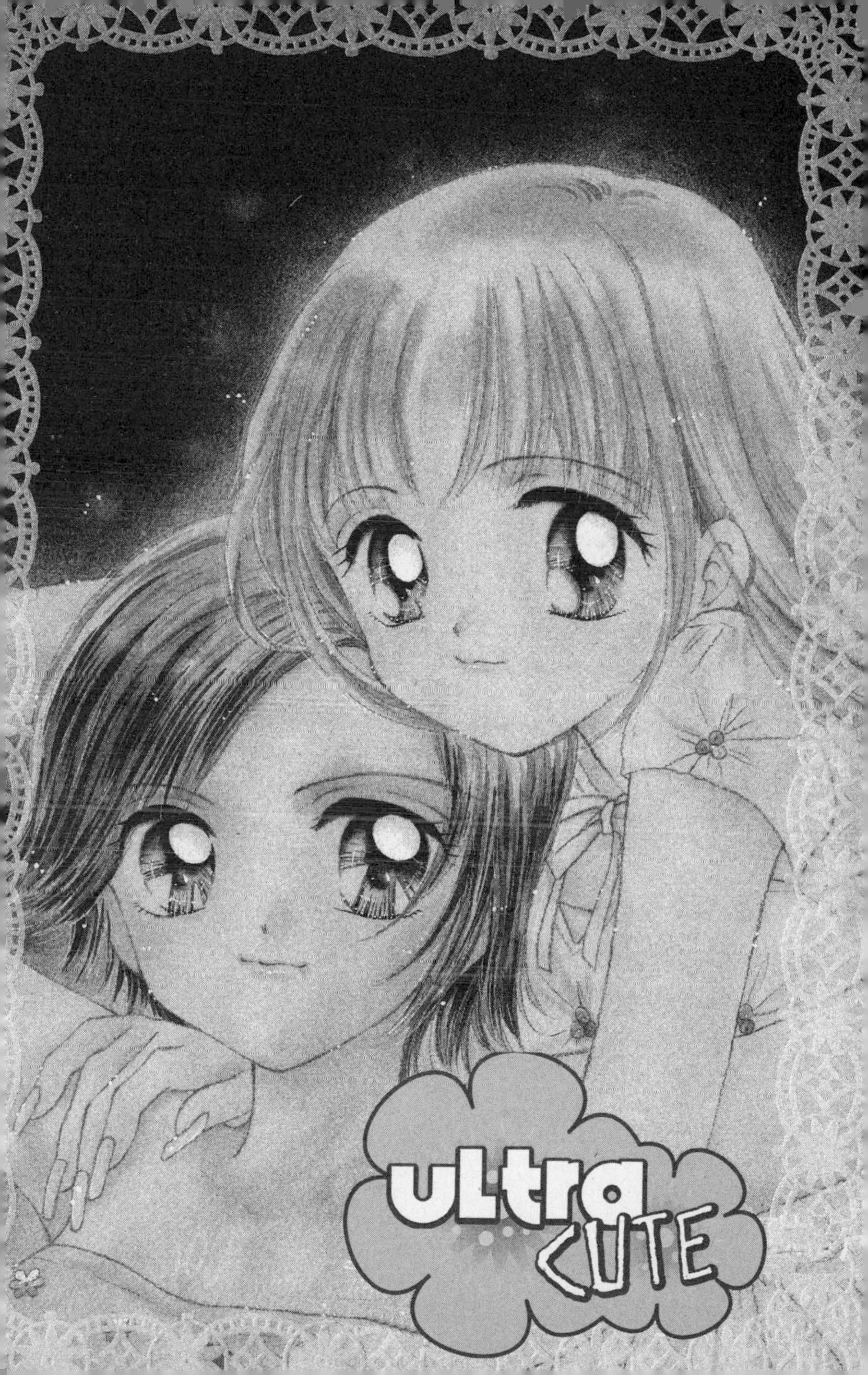
ultra
CUTE

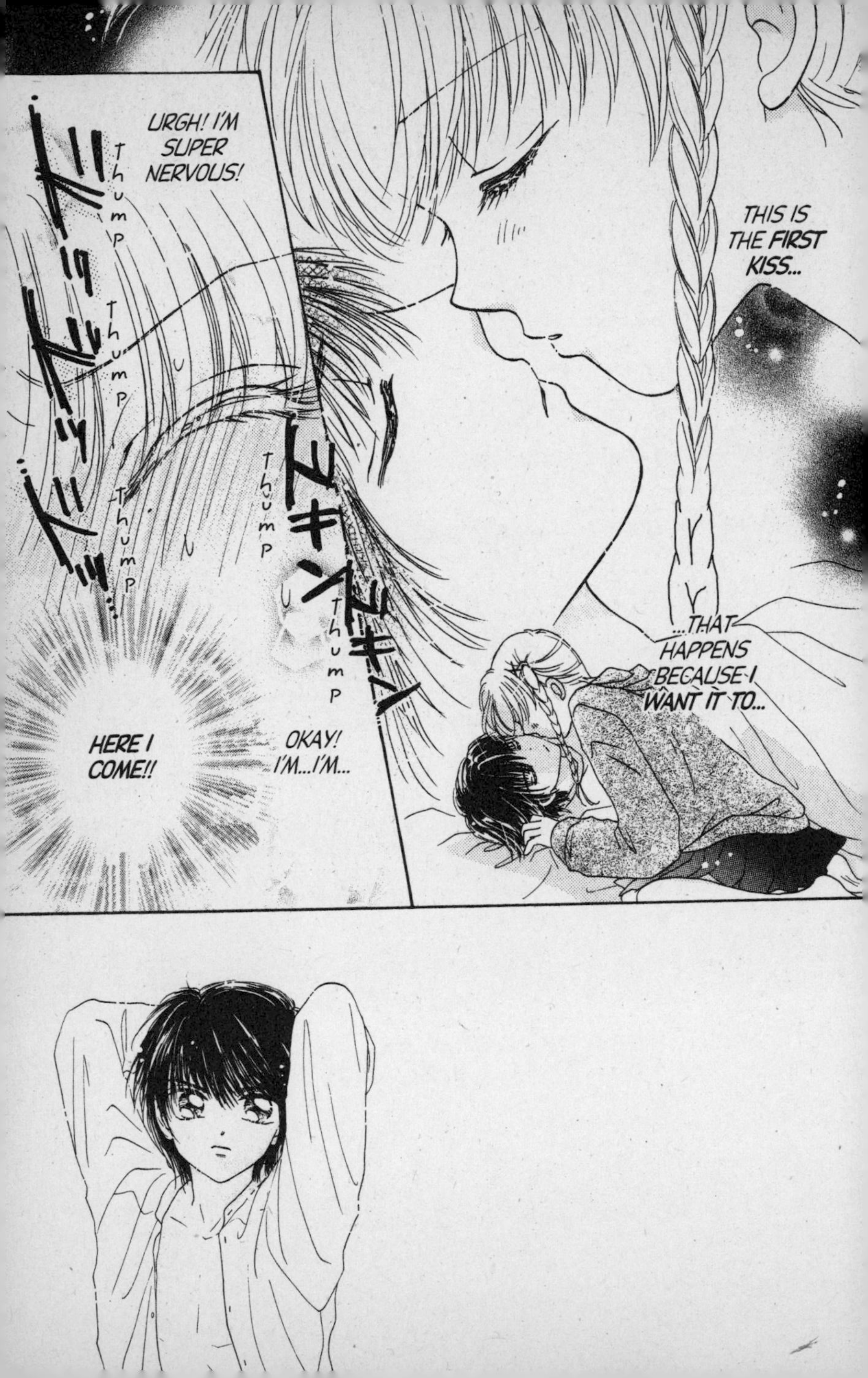
THIS IS THE FIRST KISS...
...THAT HAPPENS BECAUSE I WANT IT TO...
URGH! I'M SUPER NERVOUS!
Thump
Thump
Thump
Thump
OKAY! I'M...I'M...
HERE I COME!!

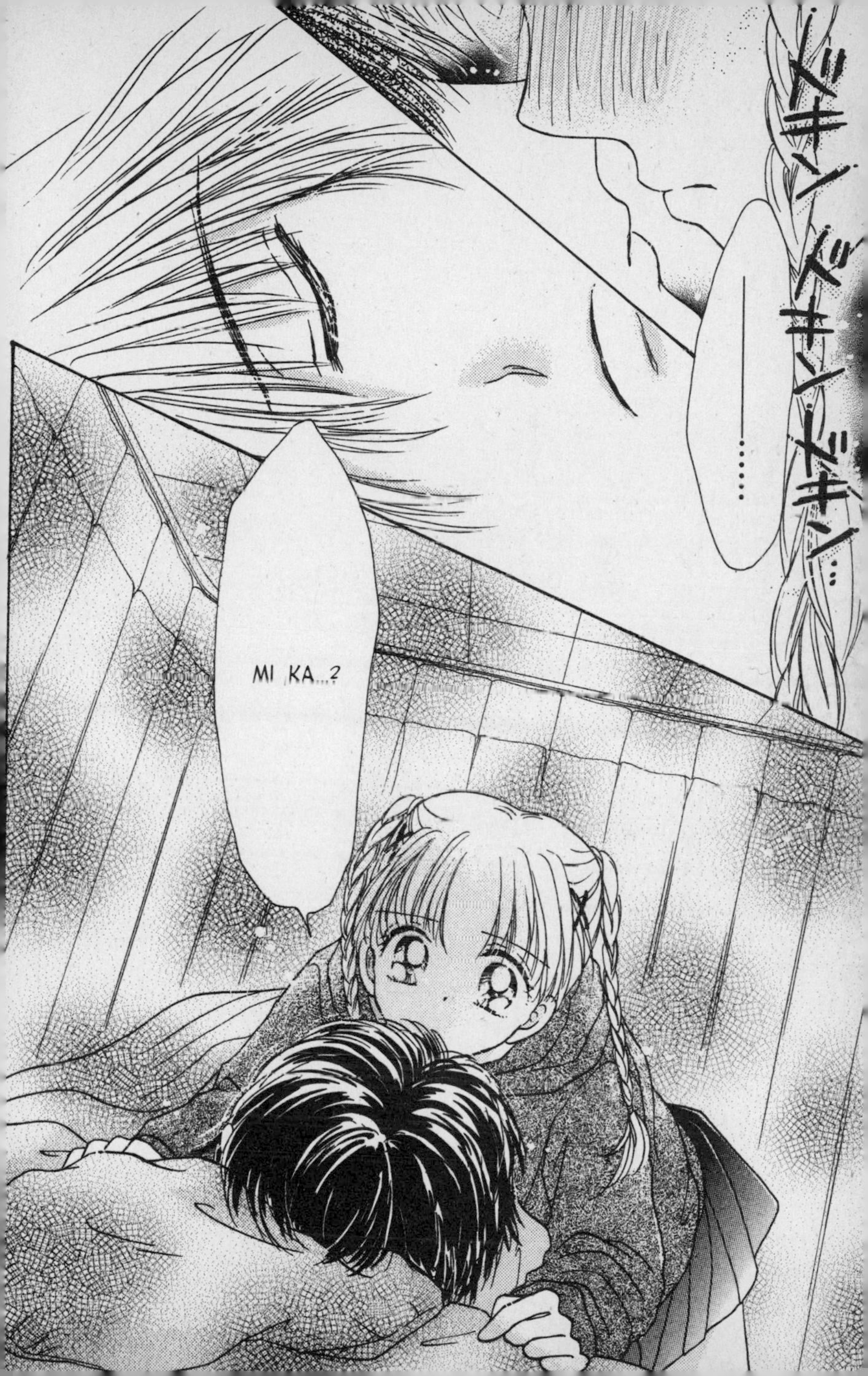
ズキン ズキン ズキン ズキン…
……
MI KA...?

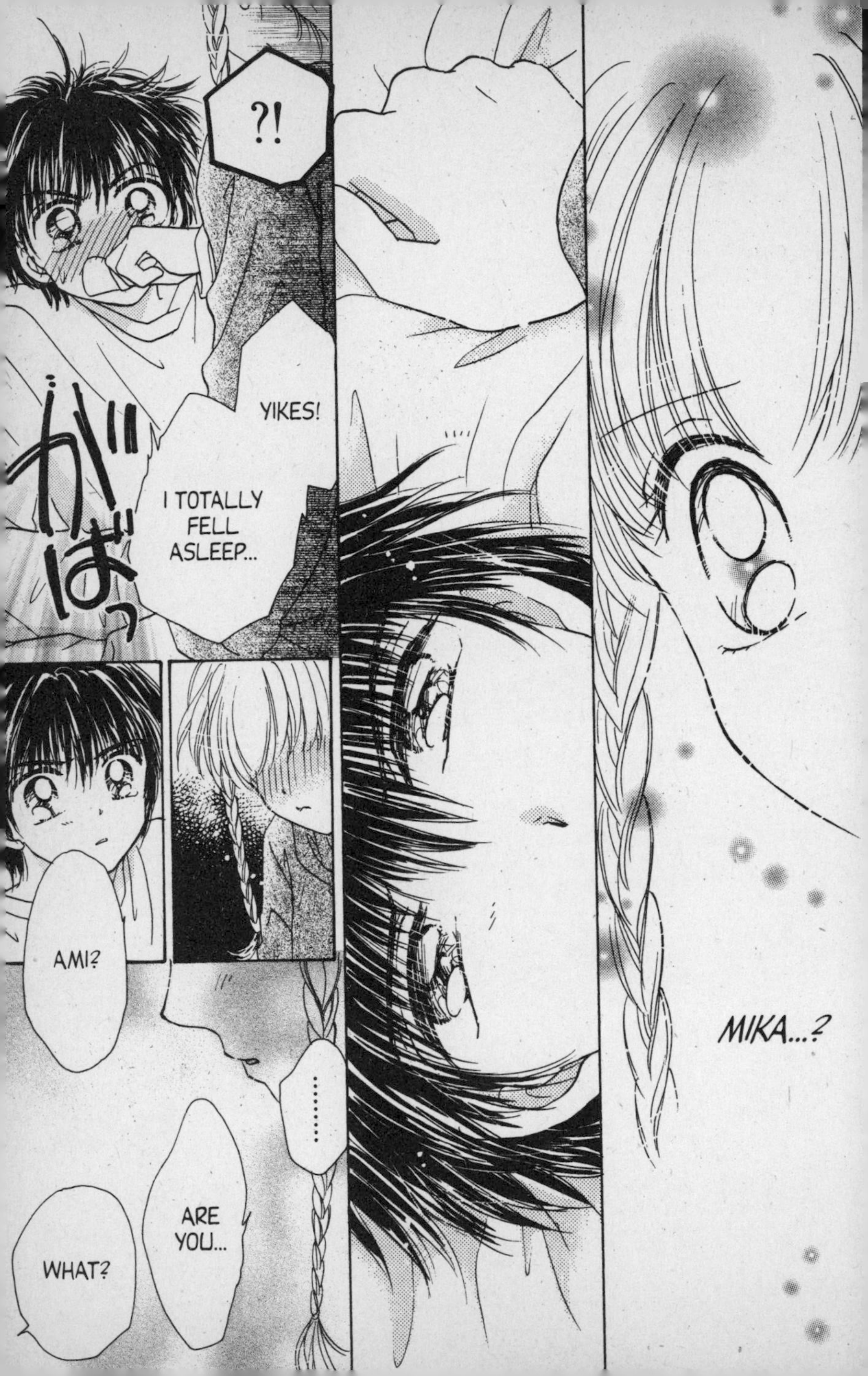

MIKA...?
?!
YIKES!
I TOTALLY FELL ASLEEP...
がばっ
AMI?
......
ARE YOU...
WHAT?

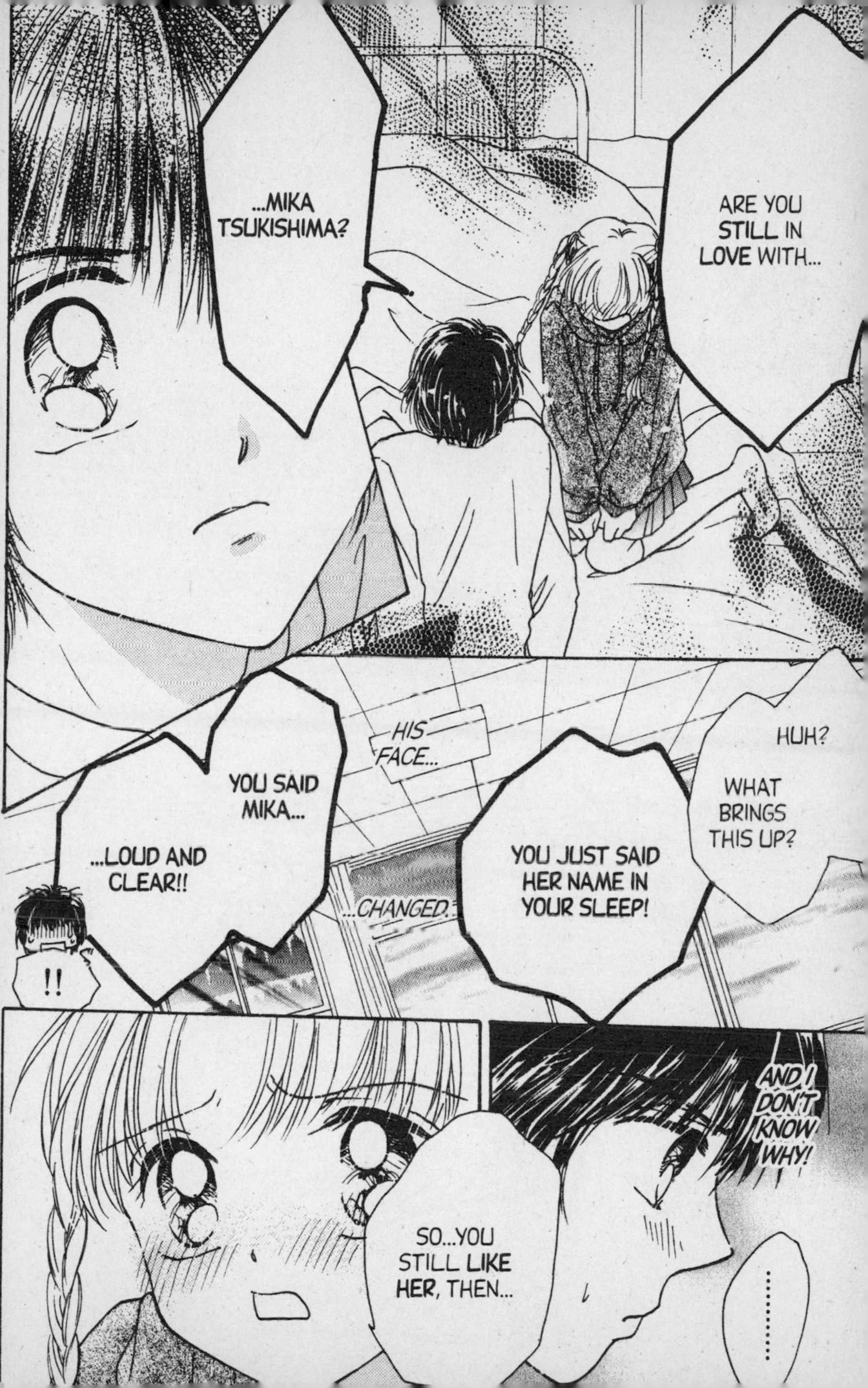
ARE YOU STILL IN LOVE WITH...
...MIKA TSUKISHIMA?
HUH?
WHAT BRINGS THIS UP?
YOU JUST SAID HER NAME IN YOUR SLEEP!
HIS FACE...
...CHANGED
YOU SAID MIKA...
...LOUD AND CLEAR!!
!!
AND I DON'T KNOW WHY!
......
SO...YOU STILL LIKE HER, THEN...

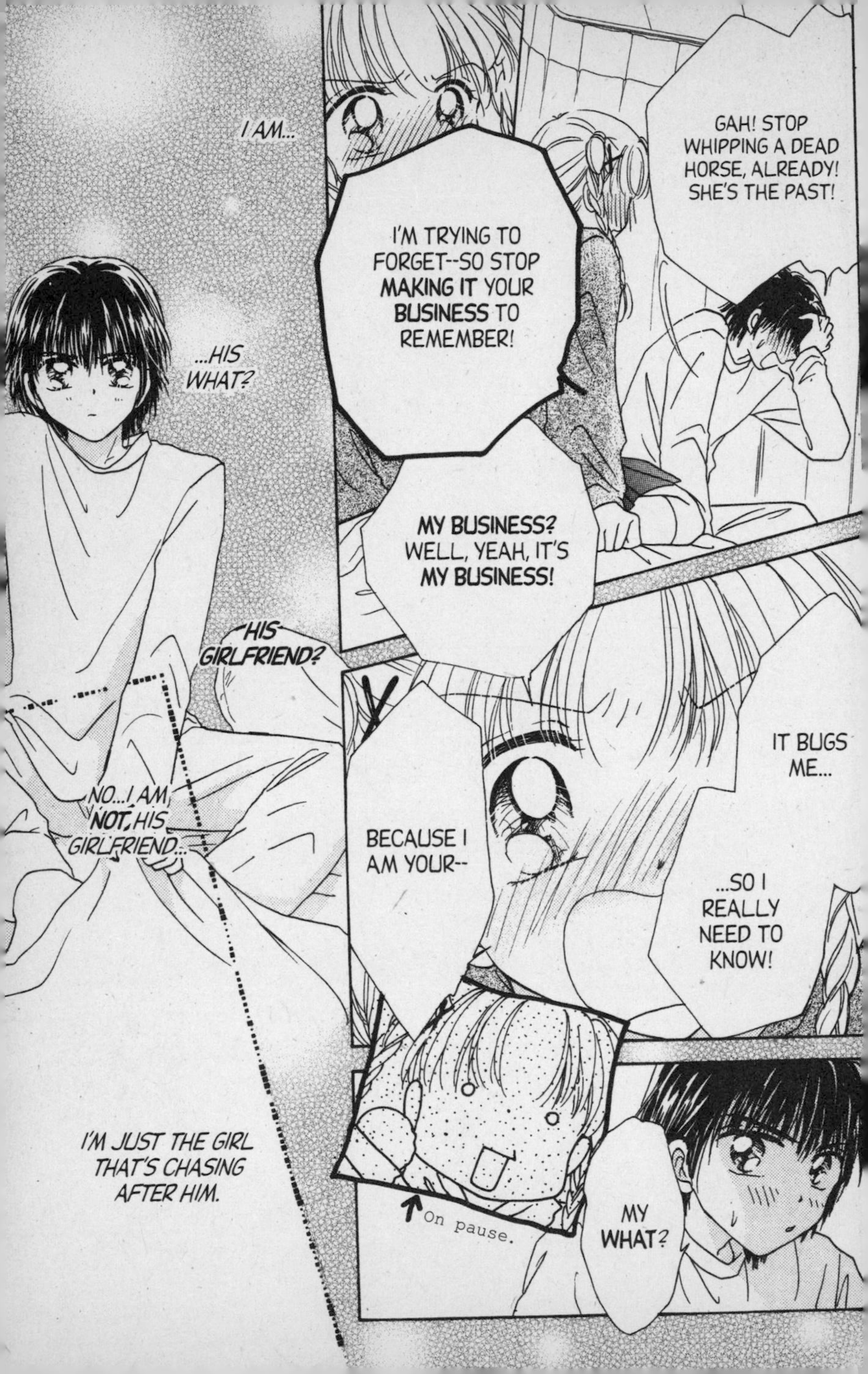
GAH! STOP WHIPPING A DEAD HORSE, ALREADY! SHE'S THE PAST!
I'M TRYING TO FORGET--SO STOP MAKING IT YOUR BUSINESS TO REMEMBER!
MY BUSINESS? WELL, YEAH, IT'S MY BUSINESS!
IT BUGS ME...
...SO I REALLY NEED TO KNOW!
BECAUSE I AM YOUR--
MY WHAT?
On pause.
I AM...
...HIS WHAT?
HIS GIRLFRIEND?
NO...I AM NOT HIS GIRLFRIEND...
I'M JUST THE GIRL THAT'S CHASING AFTER HIM.

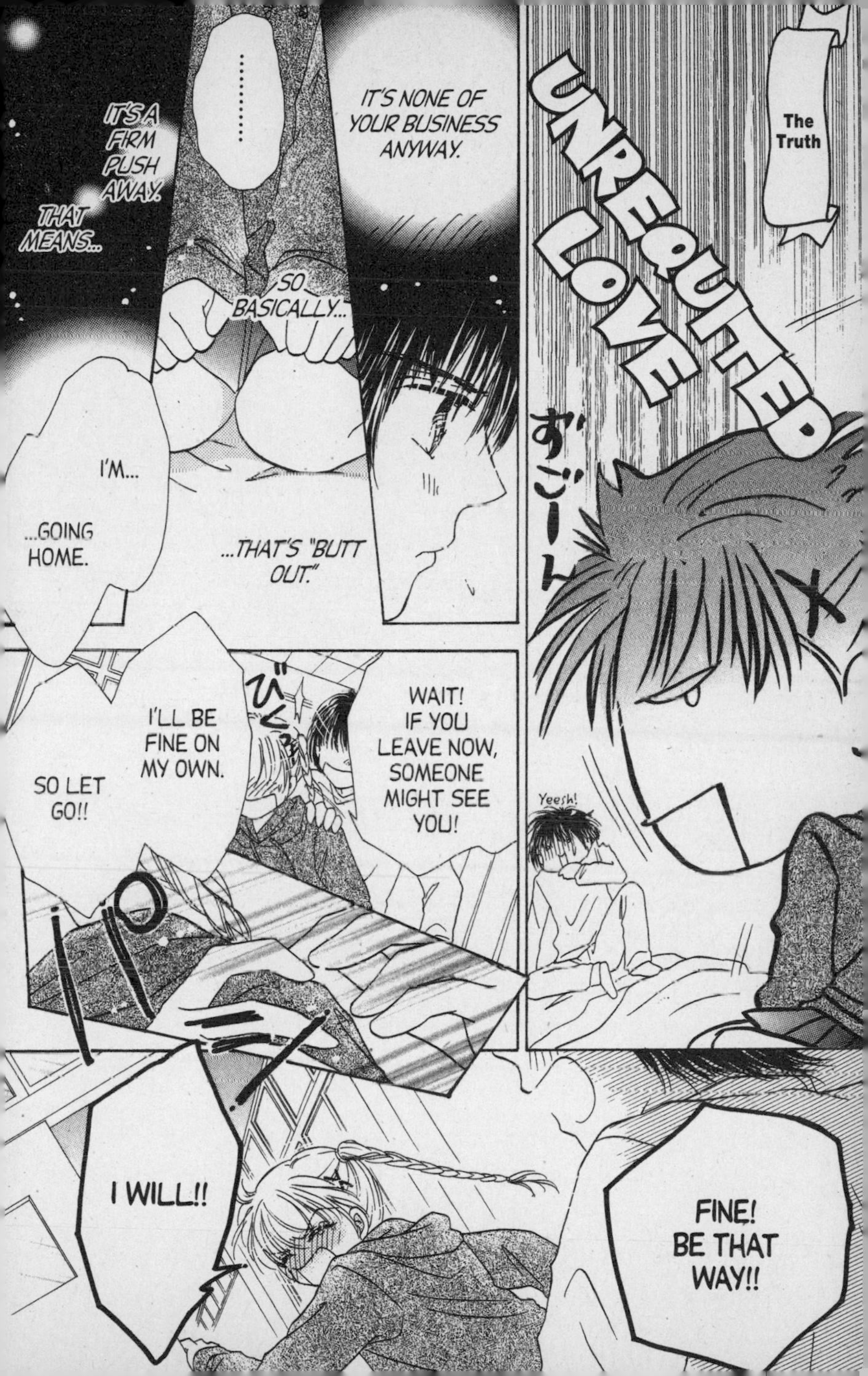
The Truth
UNREQUITED LOVE
すごーん
Yeesh!
IT'S NONE OF YOUR BUSINESS ANYWAY.
......
IT'S A FIRM PUSH AWAY.
THAT MEANS...
SO BASICALLY...
...THAT'S "BUTT OUT."
I'M...
...GOING HOME.
WAIT! IF YOU LEAVE NOW, SOMEONE MIGHT SEE YOU!
びくっ
I'LL BE FINE ON MY OWN.
SO LET GO!!
FINE! BE THAT WAY!!
I WILL!!

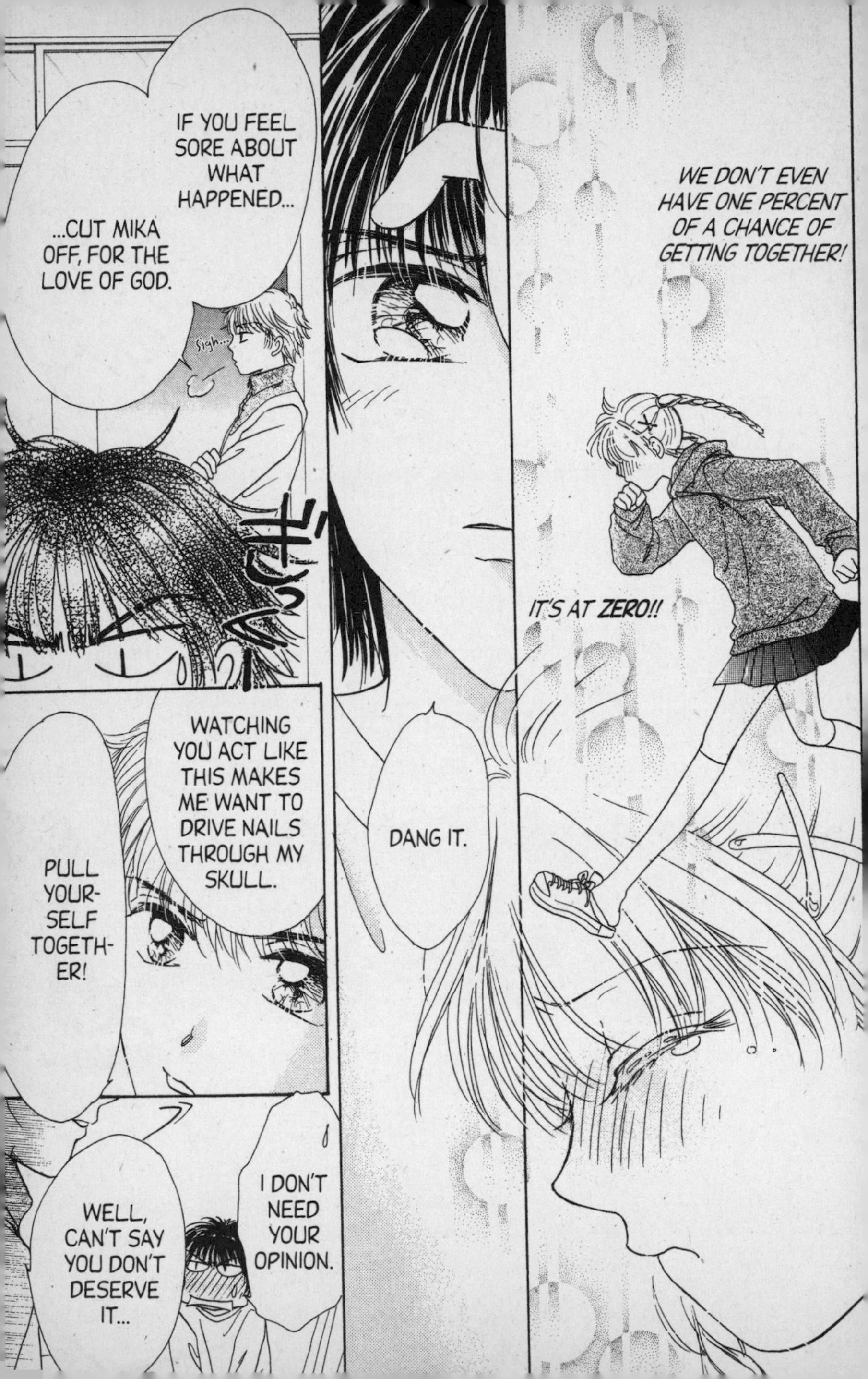
WE DON'T EVEN HAVE ONE PERCENT OF A CHANCE OF GETTING TOGETHER!
IT'S AT ZERO!!
DANG IT.
IF YOU FEEL SORE ABOUT WHAT HAPPENED...
...CUT MIKA OFF, FOR THE LOVE OF GOD.
Sigh...
WATCHING YOU ACT LIKE THIS MAKES ME WANT TO DRIVE NAILS THROUGH MY SKULL.
PULL YOUR-SELF TOGETH-ER!
I DON'T NEED YOUR OPINION.
WELL, CAN'T SAY YOU DON'T DESERVE IT...

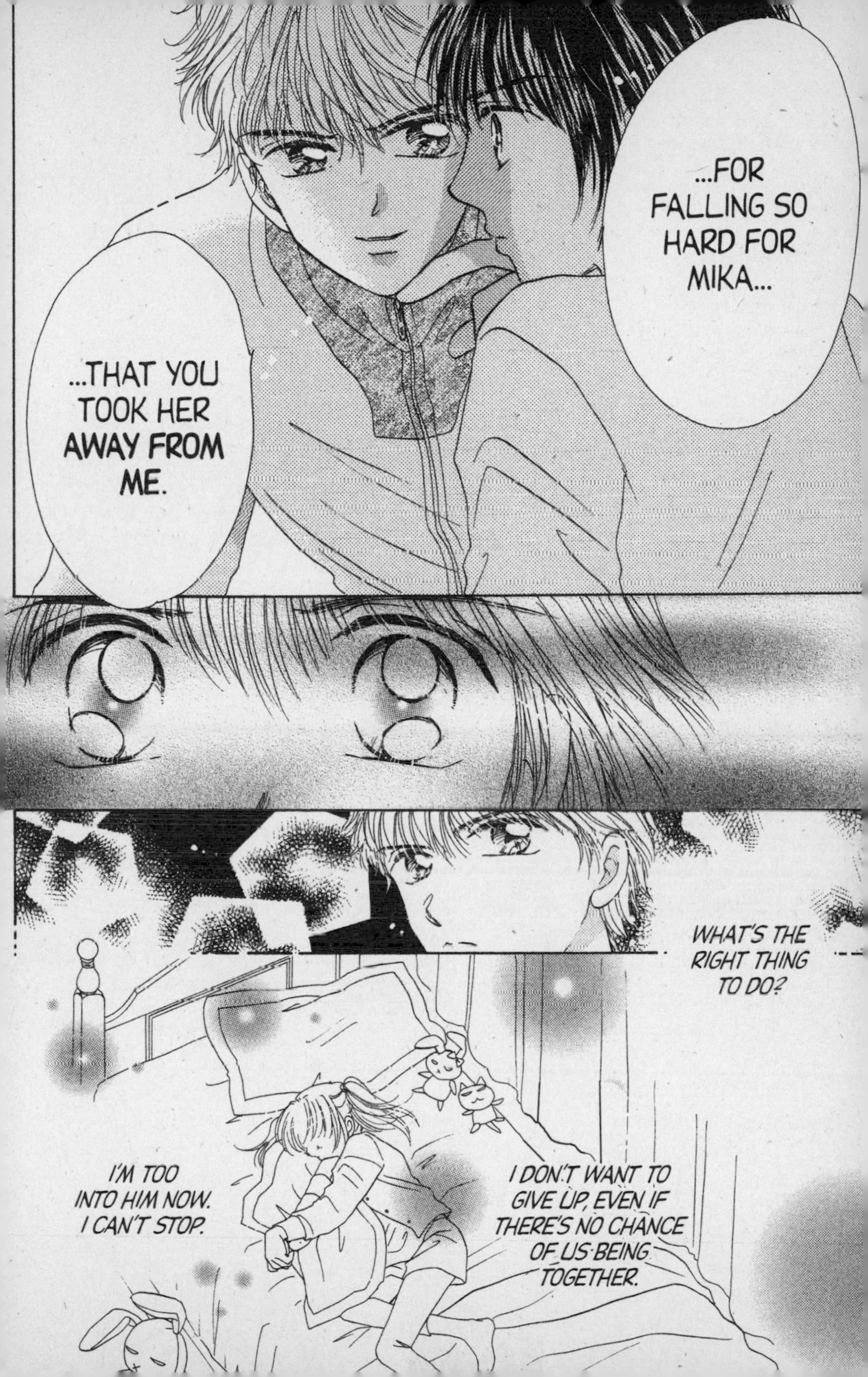
...FOR FALLING SO HARD FOR MIKA...
...THAT YOU TOOK HER AWAY FROM ME.
WHAT'S THE RIGHT THING TO DO?
I DON'T WANT TO GIVE UP, EVEN IF THERE'S NO CHANCE OF US BEING TOGETHER.
I'M TOO INTO HIM NOW. I CAN'T STOP.

There is going to be a special episode at the end of this book. It's a story from when Ami and Noa were in elementary school. It was a real joy to write, since I had been thinking of doing it for so long. If I have the chance, I would love to write an episode from when they were in junior high as well! I am totally on a roll writing the main story, too--and would love to hear your feedback on it.

Okay, then.
Let's do this again in volume three!!

Nami Akimoto

2000 MAR.

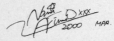

My Spring 2000 Addictions

Kimchi
Chijimi
Dry Food
Tsumire
Ricotta ice cream
Red Bean Crackers
Vilonia's Chocolate
Vodka
D & G Pink
Morning Green Tea

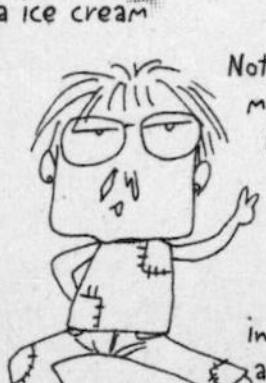

Notice they're mostly food related...

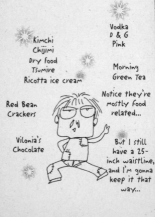

But I still have a 25-inch waistline, and I'm gonna keep it that way...

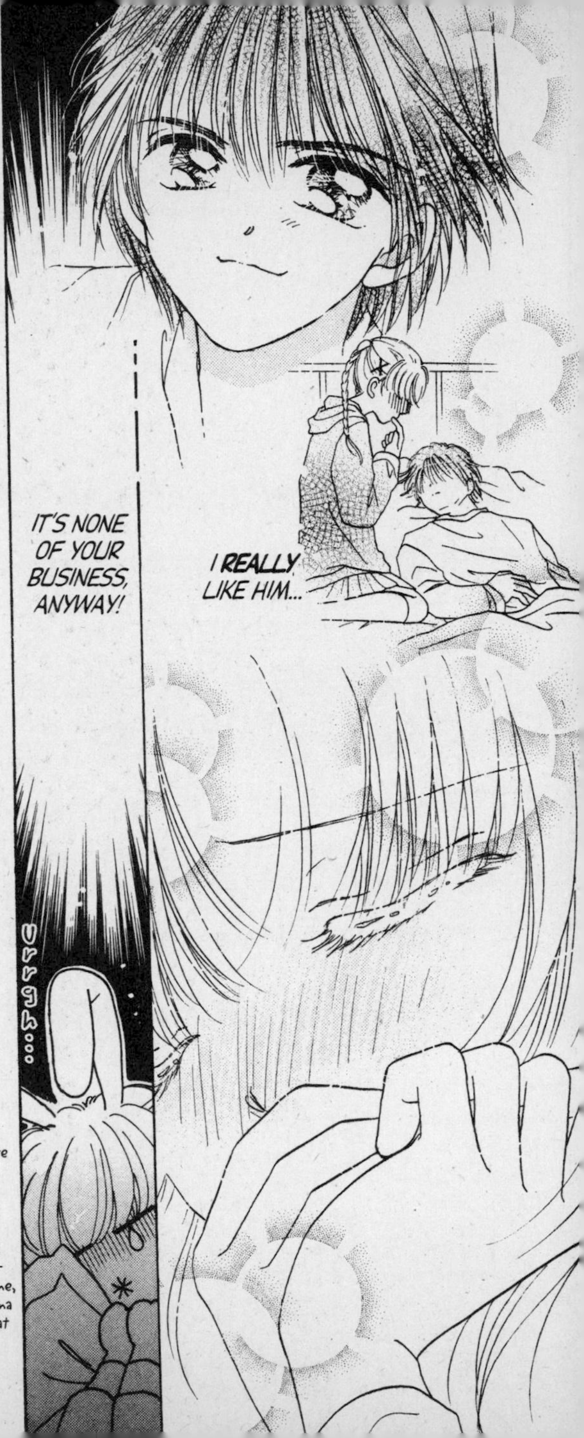
I REALLY LIKE HIM...
IT'S NONE OF YOUR BUSINESS, ANYWAY!
Urrgh...

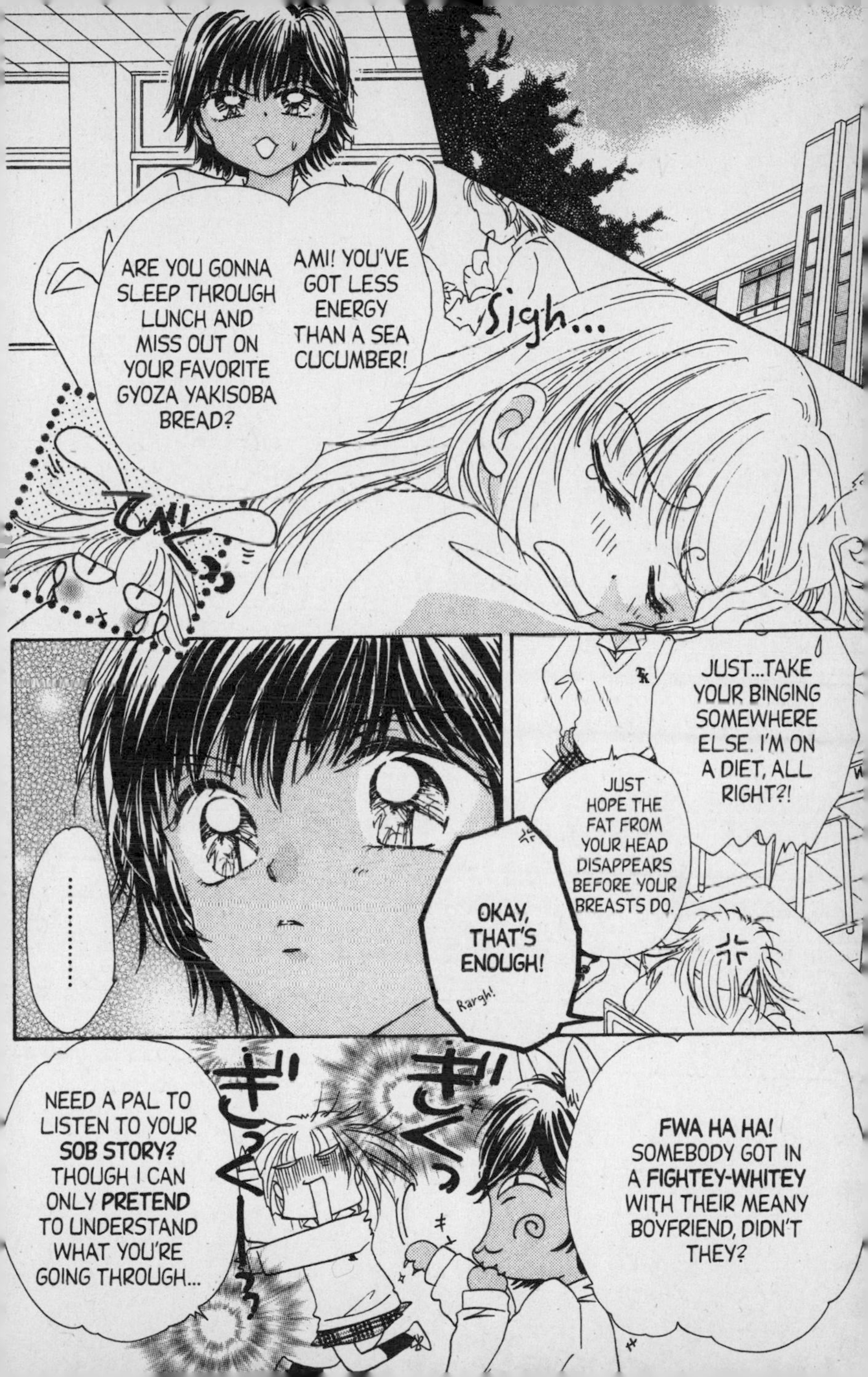
AMI! YOU'VE GOT LESS ENERGY THAN A SEA CUCUMBER!
ARE YOU GONNA SLEEP THROUGH LUNCH AND MISS OUT ON YOUR FAVORITE GYOZA YAKISOBA BREAD?
Sigh...
JUST...TAKE YOUR BINGING SOMEWHERE ELSE. I'M ON A DIET, ALL RIGHT?!
JUST HOPE THE FAT FROM YOUR HEAD DISAPPEARS BEFORE YOUR BREASTS DO.
OKAY, THAT'S ENOUGH!
Rargh!
......
FWA HA HA! SOMEBODY GOT IN A **FIGHTEY-WHITEY** WITH THEIR MEANY BOYFRIEND, DIDN'T THEY?
NEED A PAL TO LISTEN TO YOUR **SOB STORY?** THOUGH I CAN ONLY **PRETEND** TO UNDERSTAND WHAT YOU'RE GOING THROUGH...

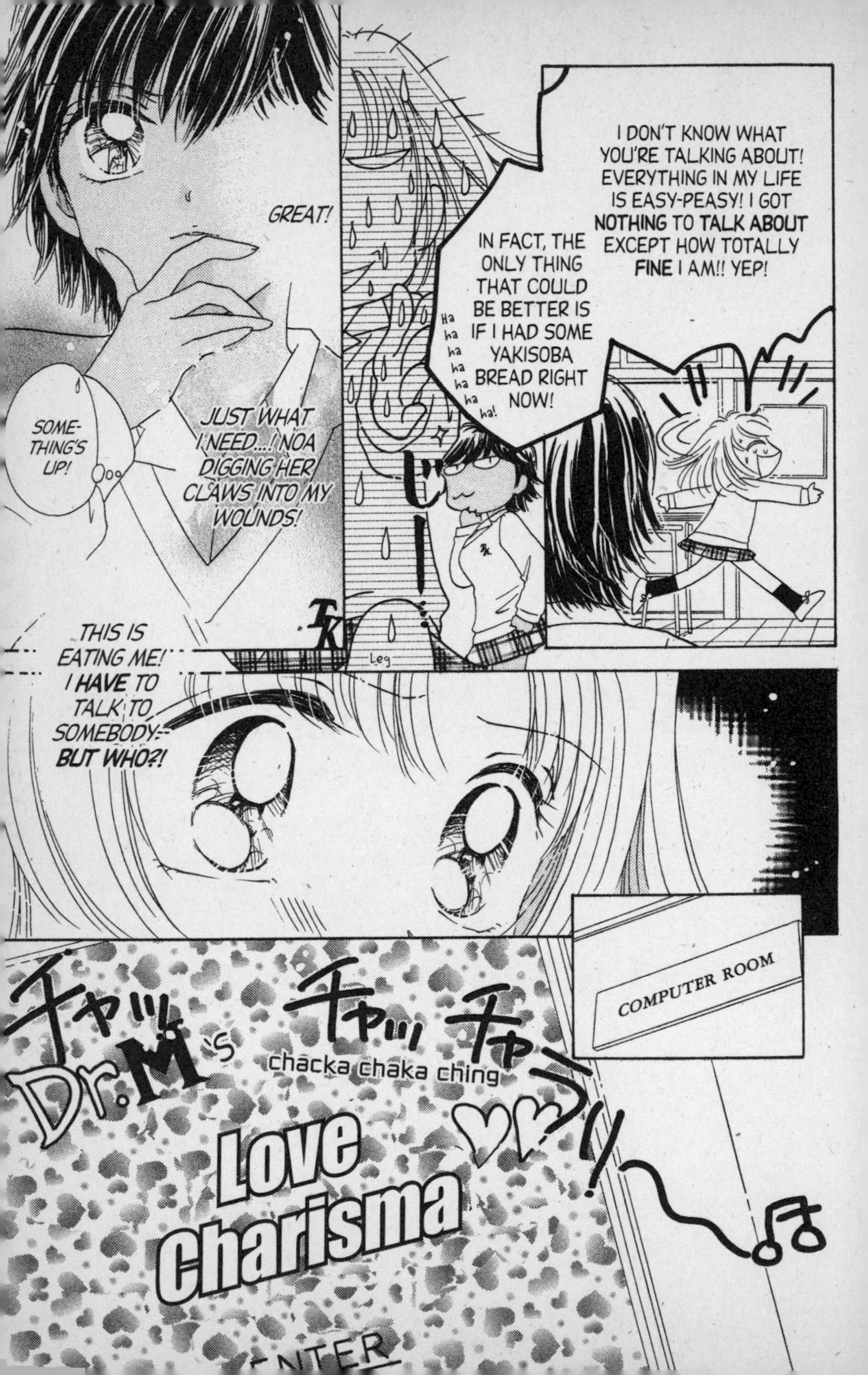
I DON'T KNOW WHAT YOU'RE TALKING ABOUT! EVERYTHING IN MY LIFE IS EASY-PEASY! I GOT NOTHING TO TALK ABOUT EXCEPT HOW TOTALLY FINE I AM!! YEP!
IN FACT, THE ONLY THING THAT COULD BE BETTER IS IF I HAD SOME YAKISOBA BREAD RIGHT NOW!
Ha ha ha ha ha ha ha!
Leg
GREAT!
JUST WHAT I NEED...! NOA DIGGING HER CLAWS INTO MY WOUNDS!
SOME-THING'S UP!
THIS IS EATING ME! I HAVE TO TALK TO SOMEBODY-- BUT WHO?!
COMPUTER ROOM
Dr. M's Love Charisma
chacka chaka ching

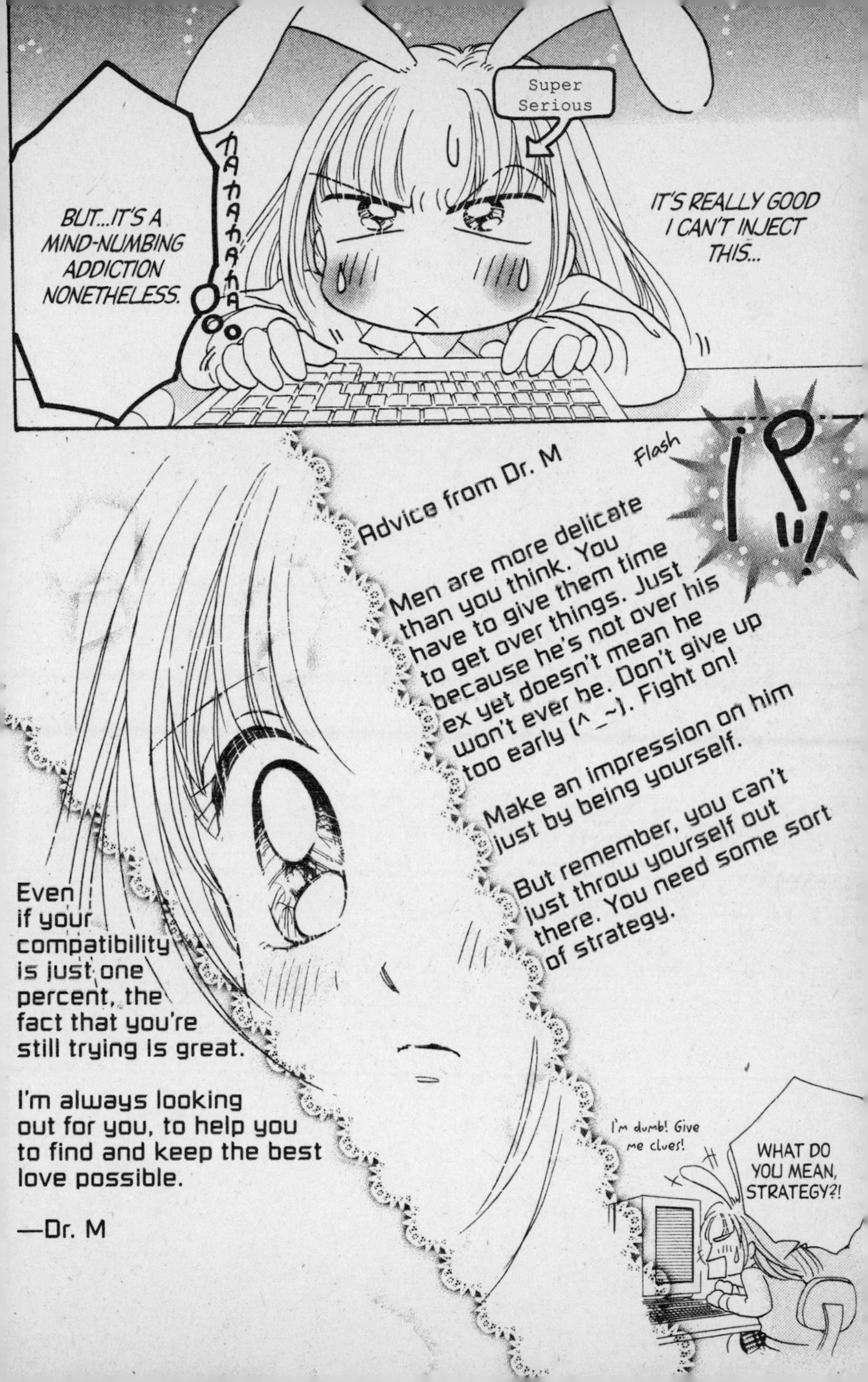

Super Serious
IT'S REALLY GOOD I CAN'T INJECT THIS...
BUT...IT'S A MIND-NUMBING ADDICTION NONETHELESS.
Flash
Advice from Dr. M
Men are more delicate than you think. You have to give them time to get over things. Just because he's not over his ex yet doesn't mean he won't ever be. Don't give up too early (^_~). Fight on!
Make an impression on him just by being yourself.
But remember, you can't just throw yourself out there. You need some sort of strategy.
Even if your compatibility is just one percent, the fact that you're still trying is great.
I'm always looking out for you, to help you to find and keep the best love possible.
—Dr. M
I'm dumb! Give me clues!
WHAT DO YOU MEAN, STRATEGY?!

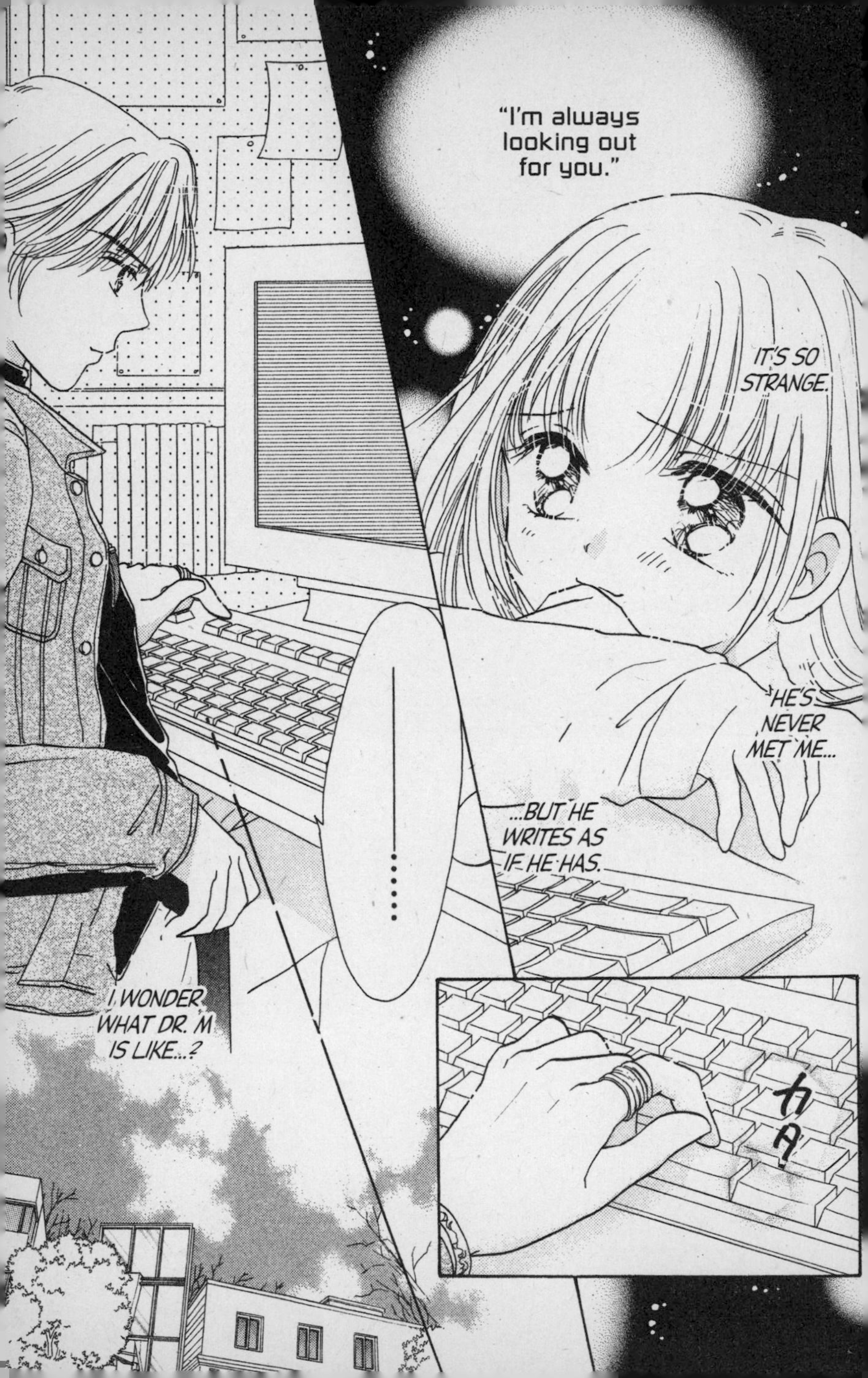
"I'm always looking out for you."
IT'S SO STRANGE.
HE'S NEVER MET ME...
...BUT HE WRITES AS IF HE HAS.
I WONDER WHAT DR. M IS LIKE...?

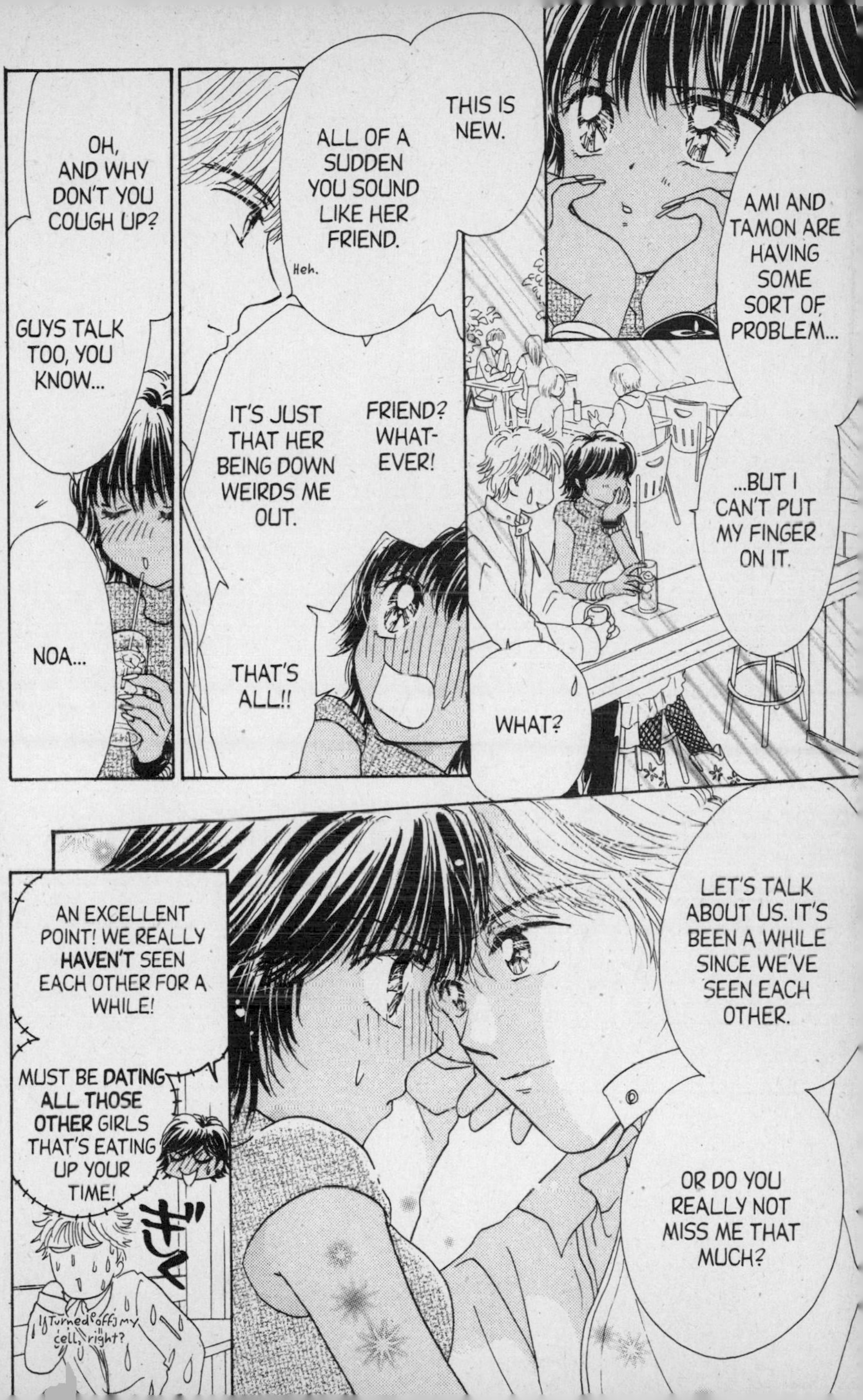
AMI AND TAMON ARE HAVING SOME SORT OF PROBLEM...
...BUT I CAN'T PUT MY FINGER ON IT.
WHAT?
THIS IS NEW.
ALL OF A SUDDEN YOU SOUND LIKE HER FRIEND.
Heh.
FRIEND? WHAT-EVER!
IT'S JUST THAT HER BEING DOWN WEIRDS ME OUT.
THAT'S ALL!!
OH, AND WHY DON'T YOU COUGH UP?
GUYS TALK TOO, YOU KNOW...
NOA...
LET'S TALK ABOUT US. IT'S BEEN A WHILE SINCE WE'VE SEEN EACH OTHER.
OR DO YOU REALLY NOT MISS ME THAT MUCH?
AN EXCELLENT POINT! WE REALLY **HAVEN'T** SEEN EACH OTHER FOR A WHILE!
MUST BE **DATING ALL THOSE OTHER** GIRLS THAT'S EATING UP YOUR TIME!
ギく
I turned off my cell, right?

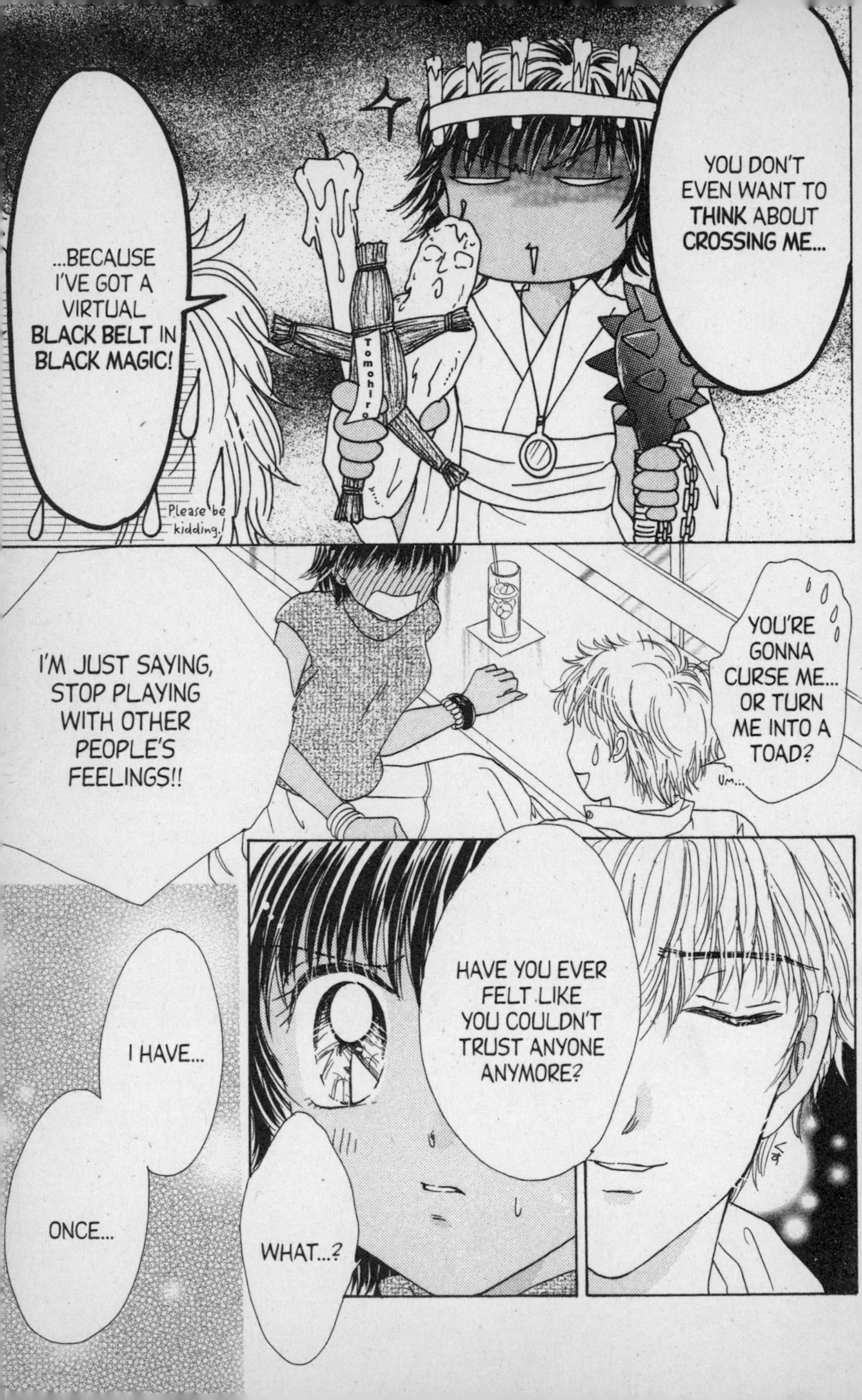
YOU DON'T EVEN WANT TO THINK ABOUT CROSSING ME...
...BECAUSE I'VE GOT A VIRTUAL BLACK BELT IN BLACK MAGIC!
Tomohiro
Please be kidding.!
YOU'RE GONNA CURSE ME... OR TURN ME INTO A TOAD?
Um...
I'M JUST SAYING, STOP PLAYING WITH OTHER PEOPLE'S FEELINGS!!
HAVE YOU EVER FELT LIKE YOU COULDN'T TRUST ANYONE ANYMORE?
WHAT...?
I HAVE...
ONCE...

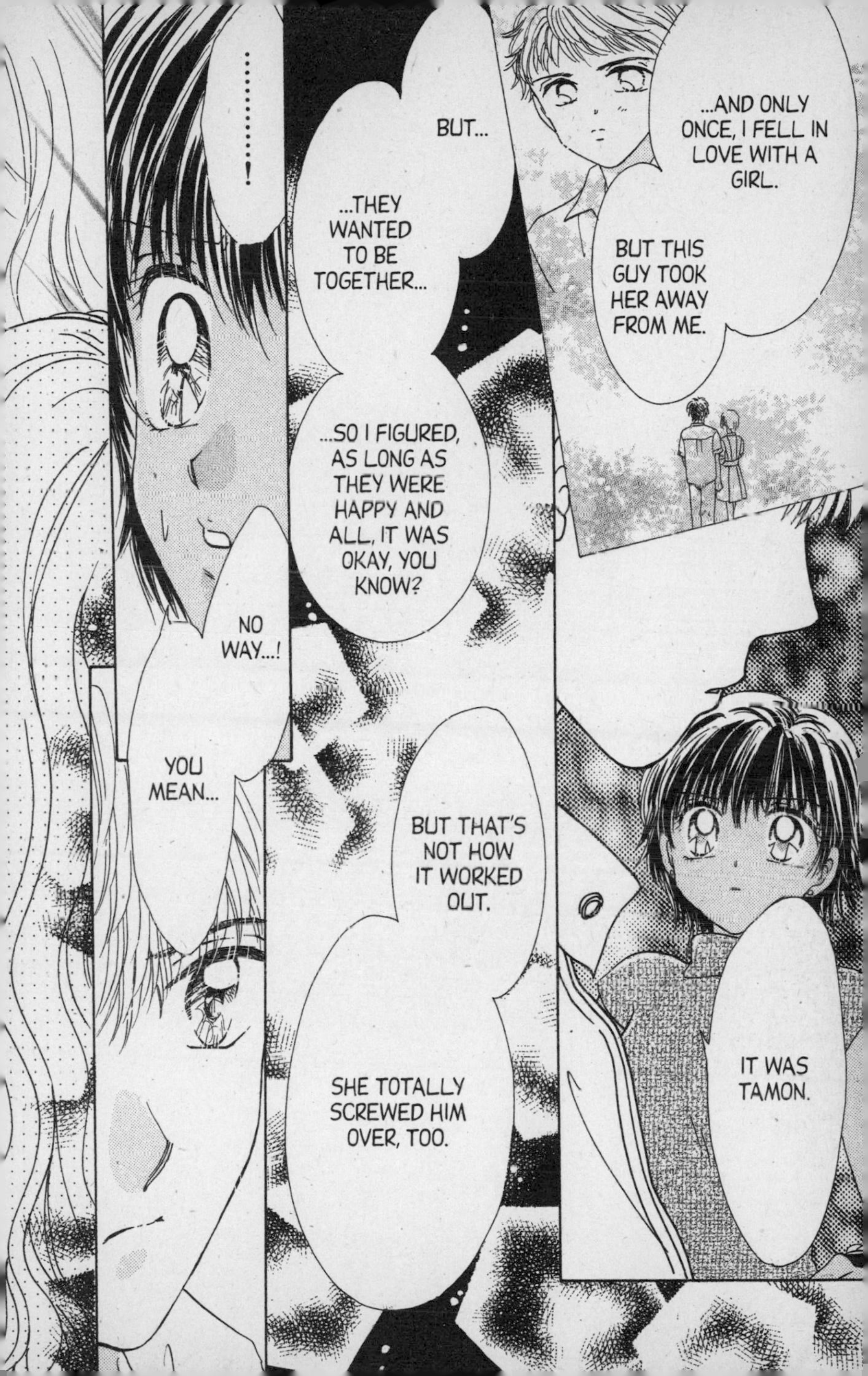
...AND ONLY ONCE, I FELL IN LOVE WITH A GIRL.
BUT THIS GUY TOOK HER AWAY FROM ME.
IT WAS TAMON.
BUT...
...THEY WANTED TO BE TOGETHER...
...SO I FIGURED, AS LONG AS THEY WERE HAPPY AND ALL, IT WAS OKAY, YOU KNOW?
BUT THAT'S NOT HOW IT WORKED OUT.
SHE TOTALLY SCREWED HIM OVER, TOO.
......!
NO WAY...!
YOU MEAN...

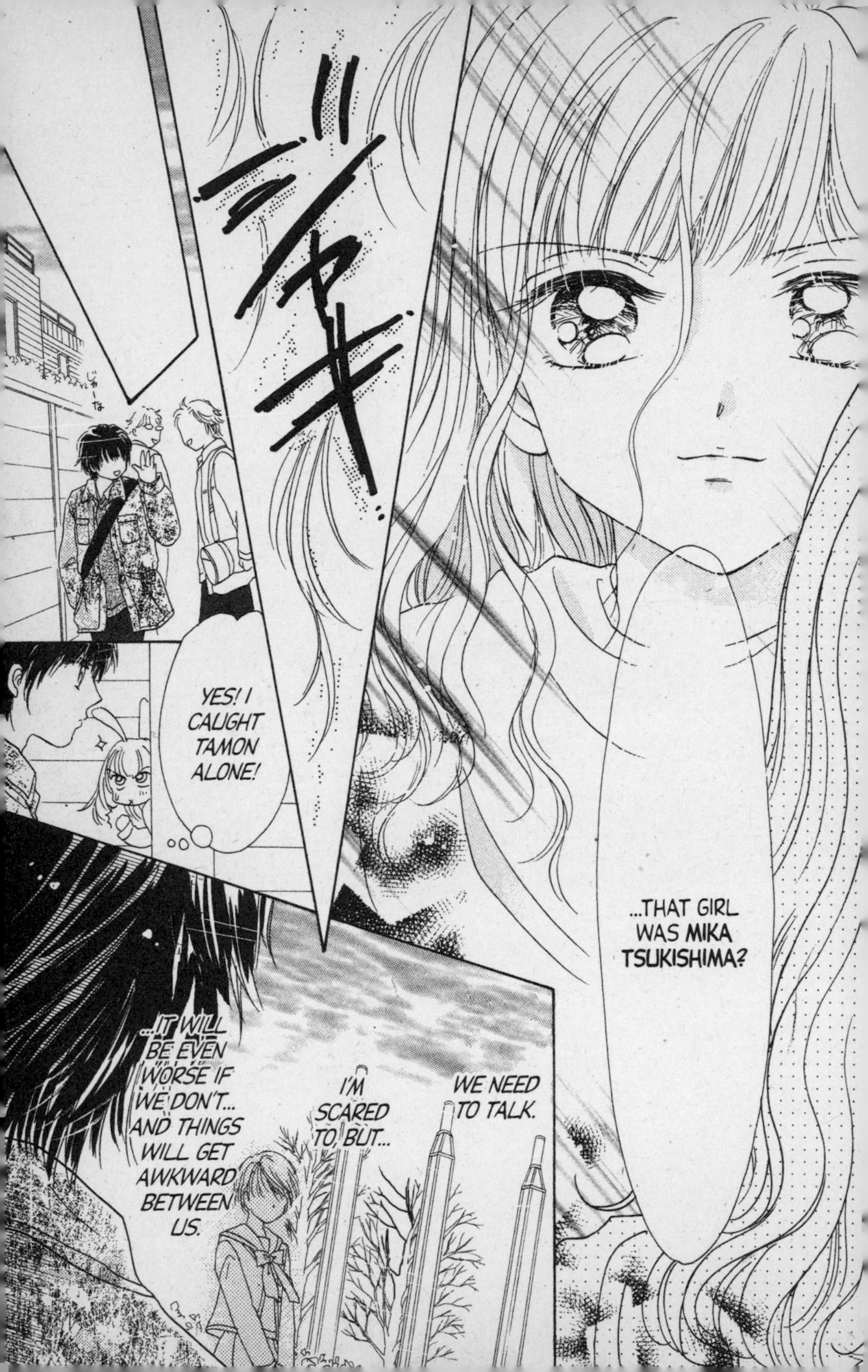
...THAT GIRL WAS MIKA TSUKISHIMA?
ジャキ
じゃーな
YES! I CAUGHT TAMON ALONE!
WE NEED TO TALK.
I'M SCARED TO, BUT...
...IT WILL BE EVEN WORSE IF WE DON'T... AND THINGS WILL GET AWKWARD BETWEEN US.

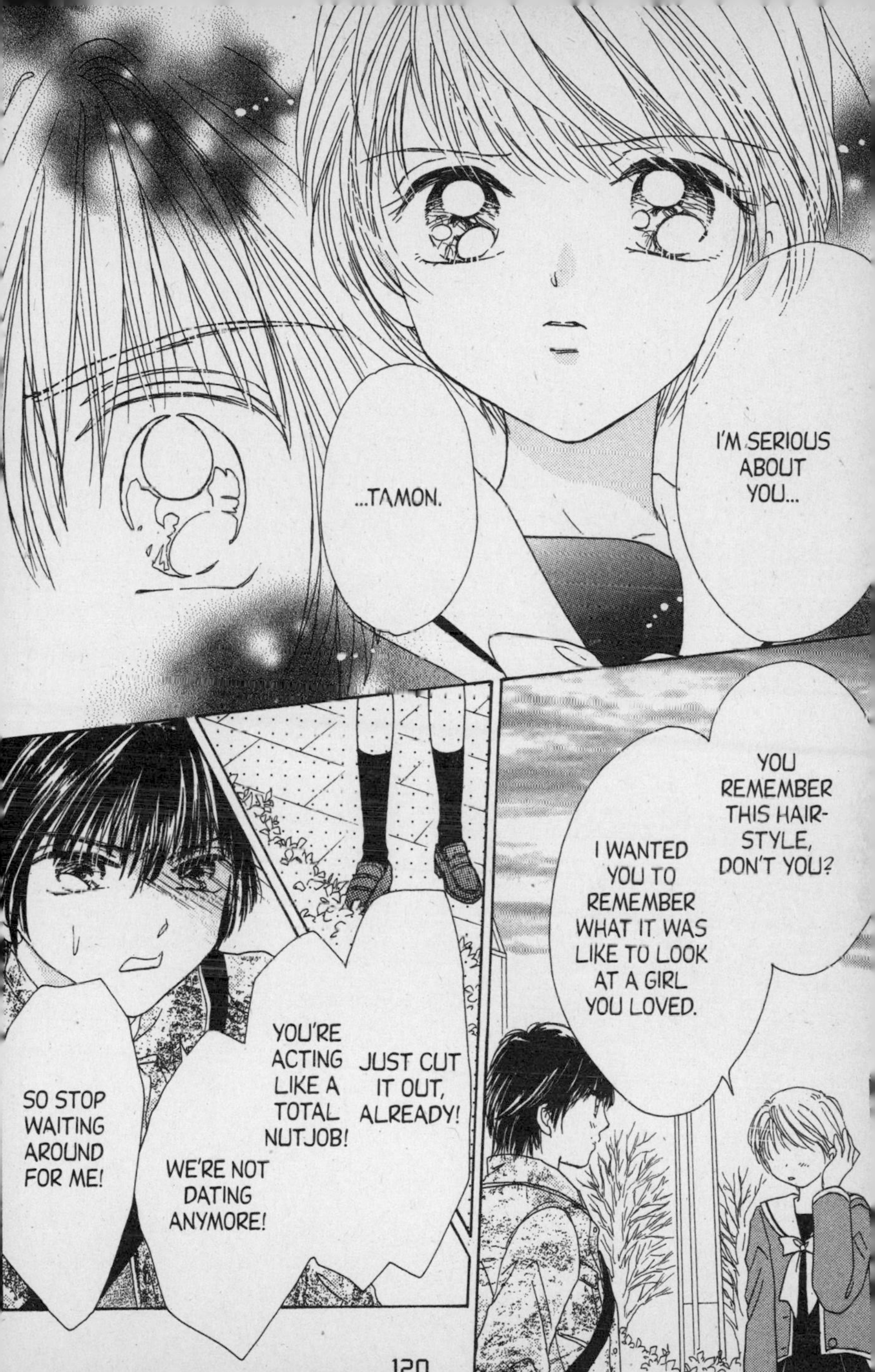
I'M SERIOUS ABOUT YOU...
...TAMON.
YOU REMEMBER THIS HAIR-STYLE, DON'T YOU?
I WANTED YOU TO REMEMBER WHAT IT WAS LIKE TO LOOK AT A GIRL YOU LOVED.
JUST CUT IT OUT, ALREADY!
YOU'RE ACTING LIKE A TOTAL NUTJOB!
WE'RE NOT DATING ANYMORE!
SO STOP WAITING AROUND FOR ME!

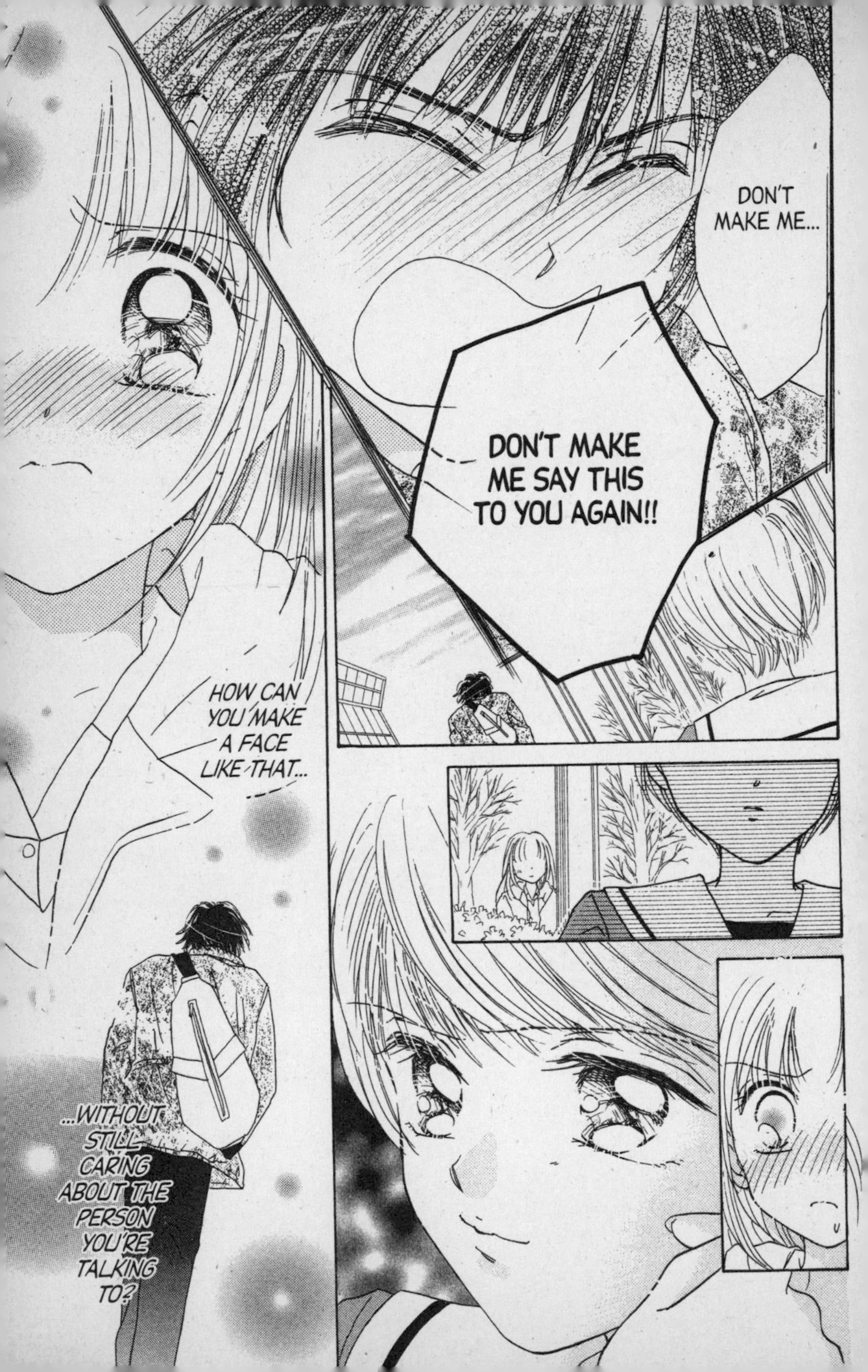
DON'T MAKE ME...
DON'T MAKE ME SAY THIS TO YOU AGAIN!!
HOW CAN YOU MAKE A FACE LIKE THAT...
...WITHOUT STILL CARING ABOUT THE PERSON YOU'RE TALKING TO?

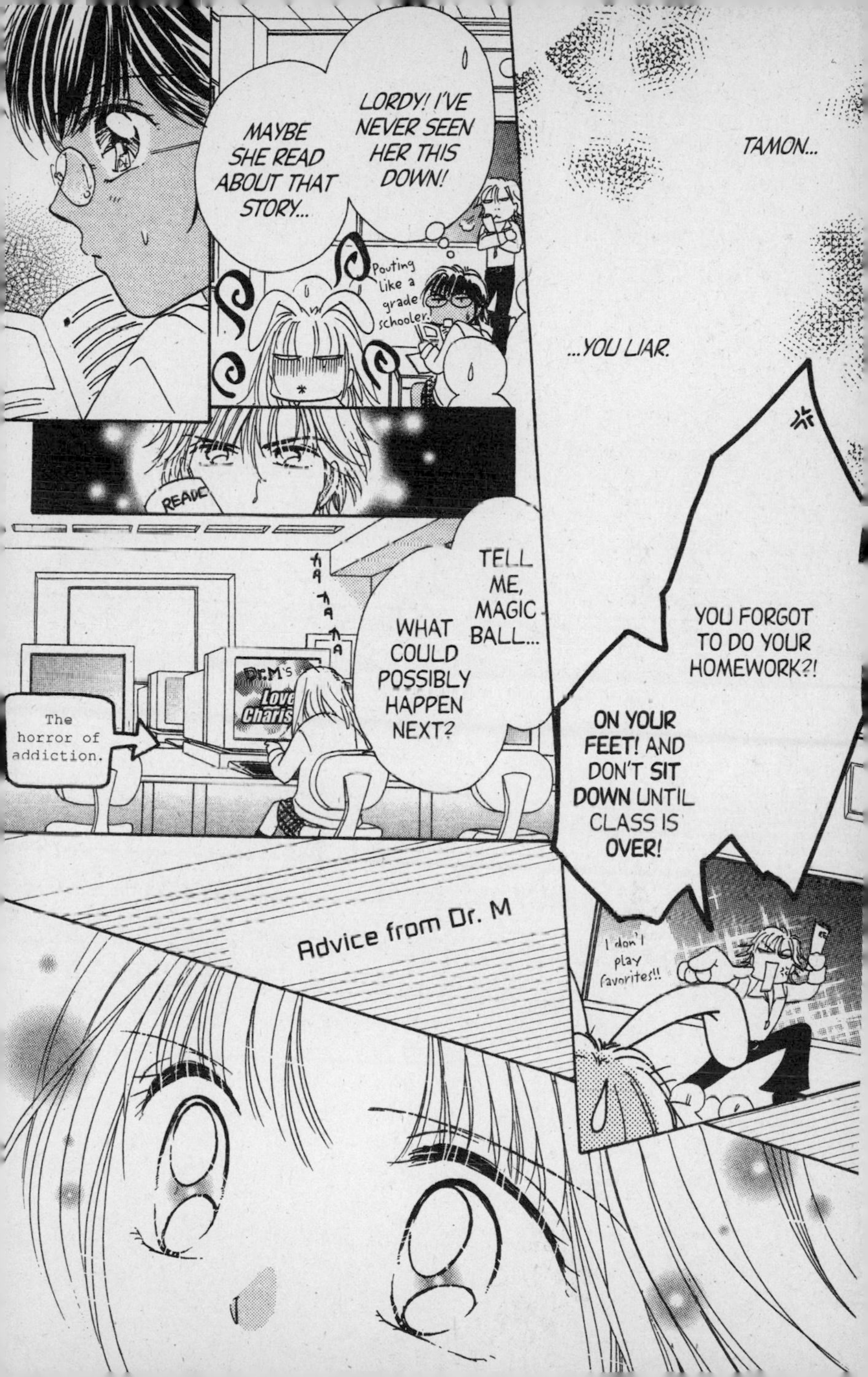
TAMON...
...YOU LIAR.
YOU FORGOT TO DO YOUR HOMEWORK?!
ON YOUR FEET! AND DON'T SIT DOWN UNTIL CLASS IS OVER!
I don't play favorites!!
LORDY! I'VE NEVER SEEN HER THIS DOWN!
MAYBE SHE READ ABOUT THAT STORY...
Pouting like a grade schooler.
TELL ME, MAGIC BALL...
WHAT COULD POSSIBLY HAPPEN NEXT?
The horror of addiction.
Advice from Dr. M

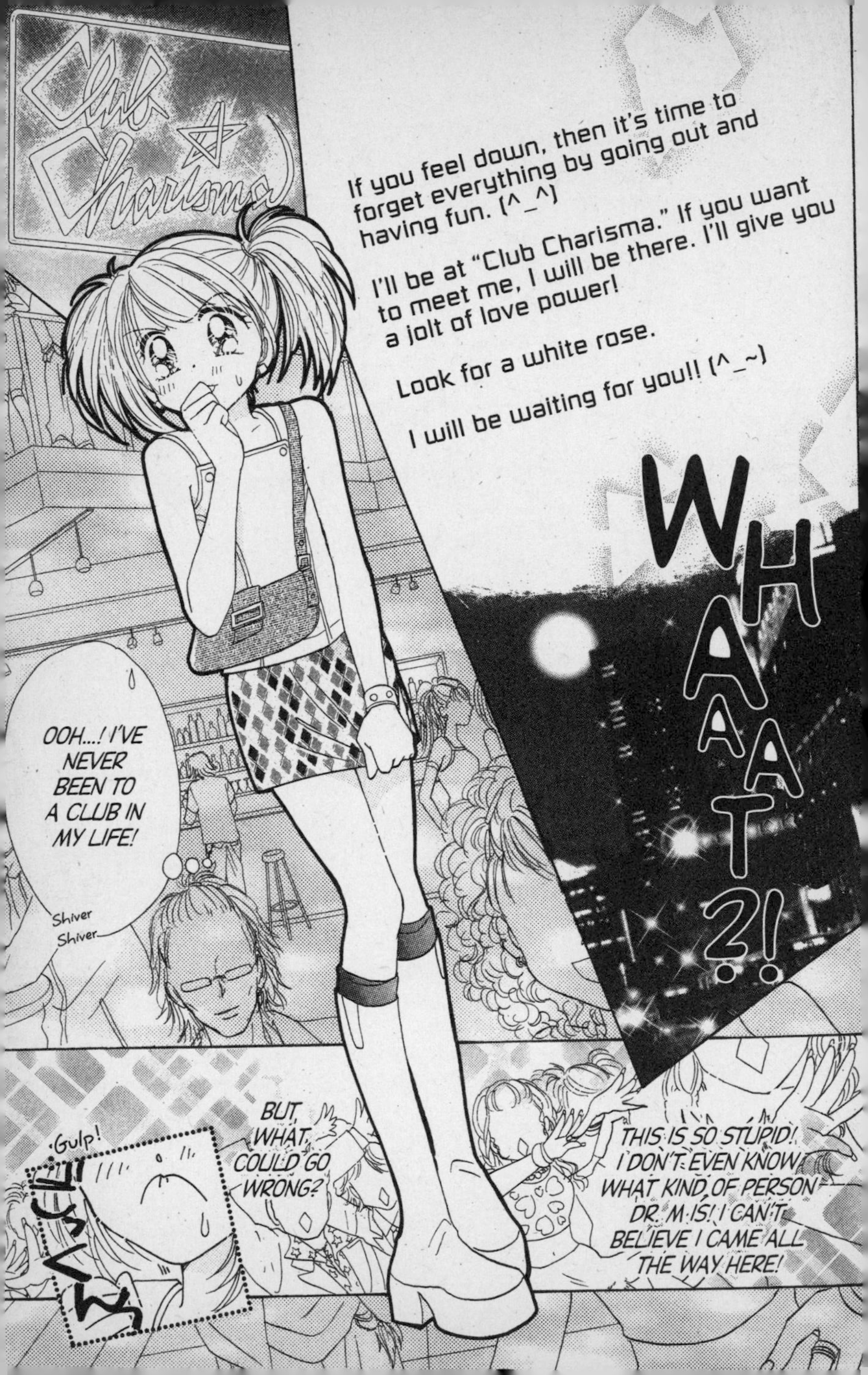
If you feel down, then it's time to forget everything by going out and having fun. (^_^)
I'll be at "Club Charisma." If you want to meet me, I will be there. I'll give you a jolt of love power!
Look for a white rose.
I will be waiting for you!! (^_~)
Club Charisma
WHAAAT?!
OOH...! I'VE NEVER BEEN TO A CLUB IN MY LIFE!
Shiver Shiver
THIS IS SO STUPID! I DON'T EVEN KNOW WHAT KIND OF PERSON DR. M IS! I CAN'T BELIEVE I CAME ALL THE WAY HERE!
BUT, WHAT COULD GO WRONG?
Gulp!

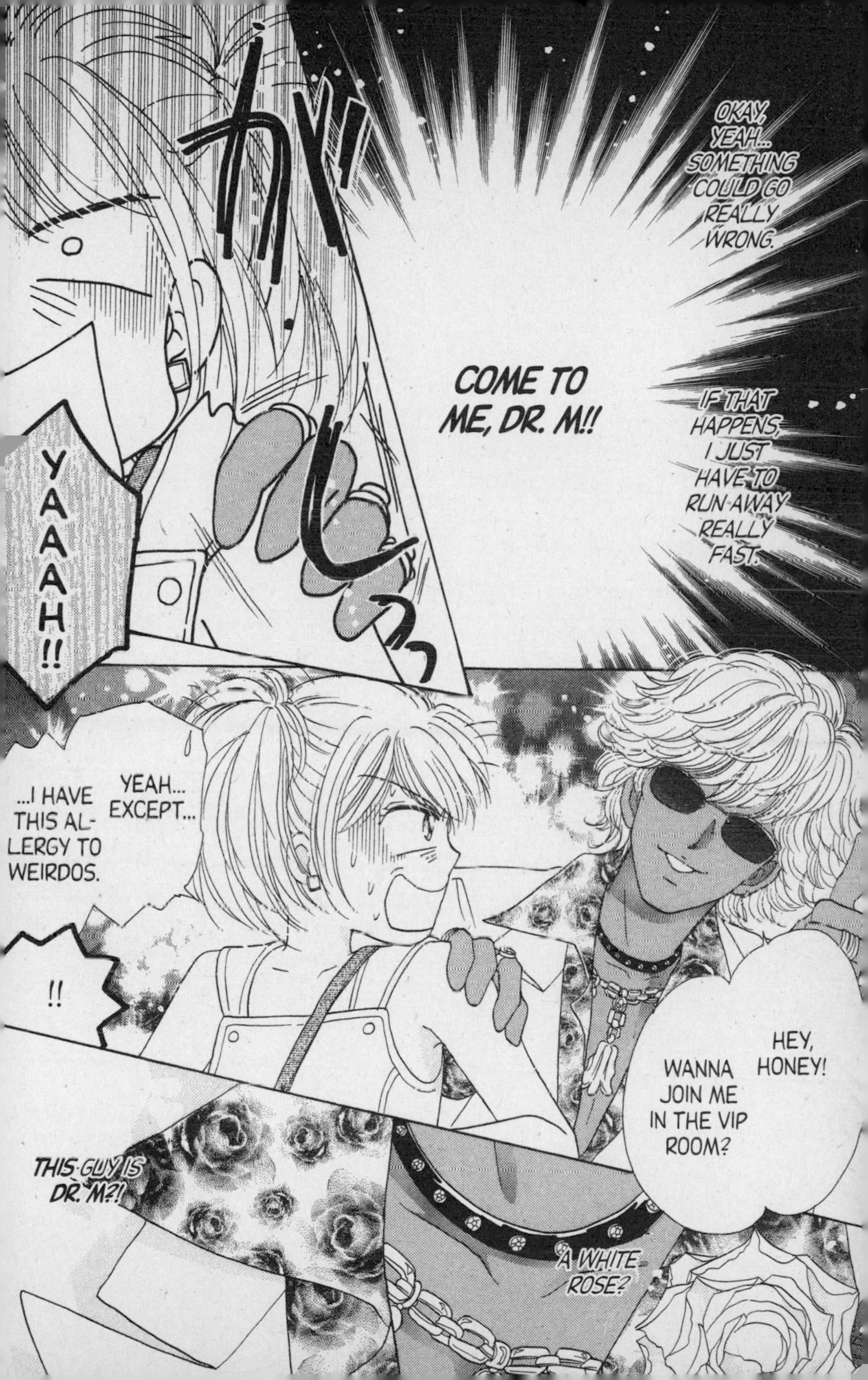
OKAY, YEAH... SOMETHING COULD GO REALLY WRONG.
IF THAT HAPPENS, I JUST HAVE TO RUN AWAY REALLY FAST.
COME TO ME, DR. M!!
YAAAAH!!
HEY, HONEY!
WANNA JOIN ME IN THE VIP ROOM?
YEAH... EXCEPT...
...I HAVE THIS AL-LERGY TO WEIRDOS.
!!
A WHITE ROSE?
THIS GUY IS DR. M?!

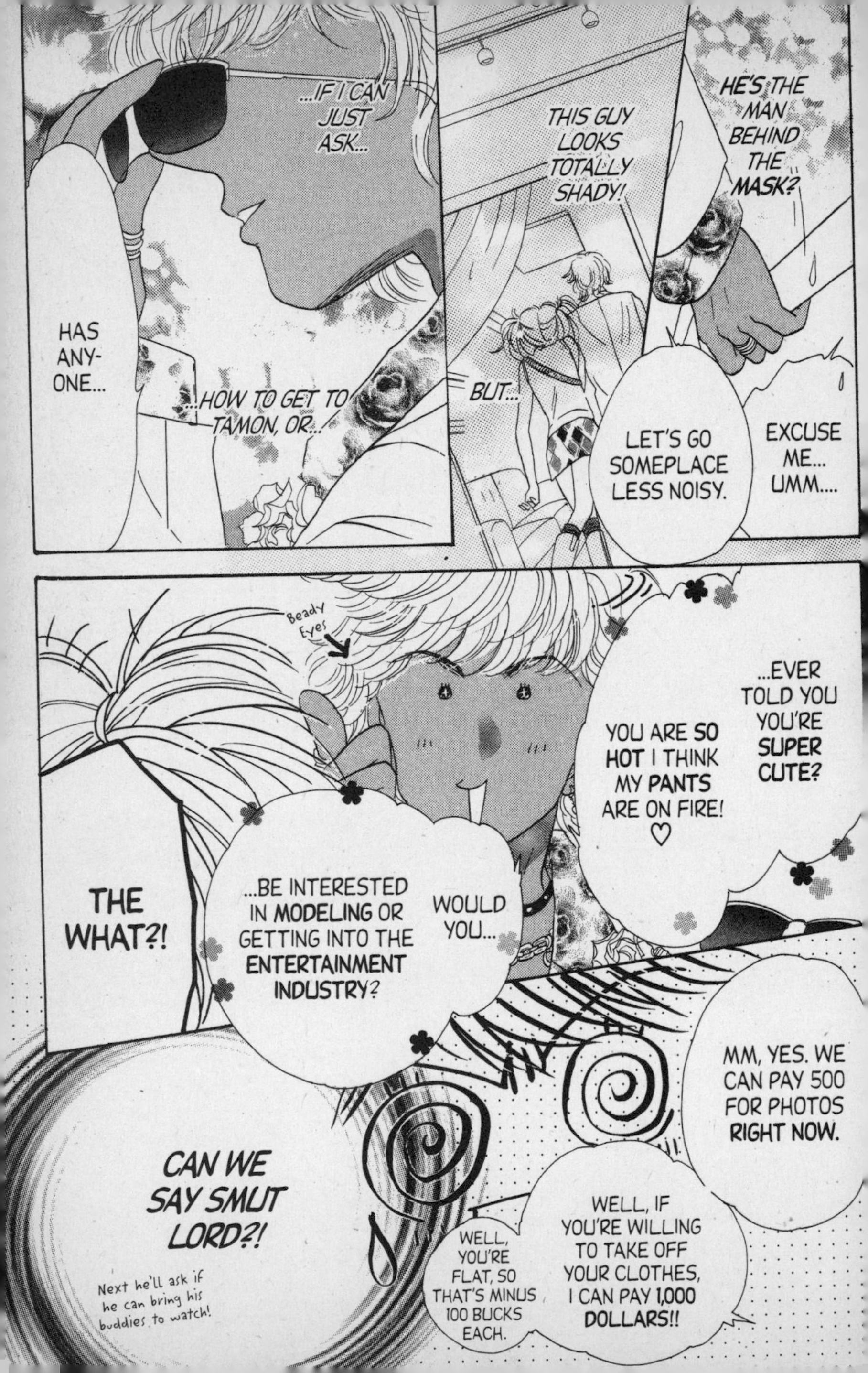
HE'S THE MAN BEHIND THE MASK?
EXCUSE ME... UMM....
THIS GUY LOOKS TOTALLY SHADY!
BUT...
LET'S GO SOMEPLACE LESS NOISY.
...IF I CAN JUST ASK...
HAS ANY-ONE...
...HOW TO GET TO TAMON, OR...
...EVER TOLD YOU YOU'RE SUPER CUTE?
YOU ARE SO HOT I THINK MY PANTS ARE ON FIRE! ♡
Beady Eyes
WOULD YOU...
...BE INTERESTED IN MODELING OR GETTING INTO THE ENTERTAINMENT INDUSTRY?
THE WHAT?!
MM, YES. WE CAN PAY 500 FOR PHOTOS RIGHT NOW.
WELL, IF YOU'RE WILLING TO TAKE OFF YOUR CLOTHES, I CAN PAY 1,000 DOLLARS!!
WELL, YOU'RE FLAT, SO THAT'S MINUS 100 BUCKS EACH.
CAN WE SAY SMUT LORD?!
Next he'll ask if he can bring his buddies to watch!

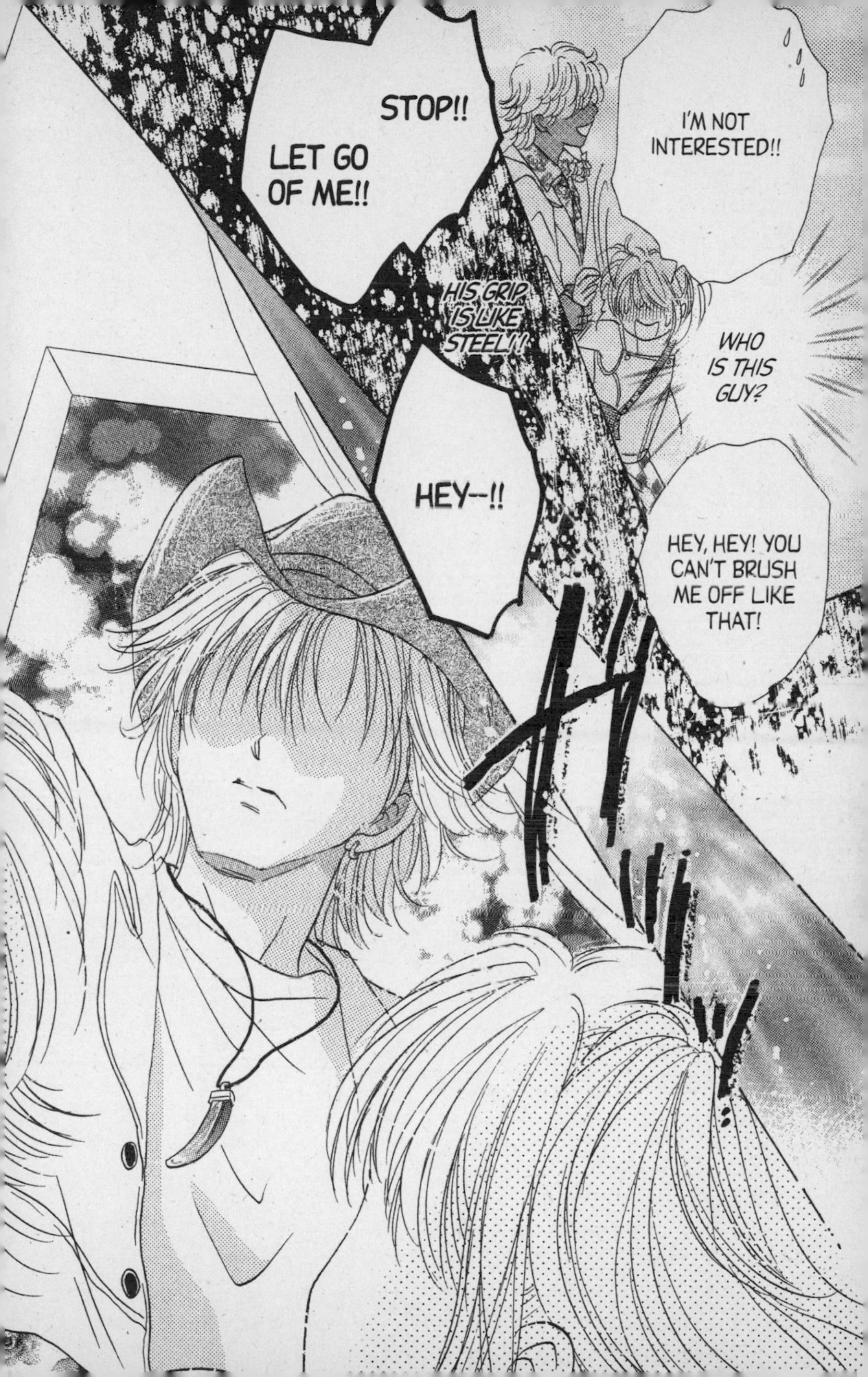
I'M NOT INTERESTED!!
WHO IS THIS GUY?
HEY, HEY! YOU CAN'T BRUSH ME OFF LIKE THAT!
STOP!!
LET GO OF ME!!
HIS GRIP IS LIKE STEEL!!
HEY--!!

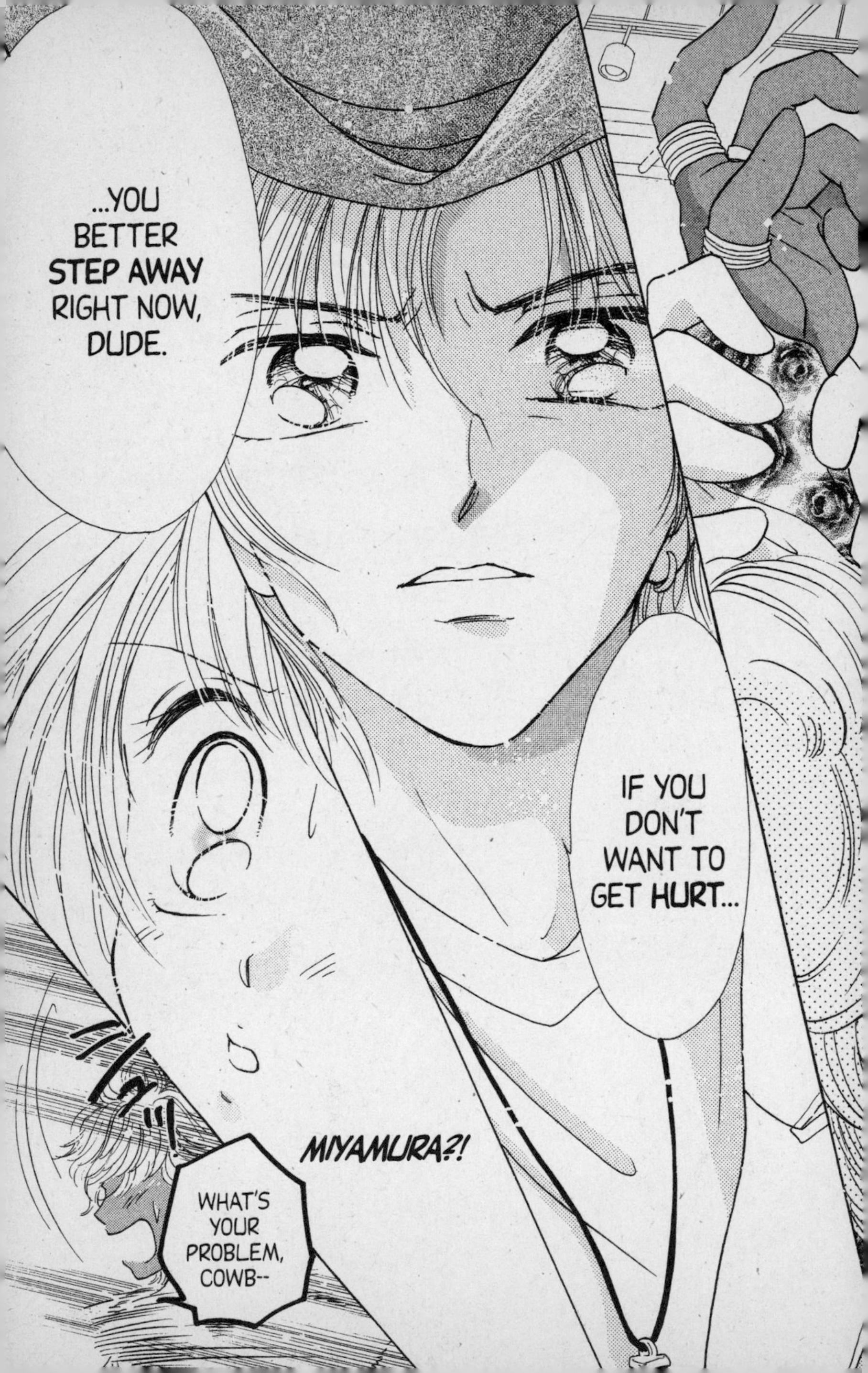
WHAT'S YOUR PROBLEM, COWB--
MIYAMURA?!
IF YOU DON'T WANT TO GET HURT...
...YOU BETTER STEP AWAY RIGHT NOW, DUDE.

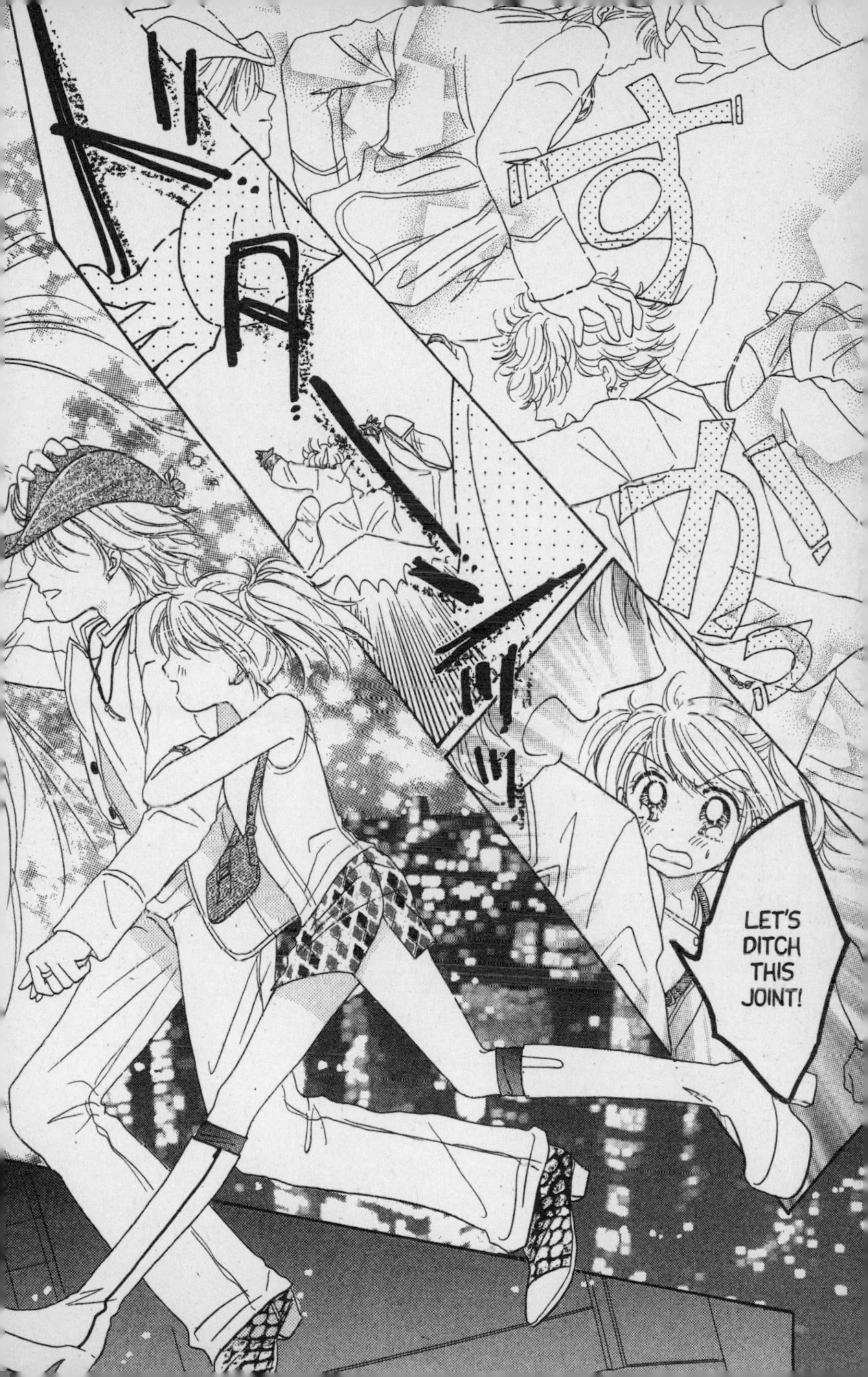
LET'S DITCH THIS JOINT!

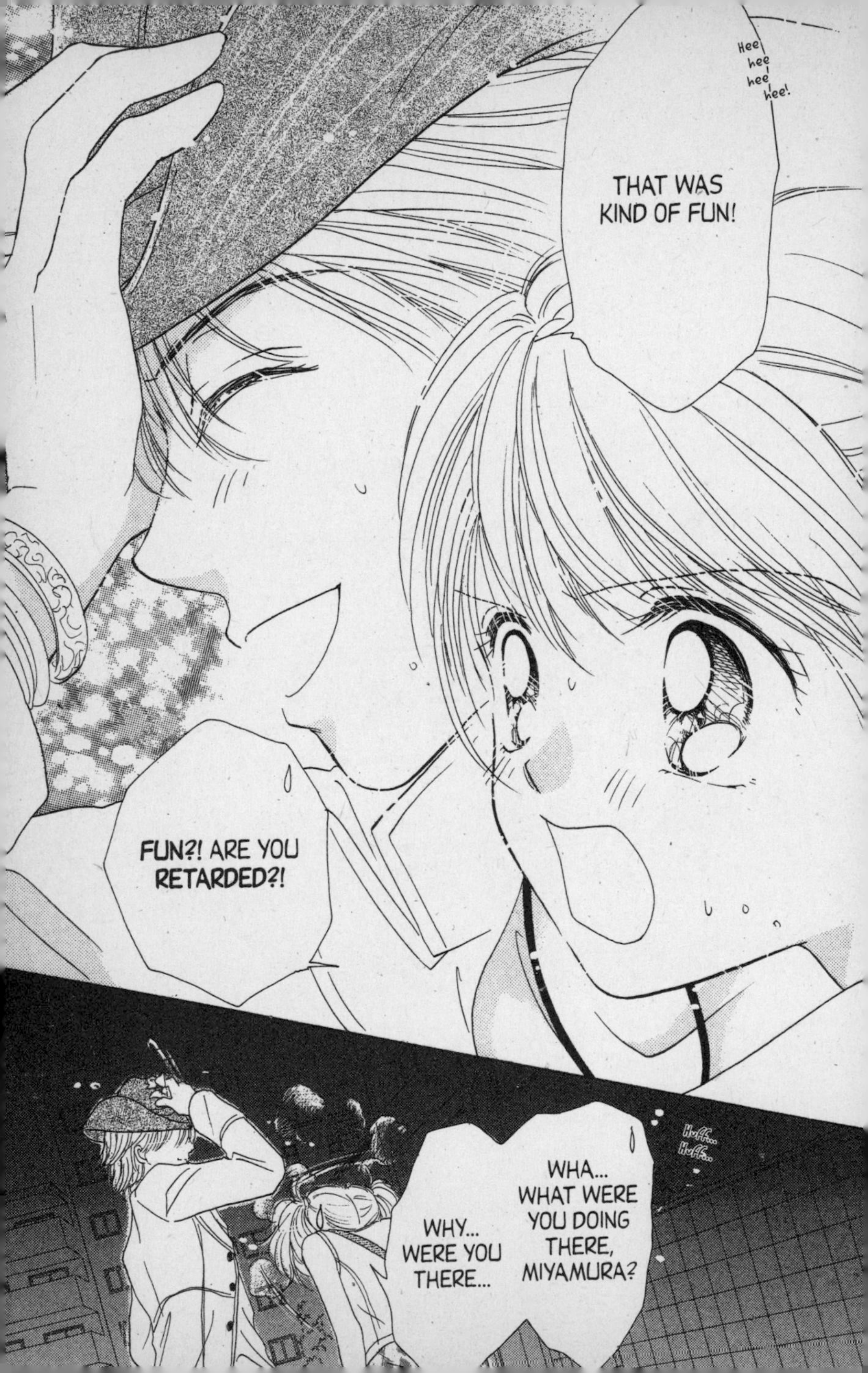
Hee hee hee hee!
THAT WAS KIND OF FUN!
FUN?! ARE YOU RETARDED?!
Huff... Huff...
WHA... WHAT WERE YOU DOING THERE, MIYAMURA?
WHY... WERE YOU THERE...

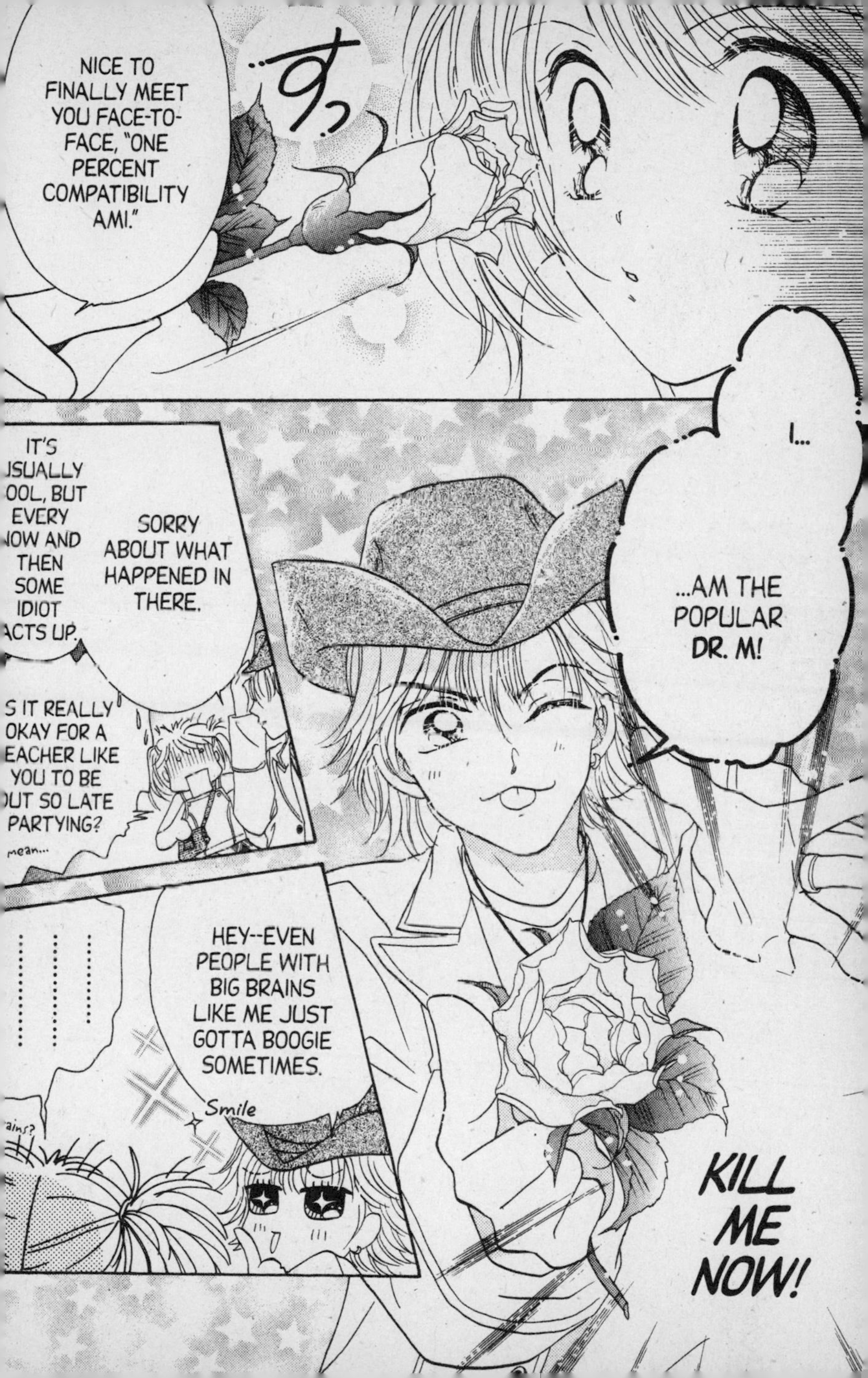
すっ
NICE TO FINALLY MEET YOU FACE-TO-FACE, "ONE PERCENT COMPATIBILITY AMI."
I...
...AM THE POPULAR DR. M!
KILL ME NOW!
SORRY ABOUT WHAT HAPPENED IN THERE.
IT'S SUALLY OOL, BUT EVERY OW AND THEN SOME IDIOT CTS UP.
S IT REALLY OKAY FOR A EACHER LIKE YOU TO BE UT SO LATE PARTYING?
mean...
HEY--EVEN PEOPLE WITH BIG BRAINS LIKE ME JUST GOTTA BOOGIE SOMETIMES.
......
Smile
ains?

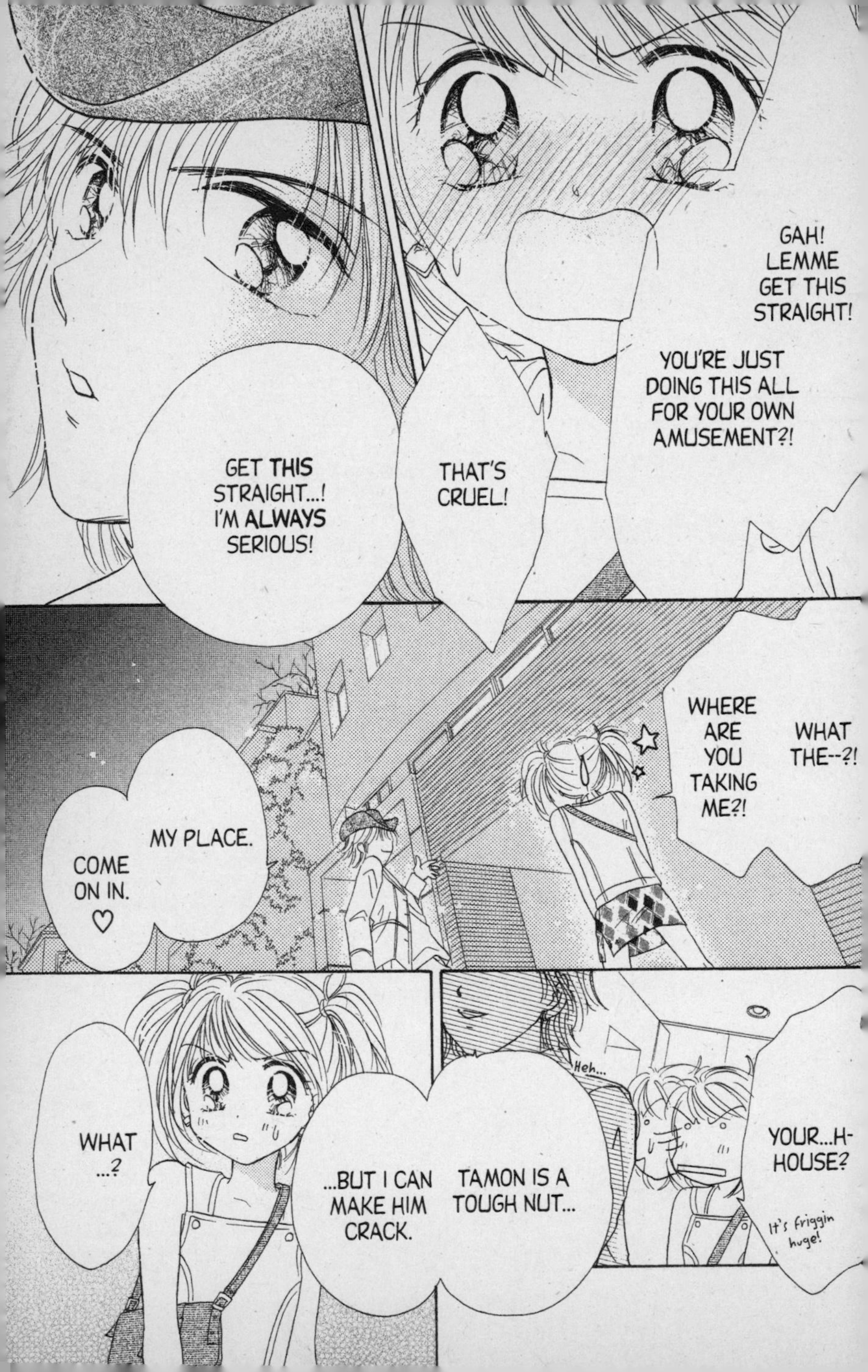
GAH! LEMME GET THIS STRAIGHT!
YOU'RE JUST DOING THIS ALL FOR YOUR OWN AMUSEMENT?!
THAT'S CRUEL!
GET THIS STRAIGHT...! I'M ALWAYS SERIOUS!
WHAT THE--?!
WHERE ARE YOU TAKING ME?!
MY PLACE.
COME ON IN. ♡
YOUR...H-HOUSE?
It's friggin huge!
Heh...
TAMON IS A TOUGH NUT...
...BUT I CAN MAKE HIM CRACK.
WHAT ...?

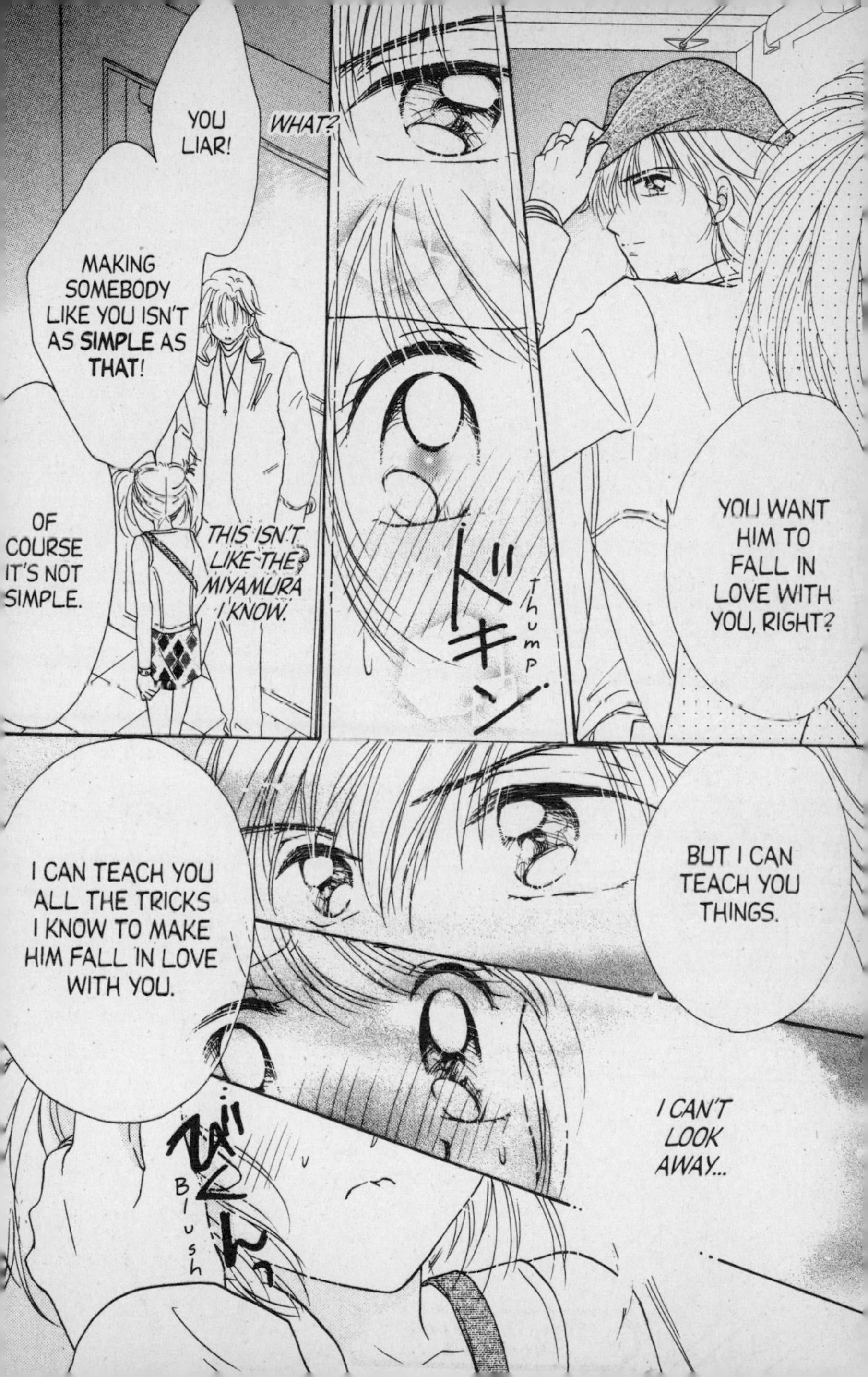
YOU WANT HIM TO FALL IN LOVE WITH YOU, RIGHT?
WHAT?
ドキン
THUMP
YOU LIAR!
MAKING SOMEBODY LIKE YOU ISN'T AS **SIMPLE** AS **THAT**!
THIS ISN'T LIKE THE MIYAMURA I KNOW.
OF COURSE IT'S NOT SIMPLE.
BUT I CAN TEACH YOU THINGS.
I CAN TEACH YOU ALL THE TRICKS I KNOW TO MAKE HIM FALL IN LOVE WITH YOU.
I CAN'T LOOK AWAY...
びくん
BLUSH

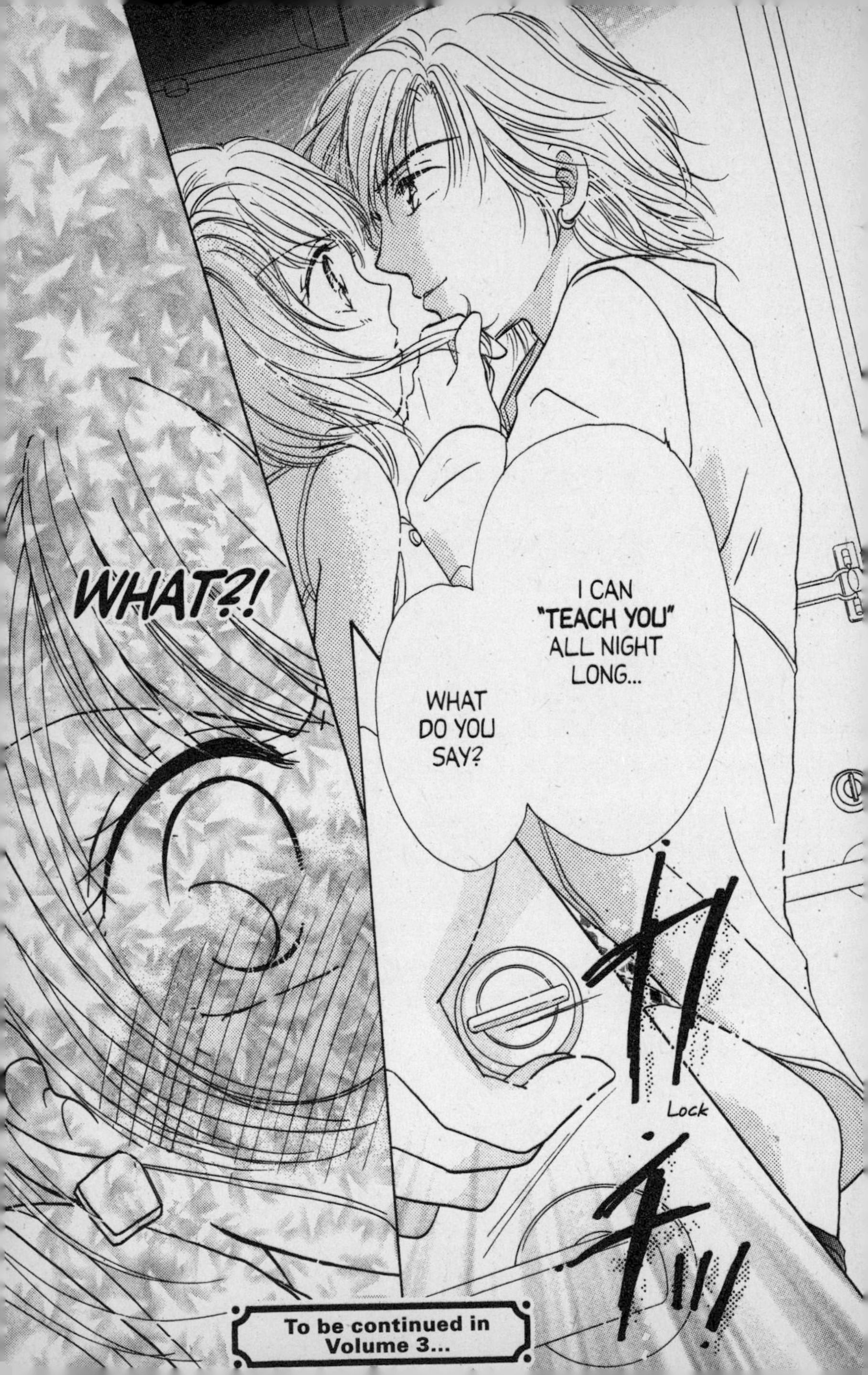
I CAN "TEACH YOU" ALL NIGHT LONG...
WHAT DO YOU SAY?
Lock
WHAT?!
To be continued in Volume 3...

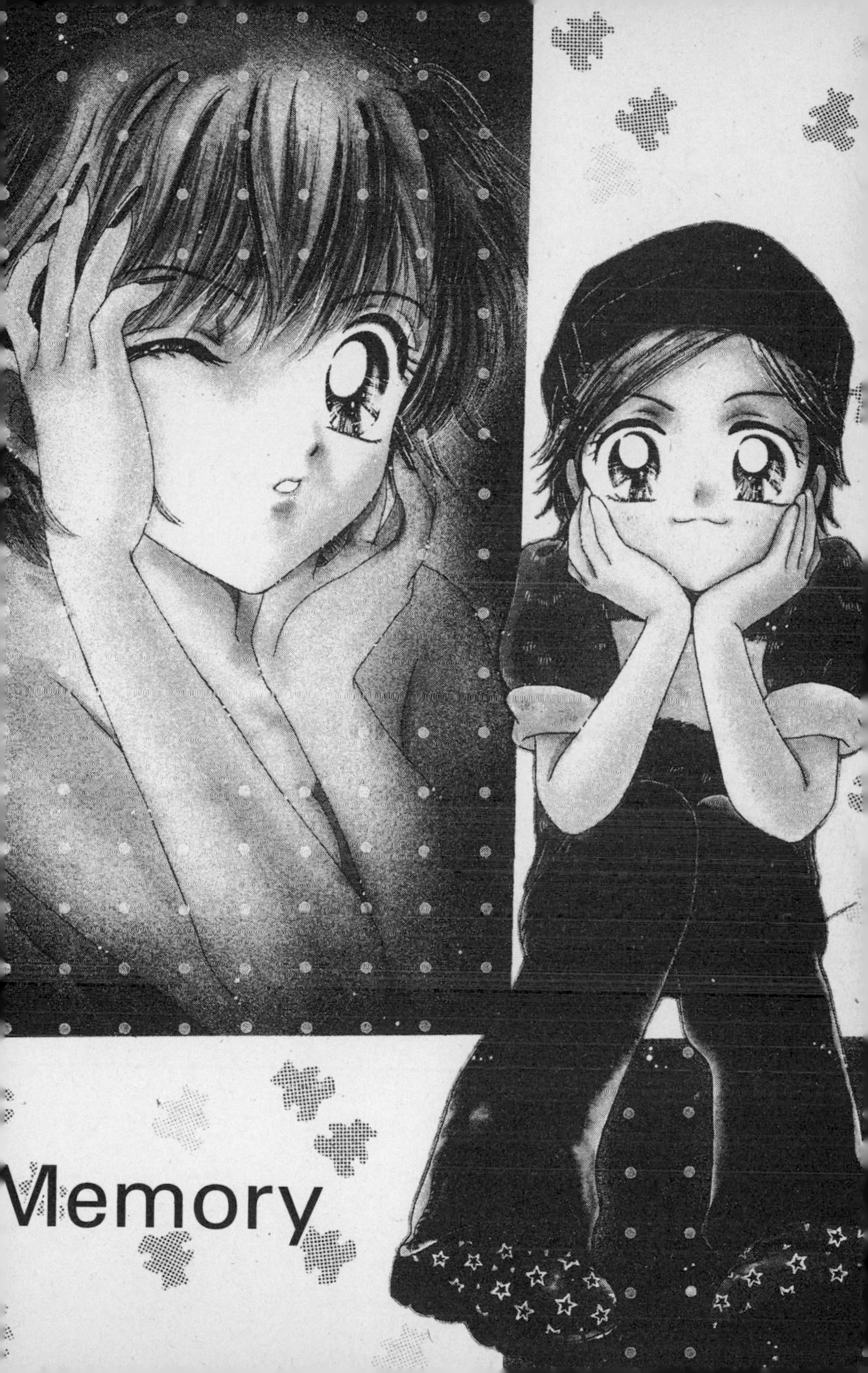
Memory

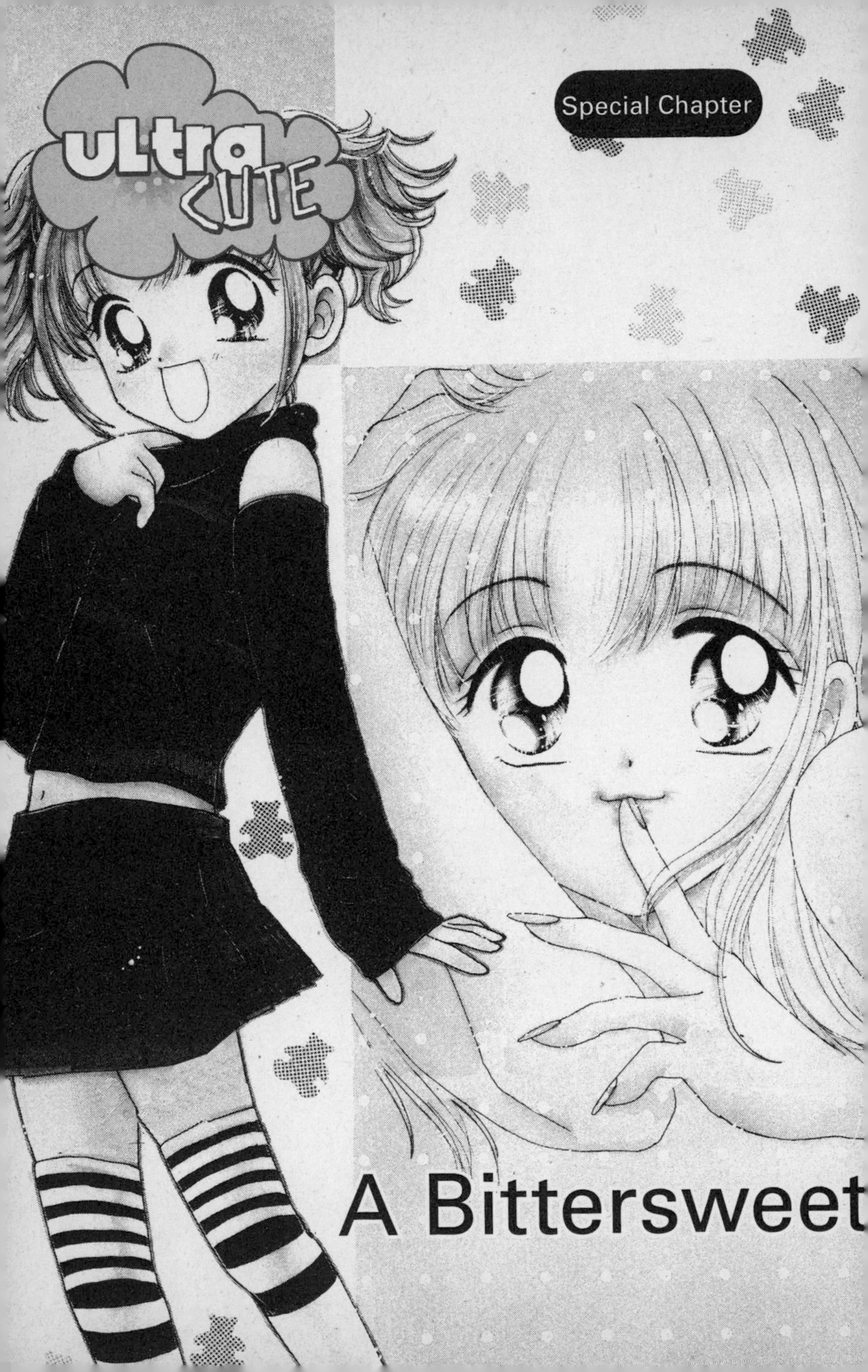
Ultra CUTE
Special Chapter
A Bittersweet

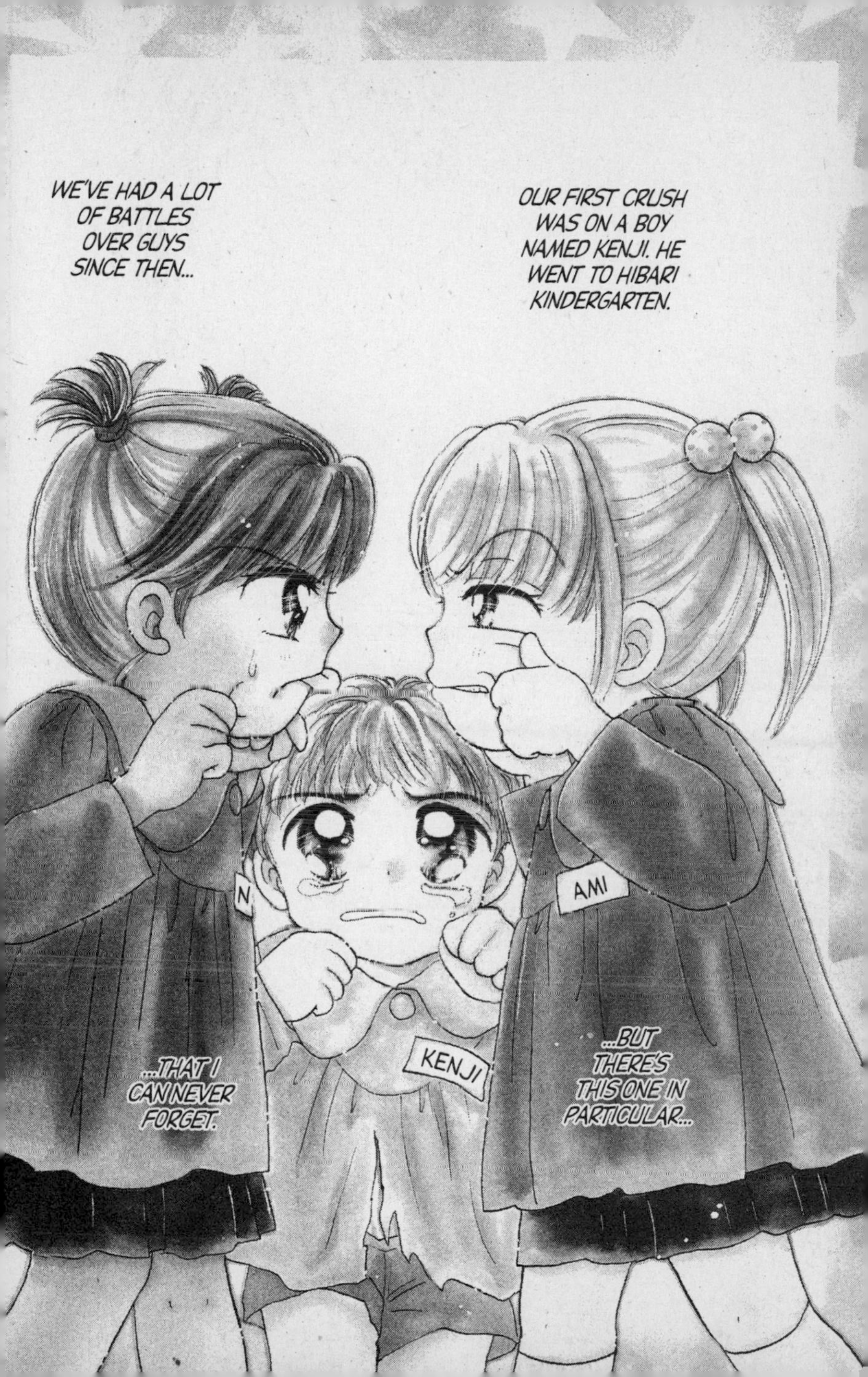
OUR FIRST CRUSH WAS ON A BOY NAMED KENJI. HE WENT TO HIBARI KINDERGARTEN.
WE'VE HAD A LOT OF BATTLES OVER GUYS SINCE THEN...
AMI
N
KENJI
...BUT THERE'S THIS ONE IN PARTICULAR...
...THAT I CAN NEVER FORGET.

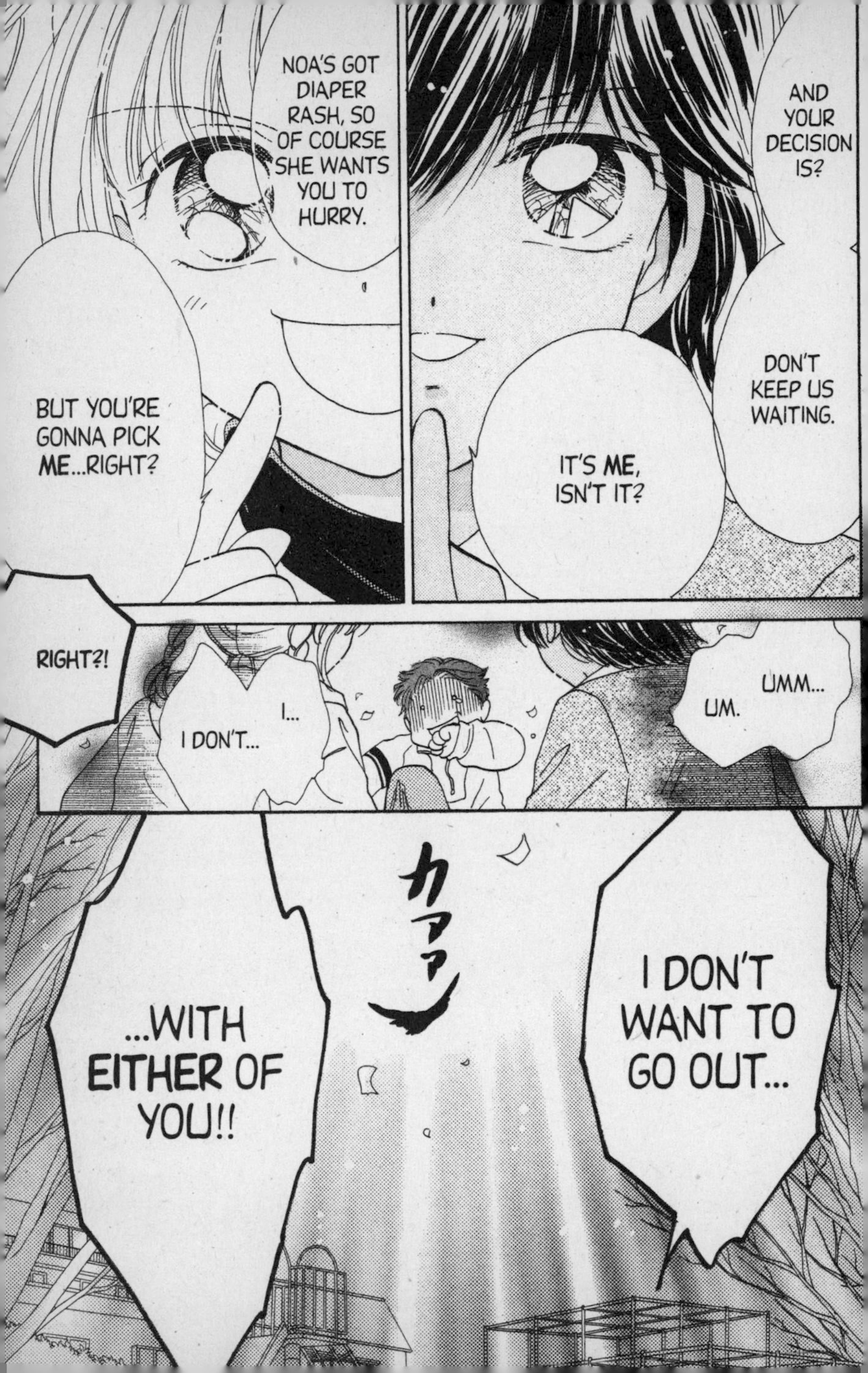
AND YOUR DECISION IS?
DON'T KEEP US WAITING.
IT'S ME, ISN'T IT?
NOA'S GOT DIAPER RASH, SO OF COURSE SHE WANTS YOU TO HURRY.
BUT YOU'RE GONNA PICK ME...RIGHT?
RIGHT?!
UMM...
UM.
I...
I DON'T...
I DON'T WANT TO GO OUT...
カァァ
...WITH EITHER OF YOU!!

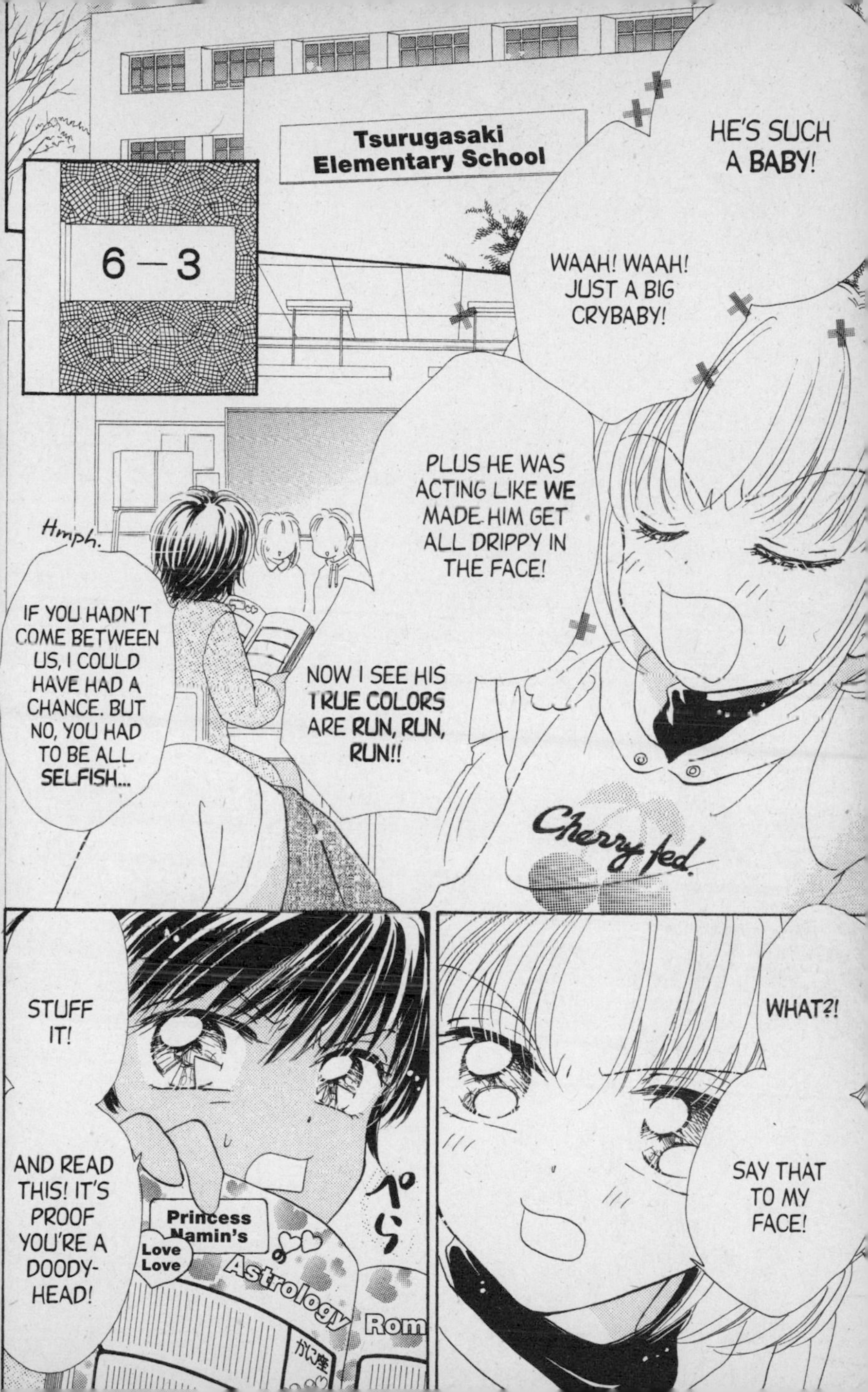
Tsurugasaki Elementary School
6—3
HE'S SUCH A BABY!
WAAH! WAAH! JUST A BIG CRYBABY!
PLUS HE WAS ACTING LIKE WE MADE HIM GET ALL DRIPPY IN THE FACE!
NOW I SEE HIS TRUE COLORS ARE RUN, RUN, RUN!!
Cherry fed.
Hmph.
IF YOU HADN'T COME BETWEEN US, I COULD HAVE HAD A CHANCE. BUT NO, YOU HAD TO BE ALL SELFISH...
WHAT?!
SAY THAT TO MY FACE!
STUFF IT!
AND READ THIS! IT'S PROOF YOU'RE A DOODY-HEAD!
ぺら
Princess Namin's
Love Love
Astrology Rom
かに座

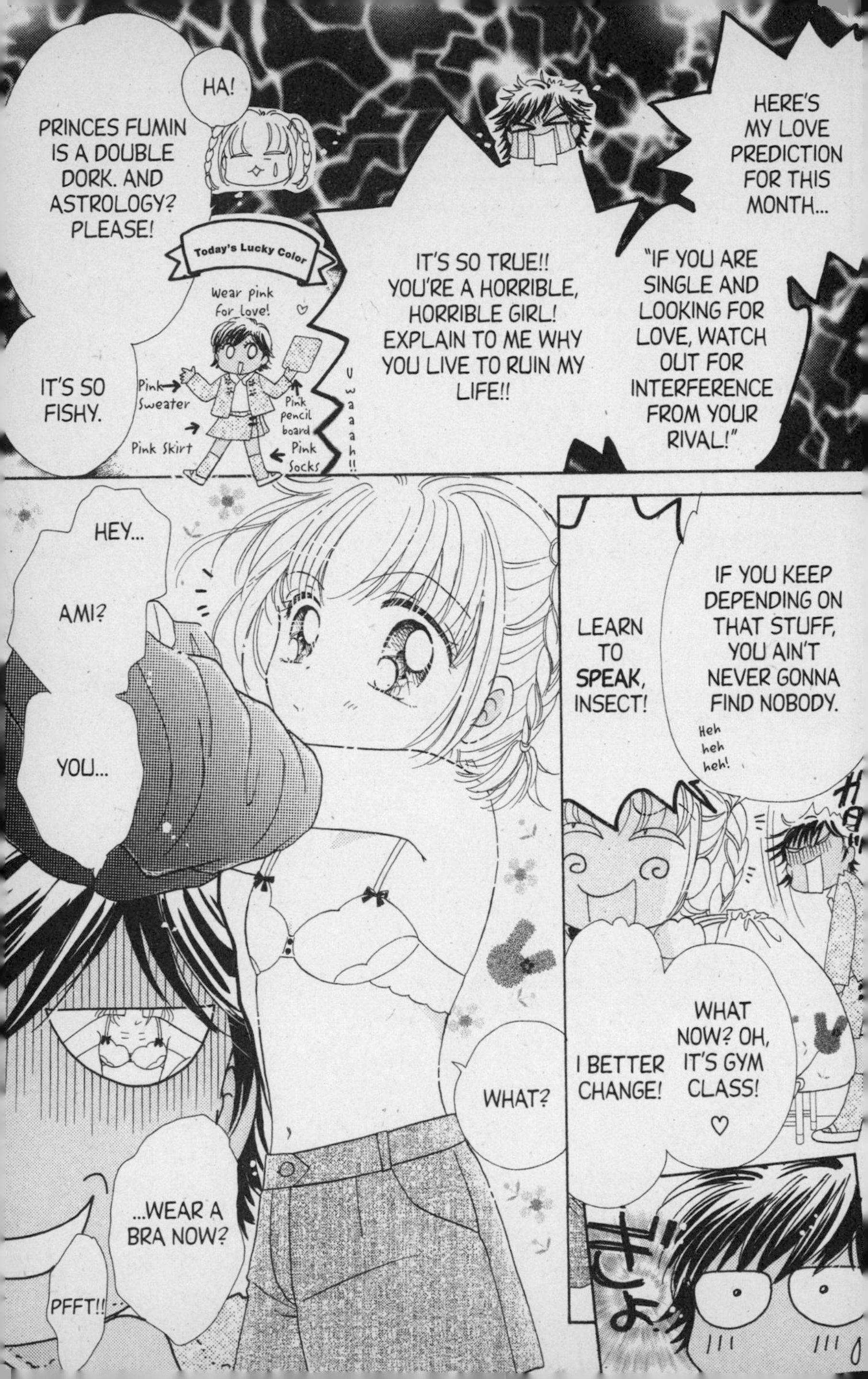
HERE'S MY LOVE PREDICTION FOR THIS MONTH...
"IF YOU ARE SINGLE AND LOOKING FOR LOVE, WATCH OUT FOR INTERFERENCE FROM YOUR RIVAL!"
IT'S SO TRUE!! YOU'RE A HORRIBLE, HORRIBLE GIRL! EXPLAIN TO ME WHY YOU LIVE TO RUIN MY LIFE!!
Uwaaaah!!
HA!
PRINCES FUMIN IS A DOUBLE DORK. AND ASTROLOGY? PLEASE!
Today's Lucky Color
Wear pink for Love!
Pink Sweater
Pink pencil board
Pink Skirt
Pink Socks
IT'S SO FISHY.
IF YOU KEEP DEPENDING ON THAT STUFF, YOU AIN'T NEVER GONNA FIND NOBODY.
LEARN TO SPEAK, INSECT!
Heh heh heh!
WHAT NOW? OH, IT'S GYM CLASS!
I BETTER CHANGE!
WHAT?
HEY...
AMI?
YOU...
...WEAR A BRA NOW?
PFFT!!

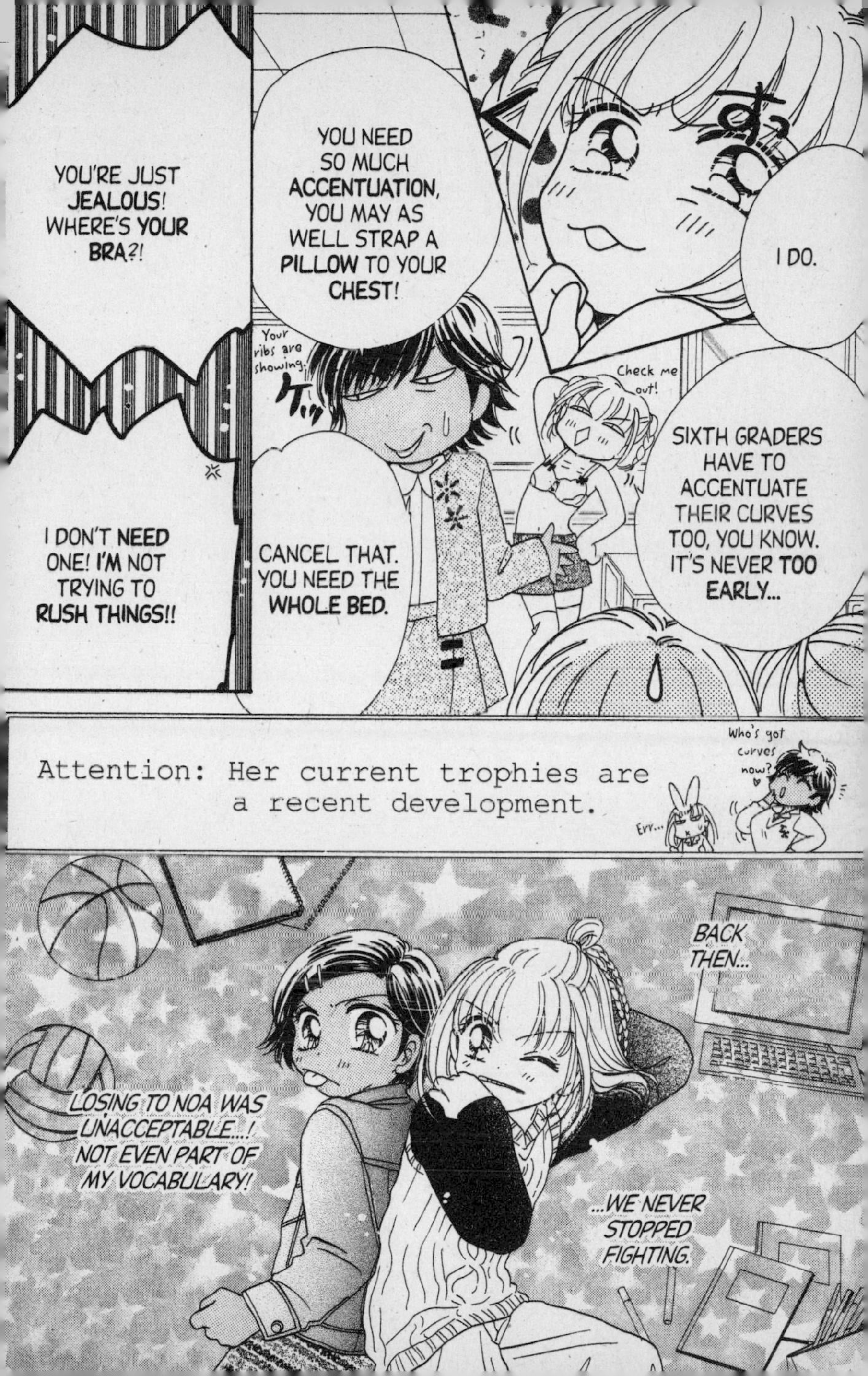
すっ
I DO.
Check me out!
SIXTH GRADERS HAVE TO ACCENTUATE THEIR CURVES TOO, YOU KNOW. IT'S NEVER TOO EARLY...
YOU NEED SO MUCH ACCENTUATION, YOU MAY AS WELL STRAP A PILLOW TO YOUR CHEST!
Your ribs are showing.
ケッ
CANCEL THAT. YOU NEED THE WHOLE BED.
YOU'RE JUST JEALOUS! WHERE'S YOUR BRA?!
I DON'T NEED ONE! I'M NOT TRYING TO RUSH THINGS!!
Attention: Her current trophies are a recent development.
Who's got curves now?
Err...
BACK THEN...
...WE NEVER STOPPED FIGHTING.
LOSING TO NOA WAS UNACCEPTABLE...! NOT EVEN PART OF MY VOCABULARY!

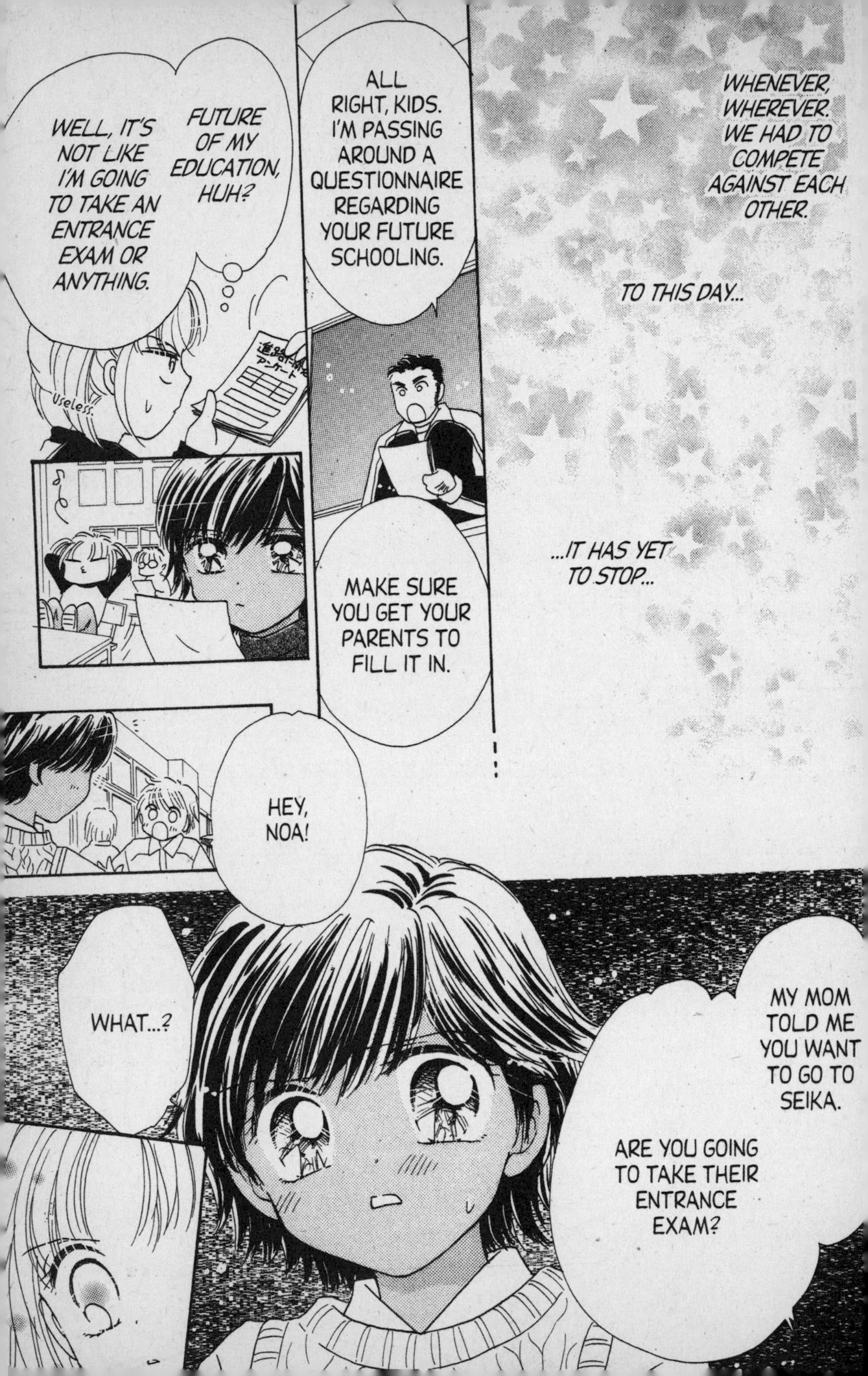
WHENEVER, WHEREVER. WE HAD TO COMPETE AGAINST EACH OTHER.
TO THIS DAY...
...IT HAS YET TO STOP...
ALL RIGHT, KIDS. I'M PASSING AROUND A QUESTIONNAIRE REGARDING YOUR FUTURE SCHOOLING.
MAKE SURE YOU GET YOUR PARENTS TO FILL IT IN.
FUTURE OF MY EDUCATION, HUH?
WELL, IT'S NOT LIKE I'M GOING TO TAKE AN ENTRANCE EXAM OR ANYTHING.
Useless.
HEY, NOA!
MY MOM TOLD ME YOU WANT TO GO TO SEIKA.
ARE YOU GOING TO TAKE THEIR ENTRANCE EXAM?
WHAT...?

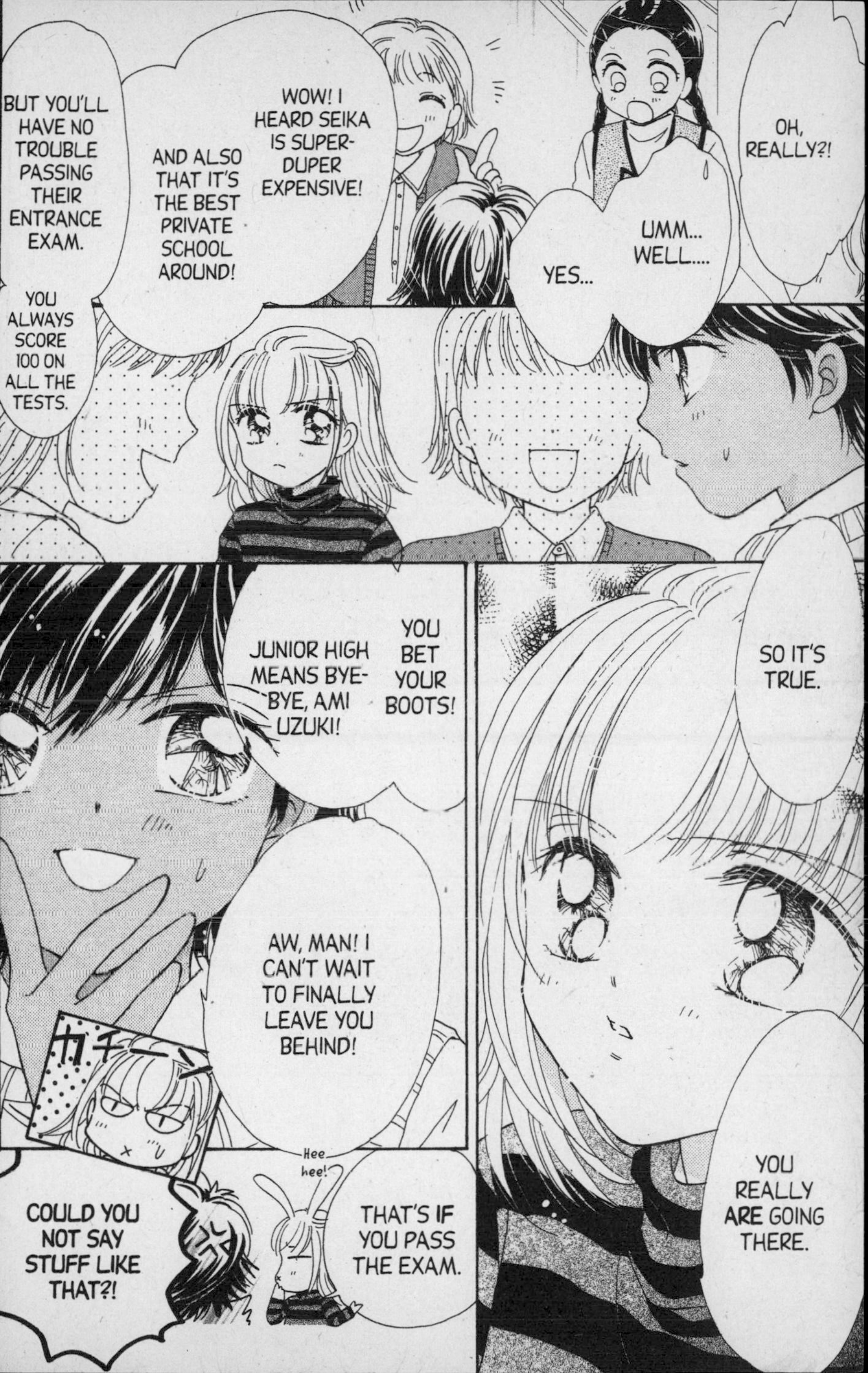
OH, REALLY?!
UMM... WELL....
YES...
WOW! I HEARD SEIKA IS SUPER-DUPER EXPENSIVE!
AND ALSO THAT IT'S THE BEST PRIVATE SCHOOL AROUND!
BUT YOU'LL HAVE NO TROUBLE PASSING THEIR ENTRANCE EXAM.
YOU ALWAYS SCORE 100 ON ALL THE TESTS.
SO IT'S TRUE.
YOU REALLY ARE GOING THERE.
YOU BET YOUR BOOTS!
JUNIOR HIGH MEANS BYE-BYE, AMI UZUKI!
AW, MAN! I CAN'T WAIT TO FINALLY LEAVE YOU BEHIND!
カチーン
THAT'S IF YOU PASS THE EXAM.
Hee hee!
COULD YOU NOT SAY STUFF LIKE THAT?!

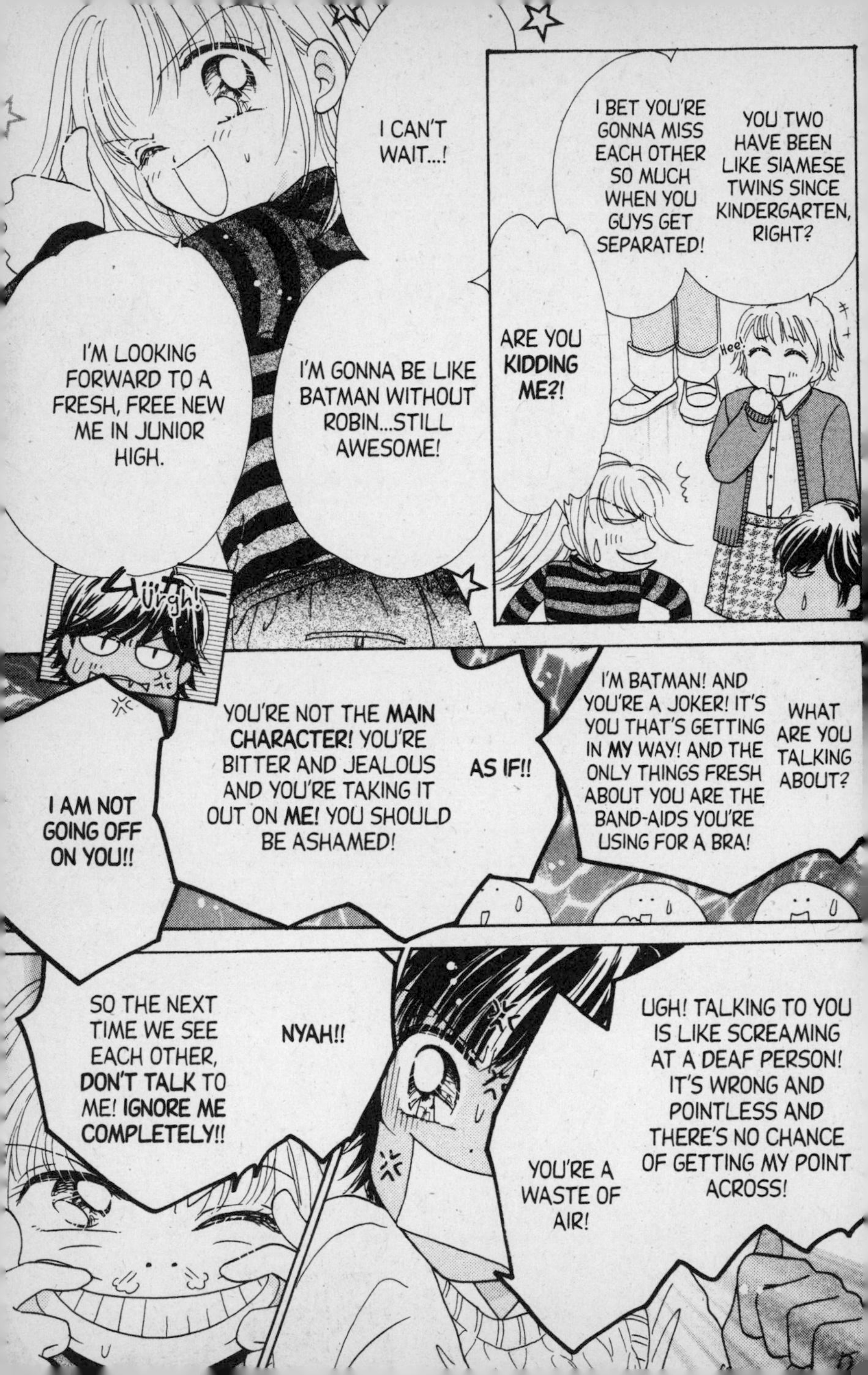
YOU TWO HAVE BEEN LIKE SIAMESE TWINS SINCE KINDERGARTEN, RIGHT?
I BET YOU'RE GONNA MISS EACH OTHER SO MUCH WHEN YOU GUYS GET SEPARATED!
Hee!
ARE YOU KIDDING ME?!
I CAN'T WAIT...!
I'M GONNA BE LIKE BATMAN WITHOUT ROBIN...STILL AWESOME!
I'M LOOKING FORWARD TO A FRESH, FREE NEW ME IN JUNIOR HIGH.
Urgh!
WHAT ARE YOU TALKING ABOUT?
I'M BATMAN! AND YOU'RE A JOKER! IT'S YOU THAT'S GETTING IN MY WAY! AND THE ONLY THINGS FRESH ABOUT YOU ARE THE BAND-AIDS YOU'RE USING FOR A BRA!
AS IF!!
YOU'RE NOT THE MAIN CHARACTER! YOU'RE BITTER AND JEALOUS AND YOU'RE TAKING IT OUT ON ME! YOU SHOULD BE ASHAMED!
I AM NOT GOING OFF ON YOU!!
UGH! TALKING TO YOU IS LIKE SCREAMING AT A DEAF PERSON! IT'S WRONG AND POINTLESS AND THERE'S NO CHANCE OF GETTING MY POINT ACROSS!
YOU'RE A WASTE OF AIR!
NYAH!!
SO THE NEXT TIME WE SEE EACH OTHER, DON'T TALK TO ME! IGNORE ME COMPLETELY!!

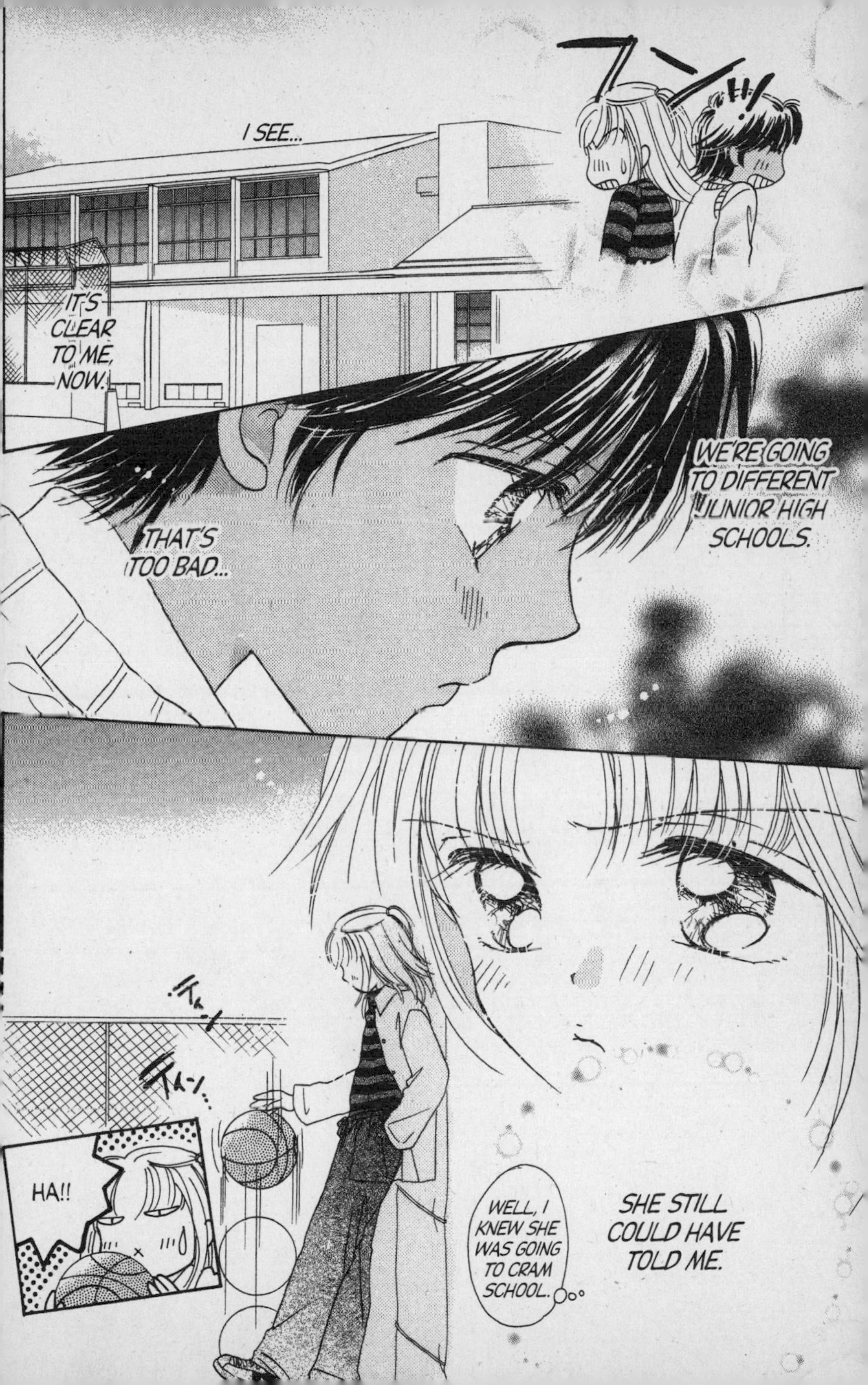
I SEE...
IT'S CLEAR TO ME, NOW.
WE'RE GOING TO DIFFERENT JUNIOR HIGH SCHOOLS.
THAT'S TOO BAD...
SHE STILL COULD HAVE TOLD ME.
WELL, I KNEW SHE WAS GOING TO CRAM SCHOOL.
HA!!

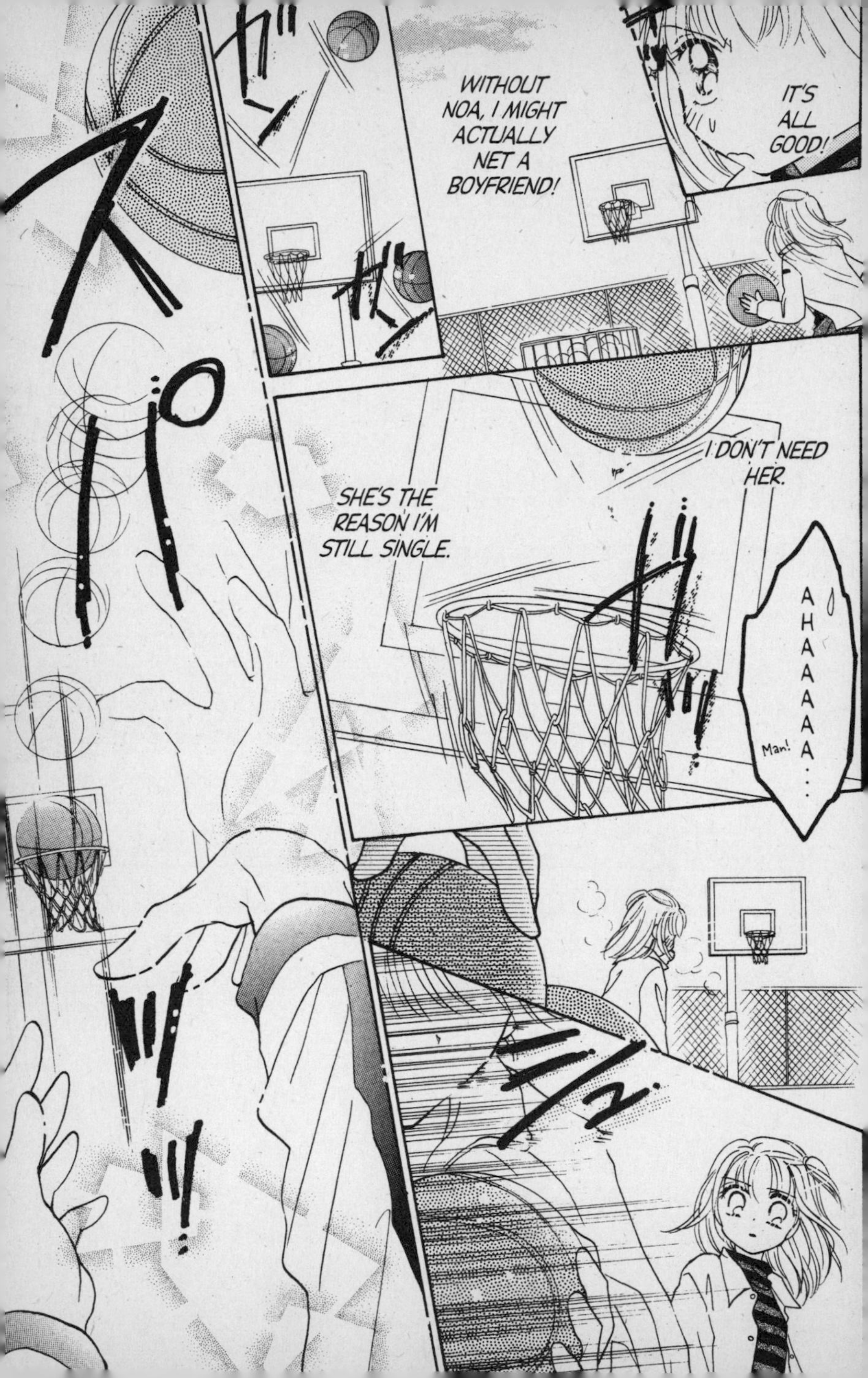
IT'S ALL GOOD!
WITHOUT NOA, I MIGHT ACTUALLY NET A BOYFRIEND!
I DON'T NEED HER.
SHE'S THE REASON I'M STILL SINGLE.
AHAAAAAA...
Man!

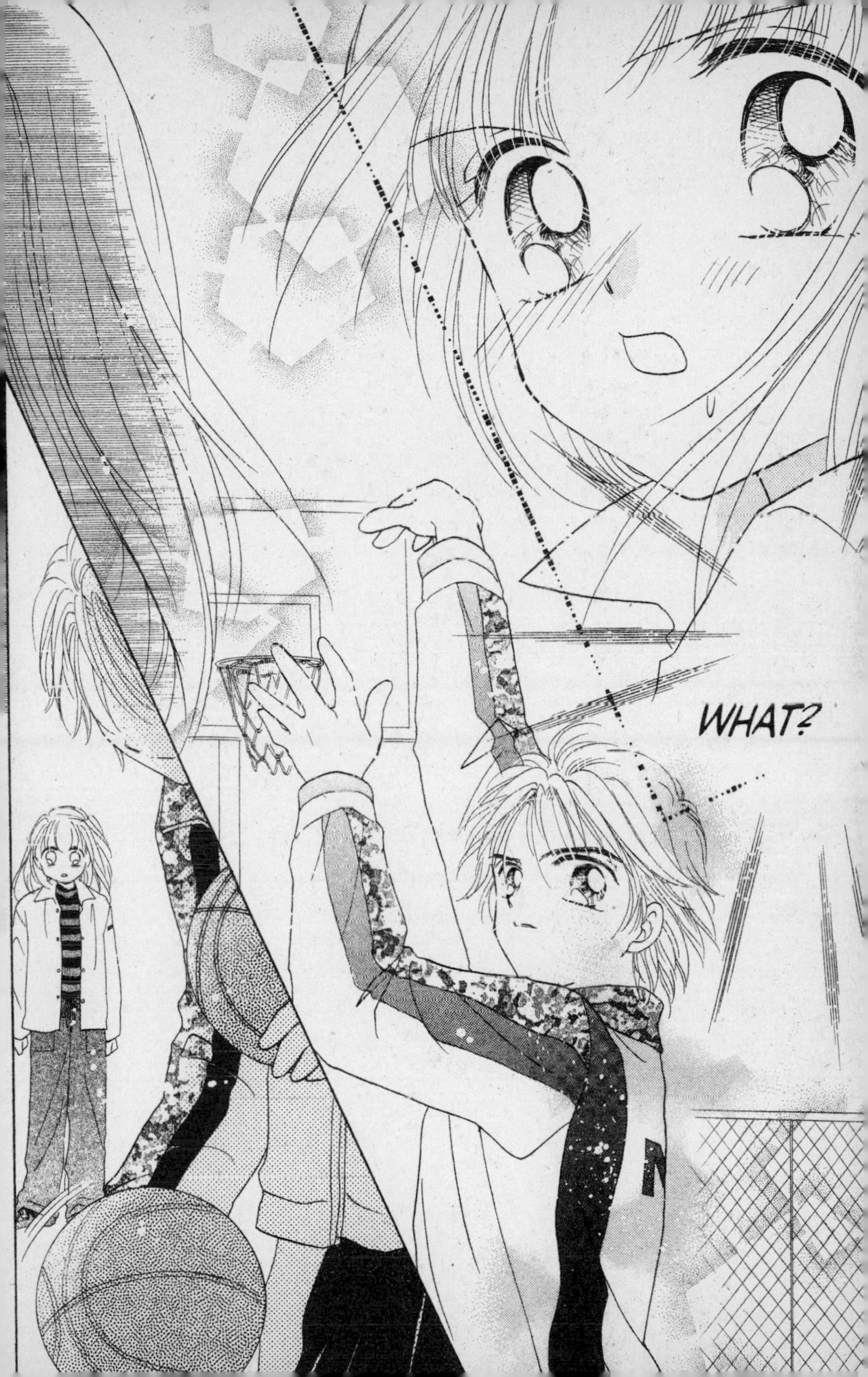
WHAT?

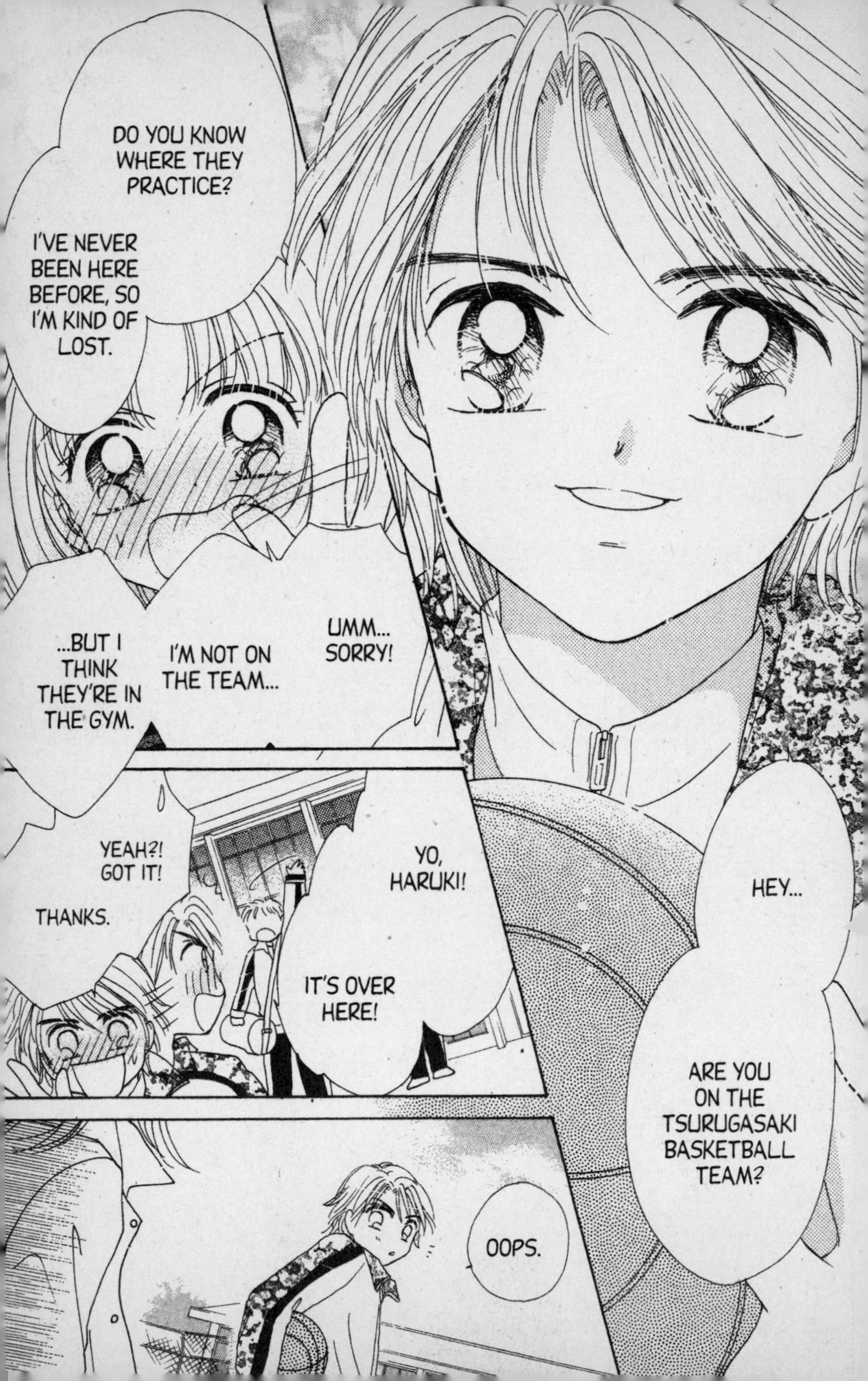
HEY...
ARE YOU ON THE TSURUGASAKI BASKETBALL TEAM?
DO YOU KNOW WHERE THEY PRACTICE?
I'VE NEVER BEEN HERE BEFORE, SO I'M KIND OF LOST.
UMM... SORRY!
I'M NOT ON THE TEAM...
...BUT I THINK THEY'RE IN THE GYM.
YO, HARUKI!
IT'S OVER HERE!
YEAH?! GOT IT!
THANKS.
OOPS.

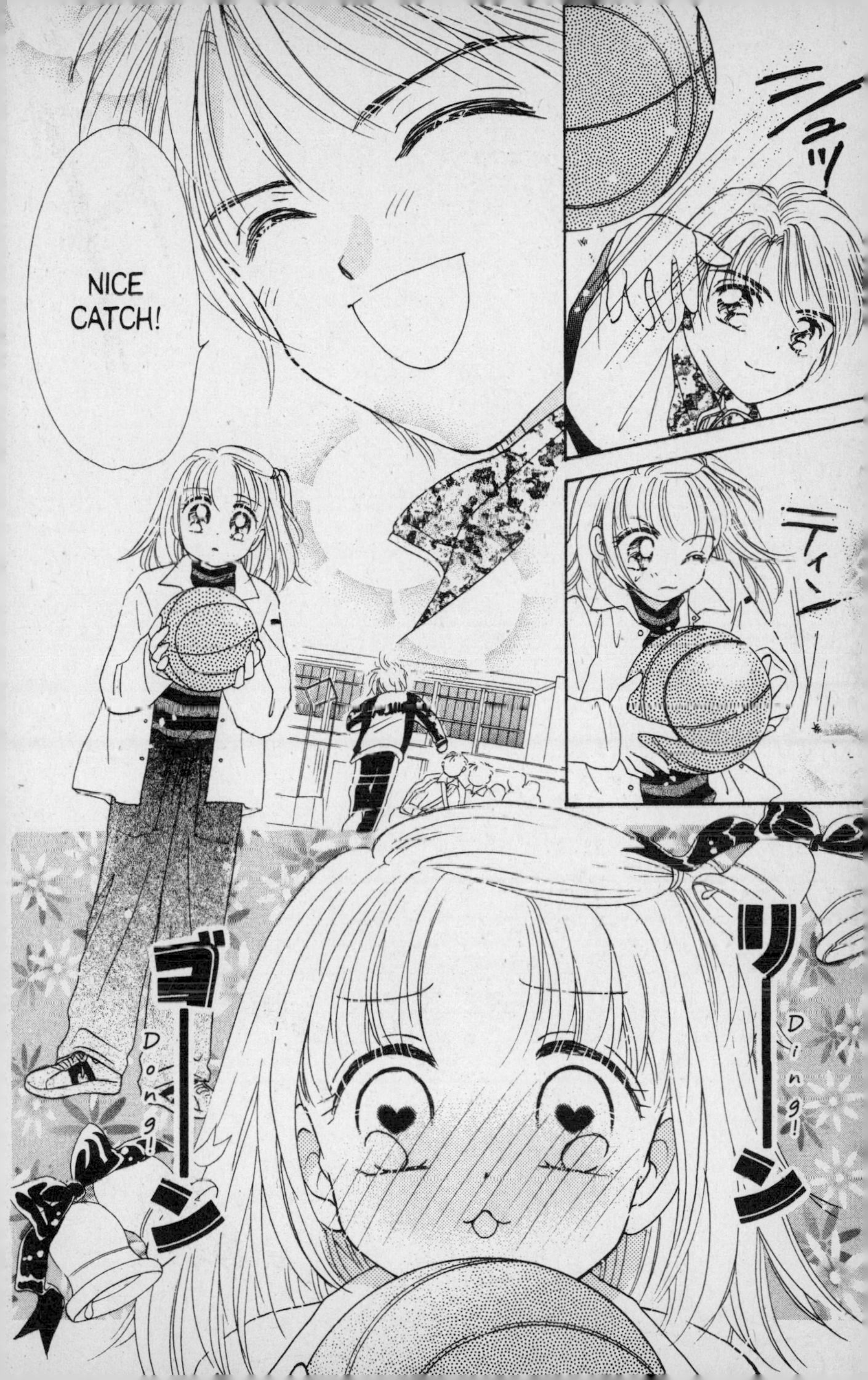

シュッ!
ティン
NICE CATCH!
リーン
Ding!
ゴーン
Dong!

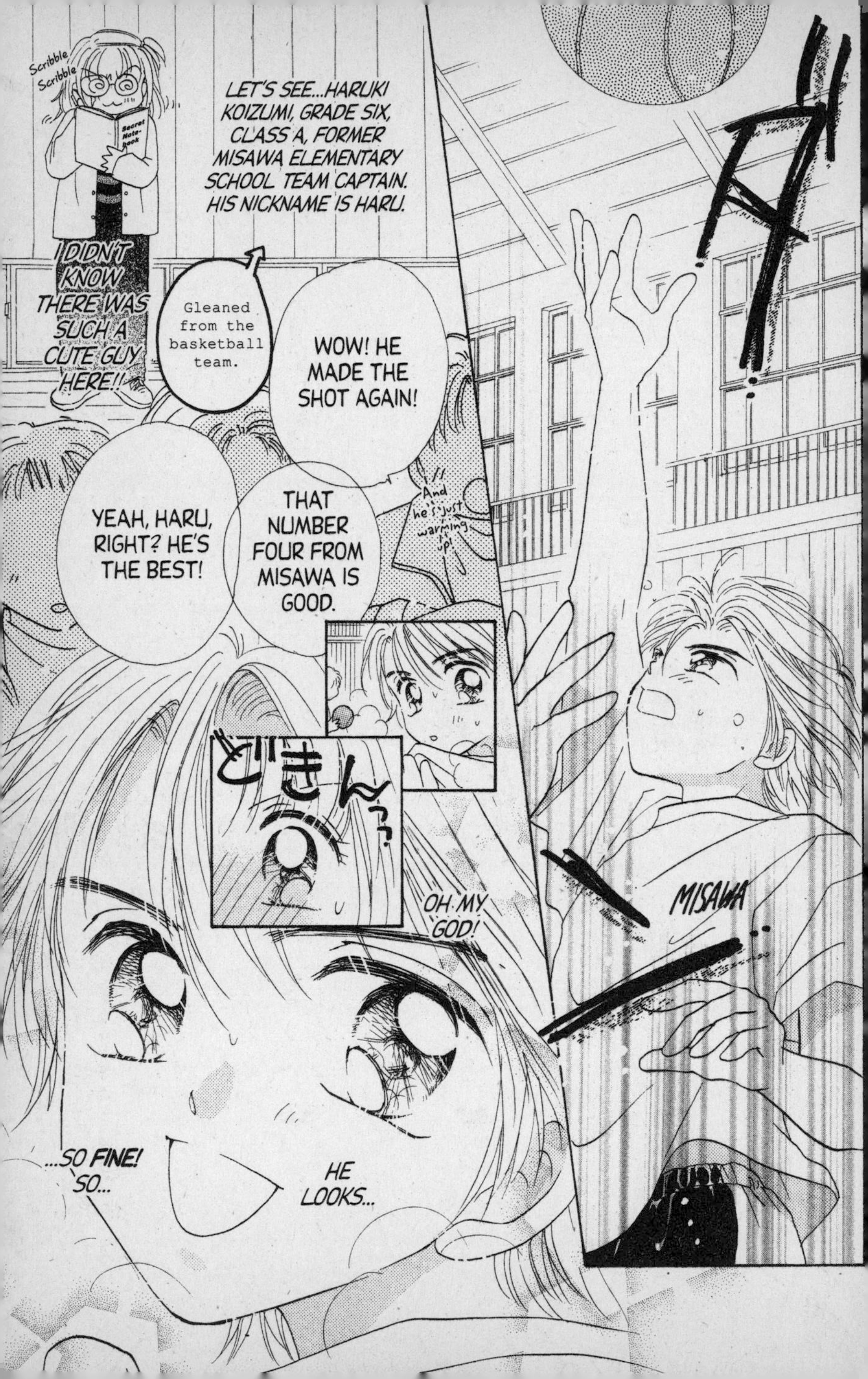
MISAWA
LET'S SEE...HARUKI KOIZUMI, GRADE SIX, CLASS A, FORMER MISAWA ELEMENTARY SCHOOL TEAM CAPTAIN. HIS NICKNAME IS HARU.
Scribble Scribble
Secret Note-book
Gleaned from the basketball team.
I DIDN'T KNOW THERE WAS SUCH A CUTE GUY HERE!!
WOW! HE MADE THE SHOT AGAIN!
And he's just warming up!
THAT NUMBER FOUR FROM MISAWA IS GOOD.
YEAH, HARU, RIGHT? HE'S THE BEST!
どきん
OH MY GOD!
HE LOOKS...
...SO FINE! SO...

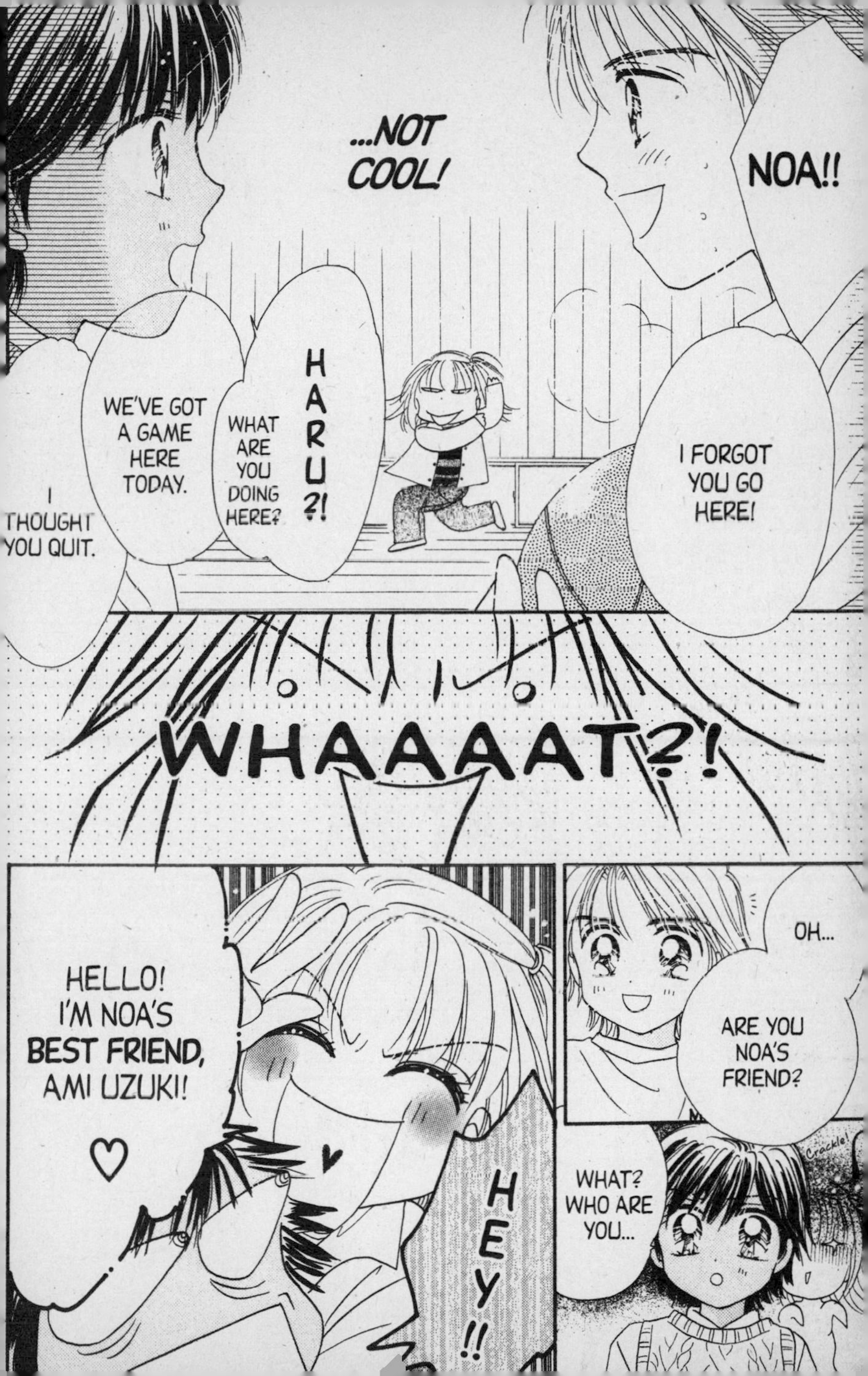
NOA!!
...NOT COOL!
I FORGOT YOU GO HERE!
HARU?!
WHAT ARE YOU DOING HERE?
WE'VE GOT A GAME HERE TODAY.
I THOUGHT YOU QUIT.
WHAAAAT?!
OH...
ARE YOU NOA'S FRIEND?
Crackle!
WHAT? WHO ARE YOU...
HELLO! I'M NOA'S BEST FRIEND, AMI UZUKI! ♡
HEY!!

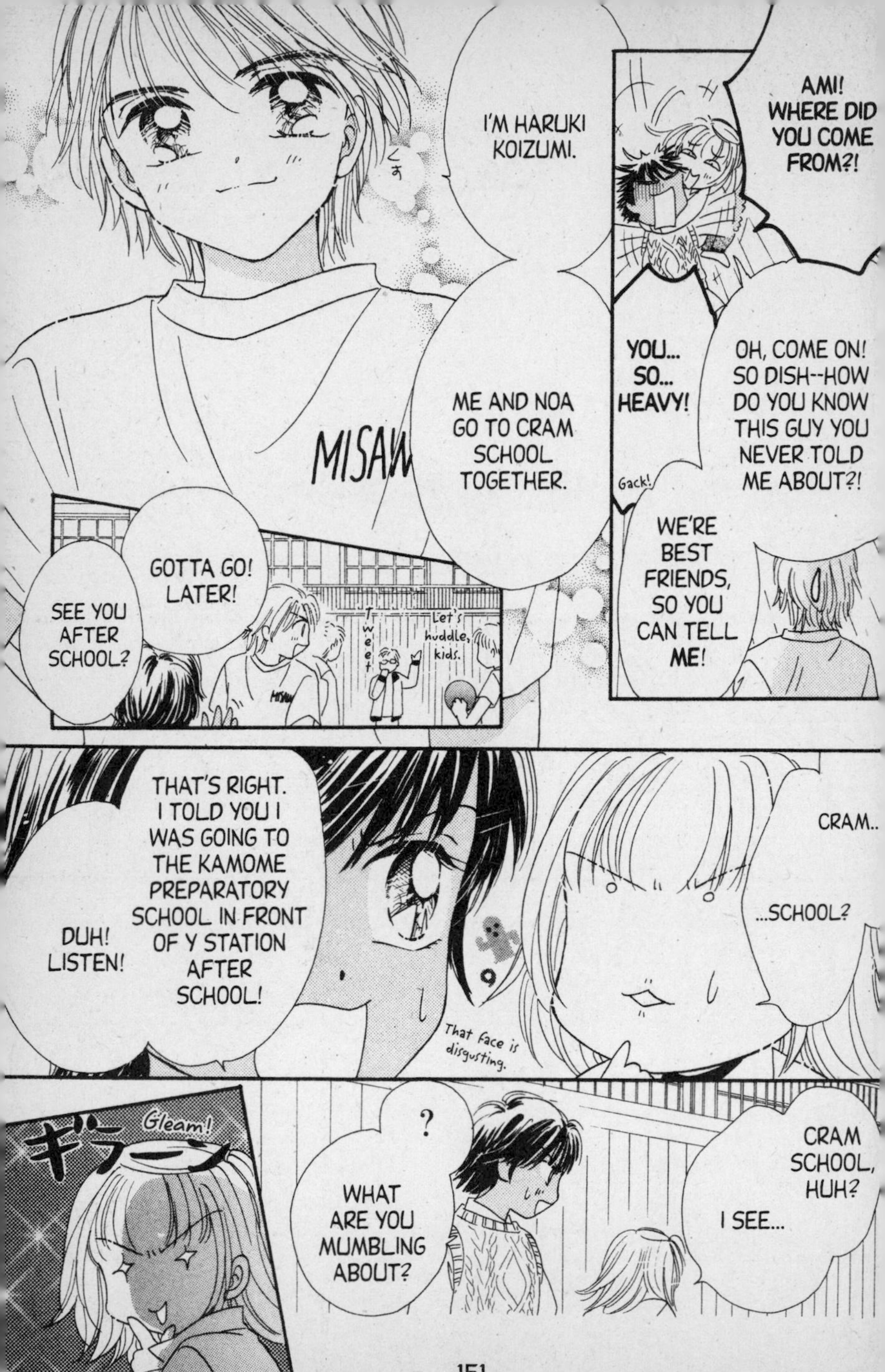
AMI! WHERE DID YOU COME FROM?!
OH, COME ON! SO DISH--HOW DO YOU KNOW THIS GUY YOU NEVER TOLD ME ABOUT?!
YOU... SO... HEAVY!
Gack!
WE'RE BEST FRIENDS, SO YOU CAN TELL ME!
I'M HARUKI KOIZUMI.
くす
ME AND NOA GO TO CRAM SCHOOL TOGETHER.
MISAW
GOTTA GO! LATER!
Let's huddle, kids.
Tweet
SEE YOU AFTER SCHOOL?
CRAM..
...SCHOOL?
THAT'S RIGHT. I TOLD YOU I WAS GOING TO THE KAMOME PREPARATORY SCHOOL IN FRONT OF Y STATION AFTER SCHOOL!
DUH! LISTEN!
That face is disgusting.
CRAM SCHOOL, HUH?
I SEE...
?
WHAT ARE YOU MUMBLING ABOUT?
Gleam!
ギラーン

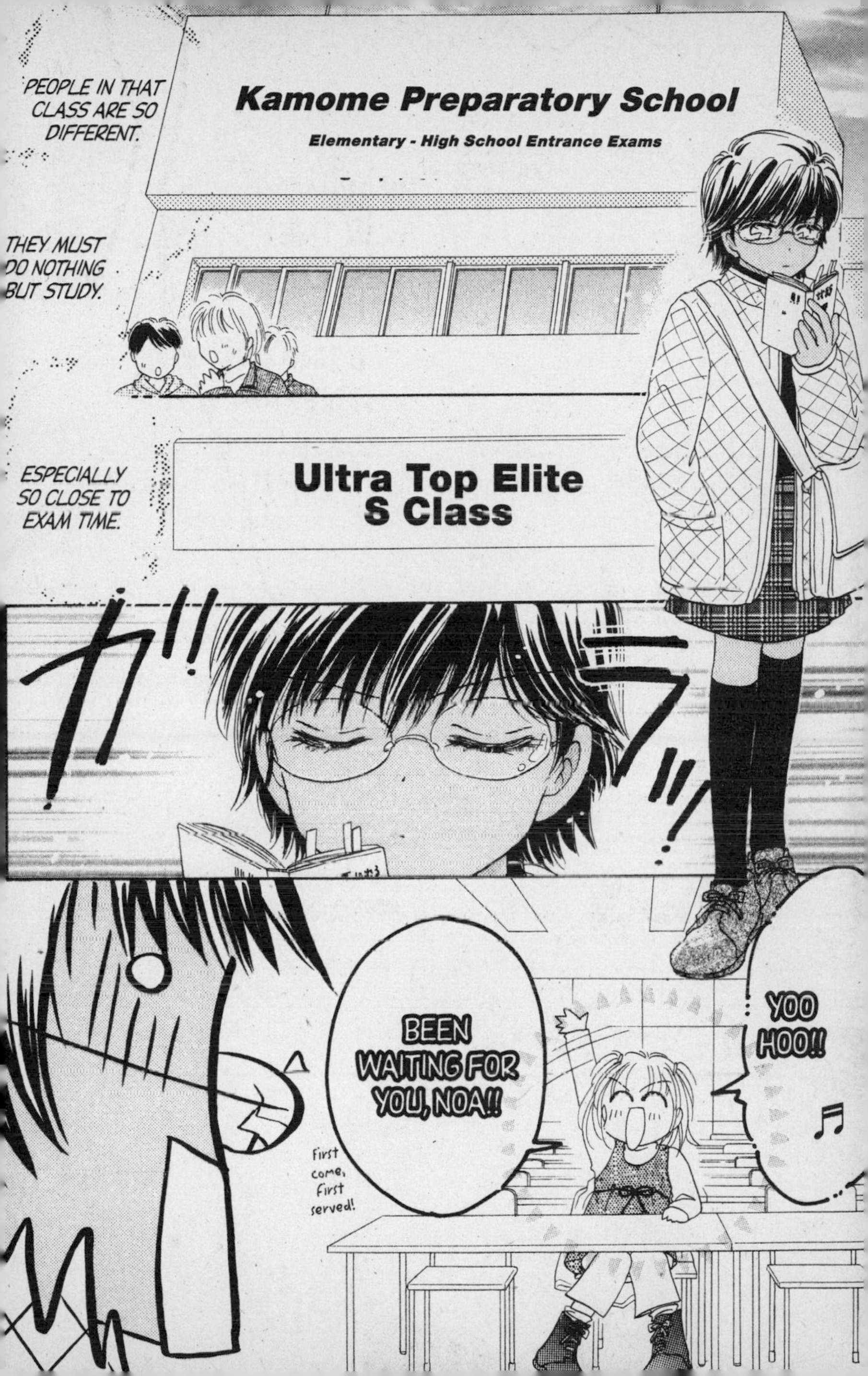
Kamome Preparatory School
Elementary - High School Entrance Exams
PEOPLE IN THAT CLASS ARE SO DIFFERENT.
THEY MUST DO NOTHING BUT STUDY.
Ultra Top Elite S Class
ESPECIALLY SO CLOSE TO EXAM TIME.
YOO HOO!!
BEEN WAITING FOR YOU, NOA!!
First come, first served!

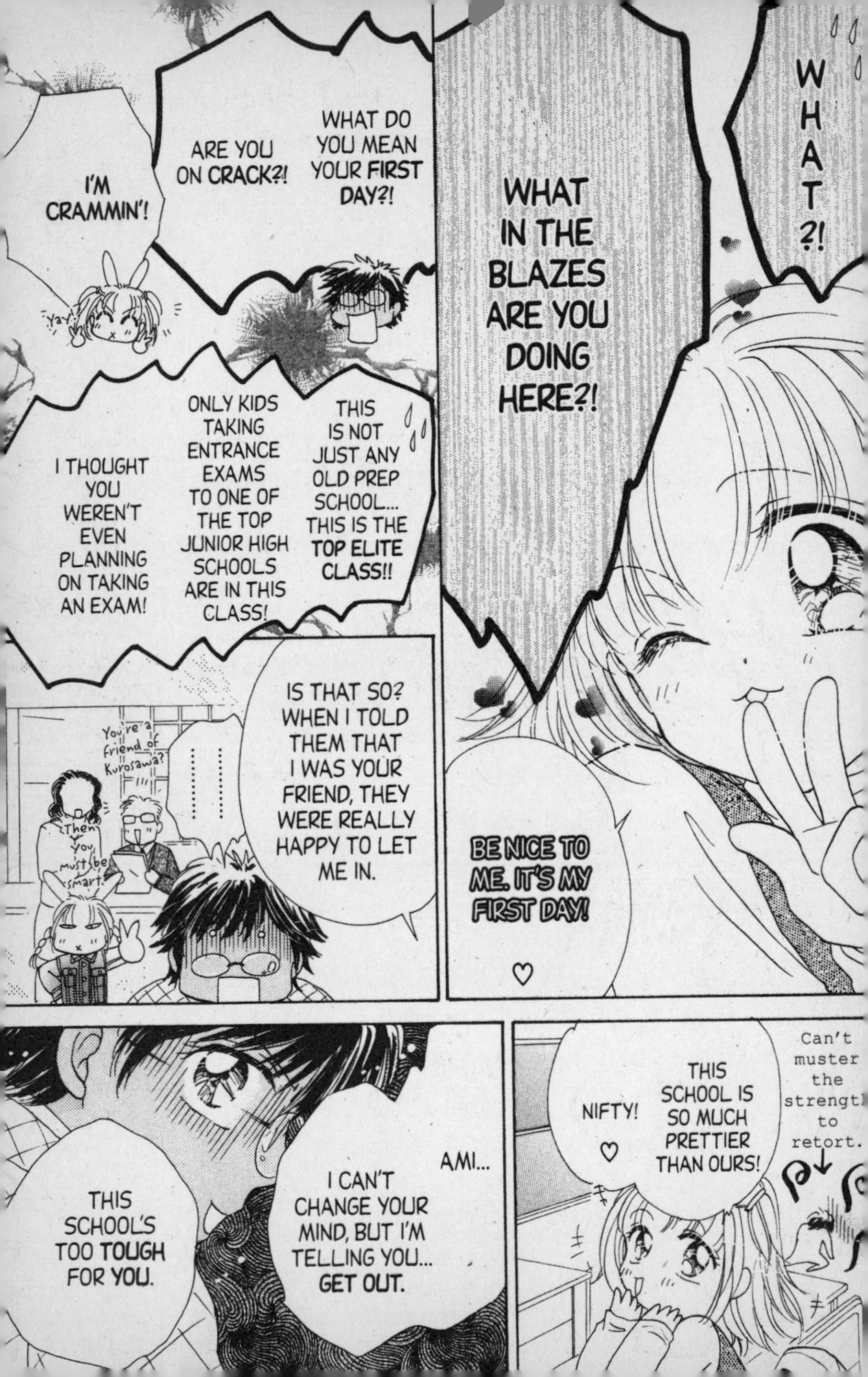
WHAT?!
WHAT IN THE BLAZES ARE YOU DOING HERE?!
BE NICE TO ME. IT'S MY FIRST DAY! ♡
WHAT DO YOU MEAN YOUR FIRST DAY?!
ARE YOU ON CRACK?!
I'M CRAMMIN'!
Yay
THIS IS NOT JUST ANY OLD PREP SCHOOL... THIS IS THE TOP ELITE CLASS!!
ONLY KIDS TAKING ENTRANCE EXAMS TO ONE OF THE TOP JUNIOR HIGH SCHOOLS ARE IN THIS CLASS!
I THOUGHT YOU WEREN'T EVEN PLANNING ON TAKING AN EXAM!
IS THAT SO? WHEN I TOLD THEM THAT I WAS YOUR FRIEND, THEY WERE REALLY HAPPY TO LET ME IN.
......
You're a friend of Kurosawa?
Then you must be smart.
Can't muster the strength to retort.
THIS SCHOOL IS SO MUCH PRETTIER THAN OURS!
NIFTY! ♡
AMI...
I CAN'T CHANGE YOUR MIND, BUT I'M TELLING YOU... GET OUT.
THIS SCHOOL'S TOO TOUGH FOR YOU.

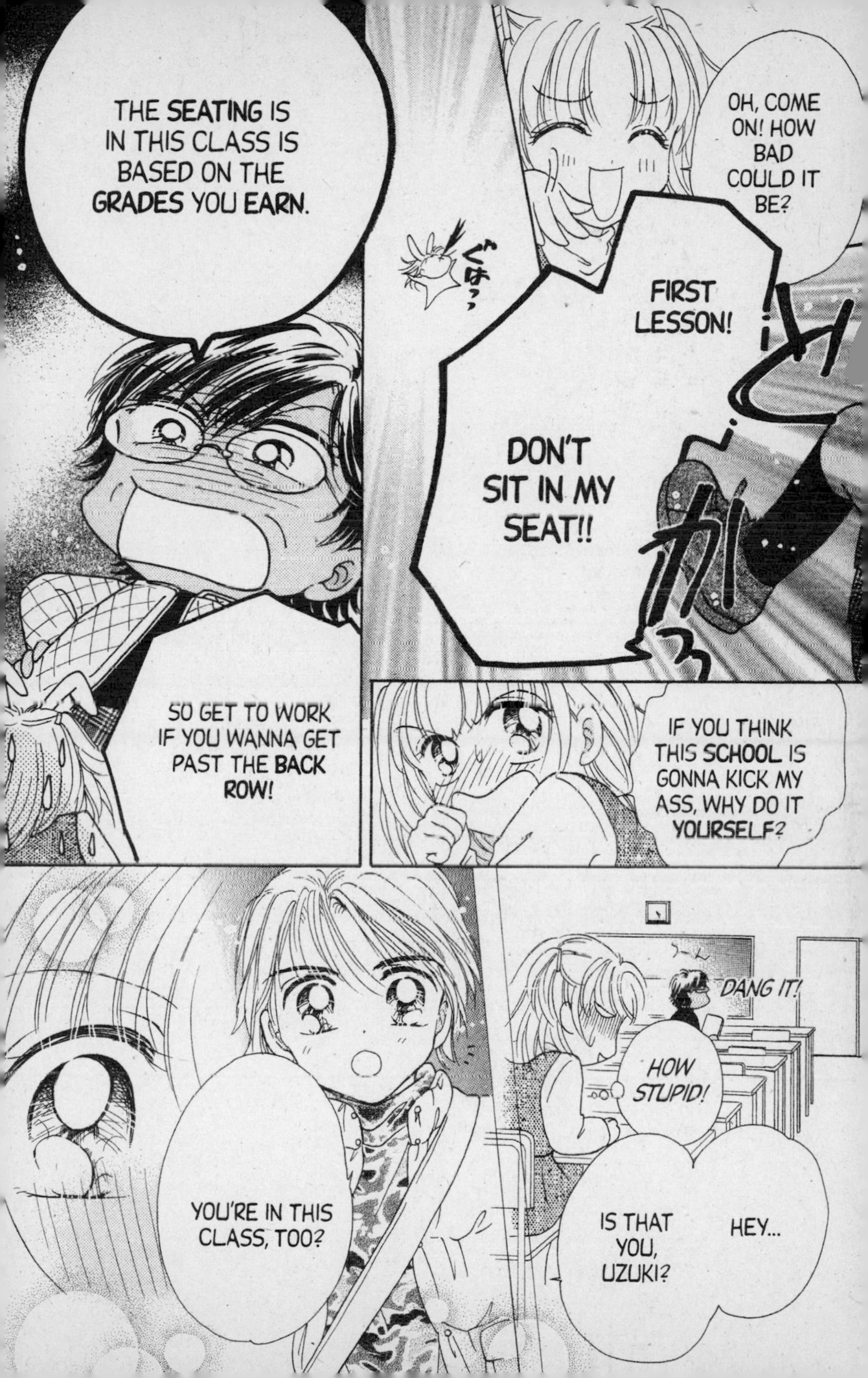
OH, COME ON! HOW BAD COULD IT BE?
ぐはっ
FIRST LESSON!
DON'T SIT IN MY SEAT!!
IF YOU THINK THIS SCHOOL IS GONNA KICK MY ASS, WHY DO IT YOURSELF?
THE SEATING IS IN THIS CLASS IS BASED ON THE GRADES YOU EARN.
SO GET TO WORK IF YOU WANNA GET PAST THE BACK ROW!
DANG IT!
HOW STUPID!
HEY...
IS THAT YOU, UZUKI?
YOU'RE IN THIS CLASS, TOO?

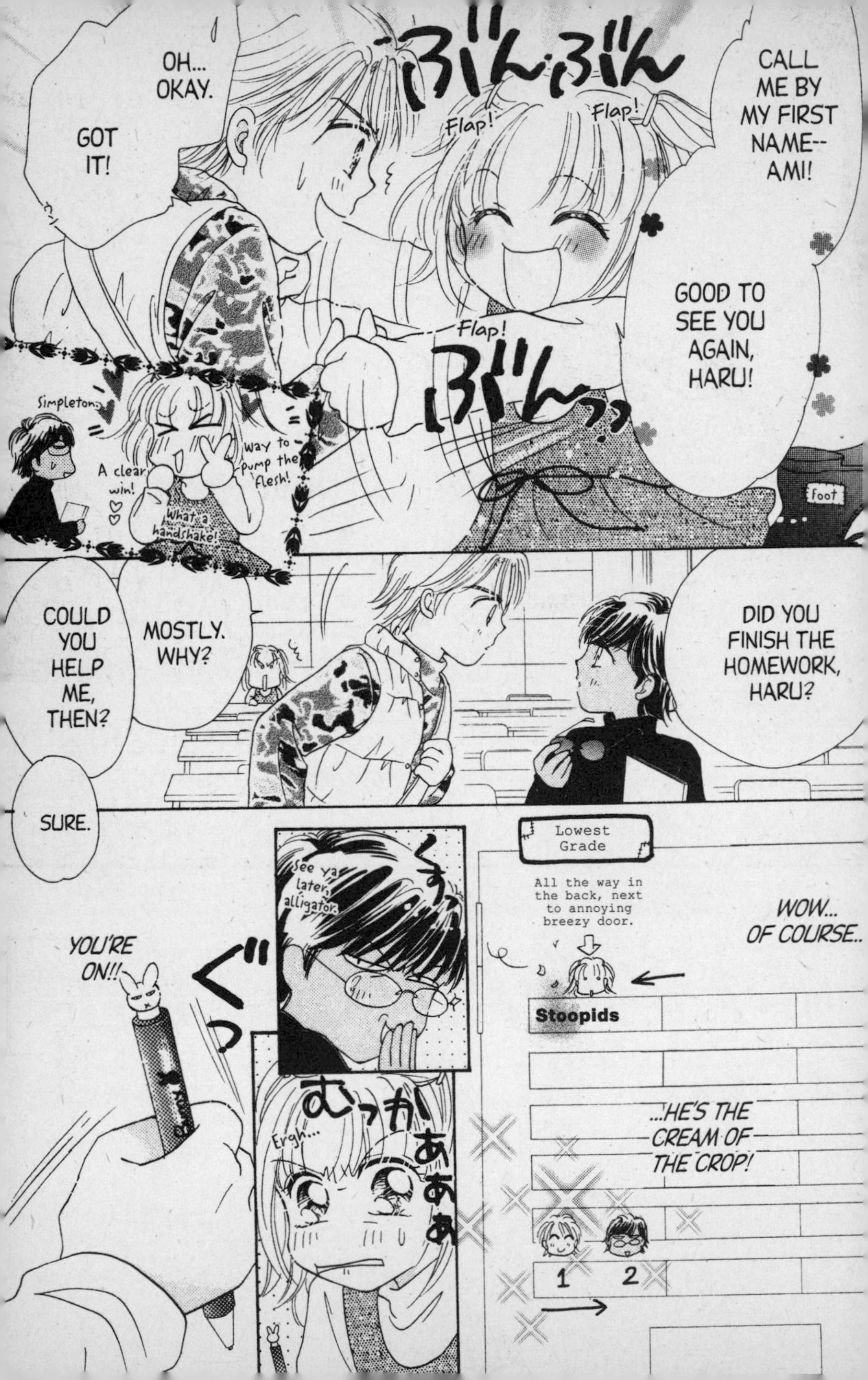
CALL ME BY MY FIRST NAME-- AMI!
Flap!
Flap!
ぶんぶん
GOOD TO SEE YOU AGAIN, HARU!
Flap!
ぶん~っ
Foot
OH... OKAY.
GOT IT!
Way to pump the flesh!
What a handshake!
A clear win!
Simpleton.
DID YOU FINISH THE HOMEWORK, HARU?
MOSTLY. WHY?
COULD YOU HELP ME, THEN?
SURE.
Lowest Grade
All the way in the back, next to annoying breezy door.
WOW... OF COURSE..
Stoopids
...HE'S THE CREAM OF THE CROP!
1
2
くすっ
See ya later, alligator.
むっかあああ
Ergh...
YOU'RE ON!!
ぐっ

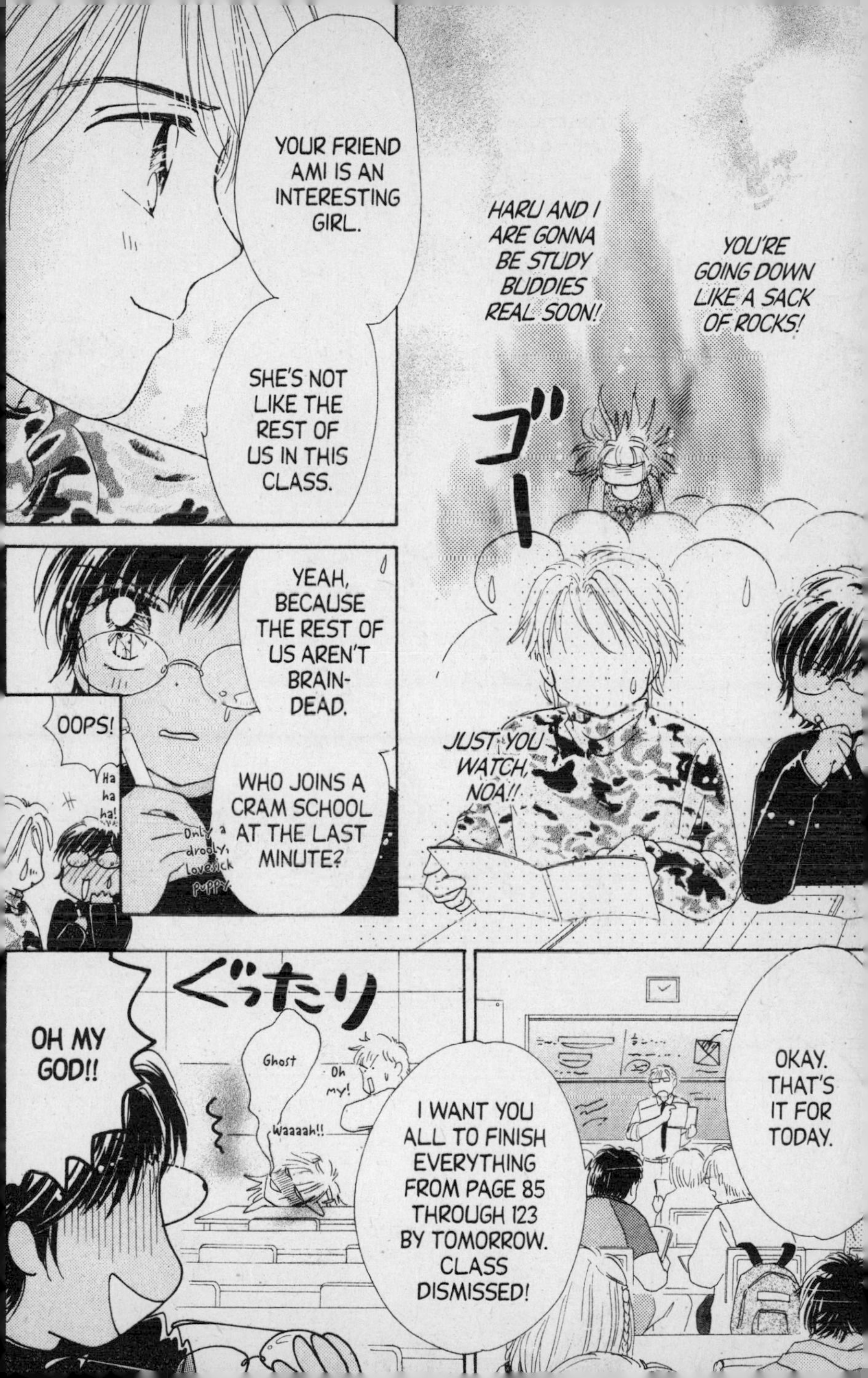
YOU'RE GOING DOWN LIKE A SACK OF ROCKS!
HARU AND I ARE GONNA BE STUDY BUDDIES REAL SOON!
ゴー
JUST YOU WATCH, NOA!!
YOUR FRIEND AMI IS AN INTERESTING GIRL.
SHE'S NOT LIKE THE REST OF US IN THIS CLASS.
YEAH, BECAUSE THE REST OF US AREN'T BRAIN-DEAD.
WHO JOINS A CRAM SCHOOL AT THE LAST MINUTE?
Only a drooly, lovesick puppy.
OOPS!
Ha ha ha!
OKAY. THAT'S IT FOR TODAY.
I WANT YOU ALL TO FINISH EVERYTHING FROM PAGE 85 THROUGH 123 BY TOMORROW. CLASS DISMISSED!
ぐったり
Oh my!
Ghost
Waaaah!!
OH MY GOD!!

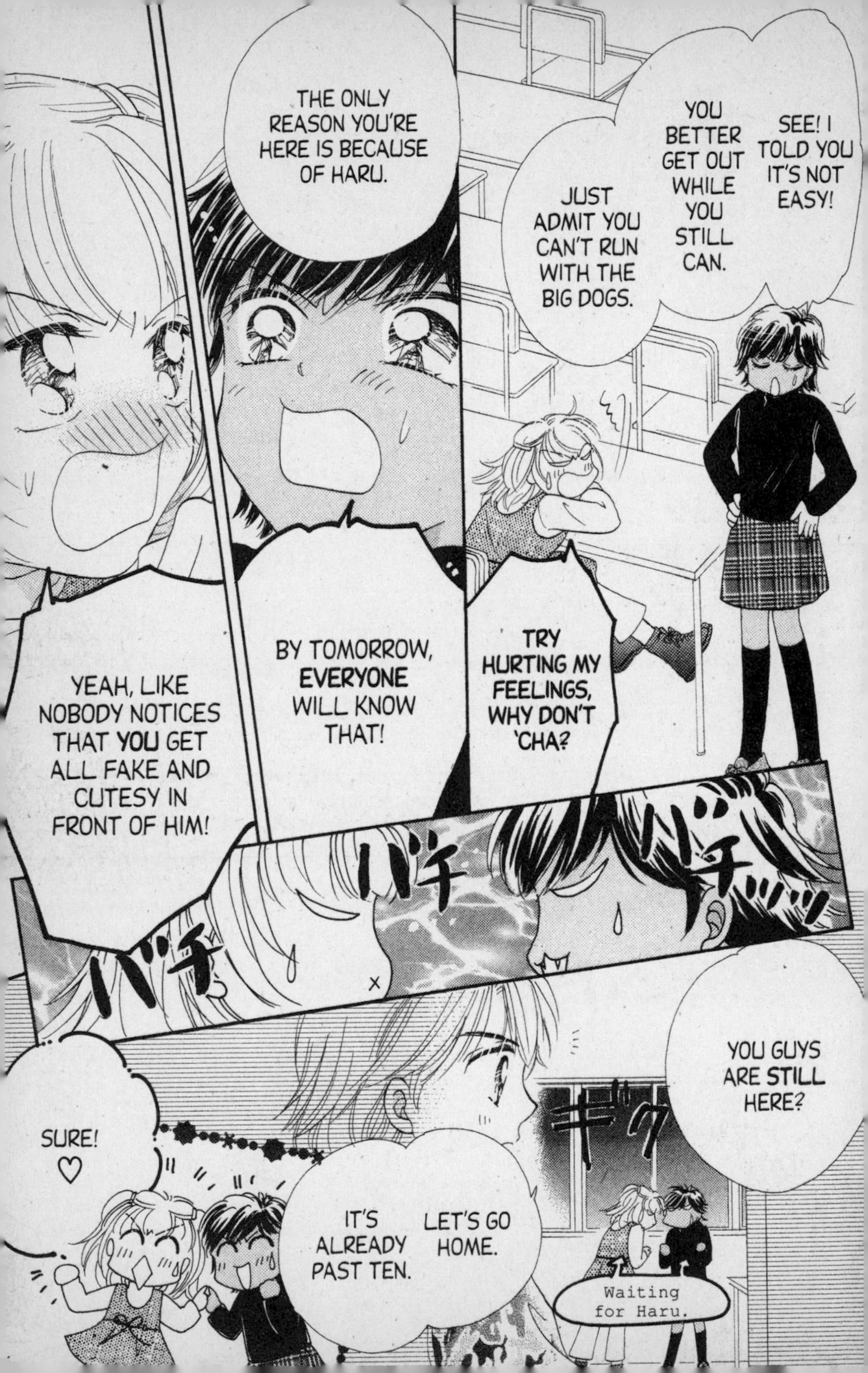
SEE! I TOLD YOU IT'S NOT EASY!
YOU BETTER GET OUT WHILE YOU STILL CAN.
JUST ADMIT YOU CAN'T RUN WITH THE BIG DOGS.
TRY HURTING MY FEELINGS, WHY DON'T 'CHA?
THE ONLY REASON YOU'RE HERE IS BECAUSE OF HARU.
BY TOMORROW, EVERYONE WILL KNOW THAT!
YEAH, LIKE NOBODY NOTICES THAT YOU GET ALL FAKE AND CUTESY IN FRONT OF HIM!
バチバチッッ
バチ
バチ
YOU GUYS ARE STILL HERE?
ギク
Waiting for Haru.
LET'S GO HOME.
IT'S ALREADY PAST TEN.
SURE! ♡

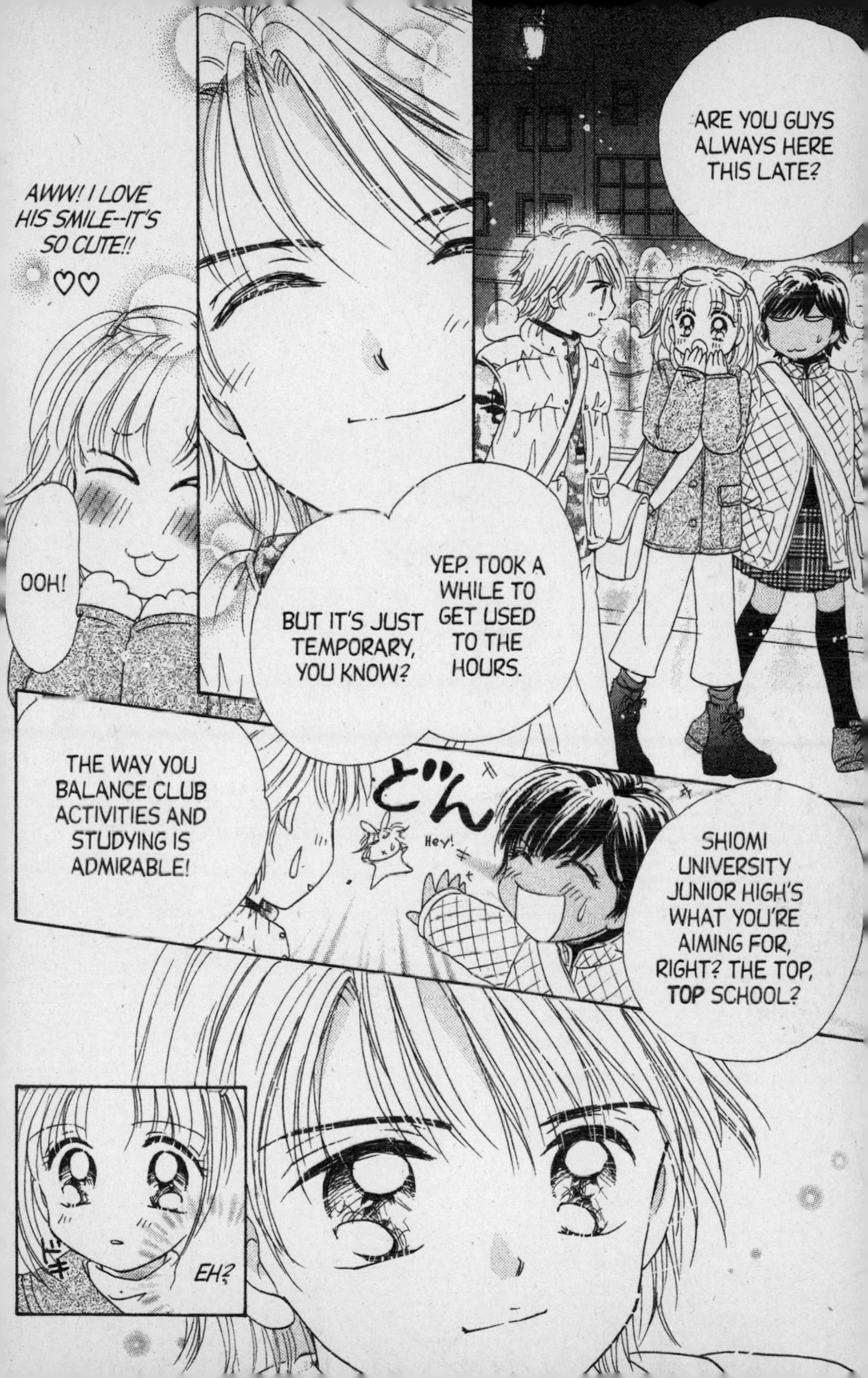
ARE YOU GUYS ALWAYS HERE THIS LATE?
YEP. TOOK A WHILE TO GET USED TO THE HOURS.
BUT IT'S JUST TEMPORARY, YOU KNOW?
AWW! I LOVE HIS SMILE--IT'S SO CUTE!! ♡♡
OOH!
SHIOMI UNIVERSITY JUNIOR HIGH'S WHAT YOU'RE AIMING FOR, RIGHT? THE TOP, TOP SCHOOL?
どん
Hey!
THE WAY YOU BALANCE CLUB ACTIVITIES AND STUDYING IS ADMIRABLE!
ドキ
EH?

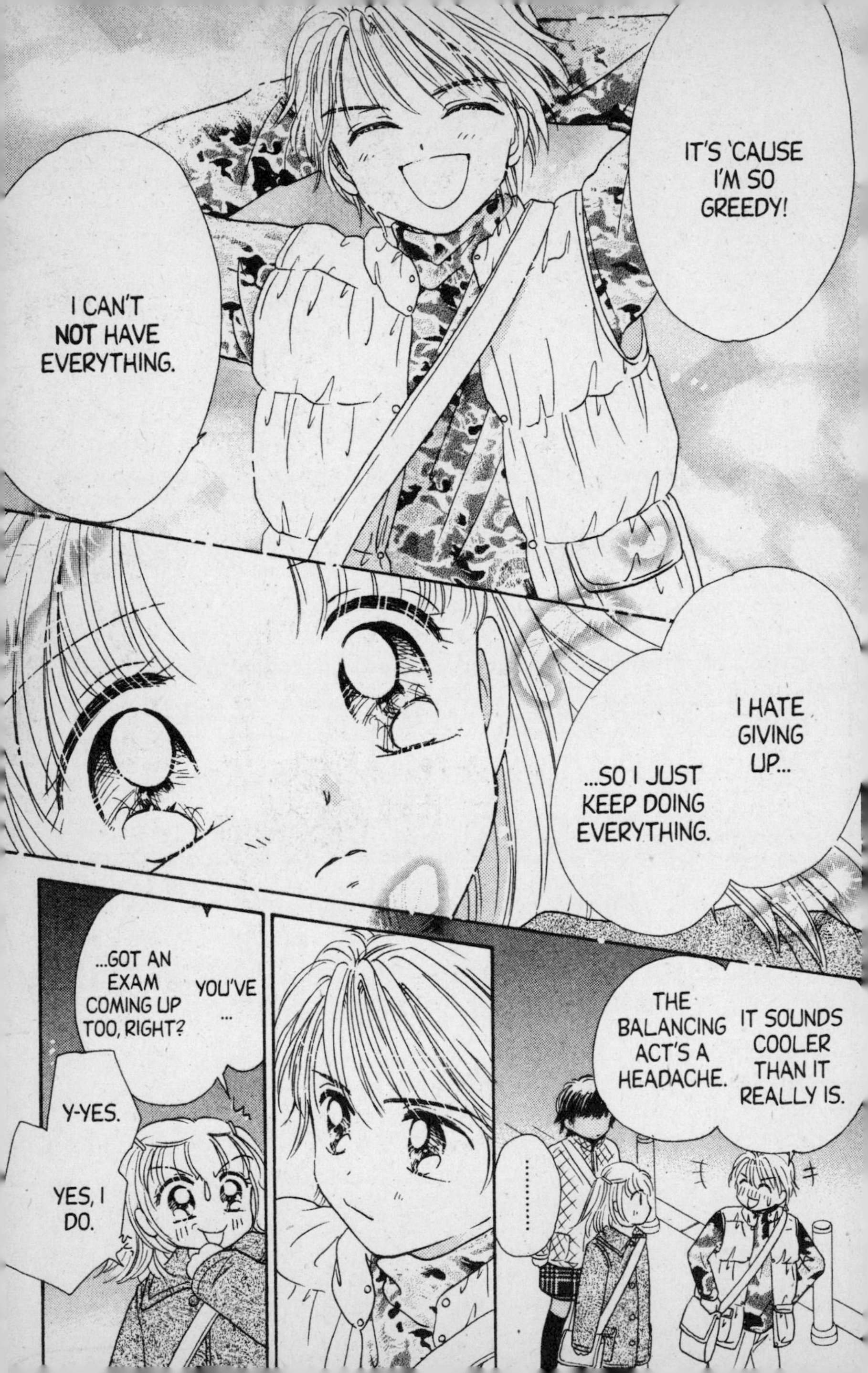
IT'S 'CAUSE I'M SO GREEDY!
I CAN'T NOT HAVE EVERYTHING.
I HATE GIVING UP...
...SO I JUST KEEP DOING EVERYTHING.
IT SOUNDS COOLER THAN IT REALLY IS.
THE BALANCING ACT'S A HEADACHE.
......
YOU'VE ...
...GOT AN EXAM COMING UP TOO, RIGHT?
Y-YES.
YES, I DO.

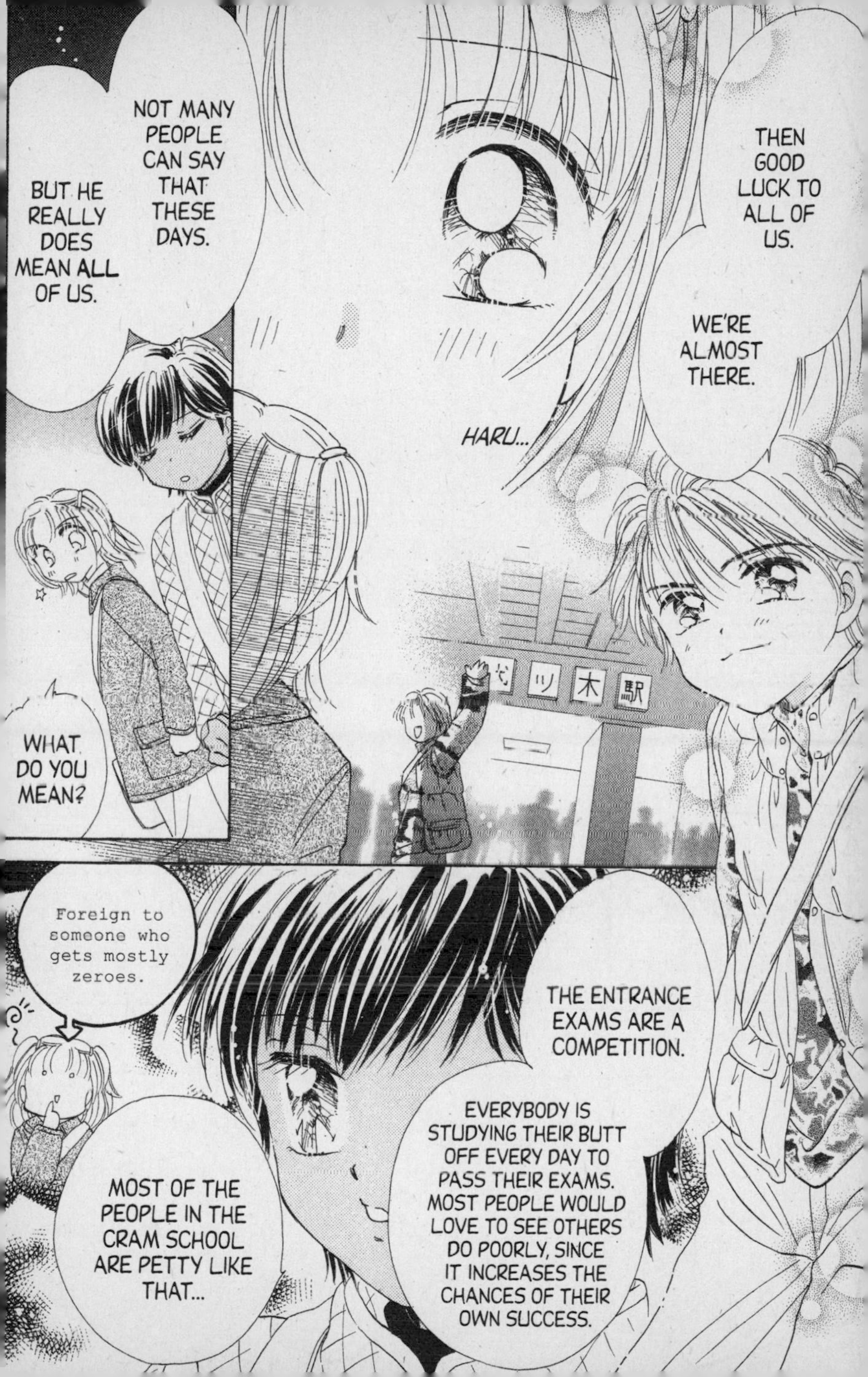
THEN GOOD LUCK TO ALL OF US.
WE'RE ALMOST THERE.
HARU...
ツ木駅
NOT MANY PEOPLE CAN SAY THAT THESE DAYS.
BUT HE REALLY DOES MEAN ALL OF US.
WHAT DO YOU MEAN?
THE ENTRANCE EXAMS ARE A COMPETITION.
EVERYBODY IS STUDYING THEIR BUTT OFF EVERY DAY TO PASS THEIR EXAMS. MOST PEOPLE WOULD LOVE TO SEE OTHERS DO POORLY, SINCE IT INCREASES THE CHANCES OF THEIR OWN SUCCESS.
MOST OF THE PEOPLE IN THE CRAM SCHOOL ARE PETTY LIKE THAT...
Foreign to someone who gets mostly zeroes.

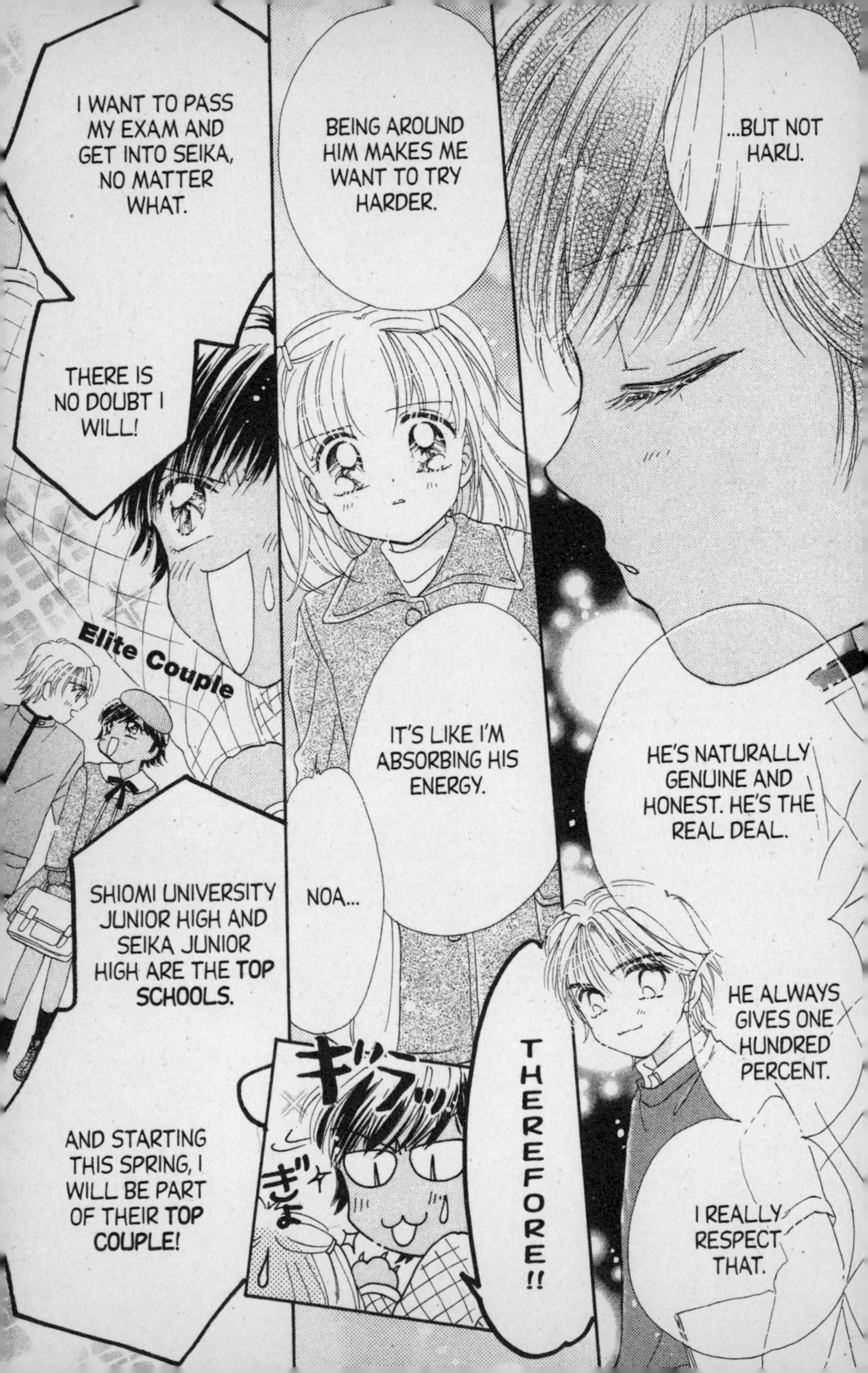
...BUT NOT HARU.
HE'S NATURALLY GENUINE AND HONEST. HE'S THE REAL DEAL.
HE ALWAYS GIVES ONE HUNDRED PERCENT.
I REALLY RESPECT THAT.
BEING AROUND HIM MAKES ME WANT TO TRY HARDER.
IT'S LIKE I'M ABSORBING HIS ENERGY.
NOA...
THEREFORE!!
I WANT TO PASS MY EXAM AND GET INTO SEIKA, NO MATTER WHAT.
THERE IS NO DOUBT I WILL!
Elite Couple
SHIOMI UNIVERSITY JUNIOR HIGH AND SEIKA JUNIOR HIGH ARE THE TOP SCHOOLS.
AND STARTING THIS SPRING, I WILL BE PART OF THEIR TOP COUPLE!

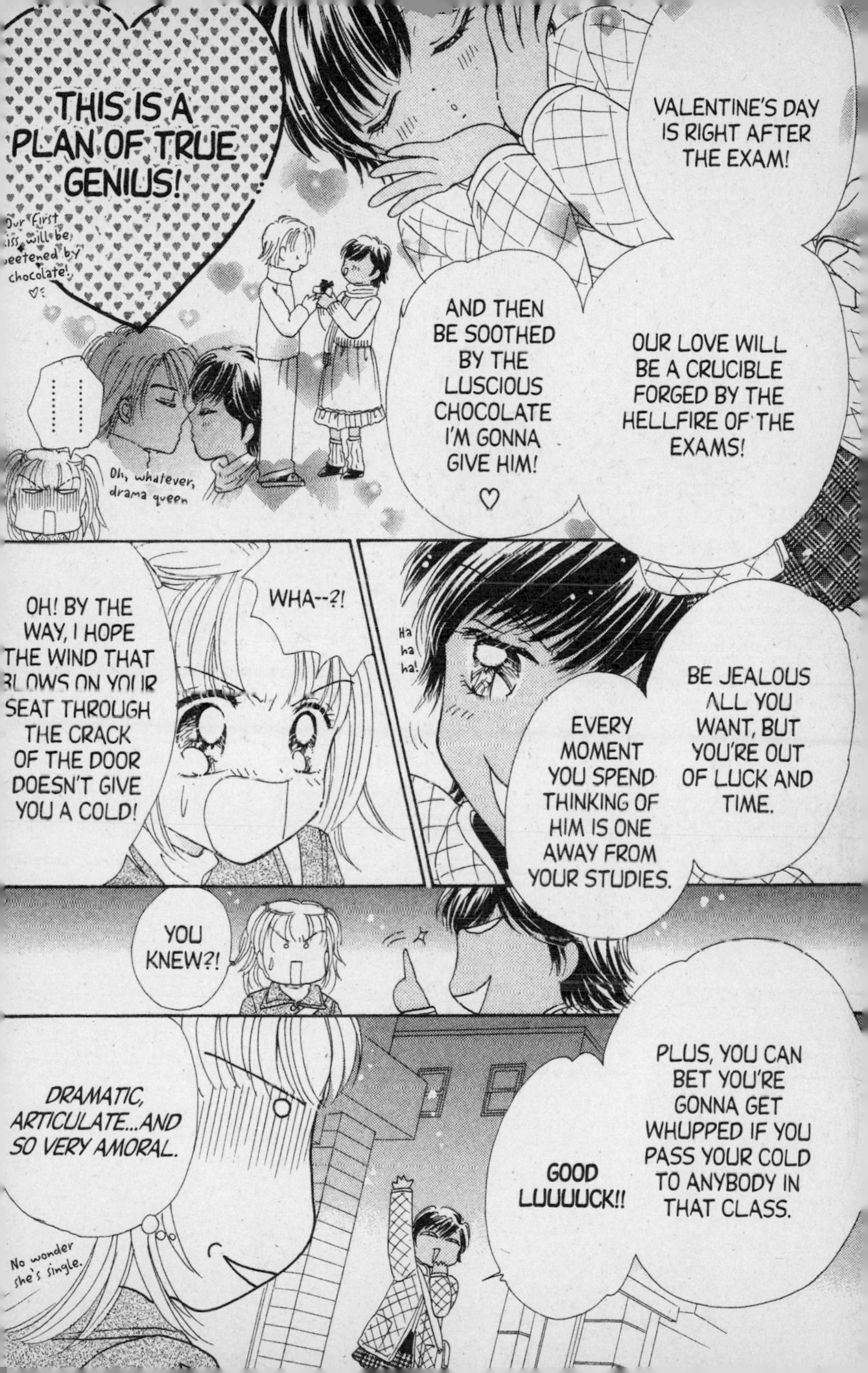

VALENTINE'S DAY IS RIGHT AFTER THE EXAM!
OUR LOVE WILL BE A CRUCIBLE FORGED BY THE HELLFIRE OF THE EXAMS!
AND THEN BE SOOTHED BY THE LUSCIOUS CHOCOLATE I'M GONNA GIVE HIM! ♡
THIS IS A PLAN OF TRUE GENIUS!
Our first kiss will be eetened by chocolate! ♡
......
Oh, whatever, drama queen
BE JEALOUS ALL YOU WANT, BUT YOU'RE OUT OF LUCK AND TIME.
EVERY MOMENT YOU SPEND THINKING OF HIM IS ONE AWAY FROM YOUR STUDIES.
Ha ha ha!
WHA--?!
OH! BY THE WAY, I HOPE THE WIND THAT BLOWS ON YOUR SEAT THROUGH THE CRACK OF THE DOOR DOESN'T GIVE YOU A COLD!
YOU KNEW?!
PLUS, YOU CAN BET YOU'RE GONNA GET WHUPPED IF YOU PASS YOUR COLD TO ANYBODY IN THAT CLASS.
GOOD LUUUUCK!!
DRAMATIC, ARTICULATE...AND SO VERY AMORAL.
No wonder she's single.

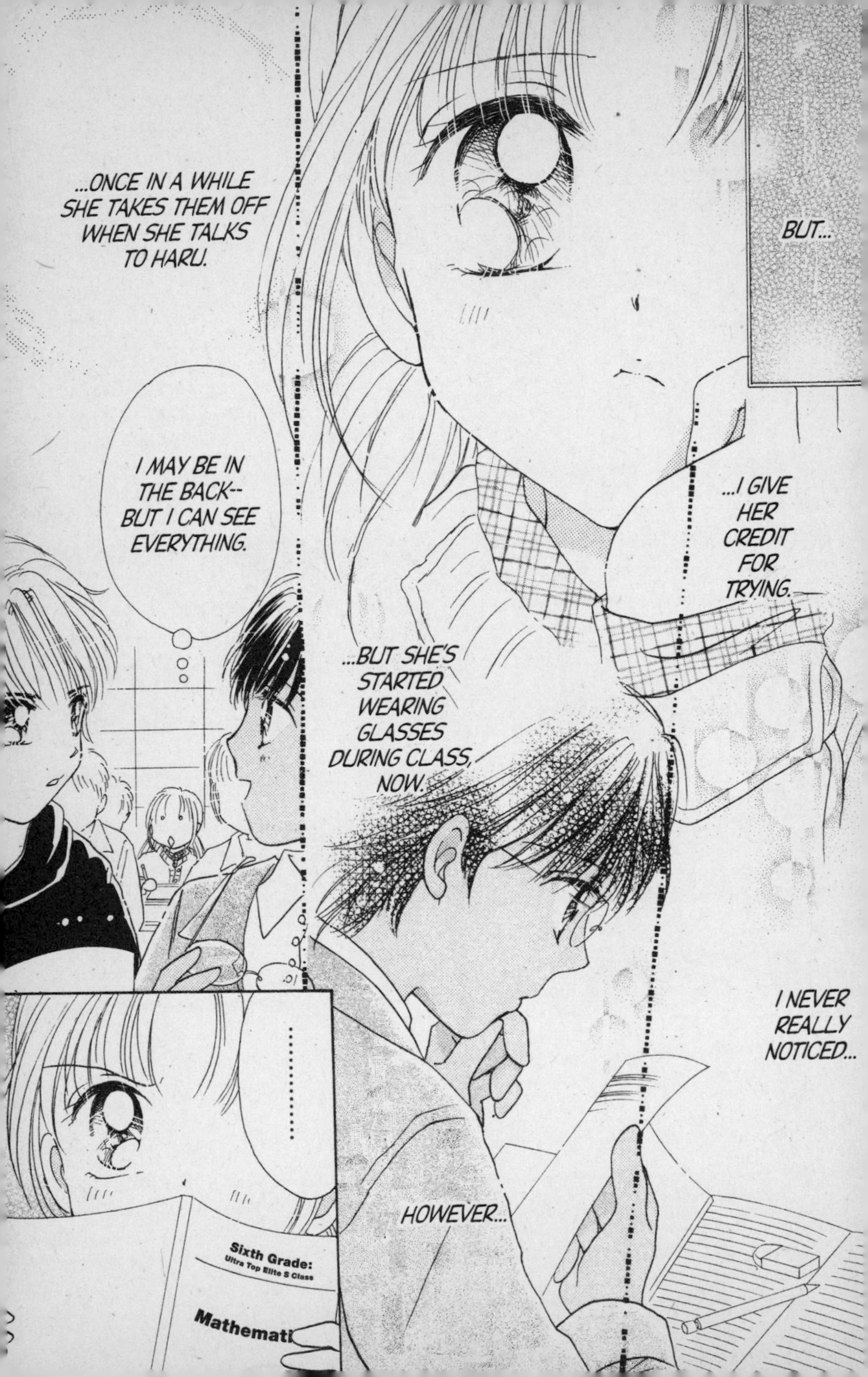
BUT...
...I GIVE HER CREDIT FOR TRYING.
...BUT SHE'S STARTED WEARING GLASSES DURING CLASS, NOW.
I NEVER REALLY NOTICED...
HOWEVER...
...ONCE IN A WHILE SHE TAKES THEM OFF WHEN SHE TALKS TO HARU.
I MAY BE IN THE BACK-- BUT I CAN SEE EVERYTHING.
Sixth Grade: Ultra Top Elite S Class
Mathemati

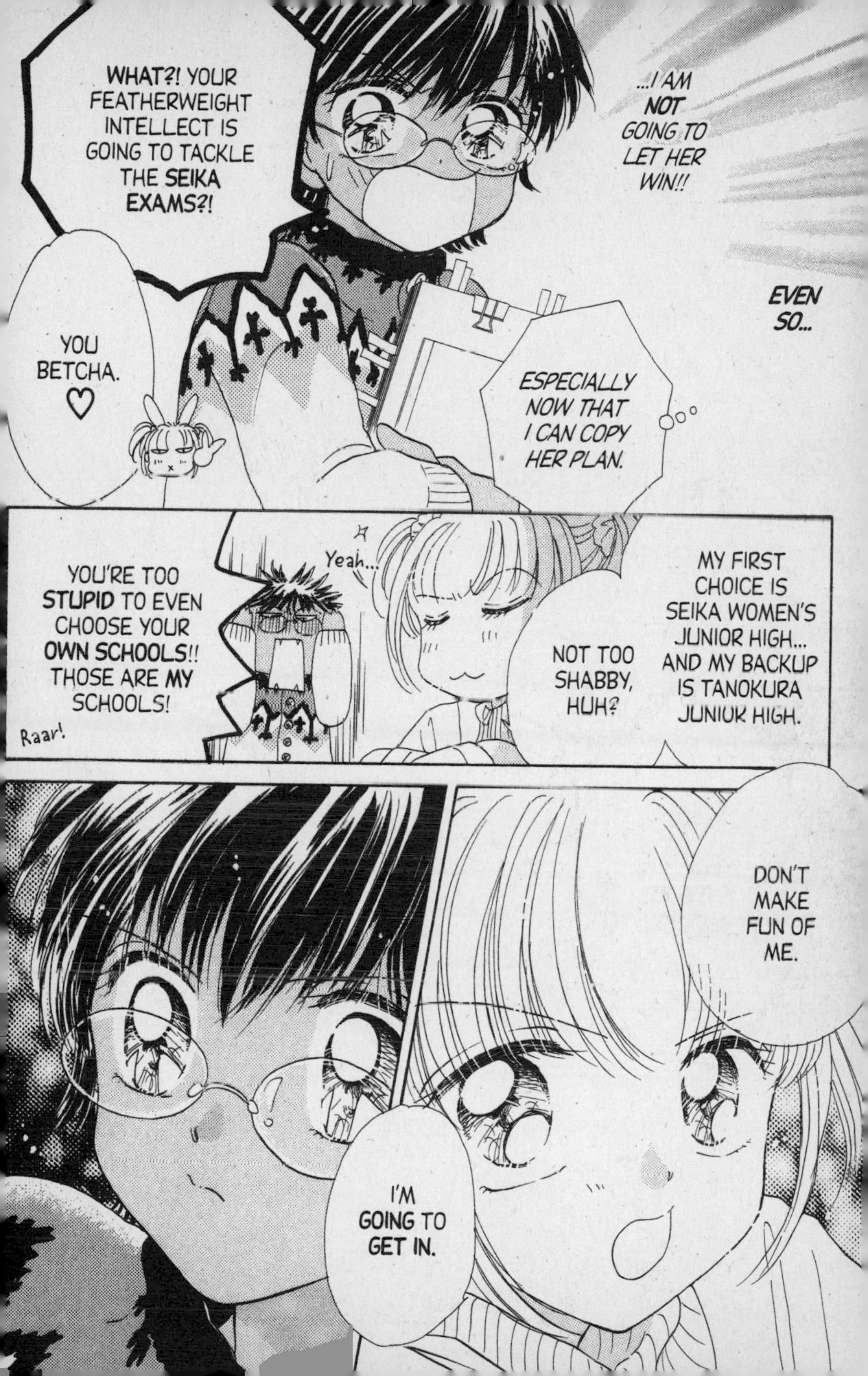
...I AM NOT GOING TO LET HER WIN!!
WHAT?! YOUR FEATHERWEIGHT INTELLECT IS GOING TO TACKLE THE SEIKA EXAMS?!
EVEN SO...
ESPECIALLY NOW THAT I CAN COPY HER PLAN.
YOU BETCHA. ♡
MY FIRST CHOICE IS SEIKA WOMEN'S JUNIOR HIGH... AND MY BACKUP IS TANOKURA JUNIOR HIGH.
NOT TOO SHABBY, HUH?
Yeah...
YOU'RE TOO STUPID TO EVEN CHOOSE YOUR OWN SCHOOLS!! THOSE ARE MY SCHOOLS!
Raar!
DON'T MAKE FUN OF ME.
I'M GOING TO GET IN.

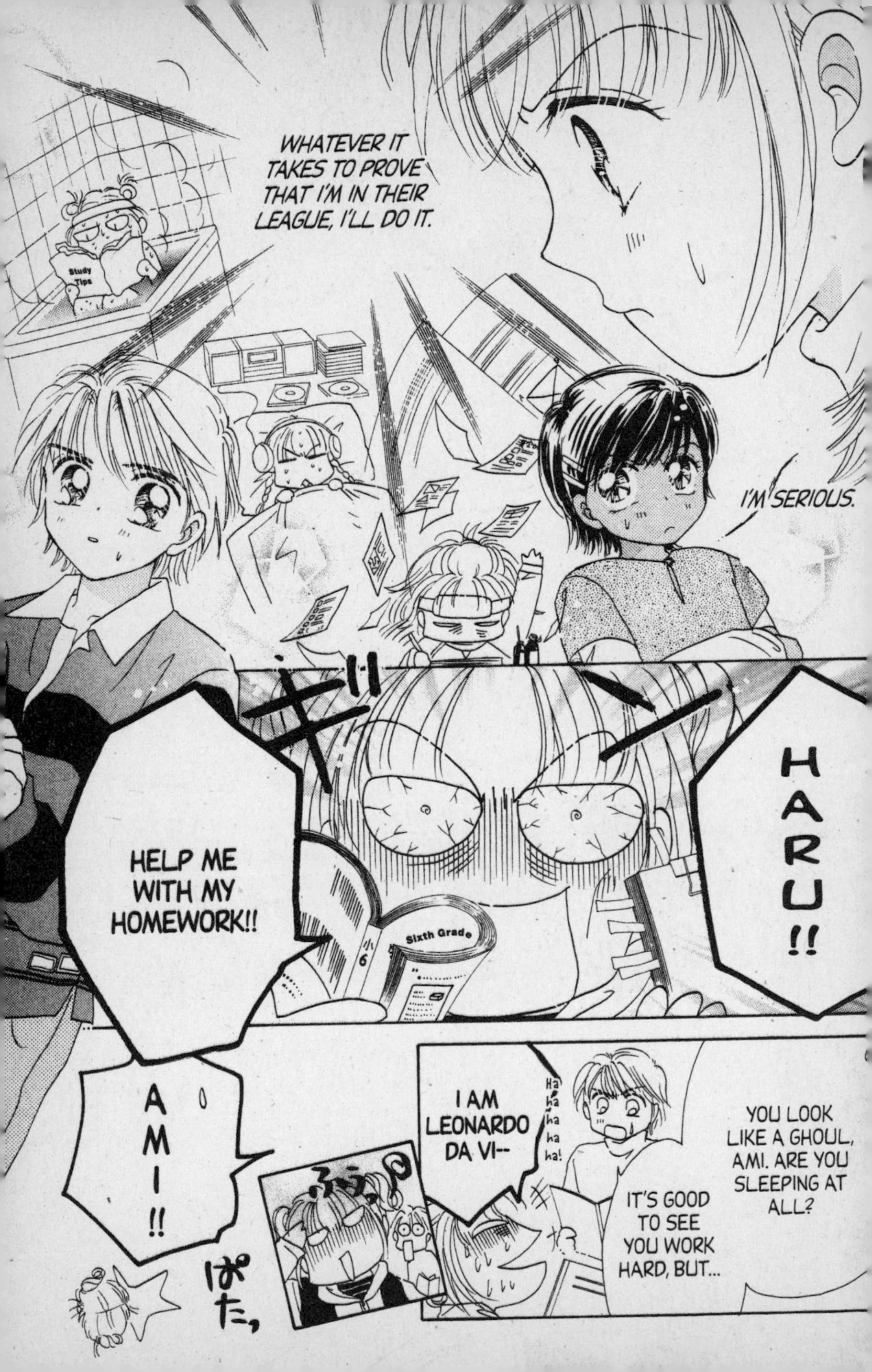
WHATEVER IT TAKES TO PROVE THAT I'M IN THEIR LEAGUE, I'LL DO IT.
Study Tips
I'M SERIOUS.
HARU!!
HELP ME WITH MY HOMEWORK!!
Sixth Grade
YOU LOOK LIKE A GHOUL, AMI. ARE YOU SLEEPING AT ALL?
IT'S GOOD TO SEE YOU WORK HARD, BUT...
Ha ha ha ha ha!
I AM LEONARDO DA VI--
AMI!!
ぱたっ

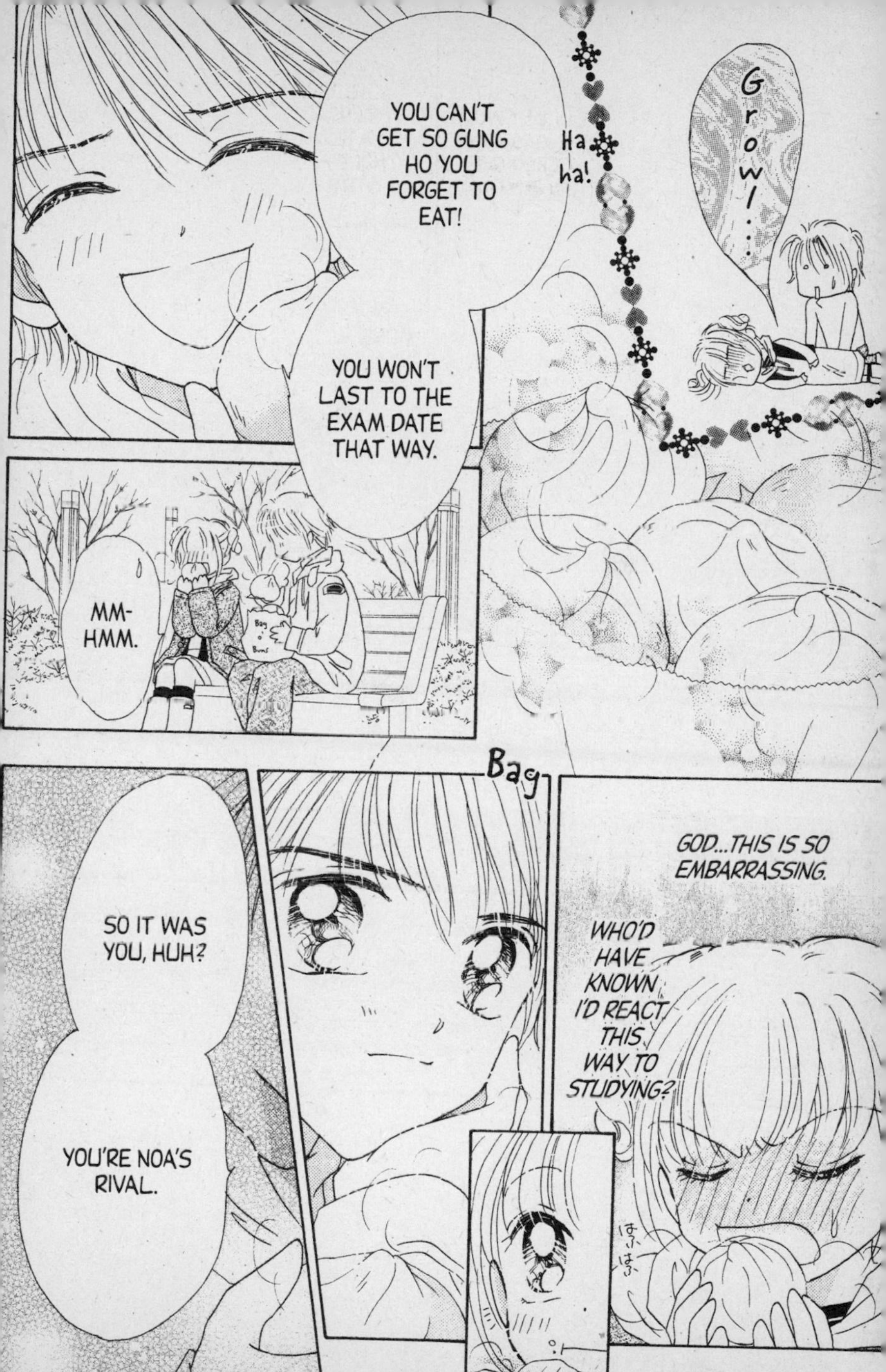
Growl...
Ha ha!
YOU CAN'T GET SO GUNG HO YOU FORGET TO EAT!
YOU WON'T LAST TO THE EXAM DATE THAT WAY.
MM-HMM.
GOD...THIS IS SO EMBARRASSING.
WHO'D HAVE KNOWN I'D REACT THIS WAY TO STUDYING?
はふはふ
Bag
SO IT WAS YOU, HUH?
YOU'RE NOA'S RIVAL.

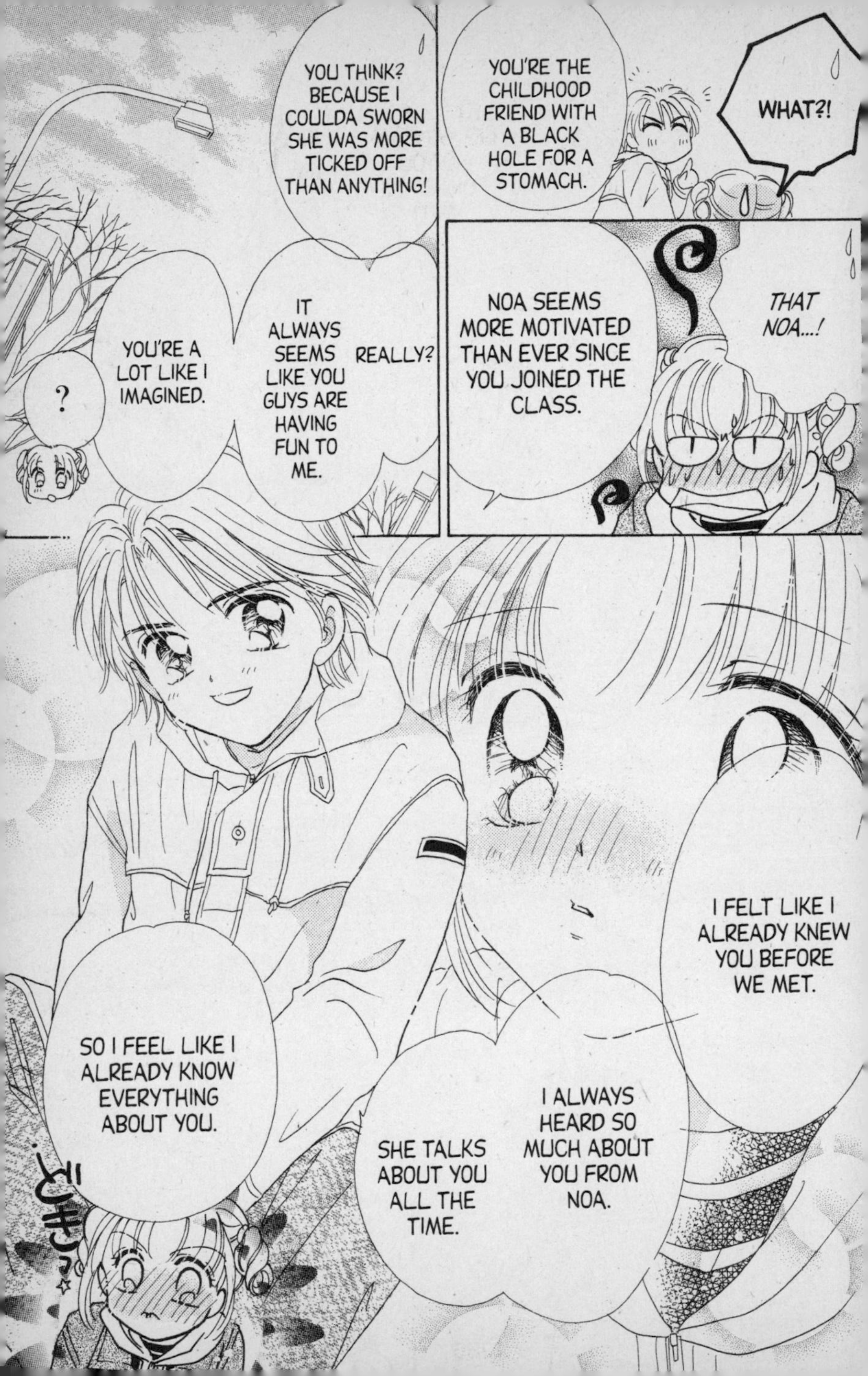
WHAT?!
YOU'RE THE CHILDHOOD FRIEND WITH A BLACK HOLE FOR A STOMACH.
THAT NOA...!
NOA SEEMS MORE MOTIVATED THAN EVER SINCE YOU JOINED THE CLASS.
YOU THINK? BECAUSE I COULDA SWORN SHE WAS MORE TICKED OFF THAN ANYTHING!
REALLY?
IT ALWAYS SEEMS LIKE YOU GUYS ARE HAVING FUN TO ME.
YOU'RE A LOT LIKE I IMAGINED.
?
I FELT LIKE I ALREADY KNEW YOU BEFORE WE MET.
I ALWAYS HEARD SO MUCH ABOUT YOU FROM NOA.
SHE TALKS ABOUT YOU ALL THE TIME.
SO I FEEL LIKE I ALREADY KNOW EVERYTHING ABOUT YOU.
どきっ

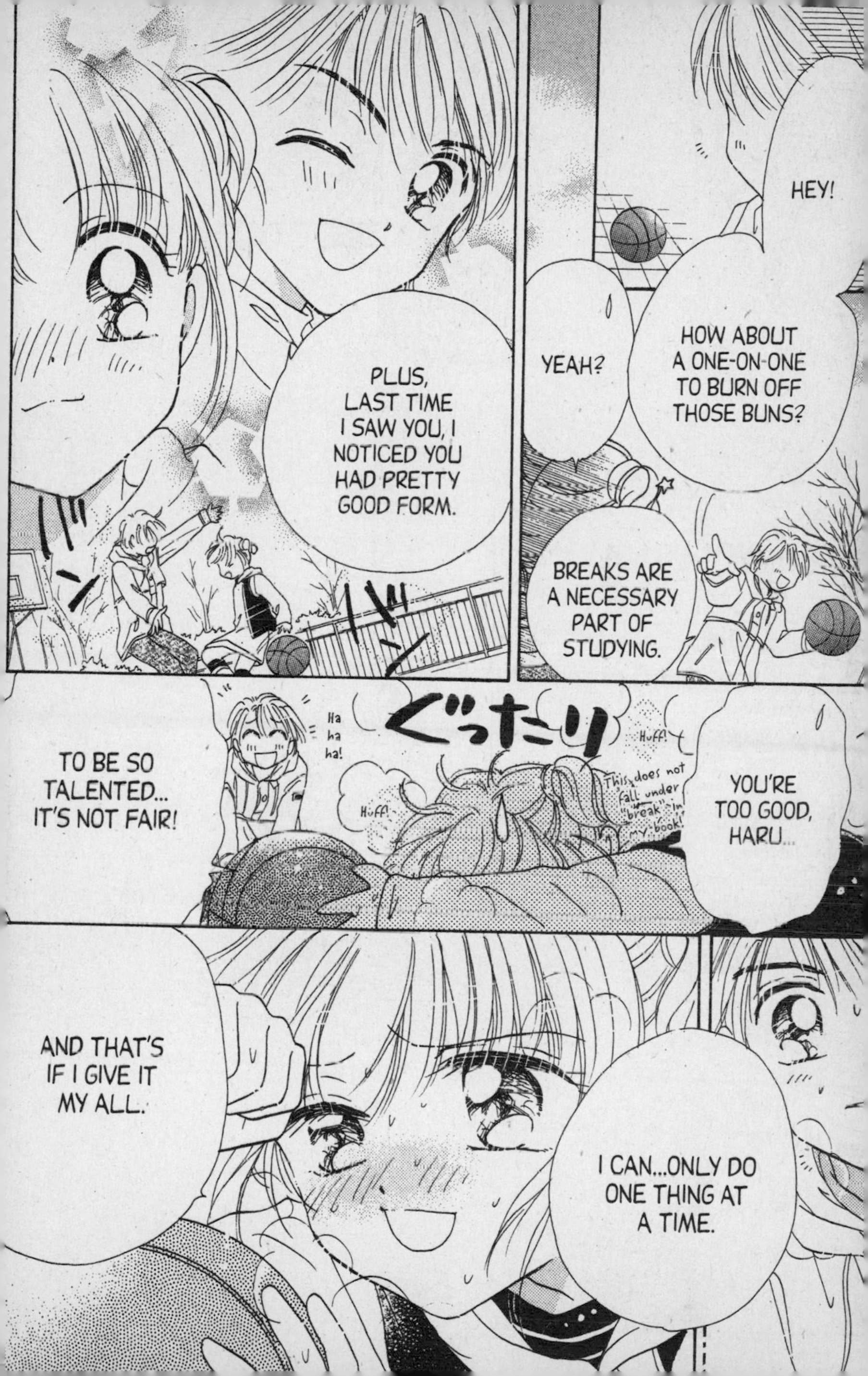
HEY!
HOW ABOUT A ONE-ON-ONE TO BURN OFF THOSE BUNS?
YEAH?
BREAKS ARE A NECESSARY PART OF STUDYING.
PLUS, LAST TIME I SAW YOU, I NOTICED YOU HAD PRETTY GOOD FORM.
YOU'RE TOO GOOD, HARU...
Huff!
This does not fall under "break" in my book!
ぐったり
Huff!
Ha ha ha!
TO BE SO TALENTED... IT'S NOT FAIR!
I CAN...ONLY DO ONE THING AT A TIME.
AND THAT'S IF I GIVE IT MY ALL.

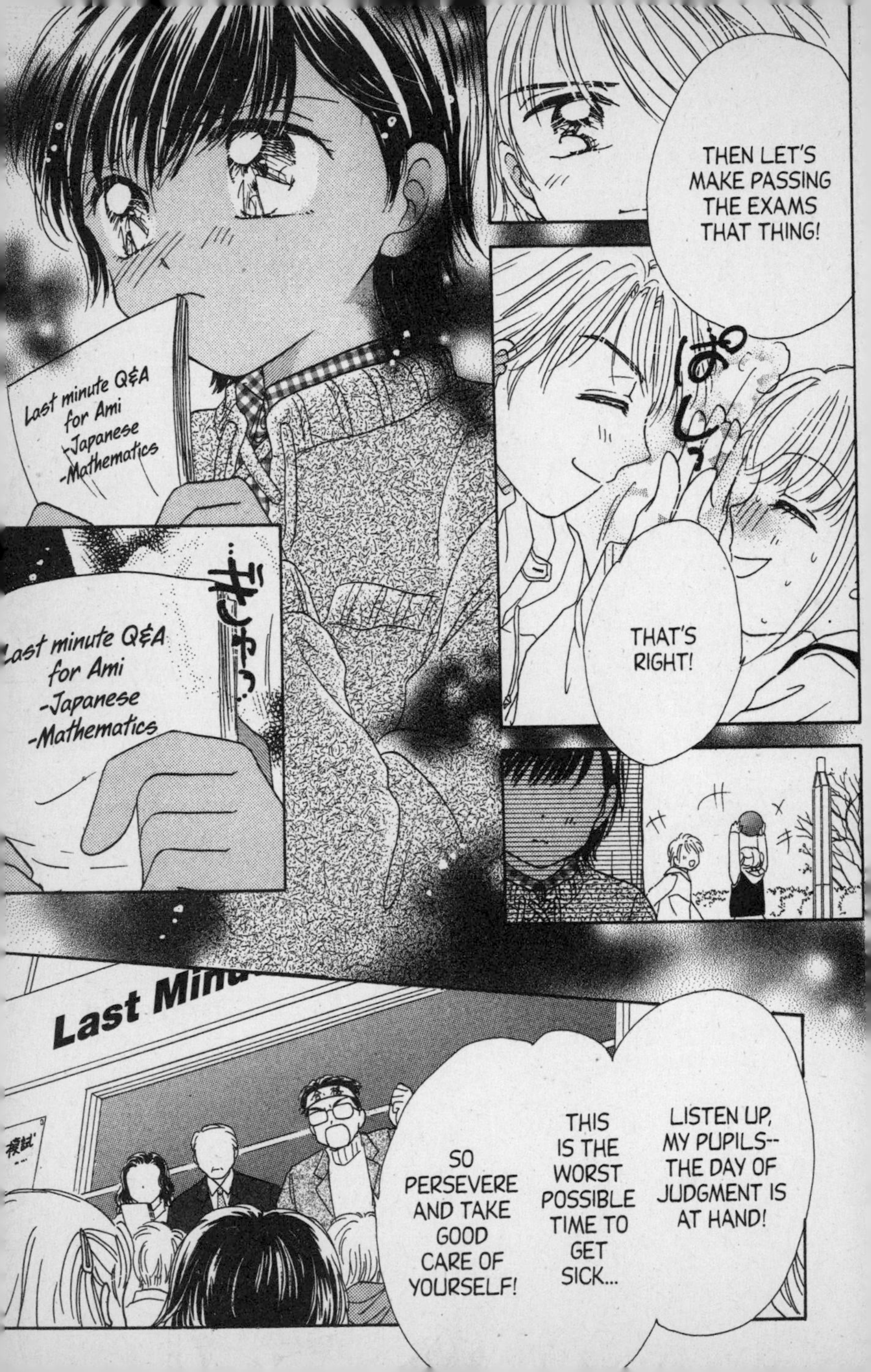
THEN LET'S MAKE PASSING THE EXAMS THAT THING!
ぱしっ
THAT'S RIGHT!
Last minute Q&A for Ami -Japanese -Mathematics
ぎゅっ
Last minute Q&A for Ami -Japanese -Mathematics
Last Min
LISTEN UP, MY PUPILS-- THE DAY OF JUDGMENT IS AT HAND!
THIS IS THE WORST POSSIBLE TIME TO GET SICK...
SO PERSEVERE AND TAKE GOOD CARE OF YOURSELF!

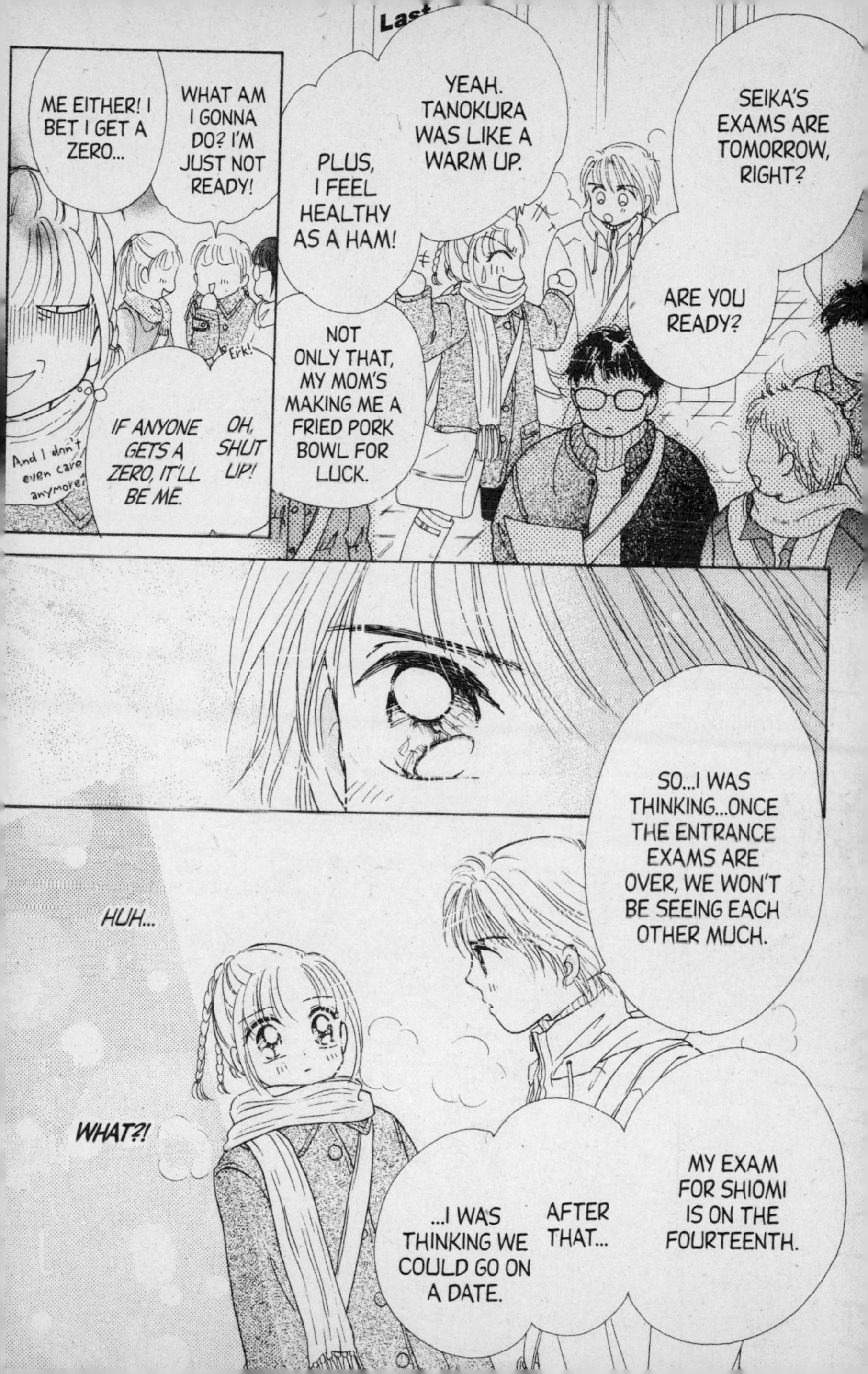
Last
SEIKA'S EXAMS ARE TOMORROW, RIGHT?
ARE YOU READY?
YEAH. TANOKURA WAS LIKE A WARM UP.
PLUS, I FEEL HEALTHY AS A HAM!
NOT ONLY THAT, MY MOM'S MAKING ME A FRIED PORK BOWL FOR LUCK.
WHAT AM I GONNA DO? I'M JUST NOT READY!
ME EITHER! I BET I GET A ZERO...
Erk!
OH, SHUT UP!
IF ANYONE GETS A ZERO, IT'LL BE ME.
And I don't even care anymore.
SO...I WAS THINKING...ONCE THE ENTRANCE EXAMS ARE OVER, WE WON'T BE SEEING EACH OTHER MUCH.
HUH...
MY EXAM FOR SHIOMI IS ON THE FOURTEENTH.
AFTER THAT...
...I WAS THINKING WE COULD GO ON A DATE.
WHAT?!

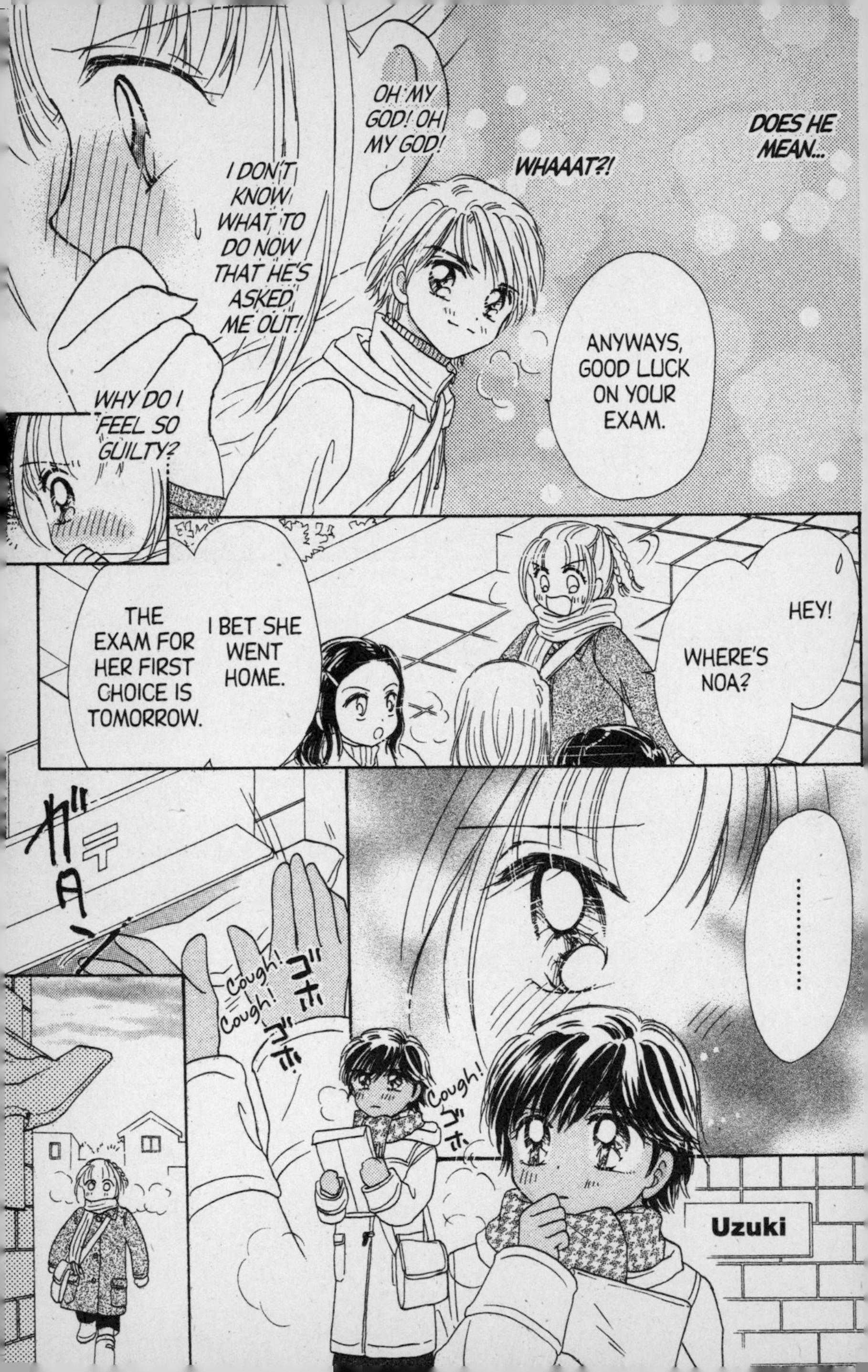
DOES HE MEAN...
WHAAAT?!
OH MY GOD! OH MY GOD!
ANYWAYS, GOOD LUCK ON YOUR EXAM.
I DON'T KNOW WHAT TO DO NOW THAT HE'S ASKED ME OUT!
WHY DO I FEEL SO GUILTY?
HEY!
WHERE'S NOA?
I BET SHE WENT HOME.
THE EXAM FOR HER FIRST CHOICE IS TOMORROW.
......
Uzuki
Cough!
ゴホ
Cough! Cough!
ゴホ
ゴホ

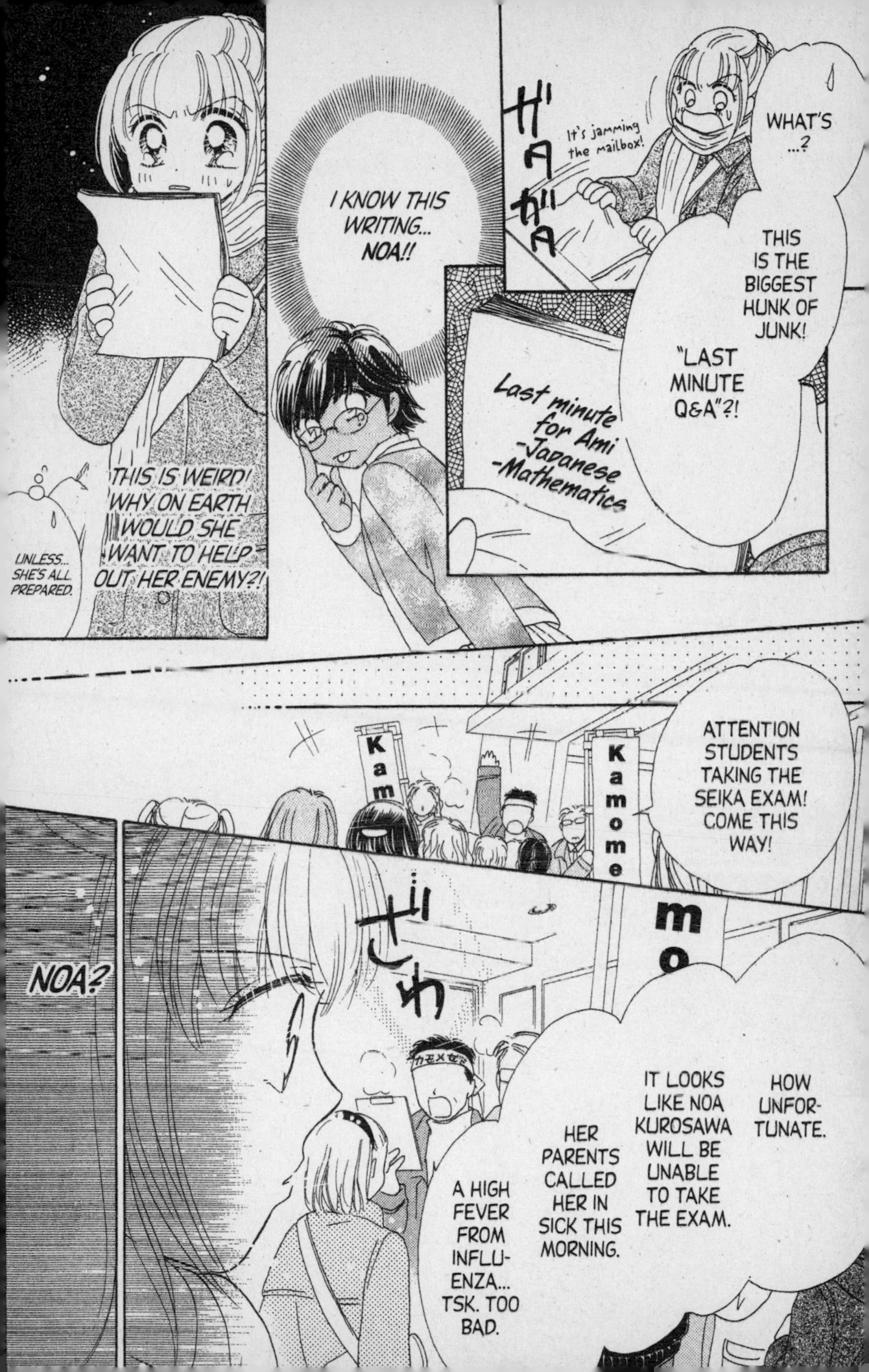
ガタガタ
It's jamming the mailbox!
WHAT'S ...?
THIS IS THE BIGGEST HUNK OF JUNK!
"LAST MINUTE Q&A"?!
Last minute for Ami -Japanese -Mathematics
I KNOW THIS WRITING... NOA!!
THIS IS WEIRD! WHY ON EARTH WOULD SHE WANT TO HELP OUT HER ENEMY?!
UNLESS... SHE'S ALL PREPARED.
ATTENTION STUDENTS TAKING THE SEIKA EXAM! COME THIS WAY!
Kamome
Kam
mo
ざわ
HOW UNFORTUNATE.
IT LOOKS LIKE NOA KUROSAWA WILL BE UNABLE TO TAKE THE EXAM.
HER PARENTS CALLED HER IN SICK THIS MORNING.
A HIGH FEVER FROM INFLUENZA... TSK. TOO BAD.
NOA?

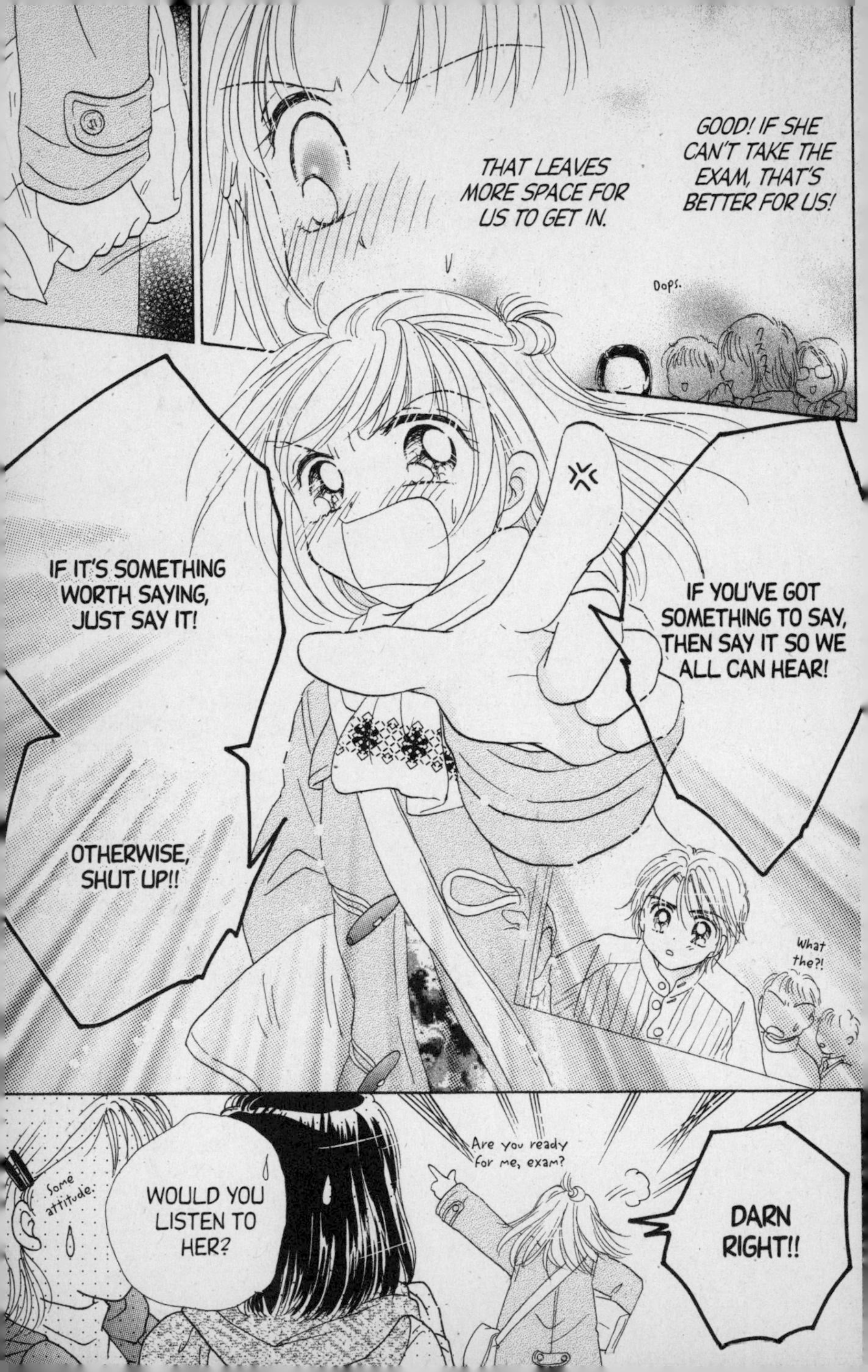
GOOD! IF SHE CAN'T TAKE THE EXAM, THAT'S BETTER FOR US!
THAT LEAVES MORE SPACE FOR US TO GET IN.
Oops.
IF YOU'VE GOT SOMETHING TO SAY, THEN SAY IT SO WE ALL CAN HEAR!
IF IT'S SOMETHING WORTH SAYING, JUST SAY IT!
OTHERWISE, SHUT UP!!
What the?!
DARN RIGHT!!
Are you ready for me, exam?
WOULD YOU LISTEN TO HER?
Some attitude.

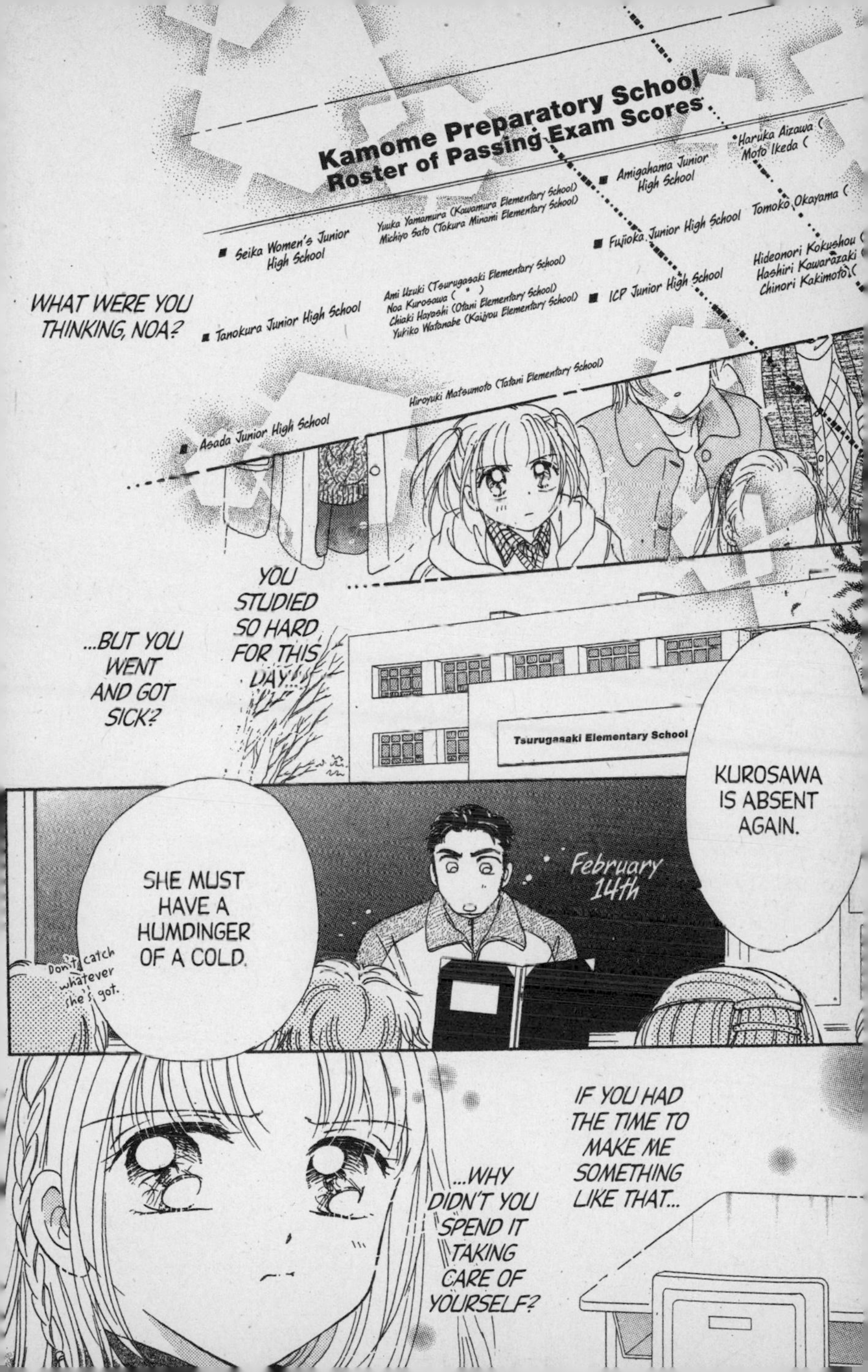
Kamome Preparatory School
Roster of Passing Exam Scores
Haruka Aizawa (
Moto Ikeda (
Amigahama Junior High School
Tomoko Okayama (
Fujioka Junior High School
Hideonori Kokushou (
Hashiri Kawarazaki (
Chinori Kakimoto (
ICP Junior High School
Yuuka Yamamura (Kawamura Elementary School)
Michiyo Sato (Tokura Minami Elementary School)
Seika Women's Junior High School
Ami Uzuki (Tsurugasaki Elementary School)
Noa Kurosawa (")
Chiaki Hayashi (Otani Elementary School)
Yuriko Watanabe (Kaijou Elementary School)
Tanokura Junior High School
Hiroyuki Matsumoto (Tatani Elementary School)
Asada Junior High School
WHAT WERE YOU THINKING, NOA?
YOU STUDIED SO HARD FOR THIS DAY...
...BUT YOU WENT AND GOT SICK?
Tsurugasaki Elementary School
KUROSAWA IS ABSENT AGAIN.
February 14th
SHE MUST HAVE A HUMDINGER OF A COLD.
Don't catch whatever she's got.
IF YOU HAD THE TIME TO MAKE ME SOMETHING LIKE THAT...
...WHY DIDN'T YOU SPEND IT TAKING CARE OF YOURSELF?

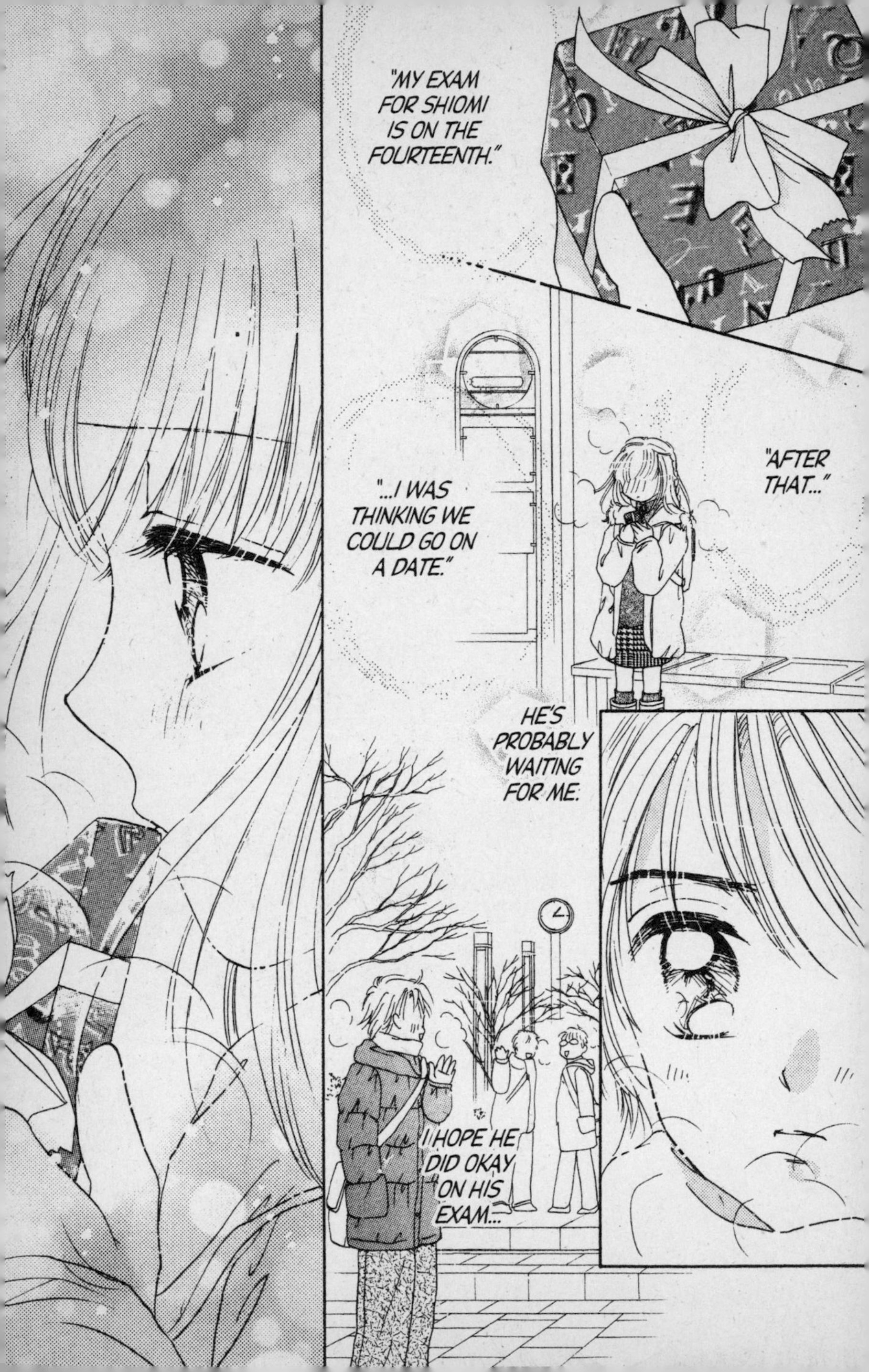
"MY EXAM FOR SHIOMI IS ON THE FOURTEENTH."
"AFTER THAT..."
"...I WAS THINKING WE COULD GO ON A DATE."
HE'S PROBABLY WAITING FOR ME.
I HOPE HE DID OKAY ON HIS EXAM...

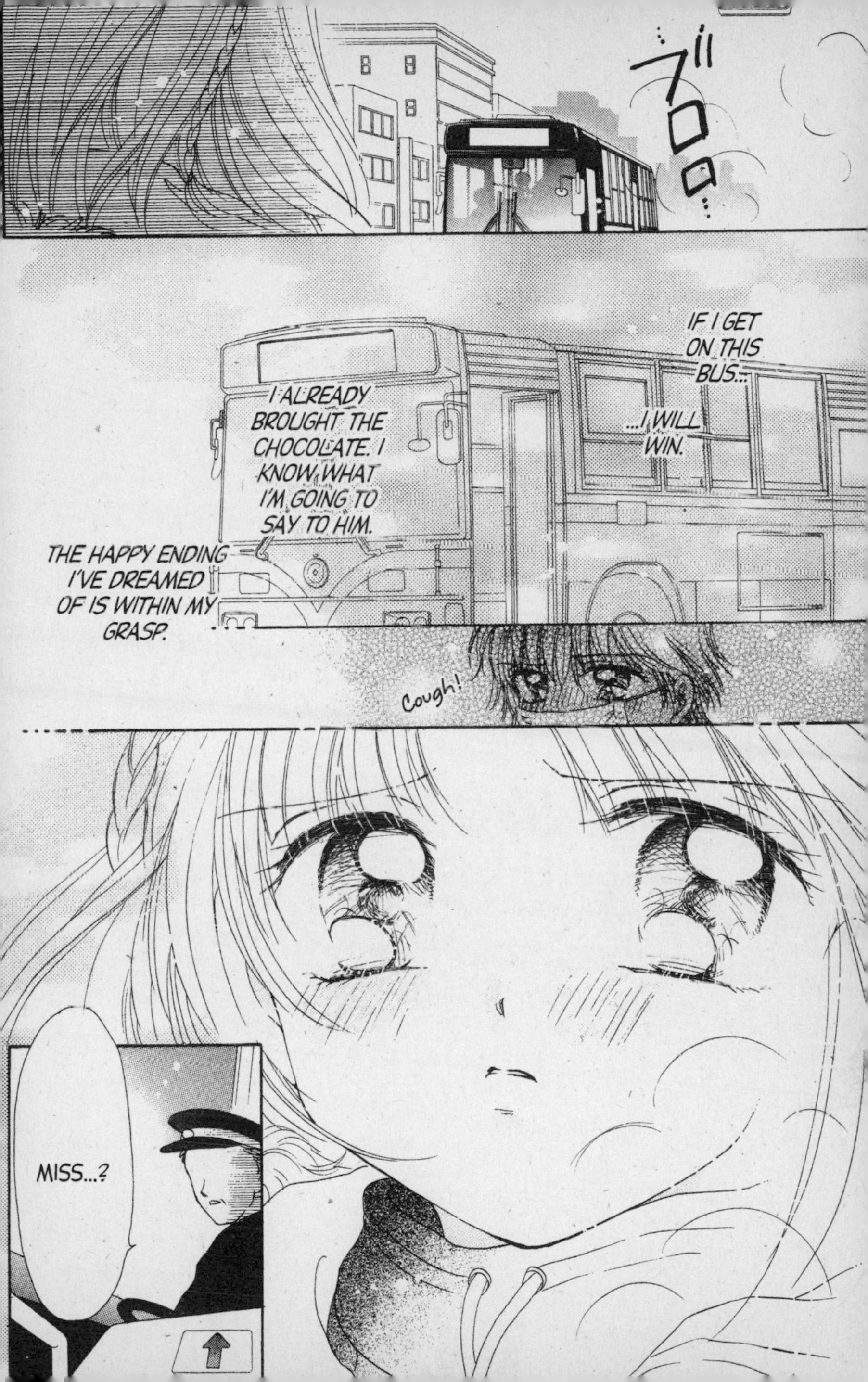
ブロロ…
IF I GET ON THIS BUS...
...I WILL WIN.
I ALREADY BROUGHT THE CHOCOLATE. I KNOW WHAT I'M GOING TO SAY TO HIM.
THE HAPPY ENDING I'VE DREAMED OF IS WITHIN MY GRASP.
Cough!
MISS...?

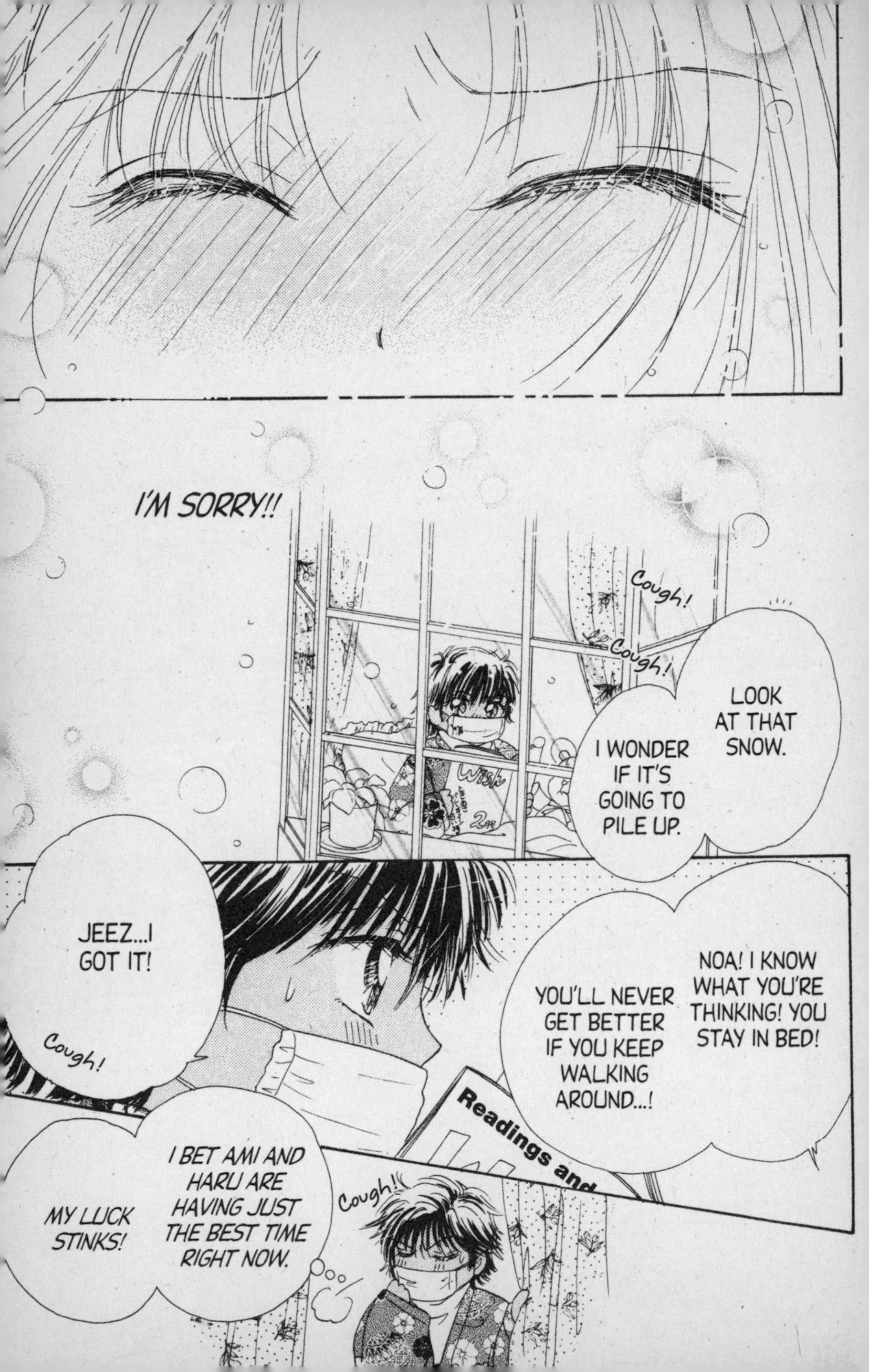

I'M SORRY!!
Cough!
Cough!
LOOK AT THAT SNOW.
I WONDER IF IT'S GOING TO PILE UP.
NOA! I KNOW WHAT YOU'RE THINKING! YOU STAY IN BED!
YOU'LL NEVER GET BETTER IF YOU KEEP WALKING AROUND...!
JEEZ...I GOT IT!
Cough!
Readings and
Cough!
I BET AMI AND HARU ARE HAVING JUST THE BEST TIME RIGHT NOW.
MY LUCK STINKS!

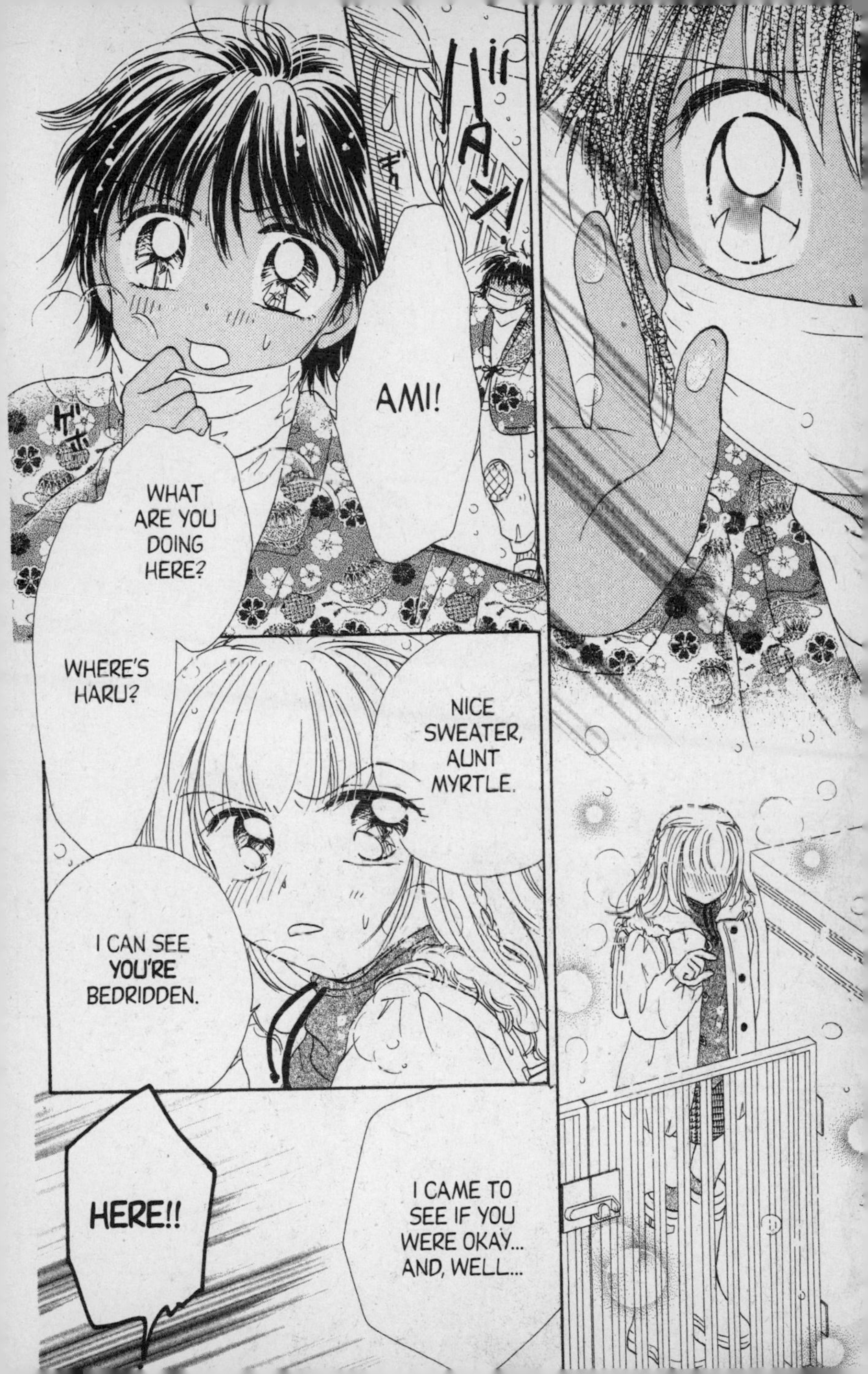
AMI!
WHAT ARE YOU DOING HERE?
I CAME TO SEE IF YOU WERE OKAY... AND, WELL...
WHERE'S HARU?
HERE!!
NICE SWEATER, AUNT MYRTLE.
I CAN SEE YOU'RE BEDRIDDEN.

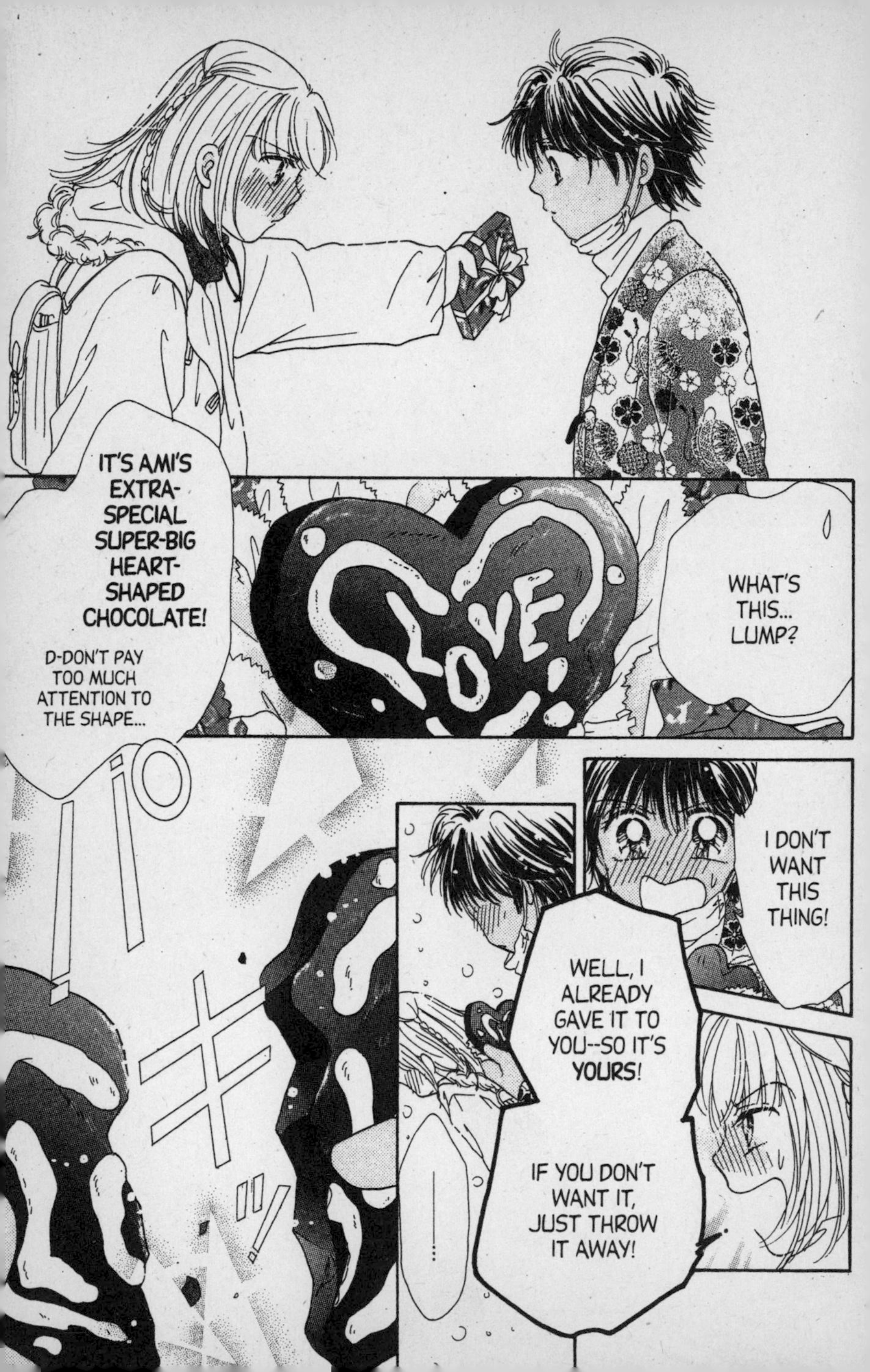
WHAT'S THIS... LUMP?
IT'S AMI'S EXTRA-SPECIAL SUPER-BIG HEART-SHAPED CHOCOLATE!
D-DON'T PAY TOO MUCH ATTENTION TO THE SHAPE...
LOVE
I DON'T WANT THIS THING!
WELL, I ALREADY GAVE IT TO YOU--SO IT'S **YOURS**!
IF YOU DON'T WANT IT, JUST THROW IT AWAY!

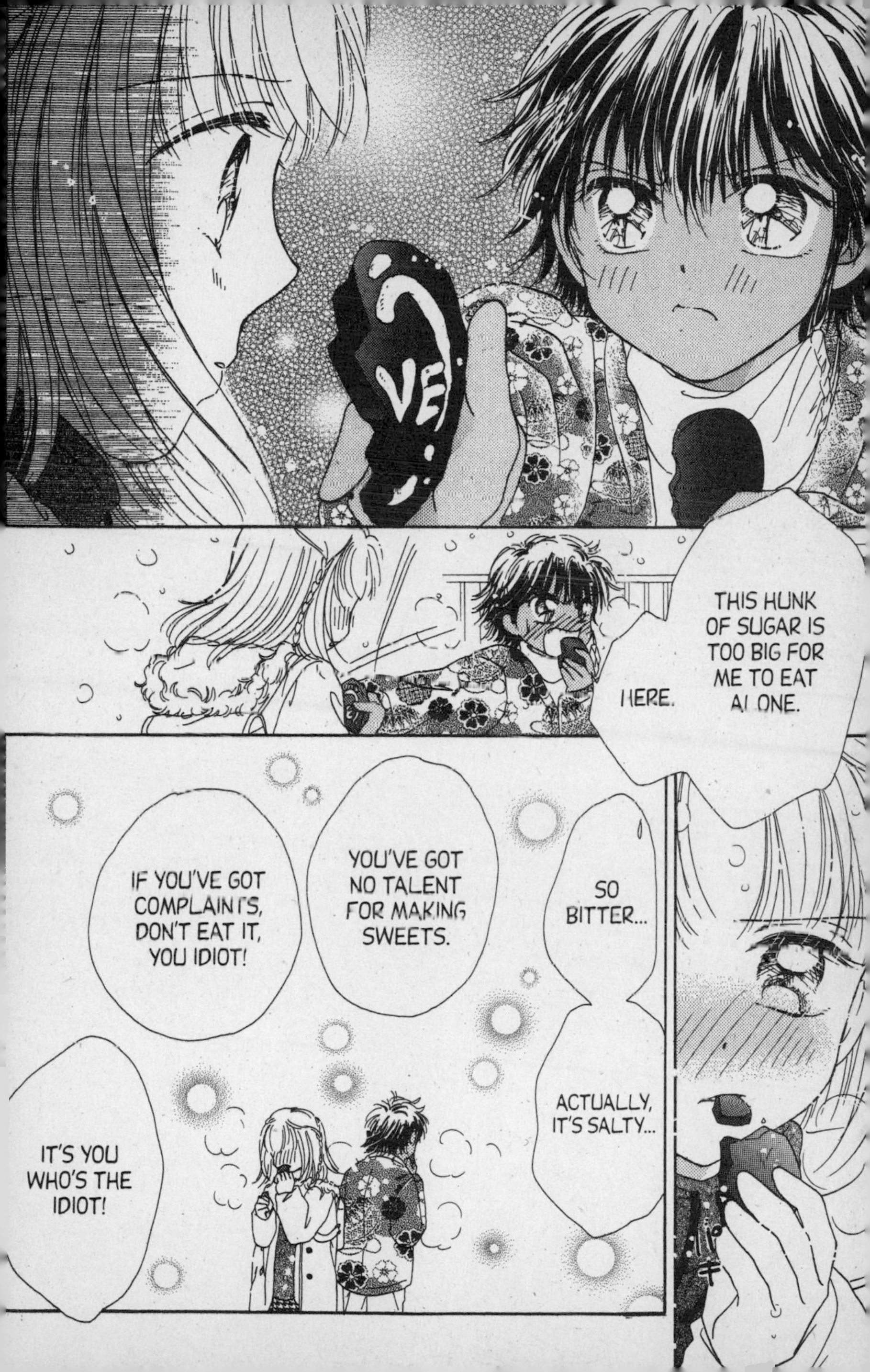
THIS HUNK OF SUGAR IS TOO BIG FOR ME TO EAT ALONE.
HERE.
SO BITTER...
ACTUALLY, IT'S SALTY...
YOU'VE GOT NO TALENT FOR MAKING SWEETS.
IF YOU'VE GOT COMPLAINTS, DON'T EAT IT, YOU IDIOT!
IT'S YOU WHO'S THE IDIOT!

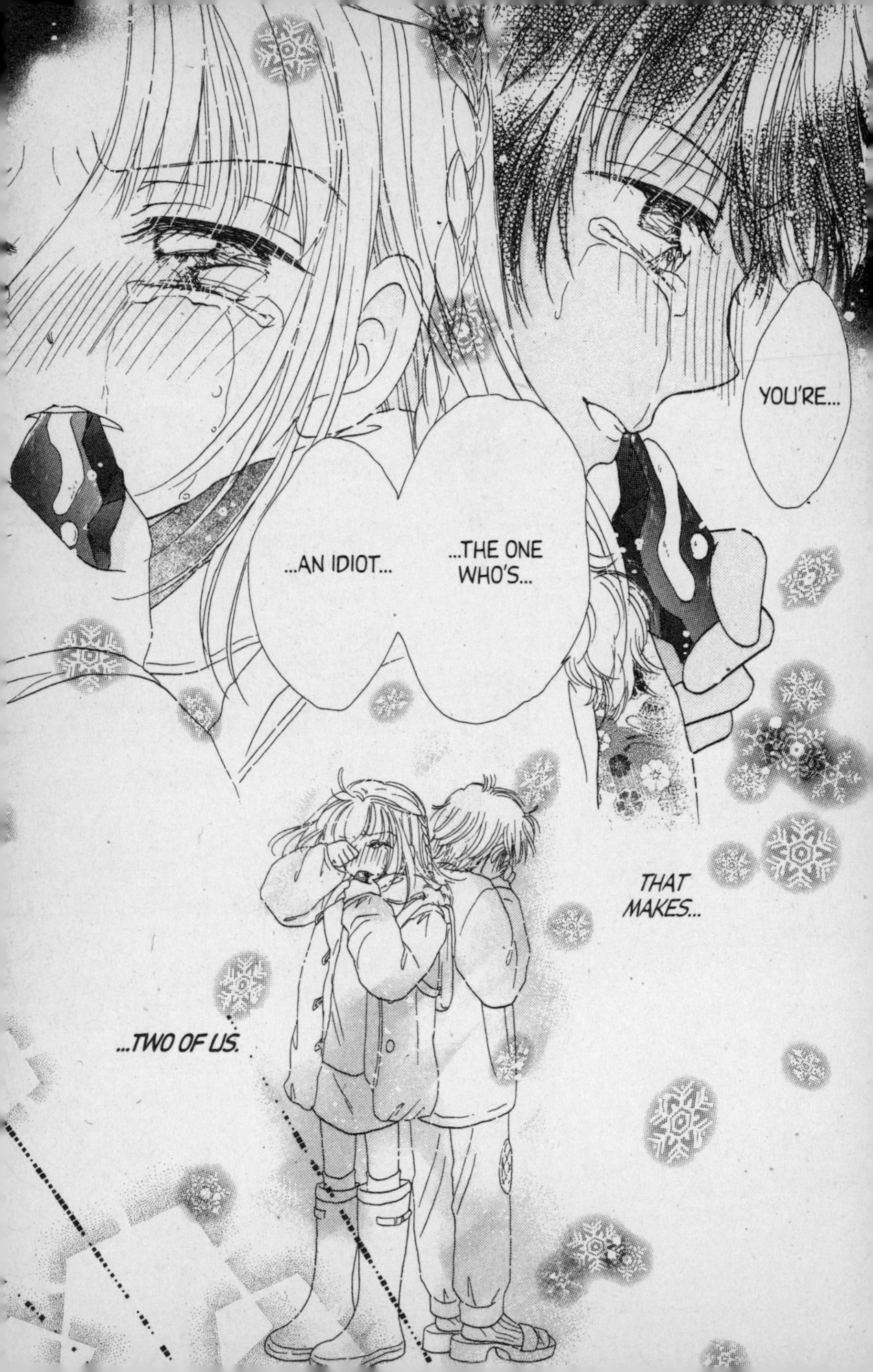
YOU'RE...
...THE ONE WHO'S...
...AN IDIOT...
THAT MAKES...
...TWO OF US.

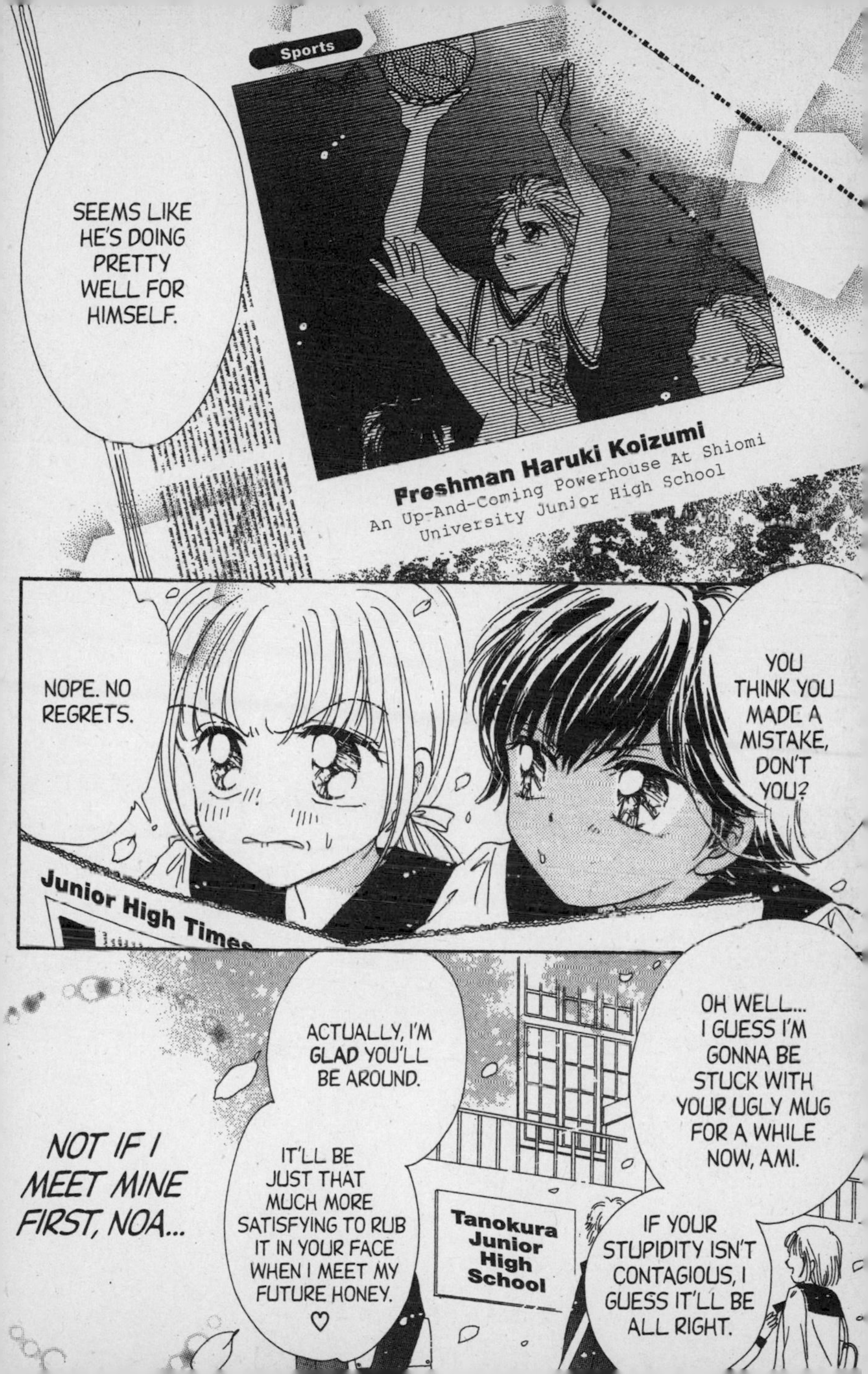
Sports
Freshman Haruki Koizumi
An Up-And-Coming Powerhouse At Shiomi University Junior High School
SEEMS LIKE HE'S DOING PRETTY WELL FOR HIMSELF.
YOU THINK YOU MADE A MISTAKE, DON'T YOU?
NOPE. NO REGRETS.
Junior High Times
OH WELL... I GUESS I'M GONNA BE STUCK WITH YOUR UGLY MUG FOR A WHILE NOW, AMI.
IF YOUR STUPIDITY ISN'T CONTAGIOUS, I GUESS IT'LL BE ALL RIGHT.
Tanokura Junior High School
ACTUALLY, I'M GLAD YOU'LL BE AROUND.
IT'LL BE JUST THAT MUCH MORE SATISFYING TO RUB IT IN YOUR FACE WHEN I MEET MY FUTURE HONEY. ♡
NOT IF I MEET MINE FIRST, NOA...

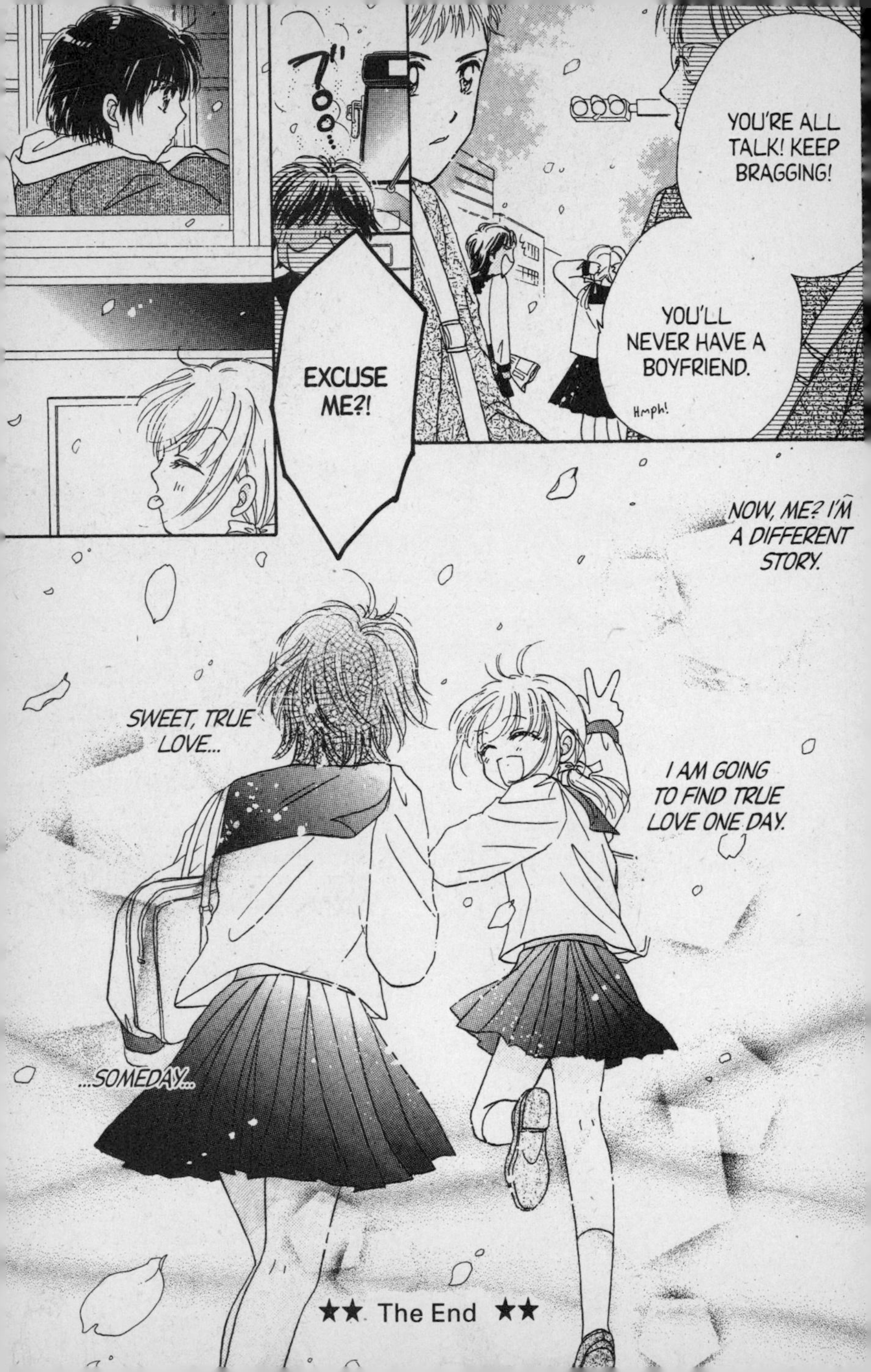
YOU'RE ALL TALK! KEEP BRAGGING!
YOU'LL NEVER HAVE A BOYFRIEND.
Hmph!
EXCUSE ME?!
NOW, ME? I'M A DIFFERENT STORY.
I AM GOING TO FIND TRUE LOVE ONE DAY.
SWEET, TRUE LOVE...
...SOMEDAY...
★★ The End ★★

IN THE NEXT VOLUME

THE FIGHT FOR TAMON'S HEART CONTINUES
AS AMI TRIES TO WIN HIM OVER--DESPITE THE
CONSTANT MEDDLING FROM MIKA. BUT JUST WHEN AMI
THINKS THINGS COULDN'T GET ANY WORSE BETWEEN HER
AND TAMON, AMI MEETS MIKA'S CUTE COUSIN, KAI. THE
SITUATION BECOMES EVEN MORE COMPLICATED WHEN
TAMON SEES AMI AND KAI TOGETHER. AMI TRIES TO MAKE
UP WITH TAMON...BUT MIKA SEES THIS AS AN OPPORTUNITY
TO KNOCK AMI OUT OF THE PICTURE ONCE AND FOR ALL!

WILL HER DASTARDLY PLAN PREVAIL?
FIND OUT IN *ULTRA CUTE* VOLUME 3!

TOKYOPOP SHOP

THIS FALL, TOKYOPOP CREATES A FRESH, NEW CHAPTER IN TEEN NOVELS...

For Adventurers...
Witches' Forest:
The Adventures of Duan Surk

By Mishio Fukazawa
Duan Surk is a 16-year-old Level 2 fighter who embarks on the quest of a lifetime—battling mythical creatures and outwitting evil sorceresses, all in an impossible rescue mission in the spooky Witches' Forest!

BASED ON THE FAMOUS
FORTUNE QUEST WORLD

For Dreamers...
Magic Moon

By Wolfgang and Heike Hohlbein
Kim enters the enigmatic realm of Magic Moon, where he battles unthinkable monsters and fantastical creatures—in order to unravel the secret that keeps his sister locked in a coma.

THE WORLDWIDE BESTSELLING FANTASY
THRILLOGY ARRIVES IN THE U.S.!

Ayumu struggles with her studies, and the all-important high school entrance exams are approaching. Fortunately, she has help from her best bud Shii-chan, who is at the top of the class. But when the test results come back, the friends are surprised: Ayumu surpasses Shii-chan's scores and gets into the school of her choice—without Shii-chan! Losing her friend is so painful for Ayumu that she starts cutting herself to ease her sorrow. Finally, Ayumu seeks comfort in a new friend, Manami. But will Manami prove to be the friend that Ayumu truly needs? Or will Ayumu continue down a dark path?

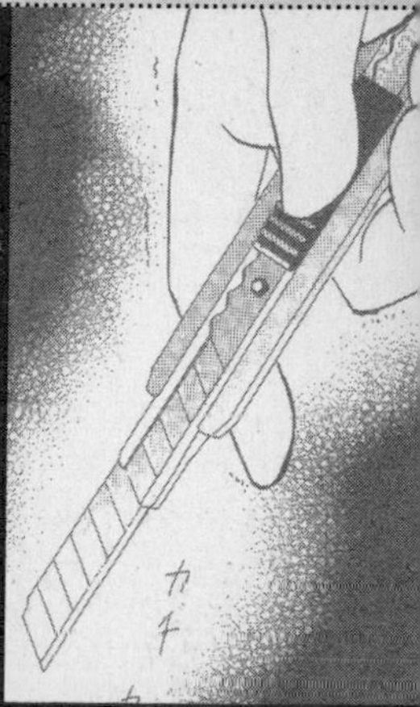

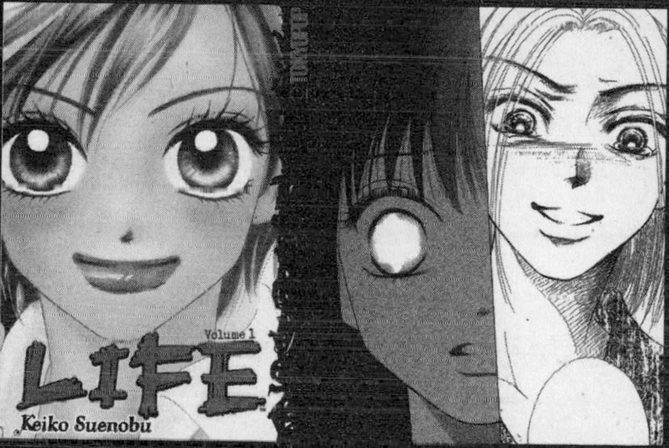
Volume 1
LIFE
Keiko Suenobu

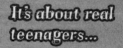

It's about real teenagers...

It's about real high school...

It's about real life.

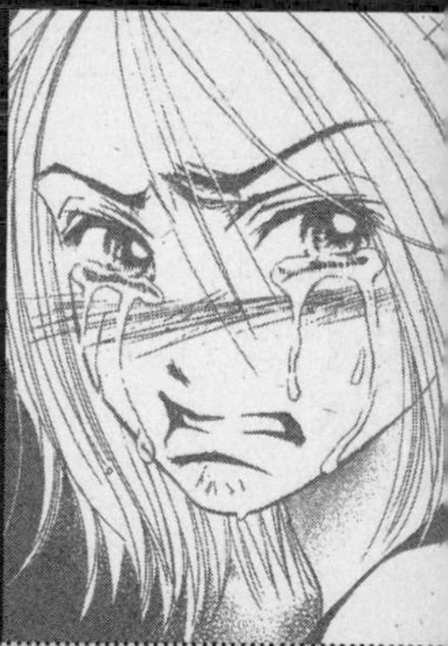

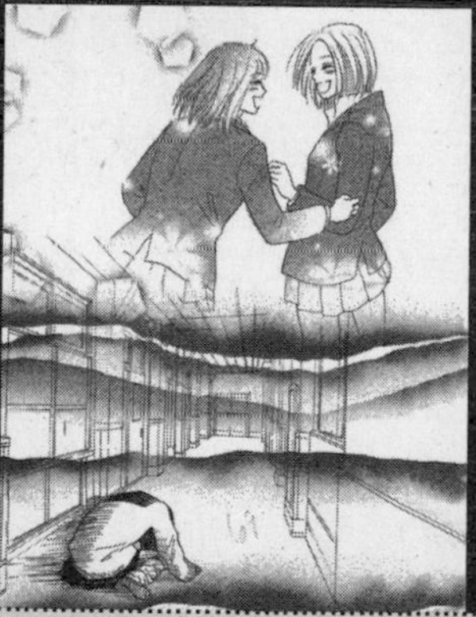

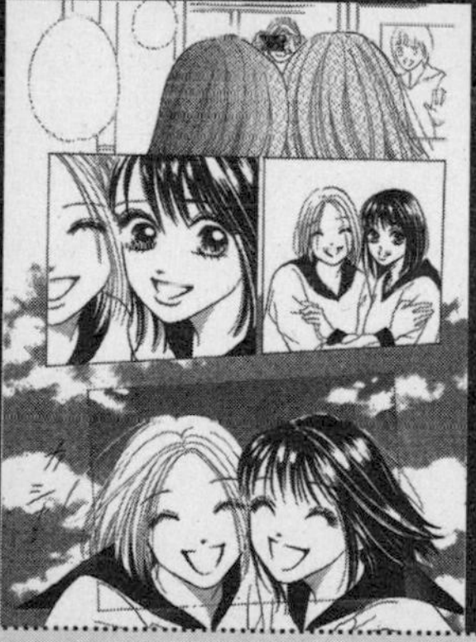

WWW.TOKYOPOP.COM/LIFE

LIFE
BY KEIKO SUENOBU

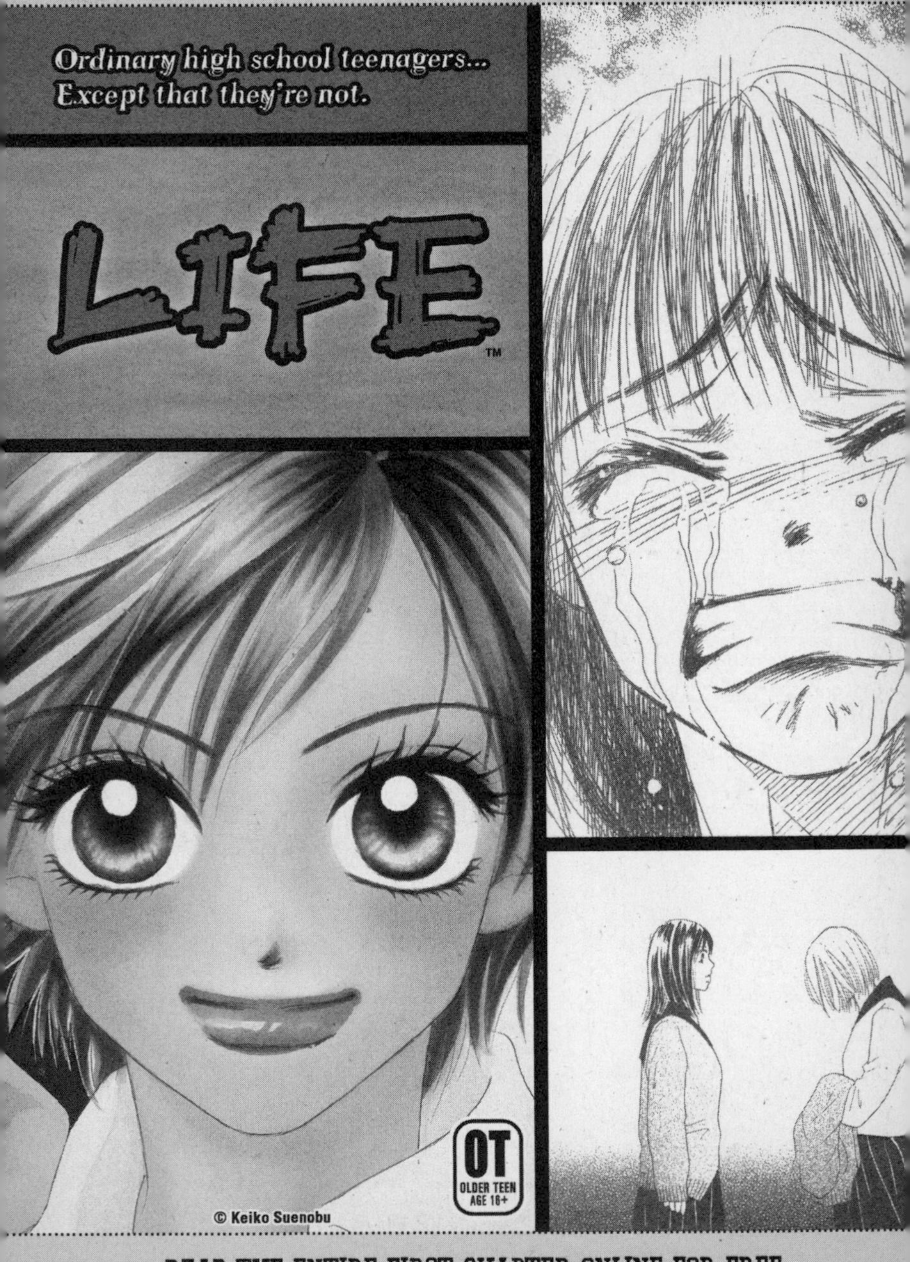

Ordinary high school teenagers...
Except that they're not.
LIFE™
OT
OLDER TEEN
AGE 16+
© Keiko Suenobu

READ THE ENTIRE FIRST CHAPTER ONLINE FOR FREE:

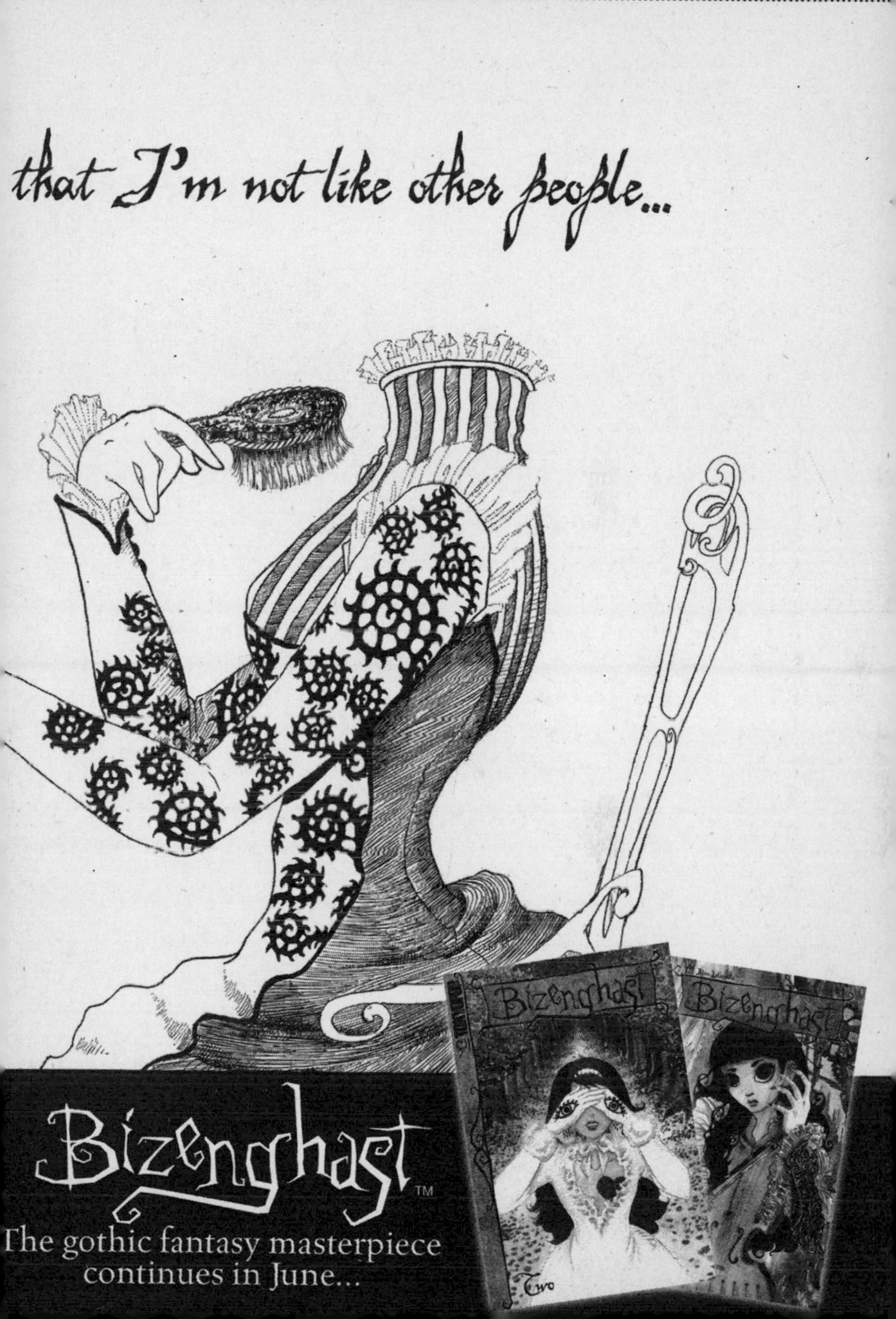
that I'm not like other people...
Bizenghast
Bizenghast
Two
Bizenghast™
The gothic fantasy masterpiece
continues in June...

BIZENGHAST

Dear Diary,
I'm starting to feel

STOP!

This is the back of the book.
You wouldn't want to spoil a great ending!

This book is printed "manga-style," in the authentic Japanese right-to-left format. Since none of the artwork has been flipped or altered, readers get to experience the story just as the creator intended. You've been asking for it, so TOKYOPOP® delivered: authentic, hot-off-the-press, and far more fun!

DIRECTIONS

If this is your first time reading manga-style, here's a quick guide to help you understand how it works.

It's easy... just start in the top right panel and follow the numbers. Have fun, and look for more 100% authentic manga from TOKYOPOP®!